James II
a study in kingship

'An excellent political biography . . . the reader always gets sufficient explanatory material to understand developments and to judge James's decisions.'   *Times Literary Supplement*

John Miller was born in Cambridge and educated at the Perse School and Jesus College, Cambridge. He became Research Fellow at Gonville and Caius College, Cambridge, in 1971 and Lecturer in History at Queen Mary College, University of London, 1975. He was appointed Reader in History in 1982 and Professor of History in 1989. His previous books include *Popery and Politics in England, 1660–1688* and *Seeds of Liberty: 1688 and the Making of Modern Britain.*

The picture on the front cover is a portrait of James II by Sir Godfrey Kneller (1684–5), and is reproduced by kind permission of the National Portrait Gallery.

D1514168

By the same author

Popery and Politics in England, 1660–1688
(Cambridge University Press)

The Life and Times of William and Mary
(Weidenfeld and Nicolson)

The Glorious Revolution
(Longman)

Restoration England: the Reign of Charles II
(Longman)

Religion in the Popular Prints
(Chadwyck-Healey)

Bourbon and Stuart:
Kings and Kingship in France and England
in the Seventeenth Century
(George Philip)

Seeds of Liberty:
1688 and the Making of Modern Britain
(Souvenir Press)

James II
a study in kingship

JOHN MILLER

Methuen · London

A Methuen Paperback

First published in Great Britain in 1978
by Wayland (Publishers) Ltd
Revised edition published in 1989
by Methuen London
First published in paperback in 1991 by Methuen London,
Michelin House, 81 Fulham Road, London SW3 6RB

Copyright © 1978, 1989 by John Miller

A CIP catalogue record for this book
is available from the British Library
ISBN 0 413 65290 4

Printed in England by Clays Ltd, St Ives plc

For James and Nicholas

Contents

Preface

At first sight it might seem that there is little need for a new biography of James II. Apart from Lord Macaulay's magisterial account of his reign, in 1948 FC Turner produced a biography which was in many ways thoroughly adequate—long and based on an impressive range of sources. This present volume goes beyond Turner's in two respects. First, it makes use of a number of major manuscript sources which Turner did not use, notably the Middleton Papers in the British Library, the D'Avaux papers in the Public Record Office, the Morrice journal in Dr Williams's Library, the Portland newsletters at Nottingham and (above all) that large proportion of the French ambassadors' dispatches which are not among the Baschet transcripts (including those of June to December 1688). These new sources make it possible to examine some aspects of James's reign, notably his diplomacy, much more fully than before.

Secondly, the present volume offers a very different interpretation of James and of later Stuart history. Turner's study reflected that complex of pre-suppositions and values usually known as "the Whig interpretation of history". These included the assumption first, that England's laws and constitution and the royal prerogative were clearly and incontrovertibly defined and second, that the seventeenth century saw an inevitable and irreversible increase in the power of the House of Commons and, conversely, an irreversible decline in the power of the monarchy. If one accepted those assumptions, for James II to try to extend his prerogatives would appear not only illegal and wicked but futile, an attempt to fly in the face of history. Recent research, however, has questioned almost every aspect of these assumptions. It can be argued that James (like his father in the 1630s) had a much better case in law than his opponents would admit. Recent studies of both early and later Stuart Parliaments have questioned whether the Commons were as eager to seize power as earlier historians assumed. Many historians of the later Stuart period (for example JR Jones and JP Kenyon) stress the inherent strengths of the Restored monarchy and argue that it owed its misfortunes primarily to failures of management. This emerges particularly strongly from Professor Kenyon's admirable biography of Sunderland, which gives a highly perceptive and scholarly account of the making of decisions in James's reign. One could argue, indeed, that the "natural" development in later Stuart England would have been towards stronger monarchy (as in France) rather than a stronger

Parliament. Seen in that light, James's attempts to extend his prerogative might be neither wicked nor doomed to failure.

But was James's attempt to extend his powers an end in itself, or was it a means to an end? I argued in my first book, *Popery and Politics in England 1660–1688*, that James's main concern was to advance the interests of Catholicism, not to strengthen the monarchy. I suggested, too, that his Protestant subjects were so used to equating Catholicism with absolutism that they were unlikely to distinguish between means and ends, even if adequate information had been available to them. (It was not, as the government censored the press and tampered with the mails.) Protestant historians have not analysed James's religious views sympathetically or even taken them seriously, while Catholics have too often confined themselves to venerating James and denigrating his opponents. Neither Protestants nor Catholics have produced a balanced picture.

My aim has been to treat James both sympathetically and critically. I have tried to understand his principles and his interpretation of events and to show how these led him into serious errors of political judgment. I have therefore assessed James's actions according to strictly practical criteria (whether they would work) rather than moral or legal criteria (whether they conformed to a particular set of constitutional or political values). It is not easy to like James: after some years of research, I must confess to feeling little affection for him. He was utterly humourless and so obsessed with his own rightness that he showed virtually no interest in the views of others. Yet in many ways he was a man more sinned against than sinning. If he failed to understand his subjects, they were full of misconceptions about him. Indeed, one major theme of the book is the extent to which the leading protagonists in the story based their decisions on assumptions or information which were dubious or downright wrong. Later historians have too often been inclined to follow them in this, to cite rumour and gossip as fact, and to assume that contemporary assumptions about James's intentions were generally correct. Having made such an assumption, it is easy to accept evidence which supports it (even if that evidence is, in itself, not very reliable), and to ignore other, more reliable evidence which contradicts it. Turner, for example, made extensive use of contemporary and near-contemporary Whig historians and Williamite propaganda, but does not seem to have used James's devotional papers. I have tried to avoid these pitfalls by basing my account on what James wrote or on what reasonably reliable observers quoted him as saying, and not on what other, less well-informed, observers conjectured.

As with James's domestic policy, studies of his foreign policy have often rested on assumptions which have recently been called into question. Traditionally English historians have seen Louis XIV as an incorrigible aggressor, whose aim was to destroy Protestantism and to bring all Europe under his rule. It therefore seemed that the natural foreign policy for England was one of alliance with Holland against France. Recent research on Louis' foreign policy by Ragnhild Hatton, JB Wolf and others has shown the defensive considerations which underlay his conduct, especially after 1678. This would imply that it would be neither irresponsible nor unpatriotic for James to have pursued a pro-French foreign policy (as contemporaries thought he did) or one of neutrality (as was in fact the case).

I should like to stress that this is intended mainly as a political and religious study. For reasons of space and of my own lack of expertise, I have said little of James's military and naval career. I have also dealt cursorily with his role in naval administration and as a colonial proprietor, both of which are subjects worthy of study in their own right, but which would require a great deal more detailed research.

In researching a work of this length, I have contracted a number of obligations and debts of gratitude. I should like to thank Her Majesty the Queen for allowing me access to microfilm copies of the Stuart papers, and to the Duke of Marlborough, the Marquis of Bath and the Warden and Fellows of All Souls' College for allowing me to consult manuscripts in their possession. I should like to thank for their helpfulness the staffs of the Rare Books and Manuscripts Rooms at Cambridge University Library, Duke Humfrey's Library in the Bodleian, the Rolls Room in the Public Record Office and the Manuscripts Students' Room at the British Library. Julia Buckroyd, Edith Johnston and James McGuire have been kind enough to comment on my first hesitant forays into Scottish and Irish history, for which I am very grateful. I should like to express my thanks to those who have given me hospitality on my travels—Professors Jean and Monica Charlot, Keith Hawkins, James McGuire and Peter Morris. Especial thanks are due to the Principal and Fellows of Brasenose College, who made me very welcome on numerous visits to Oxford. My research in the Archives des Affaires Etrangères made necessary an extended stay in Paris, which was made possible by a travel scholarship from the Wolfson Foundation, for which I am most grateful. The bulk of the research for the book was completed in the four and a half years when I was a Research Fellow at Gonville and Caius College, Cambridge. I should like to express my thanks to the Master and Fellows for electing me a Fellow, for renewing my fellowship and for making my stay at Caius a happy and profitable one. Last but not least, perhaps my greatest debt is to my wife and sons who have suffered (if not always in silence) during the composition and writing of this book.

London, May 1977   JOHN MILLER

A Note on Spellings and Dates

All spellings have been modernized and all quotations from foreign languages have been translated. Dates in the text are old style, but with the year starting on 1st January. (During the seventeenth century the English calendar was ten days behind the calendar used on the continent, and the year was taken as starting on 25th March.) In the notes, I have given the dates used by the writers themselves: new style for foreign ambassadors' reports, old style for Englishmen writing from England.

CHAPTER ONE

Childhood (1633–48)

At midnight on 14th October, 1633, Henrietta Maria, Queen of England, gave birth to a son at St James's Palace. The court was filled with joy and the citizens of London rang the church bells and lit bonfires in the streets. It was not the Queen's first child or even her first son. Charles (named after his father, Charles I) had been born in 1630 and Mary in 1631. But in an age of high child mortality a second son doubled the chances of continuing the dynasty in the direct male line. The baby was named James after his grandfather, James VI of Scotland and I of England, and the personal union of the two kingdoms under the house of Stuart was symbolized by James's being granted the two dukedoms of Albany and York.

James's first years were uneventful. Politically the country enjoyed a deceptive calm. The rumblings in Scotland in 1637–39 did little to disturb the tranquillity of London and still less that of the court: sumptuous and introverted, the court was always somewhat remote from the plain Puritanism of provincial England. Within the lush environment created by Inigo Jones and Rubens, isolated from the hard realities of the world outside, the Queen continued to produce children: Elizabeth in 1635, Henry, Duke of Gloucester in 1639 and two more daughters who died young. Van Dyck's carefully posed portraits, with the children staring with large solemn eyes and the younger boys in dresses and bonnets, make them all look almost impossibly demure. Occasional references to hide and seek suggest more normal childlike behaviour. James's was a large family and a loving one. In spite of—perhaps because of—the frequent separations soon to be forced on them by the civil war, the children showed great loyalty to their father and to each other. Neither Charles nor James showed the same devotion to their mother. Although she had great personal charm, her political advice to her husband was almost invariably bad, a point which her enemies at court made very forcefully to the young Princes. Consciously or unconsciously, they came to hold her responsible for their father's downfall. This, coupled with youth's normal resentment of parental authority, led them to resist strongly her attempts to direct their public and private affairs.

Of James's education we know little. Bishop Brian Duppa and William Harvey both served as tutors to Charles and James, at various times. James acquired the normal courtly accomplishments. He showed some interest in music, playing the guitar and dancing well. He learned, probably on his travels, to speak French fluently. He also acquired a smattering of Italian and could apparently read Spanish. Although he was a founder member of the Royal Society, his sole contribution to its proceedings was the information that a herb called Star of the Earth could cure the bite of a mad dog. In later life he acquired some knowledge of astronomy, especially as it related to navigation, and he clearly impressed his hosts on a visit to the Paris observatory in 1690. He was also typical of his time in that along with this scientific knowledge went an interest in almanacs, miraculous cures and "rules to know the weather", which Pepys found "pretty" but not very rational.[1] From his early thirties he read works of theology, devotion and church history, but there is no evidence of his having done so earlier. He received his early religious instruction from the High Churchmen patronized by his father: he had been baptized by William Laud himself. His mother, a strong Catholic, had managed to give him a Catholic nurse (which excited some comment at the time) but if she tried in other ways to influence his religious views, she did so to little effect. It seems, in fact, that James acquired most of his "education" as an adult, from experience and from private reading, and not from formal instruction when young. James was an energetic youth—like Charles, he walked very fast—and book learning seemed much less exciting than warfare. In 1647 his father sent word that he wished him "to ply his book more and his gun less".[2]

It was probably in the spring of 1641 that the children's quiet and ordered existence was first seriously disturbed. An angry crowd surged round Whitehall, demanding the execution of the King's leading minister, the Earl of Strafford. Fearful for the safety of his family Charles gave in. James later saw this as a fateful decision, but it bought a few months of peace. In December, however, after the outbreak of rebellion in Ireland, distrust between crown and Commons, court and city, built up once more. Crowds took to the streets threatening violence against courtiers and bishops and the King thought it prudent to leave London. He took Charles with him and sent the Queen off to France. James and the younger children were moved from Whitehall to St James's, a little more remote from the violence which continued sporadically around the Houses of Parliament throughout January and February 1642.

By now the breach between King and Parliament was open and the King prepared to recover by force the political ground which he had lost. In March he began to gather men and munitions in Yorkshire; Parliament had little choice but to follow suit. In this "arms race" Hull was crucially important, as it contained most of the weapons used in the Scots war of 1640–41. Parliament had ordered that these weapons should be brought to London when, late in April, the King tried to gain control of the town. He sent James, newly arrived from London, to visit Sir John Hotham, the governor. Next day, the King sent word that he was coming to dine with them, at which Hotham closed the gates. The King waited for him to open them and retired disappointed to York. James was kept a prisoner until Hotham reluctantly let him go to rejoin his father. For the King, it was a serious setback; for James, aged eight, it must have been a disagreeable and frightening experience.[3]

As the summer wore on, it became clear that the comfortable days of the 1630s would not return. By June Charles could afford to feed only his immediate family, but his military preparations continued and in August he raised his standard at Nottingham. Two months later the young Princes saw their first battle, at Edgehill. Sent away from the battlefield, they were nearly captured in the twilight by a party of enemy horse, which they mistook for the King's. After the battle the King advanced to Oxford, where James was to spend almost the whole of the next three years.

Oxford was the Royalists' capital: a centre of operations in the Thames Valley, a centre of government, the domicile of that part of the court that was not away with the King and, finally, the spiritual home of Royalism, the stronghold of Archbishop Laud's brand of High Anglicanism. While there James continued his bookish education in a desultory fashion and his training in arms with rather more enthusiasm. For much of the time his father and Charles were away and James was left to "encourage the troops" in a court that was full of factions and jealousies and increasingly poverty-stricken. By the winter of 1645-46 the Royalist cause was clearly lost. In March Prince Charles left for the Scilly Isles, whence he eventually reached France. In April the King fled to the Scots, hoping to get better terms from them than from the English. On 25th June Oxford surrendered on terms to a Parliamentarian army. Under the articles, James was to be taken to London to rejoin the three youngest children, Henry, Elizabeth and Henrietta, who had remained there throughout the war. The four of them were committed to the care of the Earl of Northumberland, who was to answer to Parliament for their safekeeping. When James eventually reached London, at the end of July, all his servants were dismissed (even his favourite dwarf) and replaced by others chosen by Parliament. However, he was glad to be reunited with Henry and Elizabeth (Henrietta having escaped to France), and the Earl and Countess of Northumberland treated them with great courtesy and respect.[4]

Although his custody was neither strict nor uncomfortable, James was soon thinking of escape. With his father in the hands of the Scots and his elder brother in France, he was the nearest heir to the throne still in Parliament's hands and already in August there was talk of deposing the King and putting James in his place. In December he received letters from his father ordering him to come to him at Newcastle, or else to flee to France. The design was discovered. James at first denied any knowledge of it, but later admitted receiving the letters, adding that he would have tried to escape, out of obedience to his father. Two of his servants were arrested. Any further thoughts of escape were prevented by a bad attack of ague in February and March 1647.[5]

By the time he recovered, the Scots had handed the King over to Parliament and gone home, disgusted at his failure to accept their demands. Meanwhile, a growing hostility appeared between Parliament and the New Model Army. On 3rd June the army took the first step towards negotiating its own settlement by kidnapping the King from his prison in Holmby House. Parliament at once brought the royal children from Syon House to St James's, but in July Parliament and the army leaders agreed to allow them to meet their father at Maiden-head. It was the first time James had seen him for over a year. In August Charles was moved to Hampton Court and the children visited him there two or three times a week. In these meetings the King expressed pessimism about the future. He realized that the army now possessed supreme power if it chose to use it and feared that it might begin to treat him more harshly at any time. If that happened, James was to try to escape, preferably to Holland to join his sister Mary, married to William II of Orange. Again and again he told the children not to desert the Church of England and to obey their elder brother. He adjured James and Henry not to accept the crown to the prejudice of the rightful heir.[6]

Such melancholy commands took much of the joy out of what were to be the children's last meetings with their father. In November he escaped to the Isle of Wight, hoping to sail for France, but he was caught and imprisoned in Carisbrooke Castle. When James heard the news he cried out, "How durst any rogues to use his father like that?" and burst into tears. He tried to kill with a longbow a servant who threatened to report his outburst to Northumberland. His first anger over, he wrote to assure the King that he would seize the first chance to escape. The letter was intercepted. James at first claimed to have destroyed the cipher, but when the Commons debated whether to send him to the Tower he handed over a copy and asked to be allowed to stay with North-umberland. The Commons agreed, although some MPs muttered that none of that family could be trusted. James, meanwhile, promised the Lords that he would show Northumberland all the letters he received. Northumberland agreed to continue his charge provided he were not held responsible for James's safe-keeping, to which the Houses agreed. He now placed a closer watch on James.[7]

This did not deter him from trying to escape. He re-established contact with his father through a Presbyterian called Colonel Bampfield, who also took charge of the arrangements for his escape. By mid-April this became an urgent neces-sity, as the army leaders revived the proposal to depose the King and put James in his place. By the 21st all was ready. For a fortnight the children had played hide and seek each evening, James hiding so skilfully that it often took half an hour to find him. That night James went straight to his sister's bedroom, locked up a little dog that followed him everywhere and set off down the back stairs. In his haste, he caught his foot on a door, making what seemed an enormous noise. He scuttled back to his bedroom and pretended to read until he was sure that nobody had heard him. The second time he descended without a hitch, passing through the inner garden and out into St James's Park. At the Tiltyard he met Bampfield, with whom he travelled by coach and boat to a surgeon's house near London Bridge. There James donned woman's clothes and they embarked on a barge with a few trusted servants. The bargemaster began to suspect that James was not all he seemed when he hitched up his stockings in a very unladylike manner and allowed Bampfield to tie his garter. They had to take the master into their confidence and persuaded him to dim his lights and slip past the blockhouse at Gravesend. Soon after, they boarded a Dutch vessel which brought them to Flushing on the morning of the 23rd. The company spent the night at an inn at Middelburg, where James scandalized the hostess by refusing to let the maids undress him and insisting on sharing a room with his "brother". William met them at Maeslandsluys and conducted them to the Hague, where James was reunited with Mary, "the affectionateness of which meeting I cannot express".[8] It had been a daring escapade in which James had shown considerable resourcefulness and courage for a boy of fourteen.

Once the joy and excitement were over, James had to adjust to the problems of exile. Under Northumberland's tutelage he had lived in considerable comfort, Parliament having voted him £7,580 a year. He had also been isolated from the backbiting and intrigue endemic in the Stuart court. Now, for twelve years, whatever James was to gain in pleasure and experience he was to suffer the constant nagging disadvantages of exile: the poverty, the uncertainty and the endless, sterile faction-fighting.

CHAPTER TWO

Exile (1648–60)

When James escaped from England he cannot have expected his absence to be more than temporary. There were many signs of dissatisfaction with Parliament and army. Riots in London were followed by risings in Kent, Essex and elsewhere. The Scots were preparing to march into England again and there were hopes of mutiny in the fleet. By the end of August, however, the scattered risings had been crushed and the Scots defeated. Moreover, the army now had the leisure to put into effect its resolution "to call Charles Stuart, that man of blood, to an account for the blood he has shed and the mischief he has done". Having decided that no settlement was possible with the King, the army resolved to have one without him. In December, when a majority of the Commons refused to break off negotiations with the King, the House was purged by Colonel Pride. The remaining "Rump" appointed a "High Court of Justice" which in January 1649 tried and executed the King.

All Europe, even republican Holland, reacted with horror to Charles I's execution, but that revulsion alone could not place Prince Charles on his father's throne. To regain his inheritance he needed a military force sufficient to defeat the New Model Army and it soon became apparent that such a force could not be found in the British Isles. The English Royalists were now a spent force. The localized risings of Penruddock (1655) and Booth (1659) were easily contained and crushed. The Irish and Scots were more formidable, although they put their own interests before Charles's and made unacceptable demands on religion. However, Irish resistance was virtually at an end by the close of 1650 and the Scots threat ended at the battle of Worcester (1651), although scattered resistance continued in the Highlands until 1655. After 1651, then, Charles could not hope to be restored by the unaided efforts of his subjects. To succeed, he would need substantial aid from abroad.

Unfortunately for Charles, the 1650s were a singularly bad time to seek such aid. The Stuarts had family connections with France (through Henrietta Maria) and the Dutch republic (through Mary's marriage to William II). The French, however, had problems of their own. Louis XIV was only eleven in 1649. A royal minority always bred faction and instability and these reached a peak in the crisis of the Frondes, between 1648 and 1652. On one occasion the young King and his mother fled from Paris; on another Cardinal Mazarin, their chief minister, went into exile for a while. To make matters worse, France was at war with Spain and the Spaniards exploited France's internal divisions to the full. Thus, once the worst of the crisis was over, Mazarin's first priorities were to prosecute the war against Spain and to rebuild the monarchy's power at home. He had no wish to annoy the English republic, with its powerful army and fleet, by gallant, quixotic gestures on behalf of his master's unfortunate young cousin. Concerned first and foremost with French interests, Mazarin sought good relations with Cromwell and in 1657 allied with him against Spain.

William II was more inclined than Mazarin to help Charles, but he too faced domestic difficulties. In 1648 the Dutch had at last secured their independence from Spain and were weary of war. Moreover, the rulers of the great towns distrusted William's dynastic ambitions, fearing (probably rightly) that he wished to change the republic into a monarchy. Their suspicions would have made it difficult for William to mobilize men and money on Charles's behalf. In fact the possibility of Dutch help disappeared when William died in October 1650, leaving a son born a week after his death. The power of the House of Orange collapsed. Its enemies, the States party, had never liked the liaison of Orange and Stuart and now sought the friendship of their fellow republicans in England. From 1651 the Stuart Princes were officially *personae non gratae* in the United Provinces. Although they visited Mary quite often and she gave them financial help in her private capacity, there was no question of any official aid or recognition from the States General.

If the French and Dutch were unable or unwilling to help, that left only the Spaniards, the rulers of the Southern Netherlands. As the Stuarts' connections were traditionally with the Houses of Bourbon and Orange, the Habsburgs were inclined to distrust the exiled Princes. Moreover, even if they had been willing to help, their ability to do so was limited. Spain's power was declining. It had been forced to acknowledge the loss of the Northern Netherlands and in 1643 at Rocroi the great Spanish army suffered its first major defeat at the hands of the French. Economically decayed and politically unstable at home, Spain's problems were compounded by problems of communication between Madrid and Brussels. The Spanish governors in the Netherlands were always waiting for money and orders. Nevertheless, once Cromwell established friendly relations with France and attacked Spanish possessions in the New World, the Spaniards began to show more interest in Charles and he and James eventually entered the Spanish service, where they raised several regiments of English, Scots and Irish exiles.

If the Stuart Princes were modestly useful to the Spaniards, the latter's main concern was the war against the French and English. Charles's restoration was for them a secondary concern, a threat to use against Cromwell, not a serious proposition. They lacked the forces and, above all, the shipping to mount a successful invasion. The exiles' dilemma remained the same throughout the 1650s. The English Royalists were reluctant to risk a major rising unless assured of substantial military help from abroad. But no foreign power would embark on a major invasion unless assured of a large-scale rising in England

and, preferably, a secure port in which to land. It was a dilemma which proved insoluble.

For the exiled Royalists, then, the 1650s were a time of frustration and depression. Again and again, hopes of foreign aid proved illusory. Conspiracies and risings which looked impressive on paper were betrayed or discovered. Some exiles gave up and made their peace with Cromwell. Others embarked on improbable negotiations with the Levellers or the Pope. These also failed and reduced the exiles' standing in the eyes of moderate Royalists at home. On top of all their other problems was that of money. Most of the exiles were unused to working for their living. Their income had come from land or the pickings of a wealthy court. Now most of their lands had been confiscated (although some managed by devious means to receive part of their landed income) while Charles and his brothers had scarcely enough to keep themselves. Nevertheless, they managed to scrape money together from a variety of sources.

The nearest to "earned" income came from prizes, English ships taken by Royalist privateers. James, as lord admiral, was supposed to receive one tenth of their value. As their value was often hard to assess, however, the income from this source was disappointing. James's pensions from first France and then Spain could also be seen as payment for his services in their armies. For the rest, the exiles depended on charity and on what they could scrounge. Mazarin granted Charles and James small pensions, but while they lived with their mother the pensions were paid to her servants who deducted her expenses before handing over the remainder. Moreover, the Queen's own pension was often in arrears during the Frondes and she then took little care to provide for her sons' servants. Only when Charles left Paris in 1654 did Mazarin pay him his pension directly and regularly, and for the next two years his finances were at their healthiest.[1] James, more in favour at the French court, had fewer financial problems until he prepared to leave Paris in 1656. Once in Flanders, the brothers' financial condition deteriorated. The Spaniards were more generous with promises than with cash and Charles received no money between March 1657 and January 1658. His followers' credit was exhausted and they often wondered where the next meal was coming from. Finally, besides the pensions there were gifts, from Royalists in England, German princes and above all Mary, who always put Charles's interests before her son's and saw his restoration as an essential preliminary to that of the House of Orange.[2]

Despite its difficulties, however, the court did not starve. Tradesmen gave credit, money could be borrowed, jewels were pawned or sold. Charles, James and their courtiers were young and exuberant. If they could not afford the splendour of their father's court, wine was cheap and women were plentiful: "They go every day here a-hunting and every night drinking, dancing and a-wenching," wrote one observer of Charles's court at Cologne. When Charles visited a monastery there his followers devoured the refreshments like a swarm of locusts. James led a similarly hectic social life at Paris. Early in 1656 he wrote that he was attending so many balls, dinners and "divertisements" that he seldom got to bed before four in the morning. Poor the exiled Stuarts might be, but they were princes none the less and were often royally entertained.[3]

Life was not all pleasure, however. Decisions had to be made and here frustration and poverty intensified the endemic factionalism of the Stuart court. If there were no great rewards for which to compete, courtiers competed vigorously for small ones (like control of Charles or James's minuscule revenues) or for hypothetical ones: for offices of state with no duties, no salaries and no power or for promises of rewards when the King was restored (and these rewards were the more inflated for being hypothetical). These battles were not meaningless, however, for if Charles was restored those who had won his favour in exile were likely to direct his affairs, with all the profit and power which that implied. Moreover, these struggles for power were closely linked to the question of the means of Charles's restoration. Those who advised the strategy which succeeded could expect enormous rewards.

The most basic division among Charles's advisers went back at least as far as the eve of the civil war. On one hand, the moderate Royalists were attached to the Church of England and the traditional constitution. Many had strongly attacked Charles I's political and religious measures in the early sessions of the Long Parliament, but from late 1641 had begun to go over to the King when they saw the traditional political and ecclesiastical order threatened by Parliament and its radical supporters. Their ideal now was to restore the monarchy as it had been after the constitutional reforms of 1641. Their main basis of support lay among the old Cavaliers and they followed Charles I in urging his son to be firm to the Church of England. The second main faction centred on the Queen and had little fondness for either the traditional constitution or Anglicanism. Much more unscrupulous about means than the old Cavaliers, the Queen's adherents were ready to sacrifice episcopacy in order to gain the assistance of Presbyterians or Catholics. In the 1650s they argued more and more that Charles's restoration depended on Catholic powers and that he should show more kindness to Catholics in England and Ireland, even at the risk of alienating the Anglicans. They also urged greater concessions to the English Presbyterians in 1659-60 than the moderates thought necessary or desirable.

The main leaders of the old Cavaliers were Edward Hyde, from 1642 one of Charles I's leading advisers, and the Marquis of Ormond, leader of the Protestant Royalists in Ireland. They were supported by Edward Nicholas, the late King's secretary of state. The Queen's main supporters were Lord Jermyn (who was probably also her lover) and Sir John Berkeley. Others joined these two parties at various times and there were also personality differences, like those involving Prince Rupert, which cut across these factional divisions. From 1651 Charles mostly followed Hyde's advice, but less vigorously or consistently than Hyde would have wished. James's position was more uncertain. He was attracted to Berkeley and Jermyn, especially when Charles was away, while they sought to build up their influence over James since Charles took little notice of their advice. Sometimes they tried to advance James's interests at the expense of Charles's and even to set James against his brother. James was usually too dutiful to be led far astray, but the conduct of James's servants annoyed Charles's advisers and caused friction between the two brothers. The fact that James patronized such unscrupulous and politically unwise people said little for his judgment of character and did not augur well for his competence as a king. Like his brother, James chose bad advisers; unlike his brother, he trusted them.

* * *

In the weeks after James came to the Hague in 1648 two related problems arose: the composition of his body of servants or "family" and what to do with that part of the Parliamentarian fleet which had just defected to the King. James's old servants had been dismissed after the surrender of Oxford. The governor named by his father, Lord Byron, had not been allowed to see him and in 1648 was actively involved in one of the Royalist risings. James arrived from Holland with only two or three servants, of whom only Bampfield had any serious claim to favour. The Queen, who claimed the right to choose James's servants, decided in view of Bampfield's humble origins and "hot and restless" temperament to fob him off with the minor post of groom of the bed-chamber. Bampfield was deeply offended, especially as the Queen named Sir John Berkeley as James's governor. Bampfield knew and loathed Berkeley and wasted no time in poisoning James's mind against him and, indeed, against his mother.[4]

On 27th May six ships of the English fleet mutinied, sailed for Holland and asked James to be their admiral. James had been appointed lord admiral at the age of three. His commission had been superseded, but it had always been assumed that his father intended him to act as admiral when he was old enough. In 1648, however, he was only fourteen and told the sailors that Rupert should command them. Bampfield, who already claimed that the seamen would not trust James while Berkeley enjoyed his confidence, now pressed some of the seamen to declare that they would not serve under Rupert and to insist that James should lead them. James dutifully disavowed these intrigues and told Rupert of them when he arrived with Prince Charles early in July. Charles promptly dismissed Bampfield from his brother's service. For a while there was some friction between the brothers. Charles declared that he would go to sea and ordered James back to the Hague. James, who had come to see the fleet as his own province, resented Charles's elbowing him out, but eventually complied. Meanwhile, Lord Jermyn tried to persuade the sailors to demand that he should be their admiral, while stirring Charles up against James; Berkeley and James's other servants, similarly, did all they could to inflame their master against his brother. These animosities and tensions simmered while Charles's fleet was away at sea and burst out when it returned to port in September.[5]

The sailors had become increasingly restless and frustrated as their commanders had failed to find and engage Parliament's fleet. When they returned to Holland, accusations of corruption and mismanagement flew thick and fast. With the fleet blockaded at Helvoetsluys and no money to pay the sailors, discipline and morale deteriorated. In November the sailors mutinied. Some wanted James to command them and Charles asked him to go to the fleet to appease them. James refused, possibly out of pique, perhaps because he did not wish to seem to advance his own interests at his brother's expense. Charles agreed that neither of them should go to sea that winter and that Rupert should command the coming expedition to Ireland. As James had sent to Rupert when the ships first came over, this arrangement probably satisfied him. Rupert was so much older and more experienced that James had no cause to feel jealous of him.[6]

By the end of 1648 Charles and James had outstayed their welcome at the Hague. They and their courtiers were insufferably arrogant, claiming precedence over even the Prince of Orange and refusing to eat with the honest bourgeois of the States General. They were also thoroughly incompetent: "Please God, our master shall have nothing more to do with these people . . ." wrote one of William's servants, "never in my life have I seen such disorder and confusion." The intrigues within and between the "families" of Charles and James created antagonism and mistrust and they imposed a great financial burden on the hosts whom they treated so rudely. It came as a great relief, therefore, when the Queen summoned James to Paris in December. He dismissed many of his servants and departed, taking the rest of his "uneasy family" with him, which helped reduce the tensions in his brother's court. His creditors tried to seize his baggage—his debts in November had been over £16,500—but the States General had it released and William gave him money for his journey. At Brussels he received a letter from his mother saying that Paris was in turmoil and that he should stay where he was. Not until 3rd February did he reach Paris, where he met his mother for the first time in almost five years.[7]

The joy of their reunion ended abruptly with the news of the King's execution on 30th January. James, like Charles, had clearly felt much more affection for his father than for his mother. Although his memoirs make only a passing reference to the execution, it clearly had a deep and lasting effect on him. It filled him with a deep hatred of the regicides so that he could consider a plot to assassinate Cromwell without any sign of compunction.[8] In the long term, his father's execution did much to shape James's political outlook. From it and from the civil war James derived two main lessons. The first was that kings should always be firm. He argued repeatedly that his father had been undone by weakness, compromise and compliance, as when he agreed to Strafford's execution. Again and again, he urged his brother not to make the same mistakes. As Burnet wrote of James: "He has an ill opinion of any that proposes soft methods and thinks that is popularity, but at the same time he always talks of law and justice."[9]

Secondly, most of the exiled Royalists explained the civil war mainly in terms of human wickedness. While some, like Hyde, were aware that Charles I's behaviour had given grounds for legitimate complaint, they believed that ambitious men had exploited these grievances in order to corrupt a basically loyal nation and turn it against the King. Charles's execution at the behest of a tiny fraction of the original Parliamentarians seemed to confirm this view. In fact, the republicanism of most of the regicides was the product of pragmatism rather than principle; their quarrel was with Charles I rather than with monarchy as an institution and hardly anyone in Parliament or army seriously considered getting rid of the King until the second civil war convinced the army that there could be no peace while he lived. In retrospect, however, many Royalists came to assume that the Parliamentarians had intended from the outset to destroy the King and the monarchy just as they had intended to destroy Laud and the Church. Thus even the Presbyterians, the most moderate of the Parliamentarians who had abhorred Charles's execution, could in some ways be blamed for it.

This explanation of the civil war and of his father's execution appealed to James. He could never differentiate between varying degrees of opposition and saw all opposition, both in the 1640s and after the Restoration, as subversive and republican. In Burnet's words, he "was for subjects' submitting in all things to the King's notions and thought that all who opposed him or his ministers in Parliament were rebels in their hearts." He thus enormously overestimated the strength of English republicanism. "Nothing will satisfy the Presbyterians but the destroying the monarchy and the setting up a commonwealth," he wrote in 1679. Moreover, his chosen monocausal interpretation of political conflict allowed no room for considerations of religious principle: "Believe me, 'tis a republic which is at the bottom of all these affairs in England and not religion."[10]

Quite apart from its emotional impact, then, his father's execution helped form James's crude and distorted views on English political conflict. The republicans, he believed, had killed his father and now wished to destroy his brother and himself. Taken together the two lessons which he derived from the 1640s help explain James's failure as king. His obsession with republicanism made him unable to appreciate the moderation, conservatism and essential loyalism of most of his opponents and the varied anxieties which motivated them. His abhorrence of weakness made him reluctant to take the conciliatory steps which would have removed those anxieties and divided the mass of moderate loyalists from the few irreconcilable radicals. Convinced that his critics wished to destroy the monarchy, he assumed that any concession would only make them greedy for more. Lacking an ability to differentiate, James saw everything in terms of absolutes, good and bad, white and black, right and wrong, "he that is not with me is against me."[11] So, ironically, the political maxims which James deduced from his father's downfall were to lead to his own.

In February 1649, however, such failures lay far in the future. The Queen and her court pressed Charles to come to Paris so that she could guide his efforts to regain his father's throne. Charles showed no inclination to be guided. He was now king, in the Royalists' eyes. The kingly power went a little to his head and much more to those of his servants, some of whom were openly disrespectful towards the Queen. When Charles eventually came to Paris in July he made it clear that he would not be directed by his mother, walking out on her when she tried to argue. The French court gave him no money, fearing to incur the hostility of the Rump, so in September Charles moved on to Jersey, hoping to sail for Ireland when his supporters there were ready to receive him. James, whom his brother now appointed lord admiral, went with him.[12]

That winter was spent in intrigue, poverty and frustrated inactivity. Jermyn tried, unsuccessfully, to establish over Charles the sort of influence he had over his mother. In February 1650 Charles travelled to Breda to negotiate with the Scots, leaving James governor of Jersey. James was bored and asked if he could go to join Rupert's fleet, then at Lisbon. He also criticized Charles's negotiations with the Scots and dismissed Byron and Berkeley from their places for supporting them. James may have opposed the negotiations because his mother supported them or because he feared that Charles would sacrifice the interests of the Church of England to the rigid Presbyterians who now ruled Scotland. If the latter, his fears were well founded. Even the Queen was disgusted at the concessions Charles was forced to make, but, as Hyde realized later, he had little choice: if the Scots could not be persuaded to help him, no one else would. While Charles was in Scotland, James fretted at Jersey, longing to undertake some bold action on behalf of the King, his brother. His irritation with his mother grew with his frustration and was eagerly fed by his "family" who played on her alleged lack of concern for James and her neglect of his servants. As a result, when James returned to Paris in September he was liable to flare up at the slightest provocation.[13]

It was soon clear that no love was lost between James and his mother. Lord Hatton wrote:

"She omits no opportunity to express her undervalue of him where she thinks she may do it secretly. . . . She lately told a lady that the Duke of York had said that the Queen in his and the opinion of all the world loved and valued Lord Jermyn more than she did all her children. . . . [The Queen added that] the King . . . was of better nature than the Duke of York, with much more of great bitterness. All which being reported again to the Duke of York, as it was, I leave it to you to consider what impressions these things may make in each of them."

He added that news had just come of Cromwell's victory over the Scots at Dunbar.[14] Rumours soon followed that Charles was dead or badly wounded. Already James was considering leaving Paris. At Jersey, James had come under the influence of Sir Edward Herbert and Sir George Radcliffe. Neither was officially his servant, but together they filled his head with dreams of serving Charles by building a great army and making himself a major European figure, like the Duke of Lorraine. (They conveniently ignored the fact that Lorraine had started off with a large army while James had nothing.) The prospect of independence from his tactless mother was alluring at any time and the rumours of Charles's death tipped the scales. On 23rd September James left Paris for Brussels. The Queen tried to stop him, "more out of policy than affection", but James was adamant. He did, however, agree to take with him Byron and Sir Henry Bennet, his secretary, although he trusted neither of them.[15]

At Brussels James was joined by Herbert and Radcliffe. Assuming that Charles was dead or dying, they proceeded to hand out offices and to conduct diplomatic negotiations as if they were the ministers of a king. Then came the embarrassing news that Charles was not dead. Herbert's negotiations to marry James to Lorraine's daughter (whom many suspected to be illegitimate) were getting nowhere and James's little stock of money was running out. His sister Mary, prostrated first by her husband's death and then by the birth of her son, could not receive him. When she recovered she refused to let him come until their mother permitted it. Charles wrote from Scotland that James should go back to Paris and follow his mother's advice. By now James was thoroughly tired of the whole escapade and would have been glad to obey, but his mother wrote that the situation in France would not allow it. James therefore diverted himself by going to The Hague with his sister and riding ostentatiously past the lodgings of the ambassadors of the English republic, while his followers taught the citizens to chant "Cromwell's bastards".[16]

James still tried to ensure that his return to Paris should not be an abject surrender. He pressed the Queen to procure him his own establishment (income and household) but the French court was reluctant to promise anything to anybody. In May 1651 Hatton wrote that the Queen and her advisers at the Louvre would not send for James "unless they can strip him unto his doublet and hose and cashier all about him but their own creatures". It was a reasonable supposition, but it was wrong. At the end of that month, the Queen sent Hyde, newly returned from Spain, with a letter inviting James to return.[17]

Hyde found James "with a family in all the confusion imaginable, in present want of everything and not knowing what was to be done next. They all censured and reproached the counsel by which they had been guided and the counsellors as bitterly inveighed against each other." They agreed only in criticizing Herbert, who still maintained his influence over James. Hyde found that James "was himself so young that he was rather delighted with the journeys he had made than sensible that he had not entered upon them with reason enough and he was fortified with a firm resolution never to acknowledge that he had committed an error." He still set off for Paris as soon as he could. His mother received him kindly, saving her reproaches for those whom she thought had led him astray. It had been a sorry episode. Secretary Nicholas, watching from The Hague, had at first sympathized with James. The Queen, he thought, wanted to "have the new modelling of him and teach him to bow to the Baal of the Louvre". First-hand experience of James's servants led him to modify his views. He still disliked the Queen's advisers but admitted that she had been given cause for complaint and declared that he wanted nothing whatever to do with James's "family".[18]

Even if James would not admit that he had been in the wrong, he had learned something from his futile gesture of defiance. At Charles's command, he no longer consulted Radcliffe and paid more heed to wiser men like Nicholas and Ormond. Unfortunately, neither of these spent much time at Paris, Nicholas because the Queen disliked him, Ormond because he was weary of business.

James's quarrels with his mother continued, partly because he still consulted Herbert but more often because of money. James lived at the Louvre, where the Queen made him pay for his food. When he could not pay enough, she deprived him and his servants of breakfasts, fire and candles. Henrietta Maria was never generous, but there was clearly calculation behind her meanness. She aimed to use her financial power over James to make him submit to her will. She refused to ask the French court for an increase in his pension unless he dismissed Herbert from his service. James's financial dependence increased his desire to secure an adequate income of his own. He began to attend the French court regularly and created a good impression "by his comeliness and personal dexterity in his behaviour and exercises".[19] He had won nothing more tangible than respect, however, when Charles returned to Paris in October, tired, dishevelled and full of stories of his adventures after the battle of Worcester.

* * *

Charles's return and the hopelessness of the Royalist cause further embittered the faction fighting at Paris. "The weakness, credulity and vanity of our friends trouble us little less than the vices of our enemies," wrote Hyde sadly. "This little court is fuller of factions than men, which were enough to destroy them if they had no other enemies," commented a more hostile observer.[20] At the heart of the disputes lay a struggle for power between Jermyn and Hyde, which reflected the efforts of the Queen and her servants to control Charles's affairs. Apart from personal antagonism, the main points at issue were money and religion. As with James, the Queen insisted that Charles should pay for his and his servants' food while he lived with her, and added that he should provide for James and his "family" as well. Again she hoped to use her financial power to force her children to do as she wished and again she failed. Hyde might bleat that he did not know how Charles would get bread in ten days' time, but Charles still refused to submit his affairs to his mother's direction.[21]

There was still greater bitterness about religion. Both Henrietta Maria and the Queen Regent of France were enthusiastic, not to say bigoted, Catholics. In the summer of 1651 the Queen Regent had forbidden Protestant services at the Louvre. When Charles returned, his mother argued that his hopes of restoration now depended on Catholic powers and that he and his brothers should turn Catholic to advance their cause. When Anglicans like Hyde argued that this would alienate all Protestant Royalists, she dismissed their fears as exaggerated and hysterical. Early in 1652 there were reports that Catholic priests, led by the abbé Walter Montagu (a great favourite of the Queen), were trying to convert Charles and James, but without success. When their younger brother was allowed leave in England early in 1652, Mary was reluctant to let him go to Paris, for fear of what the Papists might do to him. Time was to show that her fears were amply justified.[22]

Faced with this poverty and intrigue, Charles soon began to think of leaving France. Mazarin was slowly improving his relations with England, recognizing the Commonwealth in 1652 and the Protectorate in March 1654. Until these

negotiations were completed, however, Mazarin kept Charles in Paris by denying him the money he would need to go elsewhere, so that if the negotiations
broke down he could use Charles to stir up trouble in England. In June 1654,
however, Cromwell insisted that Charles, James and the other English Royalists
should leave France as a preliminary to further discussions. Accordingly,
Mazarin at last let Charles have his money and he left Paris on 28th June.[23]

While Charles lived in Paris he was naturally the main focus of political intrigue, but James lived in the same palace and his servants were bound to be
affected by the divisions within Charles's family. Those who were unable to
influence Charles tried to gain an ascendancy over his brother. These included
both the Queen and Sir John Berkeley. In the year before Charles's return
James's relations with his mother had been very strained. Thereafter they improved, partly because the Queen found herself unable to run Charles's affairs,
but more because of Berkeley's influence. When he had first been appointed
James's governor in 1648, James had disliked him. They had quarrelled violently
in 1649 and James had dismissed him in 1650. When James went to Brussels,
Berkeley had stayed in Paris, carefully building up his credit with the Queen.
Having failed to persuade Charles to make him a privy councillor and master
of the wards, Berkeley set out to establish himself as the dominant figure in
James's family, taking advantage of Herbert's transferring his attention from
James to Charles. Finding James eager to serve in the French army, Berkeley
claimed that anyone who opposed the idea wished to keep James in "pupillage"
and to deny him the chance to make a name for himself. Byron's death in 1652
removed Berkeley's only serious rival. He styled himself "intendant" of James's
affairs and encouraged James's dreams of building himself a great army with
which to serve his brother. To this end, he tried to find James a rich wife until
Charles made it clear that James should not marry before he did. By encouraging James's personal ambitions and reconciling him with the Queen, Berkeley
identified James with his mother's faction, turned him against Hyde and sowed
the seeds of a serious division between James and Charles.[24] Such developments
were to come to fruition after Charles's departure from France.

For James, however, the most memorable feature of these years must have
been his first real taste of war. As the younger son of a dispossessed king, he
needed a career to provide him with an occupation and an income and soldier-
ing was the obvious choice. At first the French were reluctant, for diplomatic
reasons, to employ him, but in 1652 James was allowed to "visit" the French
army, then under the greatest general in Europe, the Vicomte de Turenne.
James, now eighteen, took at once to the military life: the hard work, the action,
the fatigue, the danger. He "ventures himself and chargeth gallantly where
anything is to be done," noted one observer.[25] James's admiration for Turenne's
skill and thoroughness was unbounded, while Turenne seems to have developed
a real liking for this brave and enthusiastic young prince and continued to
correspond with him long after he left France. In many ways, these years in
the French army were probably the happiest of James's life. He had long lived
in his elder brother's shadow and had been further constricted by his financial

dependence on a meddling and domineering mother. The army offered an escape from both these constraints. It allowed James's limited individuality to flower and satisfied the desire for independence which he had shown by his flight to Brussels in 1650. Although he was a king's son, he could gain advancement in a foreign army only if he earned it and there is every sign that he did so, by his diligence and his courage. In 1654 he received his first commission, as lieutenant general. When Charles left Paris it is most unlikely that James felt any desire to go with him. His future, it seemed, lay in France.

* * *

With Charles gone, James came wholly under the sway of Berkeley and of Jermyn, whose charm soon captivated the young prince: Hatton wrote in 1655 that James "is not only loaded but delighted with his yoke, scarce eats without him".[26] The influence over him of the two older men was reinforced by their nephews, Charles Berkeley and Henry Jermyn. Both were about James's own age, accompanied him on his campaigns and came to enjoy his trust. It was the uncles, however, who exercised the greater influence and who tried to involve James in schemes to woo the Catholics and the Presbyterians. Their influence was clearly apparent in the Queen's attempt to convert the Duke of Gloucester to Catholicism.

Henry, Duke of Gloucester was fifteen in 1654. Hyde thought him "in truth the finest youth and of the most manly understanding that I have ever known". Despite the earlier anxiety of Mary and others that their mother might try to convert Henry, Charles left him in Paris to complete his education when he and his followers went off to Cologne. He did, however, make the Queen promise not to force Henry to change his religion and he ordered James to make sure that she kept her word. The Queen's promise was not worth much. She and abbé Montagu pressed Henry to continue his studies in a Jesuit college. They argued that only Catholic princes could help the family and that Henry's own best chance of advancement lay within the Catholic church. They claimed that Charles (whatever he said) would not really object to his becoming a Catholic and that he should obey his mother before his brother. He was made to confer with priests on matters of doctrine while his Anglican tutor was kept away from him.

Despite the Queen's efforts to stop the mails to Cologne, news soon reached Charles, who was furious. He dispatched Ormond to Paris to bring Henry away at once. The Queen claimed that his conversion would do more good than harm and that it was her duty as a mother to do what she thought best for her children's spiritual welfare. She also denied using force, but as Ormond remarked her methods amounted to "a very austere compulsion". She did all she could to hinder Ormond and James from seeing Henry and to dissuade him from going away with them. When he insisted on leaving, she turned him out of her house and refused to give him her blessing before he left for Cologne.[27]

This episode showed starkly the combination of deceitfulness and blinkered egotism which Henrietta Maria displayed so often in dealing with her children. The role of the other exiles is more problematical. Jermyn at first tried to keep the matter secret from Charles, but after a stinging rebuke from him Jermyn made every effort to keep Henry out of the Jesuits' college. Generally, though, Berkeley and the rest of the Queen's faction did little to stop her, perhaps because they feared to displease her, but they may also have hoped to blame Hyde and Ormond for having left Henry in Paris without sufficient safeguards. As Hatton wrote some months later: "I am confident that their malice against Sir E H[yde] is at that height they would ruin all the King's hopes as well as designs present to destroy [him]."[28] As for James, he returned to Paris from the army on 8th November, when the affair was already well advanced and only two days before Ormond arrived. The Queen would not let him speak of religion to his brother, except in her presence. He accompanied Ormond to see Henry at Chaillot and continued to see him after their mother had turned him out of the Louvre.[29] But Henry's letter to Charles of the 17th, mentioning those who had helped him, did not mention James, while Hatton claimed that James's lack of energy had been much criticized. Hatton blamed Berkeley for hindering "the operation of his stoutness of backing the King's commands in this business".[30] This sounds plausible, in view of Berkeley's influence over James, but there are two other possible reasons for his inaction. First, James was by no means sure of employment in the French army the following year. Mazarin had resumed serious negotiations with Cromwell and talked of finding James employment in Italy. James might have wished, therefore, to avoid giving any offence at court, especially to the Queen Regent, who was clearly on Henrietta Maria's side.[31] A second possibility is that James may have approved of what his mother was trying to do.

Throughout his exile there were occasional stories that he had become a Catholic. There were complaints at his attending Mass in Brussels, but as his chaplain remarked, he went to hear the music, surrounded by his servants and there was little else to do in Brussels. In 1652 the Queen's priests had failed to convert him. On the other hand, James complained of the prohibition of Protestant services in the Louvre only after Herbert and Ormond had bullied him to do so. His position in 1651 or 1654 was probably much as it was in 1659; when tackled about the number of Catholics in his household, he remarked that most of them were converts:

"What made them turn Papist he knew not; he was sure that he gave them no encouragement for it either by word or deed; that he himself was and would continue in profession and practice a Protestant. But he knew not how to turn away those that were Papists . . . having all his present subsistence from those of that profession."[32]

Taking this in conjunction with what James said later, it seems unlikely that, while in exile, he seriously questioned the faith in which he had been brought up. On the other hand, while carefully avoiding any association with Presbyterianism,[33] James seems to have made little effort to uphold the interests of the Church of England against those of the religion of the court which he served. Fear of displeasing the French, then, rather than incipient Catholicism lay behind his failure to bestir himself to prevent Henry's conversion.

The attempt to convert the Duke of Gloucester completed the estrangement of the two courts at Cologne and Paris. James must have felt a deep division of loyalties. Duty required that he should obey the King, his brother. Self-interest and ambition drove him to try to please the French court, and he was encouraged in this by Jermyn and Berkeley. This division of loyalties was made more acute by two sets of negotiations in 1655–56: Mazarin's continued negotiations with Cromwell and Charles's with the Spaniards.

When Charles left, Mazarin hoped that James and the other Royalists would now be allowed to stay in France. The negotiations with Cromwell proceeded slowly and James was again able to serve with the French army during the campaign of 1655. Charles raised no objection to his doing so, provided he avoided any action which could impede his negotiations with Spain.[34] In October 1655, however, Mazarin and Cromwell concluded a treaty of mutual friendship, which included a secret clause that James and all the Royalists (except Jermyn) should leave France. When James heard the news, he was commanding the army, as the other generals were away. He returned to Paris and wrote to Charles asking for orders, adding that he was waiting to see what Mazarin would propose.[35]

Mazarin was in no hurry to make him leave. Having removed the danger of English enmity he wished to avoid any closer liaison with Cromwell. Moreover, James had persuaded many Irish soldiers to desert the Spanish service for the French and Mazarin feared that if James went the Irish would go with him. As for James, while no effort was made to make him leave he made no move to go. Mary's arrival in Paris in January 1656 gave a useful pretext for delay, as did Mazarin's habitual delay in paying James's pension and providing him with the money he needed to pay his debts and depart. Reunited with his beloved sister, who had among her servants an attractive lady called Anne Hyde, James enjoyed a whirl of festivities. The last thing he wished to do was leave Paris.[36]

Charles, however, was becoming insistent. His negotiations with the Spaniards were nearing completion and a secret treaty was signed in April. As it would not help the negotiations if Charles's brother were to serve with the French against Spain, Charles ordered James to accept no employment in the field that year, and was very annoyed when he found that James had agreed to serve again. James argued that it was too late in the season for the Spaniards to accomplish anything and that it was in the family's interest not to be committed exclusively to one side in the war. He claimed too that he was honour bound to serve the French. But Charles insisted and, on 11th July, positively ordered James to come to him. James was reluctant to obey: "his removal suits not either with his inclinations nor with the end of some about him". Berkeley feared that if they rejoined Charles's court his influence over James would be attacked. The French were reluctant to provide James with money, perhaps because they feared to lose their Irish soldiers, perhaps because the young King, five years James's junior, was genuinely fond of him. Short of money and with his servants seizing every pretext for delay, James eventually left Paris on 11th

September and rejoined his brother at Bruges on the 19th. He had not seen Charles for two years.[37]

*   *   *

When James arrived, it was too late in the season for serious military operations so Charles's court began to prepare for the next year's campaign. The Spaniards allowed Charles to raise four regiments and volunteers came in from all sides: whole regiments of Irish from the French service, Englishmen from the Swedish army, wild Highlanders in their kilts (who aroused great interest in Bruges) and soldiers of fortune from all over Europe. When they saw how slowly the Spaniards provided pay and winter quarters, many had second thoughts and deserted. As Hyde spoke only English, the delicate task of liaison with Don John, the governor of Flanders, and Caracena, the Spanish commander-in-chief, was handled by the Earl of Bristol. Bristol had been secretary of state to Charles I and had served in France since 1648. Expelled from France under the treaty with Cromwell, Bristol was appointed secretary in December. Much more restless and unscrupulous than the phlegmatic Hyde, Bristol did much to provoke the domestic crisis which followed.

James had long felt dissatisfied with some of his servants. Some he trusted implicitly, like the Berkeleys and Henry Jermyn. Others had been appointed by Charles, notably Bennet, whom Charles thought was "full of duty and integrity to you". James disagreed. He thought that Bennet and Radcliffe aimed to push out the Berkeleys and Jermyn and seize control of his affairs. When sent by Charles to Paris in the summer of 1656 to urge James to hasten his departure, Bennet accused James to his face of carrying on a separate correspondence in England, through a dubious Catholic soldier and playwright called Samuel Tuke. To do so would have been against Charles's strict orders and James strongly denied it. Nevertheless Bennet and others suggested to Charles that Berkeley and perhaps James himself were conducting negotiations with English malcontents, of which Charles knew nothing. Berkeley certainly had dealings with Bampfield, now a spy for Cromwell, who claimed that Berkeley had suggested that James should marry Cromwell's daughter. Whatever the truth of Bennet's allegations, they were bound to have an effect. Charles was acutely sensitive about attempts to separate James's interest from his own or to encourage James to establish his own faction in England. He therefore hinted strongly to James that he would prefer him to leave Berkeley in Paris and when they came to Bruges Charles treated Berkeley with conspicuous coldness.[38]

It was three months before the storm finally broke. During that time, Berkeley showed himself even more arrogant than usual and made no secret of the fact that he had not wished to leave France and that he had nothing but contempt for the Spaniards. His attitude only made his enemies' task easier. They had already convinced Charles that Berkeley had turned James against him and that he should choose his brother's servants. Now Bristol claimed that Don John bitterly resented Berkeley's anti-Spanish attitude and urged Charles to send him away before he ruined Charles's relations with the Spanish authorities.

Charles agreed, ignoring Hyde's argument that Berkeley was too unimportant to be made the cause of so much fuss.[39]

It was left to Bristol to put Charles's decision into effect. First he pressed James to order Berkeley to withdraw for his own good: he claimed that both Charles and Don John were incensed against him. He then said much the same to Berkeley, adding that Charles would insult him openly if he remained at court. (Bristol admitted later that he had taken Don John's name in vain.) James was deeply distressed. He believed that honour and prudence obliged him to stand by his servants and not to let them be driven away unless good cause were shown. Mary, who had come to Bruges in November, agreed with him and so did many others at court. James feared too that if Bristol (who had virtually sole charge of the court's dealings with Don John and Caracena) could poison them against Berkeley, he could also poison them against him. As Charles seemed determined that Berkeley should go, there seemed no point in James's opposing his will, so he decided instead to go away as well. Two days after Berkeley left, James (together with Charles Berkeley and Jermyn) slipped away from a shooting party near Sluys and rejoined the elder Berkeley at Flushing.[40]

James now embarked on a bizarre and confused journey. His first instinct was to head for France, but as Cromwell's navy made it dangerous to go by sea, James and his companions decided to go overland through the Dutch republic and Germany, skirting the eastern frontier of the Spanish Netherlands. From Flushing they travelled east to Zuylestein, near Utrecht, home of the tutor to the young William III. While there, James wrote to his brother on 29th December. He apologized for having disobeyed him for the first time in his life but claimed that he could see no honourable alternative. After visiting his sister at Dieren, near Arnhem, and then travelling to Amsterdam for a wedding, James returned to Zuylestein to find a letter from Charles whose messengers had hitherto, not surprisingly, failed to find him.[41]

Charles had been dismayed by James's unexpected departure and begged him to return. In his reply James complained of being made to employ men like Bennet, who was disrespectful and deceitful and had accused James of trying to build up an independent interest in England. He complained at being ordered to serve against France and especially against Turenne "who is one of the men in the world I am the most obliged to". Above all, he complained at being forced to part with "so faithful, so eminent and innocent" a servant as Berkeley "upon suggestions falsely fathered upon the Spaniards and groundless surmises of ill offices done by him in our family, which in every way reflects more on me than upon the person himself". James was, however, prepared to return on two main conditions. First, any allegations against himself or his servants should be fully investigated and their authors punished if they proved untrue. Secondly, Berkeley should be allowed to return and prove his innocence. Charles promptly accepted these conditions, with the one reservation that Berkeley should stay away from court for a month. A few days later James returned to Bruges where Charles welcomed him with great joy.[42]

At first sight the whole episode seems to provide evidence of James's stubbornness and folly. If Berkeley was not actually a tool of Cromwell's* there is no doubt that he was vain, greedy and a most unreliable adviser. He had tried to dissuade James from leaving France and had apparently engaged in some very dubious negotiations in England on James's behalf. In defending Berkeley so staunchly James showed the mixture of loyalty and obtuseness which he was to show so often when his servants were criticized. Lacking political sense himself James was ill equipped to judge whether others possessed it, so he chose his advisers on the basis of their professions of attachment to his interests. Throughout his life he showed a touching loyalty to those he believed loyal to him. On this occasion, however, what seemed an exhibition of stubborn weakness greatly strengthened his position at court, while the creation of an open rift between the two brothers helped to reunite them. By leaving the court James had shown that, loyal and obedient though he was, he could not be taken for granted. Intentionally or not, his departure highlighted the danger of a division in the royal family, perhaps even of a rival claim to the throne. It forced Charles to concede James's immediate demands and also to treat him with more consideration thereafter. Charles had already appointed Bennet his ambassador to Spain so did not mind James's dismissing him from his service. He also allowed Berkeley to return to court, after suitable submission, and even, at James's request, made him a peer. Berkeley at once demanded an estate suitable to his new dignity.[43]

For the last four years of his exile Charles's leading adviser was Hyde, whom he appointed lord chancellor in January 1658. Bristol's credit dwindled and disappeared when he became a Catholic in 1659. The Queen and Jermyn, far away in Paris, now exercised almost no influence over Charles or James, while Bennet's departure for Spain and Radcliffe's death removed the last major sources of division in James's household. Charles and James, reconciled after the Berkeley affair, were now in the same place, which made it harder to sow dissension between them than it had been while they were apart. James's instinct was always to serve and obey his brother. Charles, having learned his lesson, took care not to give him undue cause to complain. There seemed every reason to hope that that the court would now enjoy unity and harmony.

Unity and harmony, however, were alien to Charles II's court. If there was now little dissension within James's "family", there were still restless men there who took it upon themselves to advance James's interest (as they saw it) even at the expense of the interests of his brother. Berkeley still had his little projects and intrigues, but caused far less trouble now that his position was secure. He was even reconciled to Bristol.[44] But a new intriguer of a very different stamp emerged to take his place. Peter Talbot was an Irish Jesuit whose

---

* Turner (p51) prints a letter found in both the Thurloe and Clarendon papers which purports to show this. However as this letter, supposedly from Cromwell to Mazarin, seems so out of character with the rest of the surviving correspondence between them, it is probably a forgery.

brother Richard was one of James's lieutenant colonels. Unlike most of the exiles he could speak Spanish, a great advantage in dealing with the Spanish authorities in Brussels. He also had a talent for insinuating himself into people's confidence and did much to change the Spaniards' attitude towards James. Having originally suspected him of being too pro-French, by March 1658 they were paying his pension more promptly than Charles's, much to Charles's annoyance. The next month James sent Talbot to Madrid. Charles strongly disavowed his mission, but Talbot carried letters of recommendation from the authorities in Brussels and soon won the confidence of the Spanish court. Bennet (whom Talbot hated) could not discover the purpose of his mission, but heard that it involved favours for the English Catholics and that those at Brussels had a low opinion of Charles's advisers, an opinion which Talbot may have helped to form. Bennet was sufficiently concerned to press Charles to come to Madrid to remove the misunderstandings. Cromwell's ambassador at The Hague, who was usually well informed, thought that Talbot had gone to demand a large pension for James and to threaten that James would leave the Spanish service unless he was granted greater authority in military affairs. James certainly had his pension increased and received an additional regiment of horse before the end of the year.[45]

By the spring of 1659 Talbot had transferred his energies to England. Together with Tuke and the Duke of Buckingham, he was reported to be attempting to find support for James among Presbyterians and Catholics, in opposition to the Anglicans who supported Charles and Hyde. They also hoped that Richard Cromwell's Parliament would invite James to become king. Talbot's part in these intrigues ended when his Jesuit superiors ordered him to leave England in June and, soon after, expelled him from the Society. Unabashed, Talbot returned to Spain, met Charles at the peace conference at Fuentarabia and was received back into favour. He also probably solicited further employment for James and was still in Spain at the Restoration.[46]

Talbot carried on the tradition of Catholic and Presbyterian opposition to Hyde's Anglicanism which had earlier been associated with the Queen and her circle. The only difference was that, with Charles's changed circumstances, the Catholicism was Spanish rather than French. How far James approved Talbot's activities on his behalf must remain uncertain. He certainly sent him to Spain in 1658, presumably to procure some advantages for himself, but there is no evidence that James authorized his intrigues in England in 1659.* If he did, Charles does not seem to have known of it. Whereas in 1658 there had been reports that Charles distrusted James, in July 1659 he left James in complete charge of his affairs as he prepared to go to Spain.[47] Thus while James was eager

---

* James sent Giles Rawlings to England on private business early in 1659 and Rawlings undertook some very dubious negotiations with Thurloe, the English secretary of state. There is, however, no evidence that Rawlings undertook those negotiations at James's command and it seems more likely that his orders came from Berkeley: *Cal Clar SP*, IV 154, 175.

to improve his conditions of service in the Spanish army, there is no real evidence that he sought to establish an interest for himself in England to the detriment of his brother's. It was ominous, however, that he should give such countenance to irresponsible intriguers like Talbot. His dealings with such men were later to land him in serious trouble.

Whatever his initial reservations about serving Spain, James proceeded to do so with his usual energy and diligence. Ormond wrote that the Spanish general Marsin "undertakes to succeed Turenne in our Duke's good graces, a thing I advise him to endeavour". Marsin was a competent soldier, if not a great one, but in general James found the Spanish commanders brave, but unwilling to act without orders, over-confident and lazy. Their failure to organize scouts or quarters or mining operations formed a sad contrast to the meticulous attention to detail shown by Turenne.[48] All these failures were highlighted at the battle of the Dunes. Mazarin had at last signed an offensive treaty with Cromwell, who wished to gain possession of Dunkirk. In October 1657 the Anglo-French army took Mardike and beat off a Spanish counter-attack. The following spring the Spaniards, full of distrust of Charles, ignored his warning that the French would attack Dunkirk. When the attack came, they overestimated the strength of their position and opted to fight when it would have been wiser to retreat. Despite the conspicuous courage of James and Henry, the bulk of the Spanish army broke and fled at the enemy's first charge. James was proud that the English on both sides fought better than most of the Spaniards, but there was little else to console him. The army was scattered and the loss of Dunkirk provided Cromwell with an excellent naval base which improved his control of the Channel and made a seaborne invasion well-nigh impossible.[49]

By now James's hopes of returning to England seemed slim. He and his brothers often sought relief from the tedium and poverty of Brussels and the pomposity of the Spaniards in visits to Mary at Breda or The Hague. In the summer of 1659 Charles went to Fuentarabia, where France and Spain at last agreed to make peace, hoping that somebody would embrace his cause. James, meanwhile, hoped with Turenne's help to invade England to take advantage of an expected Royalist rising. The hopes of both were dashed and they returned to Brussels for another gloomy winter. Charles's cause seemed so hopeless that when, early in 1660, the Spanish offered James the place of lord high admiral he was inclined to accept. The post carried a great salary but little power and its two previous holders had resigned in some displeasure. Spurred on by his servants, James ignored these snags and persuaded Charles to give his consent. At last, it seemed, he would have a command of his own and be able to make a name for himself.[50]

It was not to be. After all the Royalists' schemes and plots had ended in failure, Charles was about to be restored as a result of the divisions of his enemies. After Oliver Cromwell's death, the army had disintegrated into warring factions. In February 1660 the army from Scotland, led by General Monk, occupied London. It was far from clear what sort of settlement Monk wanted but it soon became apparent that only a restoration of the monarchy could command general acceptance. By March Charles's picture was displayed openly in London. In April Charles issued his declaration of Breda, promising a general pardon and liberty of conscience subject to Parliament's approval. Encouraged by this the Convention Parliament which met a few weeks later invited Charles back without stipulating any conditions. Charles and his family, meanwhile, had moved from Brussels to Breda, ignoring the blandishments of Mazarin and the Spaniards who were ready to offer him anything now that his restoration seemed assured. The States General, who had repeatedly forbidden Charles and his brothers to enter their territory, now welcomed them effusively. On 16th May Charles received a formal invitation to return. That night the States General provided an enormous feast, with cannonades after every toast, which the exiles doubtless enjoyed to the full. On the 22nd James, as lord high admiral, paid his first visit to the English fleet and was acclaimed by the sailors. Two days later Charles and his followers sailed for England, landing at Dover on the 26th.

He found England in a paroxysm of enthusiasm, not only for himself and the monarchy but for the old ways in general. On May Day maypoles, forbidden under the Protectorate, reappeared everywhere while clergymen began once more to use the book of Common Prayer. Peers and notables in their dozens converged on Dover, escorted by troops of mounted gentlemen. In London bonfires four storeys high were prepared for the King's coming, houses were hung with tapestries, the streets were strewn with flowers and the fountains ran with wine. Charles's progress to London was a royal one in every sense of the word. At Canterbury they were met by Monk. Charles and his brothers embraced him and called him "father". All three wore dark suits with coloured plumes and clearly made an excellent impression: "all very pleasing and humble with majesty". As the King approached London over a hundred thousand people waited on Blackheath to greet him and the crowds in London defied description. Looking at it all, Charles remarked that "he doubted it had been his own fault he had been absent so long, for he saw nobody that did not protest that he had ever wished for his return." Such a cynical reaction was far less typical than John Evelyn's: "I stood in the Strand and beheld it and blessed God."[51]

CHAPTER THREE

England in 1660

The England to which Charles and his brothers returned was by modern standards an underdeveloped country. The great majority of the population depended for their livelihood on agriculture, directly or indirectly. Industry in the modern sense of mass-production in factories scarcely existed. Not only did the seventeenth century not possess the necessary technology, but mass-production requires a mass market, and that simply did not exist. Primitive transportation made the carriage overland of all but the most costly items prohibitively expensive. Moreover, the bulk of the population had little money left, after purchasing food for their families, to pay for consumer products. Although a few progressive farmers were adopting the new agricultural techniques developed in the Low Countries, most continued to use the methods of their forefathers and yields remained little higher than in the middle ages. Most manufactured goods were produced by small craftsmen, using local, mainly agricultural raw materials and serving a strictly local market. The home, not the factory, was thus the normal unit of industrial production, even in the cloth industry. This was, then, a static traditional economy, where signs of growth were few and scattered. Agricultural improvers were still the exception rather than the rule while the boom in the colonial trades which began in the 1670s had, at first, only a limited impact on the rest of the economy.

In this predominantly agricultural country, the majority of people were country dwellers, ranging from unemployed migrants or squatters, through the yeomen farmers, with stone farmhouses, some silver for the table and thoughts of marrying their daughters into the gentry, to marquises and dukes, with rentrolls running into five figures. The backwardness of trade and industry meant that most provincial towns were small and that the commercial and industrial middle class was comparatively weak. (London, however, was a great metropolis of maybe half a million people—almost one-tenth of the whole population of England—and its inhabitants included some prodigiously rich merchants and financiers.) The professional middle class—clergy, lawyers, civil servants—was rather larger and its richest members could stand comparison with any London plutocrat.

Neither section of the middle class did much to shape the social values of later Stuart England, which remained profoundly rural and aristocratic. Until the very end of the century successful businessmen or lawyers almost invariably bought country estates and began to intermarry with the landed gentry. Their aim in doing so was to become accepted by their neighbours as country gentlemen. Merchants and lawyers might run the affairs of little market towns and even of the great City of London. The largest units of local government, the counties, and the nation's great representative institution, Parliament, were dominated by the landed aristocracy, the peers and gentry. They alone had the leisure and the natural authority which came from broad acres, from gentle birth and from generations of experience. They were in every sense the natural and accepted rulers of England. Their overwhelming predominance in the commissions of the peace, the militia and both Houses of Parliament both reflected and reinforced their social and economic pre-eminence. In this mainly agrarian society, political power was inevitably bound up with the ownership of land.

Pre-industrial English society was essentially hierarchical. Inequalities of wealth and status and the dominance of the nobility and gentry were seen as part of the natural order of things. The peasantry showed the aristocracy a deference which sprang not only from fear of dismissal or eviction but from generations of indoctrination and habit. The nobility and gentry showed, within limits, a paternalistic concern for the welfare of their tenants and servants. If they seldom hesitated to raise rents or hold down wages, they often tried to protect their social inferiors from the worst effects of dearth and from "unfair" exploitation by grain dealers and middlemen. They also settled their inferiors' disputes and punished their misdemeanours. Their rank obliged them to show a certain generosity in terms of hospitality and gifts to the unfortunate. The peasantry, for their part, were accustomed to look to the gentry for leadership and protection. "Gratify the gentry," wrote one of Charles II's secretaries of state, "for no disturbance can be unless they be in the head of it. The people stir not without the gentry."[1]

This is not to suggest, however, that English rural society was invariably harmonious or that all was cakes and ale in Stuart England. For much of the population dearth and disease were ever present threats. One child in six died in its first year and one child in three before the age of five. Productivity and wages were low, in agriculture and in industry. Underemployment and unemployment were endemic in both. The inflation of the century before 1640 had encouraged landlords to push up rents and to abrogate age-old common rights, which deprived landless villagers of their chance to keep a cow or pig and sometimes led to rioting. Extreme dearth and hunger could also drive the peasantry to violent self-help. To put such outbursts in perspective, however, it is worth comparing England with France. People died in England from hunger and from diseases directly attributable to malnutrition, but on nothing like the same scale as in France. Nor were the English peasantry goaded into desperate rebellion either by sheer hunger or by the crushing weight of royal and seigneurial taxation. English peasant riots, moreover, were usually limited in scope and highly disciplined and reflected a traditional and clearly articulated code of social and economic values. Despite the virtual absence of a police force, English rural society managed to absorb most of its own internal tensions. The English government did not need a standing army to maintain order, partly because the English peasantry were less catastrophically over-burdened than their counterparts in most continental countries and partly because of England's combination of peasant deference and aristocratic pater-nalism.[2]

The counties which formed the basic units of English local government were in many ways economically and socially self-sufficient. Poor communications hindered the movement of goods and people. The notorious Wealden roads of Kent and Sussex were often impassable in winter, cutting off the inhabitants of what is now commuter country from the capital. The difficulties and dangers of travel discouraged even the wealthy from moving far from their homes so, normally, the gentry married within their own neighbourhood. As Lucy Hutchinson wrote: "It had been such a continued custom for my ancestors to take wives at home that there was scarce a family of any note in Sussex to which they were not by intermarriages nearly related." These relationships were reinforced by constant social contacts, through visits and house parties, hunting and race meetings. They helped make social occasions out of meetings concerned with county business: quarter sessions and assizes, militia musters and elections. As a result the gentry élite in most counties was both closely knit and showed a surprising degree of continuity. In Kent, to take an extreme example, over four-fifths of the gentry families present in 1640 had been established in the county since before 1485.[3]

Bad roads, enforced economic self-sufficiency and gentry intermarriage, then, all helped to produce the localism which was such a prominent feature of the provincial society of Stuart England. Poor communications and press censorship together inhibited the spread of news about national affairs and for most country gentlemen local issues were at least as important as national issues. Their county was their "country" and they had a fierce pride in their ability to run their own affairs in their own way. They disliked changes to traditional routines, especially if they were imposed by civil servants far away in London who neither knew nor cared about their particular local problems.

Yet the parochialism of the county communities can be exaggerated. Region-al variations were far less marked in England than in, say, France. There was a common language (except in Wales and Cornwall) and a common legal system. There were no provincial representative bodies to provide a focus for local loyalties and to distract attention from Parliament. Handwritten newsletters and the official Gazette kept the denizens of remote manor houses and one-horse towns informed, at least superficially, of events in London and on the continent. The minority of Englishmen who could read grew rapidly in the century before 1660. More and more books and pamphlets were published and the collapse of press censorship in the Interregnum and again in the Exclusion Crisis made possible a genuinely popular debate on major political and religious issues. Parliamentary elections also helped to disseminate political information and ideas and to awaken even the illiterate and unenfranchised to the great political issues of the day.[4] The squires who ruled rural England and sat in the Commons might be conservative but they were not rustic simpletons. Members of Parliament often showed in debate an impressive range of learning, drawing illustrations from the Bible, the classics and history. It is easy, too, to over-estimate the localities' resentment and independence of central control. The massive extension of state regulation—economic, social and religious—under the Tudors would have been impossible without the co-operation of the gentry who provided the information on which legislation was based, approved it in Parliament and then enforced it in the localities. Moreover, Justices of the Peace often enforced measures which they clearly disliked, either out of duty or because they feared dismissal from the bench: a place on the commission of the peace gave a man power over his neighbours and inferiors and enhanced his standing in the county.

Thus the main features of provincial England were localism, stability and conservatism. Both agricultural methods and social relationships were strongly influenced by custom and tradition. Change (unless a very good reason could be shown) was regarded with suspicion and often with outright hostility. Thus Charles I's attempts to reform local government and to levy ship money aroused bitter hostility, much of it based on constitutional scruples but much also on a simple dislike of innovation. The opposition in the counties to Charles I was nothing, however, to that provoked by the various regimes of 1642–60. Faced with the need to defeat the King and to hold down an increasingly hostile population, the central government imposed unprecedented taxation, ignored traditional procedures and rode roughshod over time-hallowed legal rights and safeguards. By 1650 almost all the old county families had with-drawn or been excluded from county affairs. Their place was taken by lesser men, officials and above all soldiers. As they lacked the authority conferred by landed wealth and generations of involvement in local affairs, they relied increasingly blatantly on military force. The old county families disliked losing power to their social inferiors, but it was not just the gentry who resented these changes. The English did not like soldiers and they liked still less being taxed heavily in order to pay them: the excise, in particular, fell more heavily on the poor than on the rich. During the first civil war "clubmen" or peasant vigilantes appeared in over twenty counties, whose aim was to defend themselves and their property against the soldiers of both sides. The army of the 1650s, with its campaign for compulsory godliness, was no more popular. In the words of a Sussex peasant, reprimanded for spending his Sunday mornings in the alehouse: "Here I can have a cup of beer and if I should go to the church, there I should get none." Only a smallish minority of Englishmen were rabid Puritans. Most disliked the suppression of "disorderly" alehouses and of traditional sports and games. Like their social superiors, the bulk of the peasantry was essentially conservative and greeted the Restoration with relief.[5]

At the Restoration the county communities returned to normal surprisingly quickly. Few gentry families were ruined by the war: in Kent virtually all the oldest gentry families maintained their position until the end of the century and beyond.[6] The old families reappeared on the commissions of the peace and in some ways were left more to their own devices than before. Charles II's government showed far less interest than its predecessors in social and economic regulation and made only sporadic attempts to repress religious nonconformity. Despite signs of embryonic economic change, provincial society remained stable, traditional and conservative. Yet the need to secure the co-operation of the men who ran local government and the many links between centre and provinces—above all, through Parliament—meant that provincial opinion could not be ignored by those at the centre. The dukes in their palaces and the squires in their manor houses no longer posed any military threat to the crown, but to try to govern without taking account of their opinions and prejudices could prove highly dangerous, as James II was to find in 1688.

* * *

If the social values and economy of Restoration England were strongly traditional, the same was true of its political values. The dominant political concept was that of the Ancient Constitution, the traditional system of law and government stretching back unchanged and unchanging into the mists of antiquity. This provided an essentially historical justification for present institutions and procedures, which had much in common with the common law's reliance on case law and precedent. England had no systematic code of law and both constitutional and legal arguments were based more on concrete precedent than on abstract theory. Some seventeenth-century writers did, it is true, construct systems of political thought based on general principles rather than historical prescription. But none of them, even John Locke, attracted much support until well into the eighteenth century. Most English politicians continued to justify their arguments in historical terms, however weak and twisted their evidence might be.

The later seventeenth century saw a growing awareness of the possibility of progress in a number of fields. In the natural sciences phenomena which had once been explained as the actions of a wrathful and inscrutable God could now be seen to follow regular mathematical laws. In the social sciences Sir William Petty and others held out the prospect of unlimited economic growth, if the economy were properly managed, and argued that a large population could be a blessing rather than a curse. But no such concept of progress was developed in English constitutional thought, at least not one that was acceptable to more than a tiny fraction of the ruling élite. For what seemed to them good political reasons, Englishmen stuck stubbornly to the Ancient Constitution and men who see perfection in the past tend to remain both conservative and unimaginative. It is true that the events of the 1640s and 1650s had driven some thinkers to develop theories to justify the changes that were taking place. But these theories were often basically historical and, even when they were not, the very fact that they were associated with rebellion, regicide and republicanism made them unattractive after the Restoration. The concept of the people's right to resist a tyrant, for example, had had only a very limited currency in England before 1641. Under Charles II, some Whigs pointed out that kings who failed to maintain the goodwill of their subjects often came to sticky ends, but almost nobody asserted the right of resistance as such. The concept was resurrected with great hesitation and embarrassment after 1689, when supporters of the Revolution were careful to stress that the resistance used against James had been very different to that which had led to Charles I's execution.[7]

In an age obsessed with ideology and accustomed to people setting out to implement preconceived theories, it is easy to assume that our seventeenth-century forebears did the same. It is, moreover, rather hard to square the conservative constitutional views which I have outlined with the many radical things which happened. This contradiction can be explained only if we reverse the relationship which we assume between political ideas and political action. The changes which happened in 1640–60 or in 1689 happened in spite of, not as a result of, the prevailing constitutional theory. Men were forced by immediate political circumstances to take actions which directly contradicted their fundamental constitutional beliefs. New ideas were then developed, often hastily and inadequately, to justify what had been done as the result of the logic of events or of sheer chance. This could lead to considerable confusion as the new ideas were often propounded alongside older concepts, which they contradicted.*

It is, therefore, very misleading to write the history of the seventeenth century backwards, to start from 1688 or 1642 and to assume that what happened then was the product of conscious aspirations for change. To find out why these crises occurred, one must (I think) look a little more closely at the theory of the constitution and especially at the role of the monarch and consider the divergence between the theory and practice of monarchy under the early Stuarts.

It was generally agreed that England's was a mixed and balanced constitution, whose health depended on keeping a balance between the powers of the crown and the rights of the subject. On this Pym and Strafford were fully agreed. They agreed too that the monarchy was an essential part of the government. In Strafford's words, "The authority of a king is the keystone which closeth up the arch of order and government, which contains each part in due relation to the whole and which once shaken, infirmed, all the frame falls together into a confused heap of foundation and battlement."[8] The King alone was sufficiently above his subjects to do impartial justice between them. The King alone could provide the unified direction required in an emergency or in diplomacy. Few seriously questioned the necessity of either the monarchy or the royal prerogative. The source of dispute was not the general nature of the royal power but the way in which it was used in particular cases.

In theory the King's powers were supposed to be used for the common good. In practice, from at least the 1590s financial need drove successive monarchs to abuse their prerogatives increasingly blatantly in order to raise money. Worst of all, perhaps, was ship money: one of the crown's most

---

* Taken to its logical conclusion, the Exclusionists' demand that the King should always follow the wishes of the Commons would have destroyed the concept of the "mixed monarchy", to which they continued to proclaim their attachment.

essential duties (the defence of the realm in an emergency) was made the pretext for a new regular tax not approved by Parliament. Meanwhile, Charles I used his control over clerical appointments and the Church's internal affairs to impose a brand of Anglo-Catholic worship and theology which marked a radical break with the stolid middle of the road Puritanism of the Elizabethan Church. Such misuses of the prerogative seemed doubly alarming in view of the weakening of representative institutions and the advance of Counter-Reformation Catholicism on the continent. The Parliamentary opposition of the 1620s or in 1640 was thus conservative, defending the old ways in church and state against innovation. It was inspired above all by fear, fear of the twin horrors of "Popery and arbitrary government".

The members of the Long Parliament which assembled in 1640 knew what they wanted—a return to the old ways—but were far from sure how to achieve it. The proper working of the Ancient Constitution depended on the King's using his powers responsibly, for the purposes for which they were intended. If he did not do so of his own volition, the constitution provided no machinery to make him do so. The 1630s had shown that the judiciary could not or would not restrain a king who was determined to exploit his legal rights to the utmost. So in 1641 Parliament was in a dilemma. It had declared illegal many of Charles's fiscal devices and had abolished some of the institutions through which his measures had been enforced. But it had done nothing to prevent his developing new fiscal devices or institutions, nor had it begun to reverse the Laudian counter-reformation in the Church. MPs were reluctant to trust Charles to exercise his great powers responsibly in future, but they were equally reluctant to impose the novel checks which Pym claimed were necessary to make him do so: first, to make him share with Parliament his control of the armed forces, so that he could not use the army to coerce Parliament; secondly, to give Parliament a say in his choice of advisers, so that it could be sure that he would be responsibly advised even when Parliament was not in session.

At the end of 1641 the rebellion in Ireland forced Parliament to decide whether it could trust Charles with an army. A majority of MPs decided that they could not. Charles refused to abandon his control of the armed forces or his right to choose his advisers, and prepared for war. Parliament had no option but to do the same. The impossibility of trusting the King to respect both the letter and the spirit of the constitution had forced conservative country gentlemen to take up arms against their king. Once the war began, they had no choice but to try to win it. If they lost, "we shall all be hanged and our posterity made slaves." Once the war had been won, the moderates still found no satisfaction. Charles refused to make what his opponents saw as the minimum concessions needed to make the constitution work again, so the army lost patience with the moderates who wished to continue negotiating and cut off his head.

The great majority of Parliamentarians, then, were conservatives, who wished to restore the traditional order in church and state but were forced by Charles's intransigence and manifest untrustworthiness into a war which they would much rather have avoided. The experience of republicanism, sectarianism and military rule in the 1650s reinforced the conservatism of the political nation and in some ways gave it an added dimension. In religion the decades after 1660 saw a strengthening of the High Church element among the landed elite. As the old "Elizabethan" Low Churchmen died out many of their sons and grandsons imbibed very different principles, especially those who went to Oxford in the 1630s or after 1660. By Anne's reign High Church Anglicanism had infinitely stronger roots than it had had before 1640, as the Sacheverell trial was to show. This swing from Low to High Churchmanship no doubt owed something to the religious confusion of the Interregnum. "Enthusiasm" was discredited, order and authority were now deemed necessary.

There was a similar longing for order in the state. The ideal of the balanced constitution did not change. Before the civil war, however, the threat to the balance had seemed to come from crown and court, from "Popery and arbitrary government". The events of 1640-60 seemed to show that there was as great a threat from another direction. The destruction of the Church and the King's execution were seen as a conscious design carried through by Dissenters and republicans. Thus to the conservative Anglican gentry of Charles II's Parliaments, it seemed necessary to protect Church and constitution against threats from two sides: from a court which showed an undue fondness for Catholicism and absolutism and from unscrupulous Whig politicians who relied heavily on Nonconformist support.

The fact that the Ancient Constitution was now seen as facing potential threats from below as well as from above gave Charles II a real opportunity to consolidate and extend the royal authority, within the limits of what the Anglican gentry would tolerate. While they were more afraid of Dissent than of Popery, more afraid of republicanism than of absolutism, they would enthusiastically support the exercise of the royal authority—on the tacit understanding that the King should continue to protect the Church and respect the Ancient Constitution. On the other hand if the Anglican gentry were more afraid of Popery and absolutism than of Dissent and republicanism—or if they were simply annoyed by governmental incompetence and waste of taxpayers' money—they could prove just as vocal and obstreperous as any early seventeenth-century Parliament. MPs of Charles II's reign were just as loyal to the monarchy as their predecessors, but also just as intolerant of corruption and mismanagement and just as fearful of radical changes in church and state. This helps explain the apparently inconsistent behaviour of later Stuart Parliaments. Their effusive professions of loyalty in the early 1660s or in 1685 were a world away from the hysterical challenges to almost every part of the royal prerogative in 1680-81. Similarly, it might seem odd that the Parliament which had passed a severe new law against Dissenters in 1670 should have proposed a measure of toleration for Dissenters in 1673. In each case, it was the circumstances which had changed, not the basic principles of the men involved.

This view of the restored monarchy and of its relationship with Parliament is somewhat at odds with the traditional view, found in the works of both old

Whig and newer Marxist or semi-Marxist historians.[9] Both have tended to see seventeenth-century history in terms of an ineluctable progression, either constitutional or social and economic. To fit this picture, the restored monarchy has to be shown to be weaker than that of Charles I. Two basic types of argument are advanced to support this view. First, many claim that the restored monarchy was institutionally weaker,[10] but it is hard to see how. The King still chose his own advisers and directed the government. He still had overall control of the armed forces and of the conduct of diplomacy. He still had extensive powers over the Church and decided when, where and for how long Parliament should meet. Charles II was thus entrusted with the powers with which Parliament had been unwilling to trust his father in 1641–42. Moreover, the crown still controlled the law courts and could manipulate them quite grossly. As for finance, Parliament still expected the King to "live of his own" and gave him what was intended to be just enough to support the normal peacetime administration. In fact, the King's ordinary revenue at first fell far short of Parliament's estimate but by the 1680s, thanks to a mixture of luck and good management, it was producing considerably more.[11] Charles was thus able to rule for the last four years of his reign without calling Parliament.

The second main argument for the view that the restored monarchy must have been weaker than that of Charles I concentrates on ideas. The "revolution", it is claimed, unleashed new political ideas against which traditional beliefs in monarchical authority and the "divine right of kings" could not prevail.[12] Such arguments assume that contemporaries approved of what had happened between 1642 and 1660 and of the ideas which had appeared. There is a great deal of evidence to suggest that they did not. The intellectual legacy of the "revolution" was reactionary rather than progressive, authoritarian rather than liberal. After two decades of upheaval and innovation, what the conservative squires of provincial England wanted was order and stability. If a stronger monarchy was the best means of achieving order and stability, they wanted a stronger monarchy.

Similarly, it is hard to square the traditional account of Charles II's relationship with Parliament with the facts. As Macaulay wrote of the Cavalier Parliament, in a passage quoted by Hill:

"The great English revolution of the seventeenth century, that is to say the transfer of the supreme control of the executive administration from the crown to the House of Commons, was, through the whole long existence of this Parliament, proceeding noiselessly but rapidly and steadily. Charles, kept poor by his follies and vices, wanted money. The Commons alone could legally grant him money. They could not be prevented from putting their own price on their grants . . . [viz] that they should be allowed to interfere with every one of the King's prerogatives, to wring from him consent to laws which he disliked, to break up cabinets, to dictate the course of foreign policy and even to direct the administration of war."[13]

One could find many incidents in 1667–68 or 1673–74 or 1680–81 which would seem to support this view. In calmer times, however, the picture could be very different. In February 1670 the Commons agreed to vote the King money before considering the nation's grievances and Charles responded with a gracious speech. As one MP wrote to his wife:

"The Speaker then went to the Parliament House and the members were so in love with His Majesty's gracious speech that in acknowledgment thereof they voted they would wait upon the Speaker all on foot, which we did, two and two, hand in hand, through King's Street to Whitehall, all the whole House. . . . The Speaker told him the sense that the House had of His Majesty's most gracious speech did ravish them and he was commanded to return him their thanks. . . . All persons there present could not forbear their acclamations of joy and many did express it in tears. The King's servants then invited the Speaker and us all into the cellar. Old and young, grave and mad went . . . and each man drunk the King's health so long that many will want their own tomorrow."[14]

Such a scene of exuberant harmony was rare but the fact that it was possible shows that the picture of an aggressive Parliament, steadily whittling away the King's power, is misleading. Parliaments were emotional bodies. Several hundred men, crammed into a confined space, could easily be moved to extremes of joy, fear or anger. The fact that fear and anger predominated under Charles II tells us more about the political failings of the King than about the "aspirations" of Parliament. For in the last analysis, the limitations on the monarchy were political rather than institutional. Charles I's Personal Rule had shown that no mechanism existed to force a king to rule responsibly or to stop him stretching his powers to the limit. The conventional checks on the crown provided by the law courts and Parliament could prove inadequate. Both in the 1630s and under James II the judges approved actions which were widely regarded as unconstitutional, while there was no way to force a king to call Parliament if he did not wish to do so. But if the king could get his way in the short term, he paid a heavy price in accumulated ill will, which became only too apparent if he ever had to rely on his subjects' support, as Charles I found to his cost in 1640 and James II was to find in 1688.

The art of kingship, then, did not consist of stretching the prerogative to its limits: "When a king extendeth his uttermost authority, he loses his power."[16] It consisted of making full use of the royal power within the limits which were regarded as customary and acceptable. To have to rule without Parliament was a sign of weakness, not strength, for without Parliament the king could not wage war or pursue a positive foreign policy. The king was at his strongest when he ruled with Parliament, above all when he could *control* Parliament. Parliaments were never easy to control. They were suspicious of courtiers and civil servants and watched vigilantly for waste, corruption and incompetence. But they could be managed if the monarch could convince the Houses that his interests and theirs were fundamentally the same, as Elizabeth had managed to do. It required good public relations, expert spokesmen in the Commons and above all sound political sense. To preserve his freedom to direct the government, a king had to avoid measures which would make MPs angry or fearful.

Charles II lacked this political sense. The reaction against the upheavals of the Interregnum and the appearance of the new bugbear of republicanism and Dissent should have made Parliament easier to manage. But it did not. The Anglican squires expected cheap, "clean" government, a Protestant foreign policy and the maintenance of Anglican supremacy against both Dissenters and Catholics. Charles's government failed to match their expectations. In the 1660s it was flagrantly inept and wasteful and tried to secure toleration for Dissenters. In the 1670s James's conversion and the French alliance aroused violent fears of Popery. Only after 1680, when the Whigs' behaviour once again made the republican threat seem greater than the Catholic one, did Charles at last give the Anglicans the policies they wanted. The results were spectacular. First, there appeared for the first time an authoritarian political theory which won quite wide acceptance. Sir Robert Filmer's works were republished. Historians like Robert Brady attacked the historical basis of the myth of the Ancient Constitution and did not hesitate to draw quasi-absolutist conclusions from their researches.[16] Secondly, with the Tories' enthusiastic support Charles prepared to pack Parliament, something which Charles I or Elizabeth had never dared to attempt. What was more, it worked. James II's Parliament oozed loyalty and had he only confined himself to the politically possible and not tried to procure benefits for the Catholics it should have proved easy to manage. The early 1680s showed the great opportunity given the later Stuarts to control Parliament, provided they observed certain elementary political conditions. The fact that they twice failed to exploit this opportunity—in the early 1660s and again in James's reign—only showed their political incompetence.

CHAPTER FOUR

Clarendon (1660–67)

For a quarter of a century after the Restoration James lived in the shadow of his elder brother. Not only was James very conscious of the obedience he owed to Charles, as his king, but Charles outshone James in both charm and intelligence. "The King is certainly the best bred man in the world . . ." wrote Burnet. "The Duke would also pass for an extraordinary civil and sweet tempered man, if the king were not much above him in it." "He was affable and courteous", recalled Roger North, "and frequently laid aside kingship to enjoy himself in company. . . . As he was very witty himself, he loved it immoderately in others." Although he read little he had a quick mind and retentive memory and could talk intelligently on many subjects. He was often highly amusing and was an excellent storyteller, although he told his favourite stories rather too often. Like James, he was physically very active and walked very fast with overfed courtiers panting behind him. His intellectual curiosity led him to dabble in "natural philosophy" and made him interested in all sorts of people—even dull people—and what they had to say. As Halifax remarked, if his affability originated in a conscious policy, it became second nature and Charles became the most charming and approachable of kings.[1]

More was required of a king, however, than charm and wit. Monarchy was a demanding profession. The king was responsible for the day-to-day conduct of government, laid down broad lines of policy and made innumerable decisions about appointments to office and matters of administrative detail. Since the king was the mainspring of government his capacity to govern was crucially important and his court was the prime source of political power. Influence in Parliament could supplement but never replace influence at court. The court was the centre of politics and the character of Charles ll and his court did much to determine the character of Restoration politics.

Perhaps the most fundamental weakness of Charles's kingship was a dislike of hard work. Louis XIV believed that he could make the right decisions only if he knew all the relevant facts, so spent hours each day going through the reports of his officials and ambassadors. Charles was quite incapable of such sustained application. He could show great intelligence and perception if a subject really interested him (the navy, for example), but it was hard to hold his attention for long: "It was not his nature to think much or to perplex himself," remarked Sir John Reresby. Charles always preferred pleasure to business.

As Halifax wrote: "His ministers were to administer business to him as doctors do physic, wrap it up in something to make it less unpleasant; some skilful digressions were so far from being impertinent that they could not many times fix him to a fair audience without them." "His humour", wrote North, ". . . was to be easy himself and to make everybody else so, if he could, that he might have no trouble." Such indolence, in a king, amounted to a dereliction of duty. Apocryphal or not, Pepys's story that Charles and his mistress "were all mad in hunting of a poor moth" while the Dutch burned his ships in the Medway symbolized Charles's failings. A year earlier Pepys had written "nothing in this world can save us but the King's personal looking after of business." Charles had not been prepared to make the necessary effort.[2]

Along with Charles's indolence went a dislike of formality and routine. "He had so natural an aversion to all formality [that] . . . he could not on premeditation act the part of a king for a moment . . . which carried him to the other extreme . . . of letting all distinction and ceremony fall to the ground as useless and foppish." He was too sociable to maintain the aloofness normally associated with monarchy and his casual habits had been reinforced by his years as a "private person" in exile. While Louis XIV's court displayed an elaborate formality, Charles's was chaotically informal. He dined surrounded with crowds of people "in that dirty pickle as I never saw man in my life". His spaniels followed him everywhere and slept in his bedchamber "where often times he allowed the bitches to puppy and give suck, which rendered it very offensive and indeed made the whole court nasty and stinking."[3] He showed a similar informality in his government. Privy council meetings bored him and he relieved the tedium by exchanging little notes with Clarendon. He also preferred to meet ambassadors informally in the Queen's apartments rather than in formal audiences.

This preference for informality pervaded the whole of Charles's kingship. Experience of civil war and exile had given him a cynical view of human nature. He did not believe that anyone could serve him out of affection and feared that his servants would exploit and mislead him for their own ends. To quote Halifax again:

"He lived with his ministers as he did with his mistresses; he used them, but he was not in love with them. . . . He had backstairs to convey informations to him as well as for other uses; and though such informations are sometimes dangerous (especially to a prince that will not take the pains necessary to digest them) yet in the main that humour of hearing everybody against anybody kept those about him in more awe than they would have been without it. I do not believe that ever he trusted any man or any set of men so entirely as not to have some secret in which they had no share; as this might make him less well served, so in some degree it might make him the less imposed upon."[4]

Charles's accessibility, then, enabled him to play off one politician against another and to maintain contact with leaders of the opposition in Parliament or the City. Such contacts were facilitated by the layout of Whitehall Palace, a great rabbit-warren of apartments, cubby holes and corridors—maybe two thousand rooms in all—through which courtiers and politicians scuttled like rats in a granary. It was easy to smuggle in whores, opposition politicians or Catholic priests and impossible for any minister to prevent the King from seeing his rivals.[5]

In theory, playing ministers off against each other might have enabled Charles to maintain control of the government. In practice, it could work only if he maintained a much firmer grip on the conduct of government than Charles in fact did. His lack of firmness showed in three ways. First, he could not be bothered to master administrative details and feared that those who had mastered them would use their expert knowledge to mislead him. His tendency to distrust those who were best informed led him too often to follow the advice of those who were badly informed. Secondly, he found making decisions very difficult, and in particular never liked saying "no" to anybody. Thirdly, despite his fear of being dominated, Charles was easily influenced by those closest to him. As Clarendon complained:

"The King was too irresolute and apt to be shaken in those counsels which, with the greatest deliberation, he had concluded by too easily permitting . . . any men who waited upon him or were present with him in his recesses to examine and censure what was resolved; an infirmity which brought him many troubles and exposed his ministers to ruin."

Charles accepted that he needed honest drudges like Clarendon or Sir William Coventry to handle his paperwork. Often, however, he ignored their advice and took that of the "men of pleasure", especially the gentlemen of the bed-chamber, who were amusing and made Charles believe that the "men of business" sought to deprive him of his freedom of action. His mistresses enjoyed a similar influence, despite Charles's claim that they had no say on matters of policy. Indeed, the most insidious feature of the political influence of the "little people" was that Charles did not realize that it was being exercised. Because they were always with him, the mistresses and men of pleasure could badger Charles day and night to do as they wished, so their pressure was often more effective than weighty arguments in the privy council. Often Charles gave in to them, if only for a little peace. Often he seemed to give in and was then persuaded to change his mind, so the nagging resumed. Only rarely did he assert his authority and take a firm line of his own.[6]

Charles's attempts to balance factions and interests, then, were the actions not of a strong king firmly in control of affairs, but of a weak king, struggling to minimize the effects of his own idleness and indecision. He could show real insight and decisiveness, but only if forced to by events and seldom for long. In general, the weaknesses of his kingship encouraged the factionalism and instability which characterized Restoration politics. Although Charles was to protect Danby and Lauderdale in the 1670s, his encouragement of Clarendon's prosecution in 1667 meant that no minister could rely on Charles to support him against his enemies. High office was thus very precarious. The court was a jungle where ministers saw each other as rivals rather than colleagues and organized attacks against each other in Parliament. As they could not trust Charles to back them up they were concerned more with short term expedients (to stave off financial disaster and to forestall criticism in Parliament) than with long-term planning. They were also eager to grab as much as they could during what might be only a short period in office. As the Venetian resident noted: "At the court here no progress can be made and nothing obtained without presents and without money."[7]

Despite so many factors making for instability and inconsistency, one can detect one or two consistent themes in Charles's behaviour. In politics he had little respect for the Ancient Constitution. Clarendon was shocked that he

"had in his nature so little reverence or esteem for antiquity and did in truth so much contemn old orders, forms and institutions that the objections of novelty rather advanced than obstructed any proposition. He was a great lover of new inventions and thought them the effects of wit and spirit and fit to control the superstitious observation of the dictates of our ancestors."

His courtiers flattered him with ideas of absolutism and he remarked that "he did not think he was a king so long as a company of fellows were looking into all his actions." His common sense and love of ease, however, combined to make him accept the need to work within the existing system. As the French Ambassador remarked in 1678: "Changing the government is contrary to his humour . . . and I believe that he does not care to be any more absolute than he is."[8]

Charles's religious outlook was more complex. He had a good knowledge of Scripture and liked to discuss religious topics but does not seem to have had a deep religious faith. Unlike James, he apparently felt no guilt at his endless adulteries. He believed that "to be wicked and to design mischief is the only thing that God hates" and that "God would not damn a man for a little irregular pleasure." His attitude towards institutional religion seems to have been guided mainly by political and social considerations. After his experiences in Scotland in 1650–51 he strongly disliked Presbyterianism, which he thought no religion for gentlemen. He especially resented the kirk's claim to direct the state. He "lamented that common and ignorant persons were allowed to read [the Bible] and that this liberty was the rise of all our sects." "He thinks an implicitness in religion is necessary for the safety of government and he looks upon all inquisitiveness into these things as mischievous to the state." He argued sometimes that it was illogical for the Church of England to complain of the Dissenters' nonconformity when it had itself separated from Rome. Charles clearly inclined towards Catholicism long before he was received into that church on his deathbed, but unlike James he seems to have distrusted clerics of all denominations and showed little interest in religious observance. His was a very personal idiosyncratic faith. He had his own sense of morality and thought matters of doctrine and church government comparatively unimportant, to be subordinated to political considerations. For this reason, he conformed without difficulty throughout his life to a Church for which he had only limited sympathy.[9]

Charles was at his most consistent in foreign policy. He soon forgave Mazarin his alliance with Cromwell and pressed for a close Anglo-French alliance. He said that he regarded himself as a Frenchman, that the Dutch were the greatest scoundrels in the world, fit only to be common sailors, while the Spaniards were penniless and worthless. The decay of Spain's power left Charles with a straight choice between a Dutch and a French alliance, and he unhesitatingly chose the latter. There are several possible reasons for his dislike of the Dutch: commercial jealousy, resentment of their treatment of his sister Mary, a desire to avenge the humiliation of the Medway disaster and perhaps a patrician disdain for a bourgeois, money-grubbing republic. On the other hand, Charles liked French manners, culture and language, but he also had more practical reasons to seek a French alliance. Like all the Stuarts, Charles exaggerated the strength of English republicanism and the likelihood of a rebellion. As he could not afford a substantial army, he felt that he needed an ally who possessed one. The Dutch army was a shambles until William III began to reorganize it after 1672, but Louis XIV's went from strength to strength. Several times Charles asked Louis for promises of military aid in case of an insurrection in England.[10] In pursuing a policy of alliance with France he never considered the reactions of his subjects, fearful as they were of "Popery and arbitrary government". Indeed, the vigour of their reaction made Charles still more determined to stick to Louis, in case he should need his help.

Thus Charles's views on politics, religion and foreign policy differed markedly from those of the Anglican peers and gentry who filled Parliament. His life-style, too, was alien to them. His father's court had been remote, introspective and Italianate. Charles was far from remote, but his court followed foreign fashions and was conspicuously extravagant. Worst of all was its identification with debauchery and sexual promiscuity. One need not, perhaps, place too much weight on Burnet's allegations of Charles's incest with his sister or his claim that "even a modest whore was unacceptable to him, for studied brutalities were the only things that recommended women long to him." Even so, Charles's aggressive sexuality, which set the tone for his court, outraged the morality of his day. As Pepys noted, it was necessary to keep at least a show of religion and sobriety for "that is so fixed in the nature of the common Englishman that it will not out of him." Charles's behaviour undermined respect for his person, if not for the institution of monarchy. It made Parliament more resentful of his misuse of taxpayers' money and made financiers reluctant to advance loans.[11] The old Cavaliers' disillusionment was completed by their failure to gain the rewards they expected, which went to the Presbyterians who had helped to bring about the Restoration or to younger men who had been with Charles in exile. Small wonder that the euphoria of 1660 soon evaporated in bitterness and recrimination.

* * *

On returning to England James was able at last to set up his own household and enjoy his own revenue. Much of the time he lived with Charles at Whitehall or travelled with him to Windsor or Tunbridge or Newmarket, but he spent the summers at St James's and had his own separate establishment. Lord Berkeley and his other servants had pressed James to demand his own household, like those of the French King's younger brothers. They also ensured that his household should be large and its officers well paid. By 1662 James had over a hundred servants, plus thirty for his Duchess. He had his own groom of the stole and master of the horse, his own attorney general, solicitor general and revenue commissioners.[12] To maintain this state, he had various sources of income, including that from wine licences, the profits of the post office and £200 a week from the King for his "diet". Even so, by 1663 he was living well beyond his means, with expenditure of almost £75,000 a year and an income of under £47,000. His commissioners therefore set out to cut his expenditure to £60,000, including £10,000 for food and drink, £15,000 for wages, £15,000 for the stables and £12,000 for clothes, linen and the like. By 1667 his expenditure had been reduced to this level, but his basic income was still only about £40,000.[13]

In time, however, his income grew substantially. In the course of the reign, James's annual revenue from the post office and wine licences grew from about £16,000 each to £50,000 and £24,000 respectively. As Lord Admiral, he received the profits of the court of admiralty as well as one-tenth of the value of all prizes: he should have received over £50,000 from the latter source during the two Dutch wars. The revenue from his Irish lands also rose to maybe £8,000 a year.[14] This rise in revenue enabled James to enlarge his and his wife's household in the second half of Charles's reign: by 1682 his wages bill was a third higher than in 1662, and he still had a substantial surplus to invest in the money markets of London and Amsterdam. He had a reputation as a careful financial manager: "His household is very well regulated, all his servants are paid punctually and he owes nothing," commented the French Ambassador in 1677.[15]

James's servants naturally benefited from his new-found wealth. Apart from places in his household, he had many other offices and rewards at his disposal. He had a large say in the granting of places in the fleet, army and dockyards. The post office was his personal preserve and he influenced appointments in the civil service, the Church and even the Queen's household. He could secure other types of favour too. Thanks to James, Sir Charles Berkeley was granted a lease of all the chains in the Thames to which ships tied up (and paid a fee for doing so). Those in favour at court could make rich pickings. They could secure grants of sinecures or of the goods of convicted felons. They might receive pensions or be included in government contracts or revenue farms, whereby they paid for the right to collect a certain duty and kept the profits. Alternatively, they could procure such favours for others, in return for money or services. Such rewards, distributed in return for services rendered, enabled James to build up a large following at court, in the armed services and in Parliament. James possessed some electoral patronage, notably as lord warden of the Cinque Ports, and a number of his servants and clients sat in both Houses. A list of 1669 showed nine MPs who were directly dependent on him and many others who were said to be amenable to his influence. Not all these clients were courtiers. Sir John Reresby was a Yorkshire squire who first attracted James's attention by his skill in speaking French. James had him appointed sheriff of Yorkshire in 1666 and governor of Bridlington in 1678, with a salary of £200 and a commission to raise his own company of foot. James also made Reresby's nominee postmaster of Doncaster and helped secure his election to Parliament. Reresby, in turn, defended James's interests in the Commons.[16] Thus James's favour gave Reresby a useful addition to his income and enhanced his influence in his county. Such a relationship of client and patron, based on service and reward, gave some cohesion both to a Parliament whose members were independent country gentlemen and to the jungle warfare of the court. Most great men had their clusters of clients and dependants. James, as the greatest patron under the King, had far more clients than most. His influence stretched throughout the nation and all the branches of government. It was not surprising that his enemies regarded him as a foe to be reckoned with.

Many of James's servants now were men who had served him in éxile: Charles Berkeley, Henry Jermyn, Richard Talbot and so on. His servants mostly resembled Charles's in their rapacity, their incapacity for business and their love of intrigue. There was considerable contact between the two "families", which were often in the same place, and many who started in James's moved into Charles's—Sir Charles Berkeley and Baptist May, for example. James's servants were at least as wild and violent as Charles's. Giles Rawlings was killed in a duel and Talbot was sent to the Tower for threatening to kill Ormond. Both of these were Catholics and many noted James's fondness for Catholics and Irish. Like Charles, James apparently made little effort to discipline his servants and his fondness for the company of men like Berkeley or Talbot gave little hint of the prudery he was later to show (except, perhaps, that he seldom got drunk)[17]. In such dissolute company James's secretary, the sober and industrious Sir William Coventry, was rather out of place, but his appointment showed that even James could sometimes recognize talent.

After some years spent in armies, James soon found court life boring. The ferocity with which he hunted suggests that he may have seen hunting as a pale substitute for war. "All his life had been passed in arms and he disliked private ease," he told the Venetian Ambassadors in 1661. They added that he "applies himself but little to the affairs of the country and attends to nothing but his pleasures." Soon, however, as the merchant community clamoured for strong measures against the Dutch, James became more interested in naval affairs. By the end of 1663 Pepys commended his zeal and diligence, adding that James alone possessed the authority to maintain discipline in the fleet. Even so, James could still be distracted by women. At the end of 1666 Pepys grumbled: "The Duke is gone over to his pleasures again and leaves off care of business." Such lapses were rare, however, and James continued to play an active part in naval administration until the Exclusion Crisis.[18]

He also showed some interest in trade and colonization. He was a member of the committee for trade and plantations. In 1663 he put up the money for a trading voyage to Brazil, from which he hoped to make si orx seven thousand pounds. In 1664 he was granted a vast tract of land in North America, including what was to become New York. He watched over the colony's development, granting liberty of conscience to the mixed population of English, French and Dutch and resisting their demands for a representative assembly. In 1683 he became governor of the Hudson's Bay Company, but refused to take an active part in its affairs, remarking "that he did never sign any orders or papers of any company that he was governor of". He showed more interest in the Royal Africa Company, perhaps because it offered the chance of action against the Dutch. Started by courtiers who proved too inept to run it, the company welcomed merchant capital and expertise, but the courtiers (led by James) successfully resisted the merchants' attempt to take it over. James invested £12,000 in the company and eventually became its governor. Again, he played little part in running the company, whose financial health gradually improved, so that it could pay modest dividends in the 1680s.[19]

* * *

In 1655 Mary took into her service Hyde's daughter, Anne, much to the annoyance of the Queen, who loathed Hyde. In January 1656 James met Anne, when Mary came to Paris to visit their mother. During the years that followed, Anne's presence was doubtless one of the reasons for James's frequent visits to his sister. In 1659 James signed a paper promising to marry Anne, although he later recovered and destroyed it. Afterwards he slept with her regularly on his visits to Mary and in the spring of 1660 she discovered that she was pregnant. Charles refused to give James permission to marry her, so James came to England morally obliged (if no more) to marry a woman who by now was some four months pregnant. James continued to badger Charles to consent to his marrying her and at last Charles agreed. On 3rd September, 1660, James and Anne were married, secretly, by one of James's chaplains.[20]

The marriage was only the start of the couple's problems. Hyde, now confirmed as lord chancellor, had many enemies at court and in James's household. Those who argued that Hyde was already too high and mighty criticized his presuming to marry his daughter into the royal family. Hyde had been aware of James's fondness for Anne but not of how far their liaison had gone. When he found out he suggested that Charles should send Anne to the Tower and even cut off her head. Charles regarded this as unnecessarily melodramatic, but Hyde insisted on confining Anne to her room, where James often visited her with her servants' connivance. By early October, however, he was having second thoughts. He had kept his marriage secret and now began to deny its validity, thanks to the influence of his servants. Some claimed that the disparity of rank between James and Anne invalidated the contract. Others alleged that they had enjoyed Anne's favours on various occasions, one even claiming "that he had found the critical minute in a certain closet over the water, for a purpose very different from that of giving ease to the pains of love." James rebutted such allegations, but was sufficiently worried to tell Hyde that he had decided never to see his daughter again. He added that if Hyde tried to insist that the marriage was valid, he would be obliged to leave England. Lords Berkeley and Jermyn (now Earl of St Alban's), together with Mary, pressed Charles to declare the marriage null and void. Charles refused, perhaps out of loyalty to Hyde, perhaps because he could see no way of doing so legally, perhaps because he believed that James should accept the consequences of his folly. Some claimed, indeed, that Charles wished to mortify both James and the Queen, since Charles believed that she had always preferred James to him.[21]

The next stage in the drama came on 22nd October, when Anne gave birth to a son. Throughout her labour, she affirmed that she was married to James and that he was the child's father. James now avowed the marriage, but his doubts soon returned. Letters from the Queen's household renewed the allegations of Anne's misconduct and on 2nd November the Queen herself arrived in London. Her first aim was to break the marriage but she and her servants also hoped to break Hyde's influence and to gain control of Charles's affairs. Pressed by his mother and sister, James again denied that he was married, especially after Charles Berkeley swore solemnly that he had slept with Anne. Charles, however, insisted that the marriage should stand unless valid legal reasons could be found against it—and none could. He refused to consider annulling it by Act of Parliament, saying that he would not let Parliament meddle with the succession to the throne. The Queen accused Charles of protecting Hyde, Charles's servants accused the Queen of trying to run his affairs, all the old coldness reappeared between mother and son and she began to talk of returning to France.[22]

If Charles was adamant, James was not. The Queen and her servants spared him nothing in their allegations of Anne's "whoredom". Distraught and ashamed, James talked of it to everyone "with all the confusion and pain imaginable". The storm soon abated. James's obvious distress touched Charles Berkeley's heart and he confessed that he had lied, claiming in extenuation that he had done only what he thought was best for James's service. Infinitely relieved, James sent to Anne to have a care of his son. On 11th November he had a long meeting with Hyde. The courtiers, sensitive to signs of change, stopped their coarse stories and began to visit Anne. Before the end of the month James began to spend the nights secretly at Hyde's house and on 12th December he did so openly. The Queen, who now saw that she could not break the marriage, became bored and miserable. Charles refused to tell her anything about his affairs and when she asked him questions, he whistled or turned his back on her. Both Charles and James were clearly eager for her to return to France, but she refused to leave until her pension was settled. At last, James's impatience got the better of him. On 20th December he publicly owned Anne as his wife. The Queen and her servants failed to compliment her, but not for long. Mazarin stressed the harm that her intransigence was doing to Anglo-French relations and insisted that she should be reconciled to her sons. On New Year's Day 1661 she received Hyde and Anne. Hiding her feelings with difficulty, she kissed Anne and gave her her blessing with the rest of the family. Soon after, she returned to France, bitter and humiliated.[23]

With the Queen gone, the rifts of the past months soon healed. Anne received the humble submission of those who had slandered her. Charles clearly liked his new sister in law. If she was not a great beauty, she had "a pretty good shape" and a natural authority which developed later into haughtiness. Her conversation was witty and she possessed considerable intelligence and determination: Reresby was impressed by her picking up his pet snake with no sign of fear. At first she and James were devoted to each other. When he went to sea in 1664 she shut herself away to pray for his return. She did her duty as a royal wife by producing seven children in eleven years. The son born in October 1660 died in 1661. Pepys noted that even James and Anne seemed little concerned at his death, perhaps because of the dubious circumstances of his birth. James was not much pleased at the birth of a daughter Mary in 1662: he would no doubt have preferred a son. He soon became fond of the child, however, and Pepys saw him "with great pleasure play with his little girl, like an ordinary private father".[24] Three more sons followed, none of whom reached the age of four, and two daughters of whom Anne (born in 1665) survived to adulthood. The loss of his sons must have been a grave affliction to James. His enemies claimed that most of his children died young because James contracted a venereal disease in the later 1660s which he passed on to both his wives. This seems highly unlikely. Two of his children by his second wife grew to maturity and he continued to father illegitimate children of undoubted health and vigour, like the Duke of Berwick (born in 1670). If so many of his children died in infancy, they did so probably because the court physicians were liable to prescribe the most harrowing treatments for the royal infants at the slightest sign of illness, or else because of the bizarre methods of feeding children which the doctors favoured.

James shared his brother's frenetic sexual energy, and marriage interrupted his affairs only briefly. He was not the most eloquent of lovers.

"Not daring to tell [Miss Hamilton] of what lay heavy on his heart, he entertained her with what he had in his head, telling her miracles of the cunning of foxes and the mettle of horses, giving her accounts of broken legs and arms, dislocated shoulders and other entertaining adventures; after which his eyes told her the rest."

What he lacked in fine words, he made up in boldness and determination: he was the "most unguarded ogler of his time". Pepys noted with mingled pride and dread that James "did eye my wife mightily". Although some husbands carried their wives off to the country to save them from James's attentions, neither chastity nor marital fidelity were in fashion at court and few could resist the King's brother, however clumsy his advances. James's servants took care to provide for his needs. Pepys heard that "he hath come from his wife's bed and gone to others laid in bed for him," and so James lunged from one affair to another.[25] Anne complained about Lady Chesterfield in 1662 but afterwards seems to have taken James's infidelities in her stride, seeking consolation in food. She became "one of the highest feeders in England", growing fat while James "exhausted himself by his inconstancy and was gradually wasting away". When she flirted with Henry Sidney, however, James refused to speak to her and had him banished from court. As she grew fatter and less attractive, she concentrated her considerable intelligence on administering James's finances and influencing his political activities. Pepys was told late in 1668 that "The Duke of York, in all things but his codpiece, is led by the nose by his wife." As his wife was the Chancellor's daughter, her influence over James was to be of considerable importance in the politics of the 1660s.[26]

*   *   *

The salient feature of James's political activities in the 1660s was his loyalty to his father-in-law, created Earl of Clarendon in 1661. Turner treats this as entirely natural: "it was Clarendon's high sense of the royal prerogative which made James his consistent, almost blind supporter." This is highly dubious. James had been hostile to Hyde through most of the exile and had been reconciled to him at the Restoration, when he married Hyde's daughter and Charles had ordered him to live well with his ministers. Even then James's servants almost all disliked Clarendon and sought to prejudice their master against him, while James disagreed with him on many major issues of policy. It was only James's strong sense of family loyalty, strengthened by his wife's influence and the King's determination to stand by Clarendon, which led James to support the Chancellor so consistently.[27]

Clarendon had been born in 1609 and so was a generation older than Charles, James and most of their courtiers. Self-confidently insular, he had failed to learn a foreign language in ten years of exile, and clearly disliked the foreign fashions, foods and manners at Charles II's court. Having advised Charles I, he lectured his son like a schoolboy on the need to leave his pleasures and apply himself to business. His friend Nicholas saw clearly why he was both indispensable and unpopular.

"He is wiser than all men in all things and it seems because he can speak well he thinks he may do anything and never consider how great envy attends him and how few friends he has in this court; but he is very industrious and able in the King's affairs, exceedingly faithful to his master, though no kind friend even to those he has reason to esteem."

Charles, however, had stood by Hyde in exile and gave him much of the credit for the Restoration. However much Charles might be irritated by Clarendon's pomposity, he knew that his integrity, his past services and his willingness to do the work which Charles was not prepared to do made him too valuable to lose.[28]

Charles and James accepted that Clarendon was indispensable, but they still disagreed with him on several fundamental issues. If Clarendon had a "high sense of the royal prerogative" it was of a prerogative confined within the limits of the Ancient Constitution. Both Charles and James would have liked to extend the crown's powers and James later came to accept the claim of many at court that at the Restoration Clarendon deliberately failed to seize the chance to strengthen the monarchy by securing a larger revenue.[29] Clarendon's obsession with formal and traditional procedures may have contained an element of self-interest—he could dominate the privy council but not the bedchamber—but it was at odds with Charles's preference for informality and did not always make for efficiency. At times Clarendon showed an obscurantist hostility to innovation, for example to placing great offices in commission, which he thought more suited to a republic than a monarchy. Charles and James disagreed and the new treasury commission of 1667 proved one of the major administrative advances of the reign.[30] In religion, too, Clarendon came to differ from Charles and many of his courtiers. By 1664 Clarendon had come to oppose any further toleration of Catholics or Dissenters, while many at court argued that toleration was both desirable and necessary.

James's marriage, then, impelled him into what was otherwise an unlikely alliance with the Chancellor. Both his support for Clarendon and the implications of his marriage were to lead him into conflict with Charles. There had been friction between them in exile, and although the Berkeley affair cleared the air, there were still occasional petty tensions. It was said that Charles resented James's greater military experience and his dominance of military affairs. Sometimes there was jealousy over women, as when both of them fell in love with "la belle Stuart". There was always a contrast of temperaments: James was slow and diligent, Charles quick and indolent. As Halifax wrote years later:

"His brother was a minister and he had his jealousies of him. At the same time that he raised him he was not displeased to have him lessened. The cunning observers found this out and at the same time that he reigned in the cabinet he was very familiarly used at the private supper."[31]

The biggest cause of jealousy was Charles's marriage to Catharine of Braganza in 1662, for which Clarendon had been largely responsible. The Queen was not unattractive, although her Portuguese fashions and piety seemed rather incongruous in Charles's court. She was also rather aloof and was upset by her husband's conspicuous infidelities. Her most grievous fault, however, was her failure to produce children. From the start, Clarendon's enemies had alleged that she was sterile. In fact she was not. She miscarried in 1666 (although Charles was persuaded to believe otherwise) and again in 1668 and (apparently) in 1669. Nevertheless, it was all too easy to contrast the unfortunate Catharine's childlessness with Anne's fecundity and to allege that Clarendon had arranged for Charles to marry a barren woman so that his own grandchildren should succeed to the throne. Moreover, some at court suggested that to compensate for the Queen's failure to produce a legitimate heir, Charles should legitimize his beloved bastard son, the Duke of Monmouth. This suggestion was made as early as October 1662 and recurred frequently over the next twenty years.[32]

James's role in the political conflicts of the 1660s is somewhat obscure. In religion, for example, his behaviour appears thoroughly inconsistent, even given the great complexity of religious affairs at the Restoration. Before the civil wars almost all English Protestants saw themselves as members of the Church of England, even when they greatly disliked the forms of worship and doctrine imposed by the bishops. The Interregnum saw the emergence of a number of sects who wanted nothing to do with any national church. Only the more moderate Presbyterians were prepared to rejoin the Church, provided it modified its organization and ceased to insist on certain practices which they disliked. At the Restoration, it was generally agreed that the Church of England should be re-established, but there was less agreement about the form that it should take. Two main points were at issue. First, should the Church's worship and doctrine remain as they had been before 1640 or should they be adapted to accommodate the Presbyterians? Secondly, should those who refused to conform to the established Church be tolerated or persecuted?

The majority of the House of Commons elected in 1661 wanted exclusive Anglicanism: no concessions to the Presbyterians and no toleration. Charles and Clarendon, for reasons of principle or policy, wished to make the Church more comprehensive and flexible. The Catholics and the sects wanted toleration and usually opposed comprehension, arguing that the more broadly based the Church became, the less it would need to tolerate those outside it. While the new Act of Uniformity was going through Parliament, Charles and Clarendon tried to make it more comprehensive. Once it came into force, in August 1662, the court (apparently with Clarendon's approval) tried to mitigate its effects by granting a measure of toleration.[33]

What position did James take in all this? Burnet claimed that James, like the Catholics, supported toleration and opposed comprehension, but this is not entirely true. In July 1663 he signed a protest in the Lords against a measure to weaken the degree of "assent and consent" to the Prayer Book which was demanded of the Anglican clergy. On the other hand, in the spring of 1662 he supported several measures in favour of comprehension, for which he was bitterly attacked by Bristol, one of the Catholics' leaders. It was remarked, however, that James was here following Clarendon's wishes.[34] His advocacy of toleration was not consistent either. In 1661 he was said to support proposals to remove some of the laws against Catholicism. In December 1662 he did not oppose a royal declaration intended to grant toleration to both Dissenters and Catholics. He had, however, opposed a Presbyterian proposal to suspend the Act of Uniformity for three months. It is worth noting too that when, in February 1663, James was deputed to propose in the Lords that Parliament should give statutory force to Charles's declaration of toleration, the proposals he outlined specifically excluded any toleration for Catholics. Finally, in 1665 James joined Clarendon in opposing yet another proposal to relieve Catholics and Dissenters from the penalties imposed by law.[35]

Amidst such apparent inconsistency, one can, I think, detect a certain pattern. First, one should distinguish clearly between the occasions on which James was acting under orders and those when he was not. In supporting the comprehension proposals in 1662 and proposing a form of indulgence which excluded Catholics in 1663, James was clearly doing as he was told. Secondly, it seems that James was more sympathetic towards Catholics than Presbyterians or other Dissenters, as he had been in exile. He still had many Catholic servants, but was not yet a Catholic himself. His protest in the Lords in 1663 suggests that he was a High Anglican, an impression confirmed by his claim that he had always been taught that belief in the real presence was the accepted teaching of the Church of England. He had been educated by High Church divines like Brian Duppa, and the chief Anglican chaplain to the exiles at Paris had been the extreme Laudian John Cosin, who called the Reformation a "Deformation" and the communion service "Mass". As his religious views had been formed by such men, it is not surprising that he saw little difference between the Anglican and Catholic churches. As yet, however, he seems to have seen no reason to leave the Church of England. The scraps of evidence we have suggests that he was a very High Anglican who was comparatively tolerant towards Catholics. His religious principles were not, however, so strongly held that he would not act against them if Charles or Clarendon told him to.[36]

James's views on foreign policy were much more clear-cut. Always more francophile than Charles, he believed firmly in the need for a close liaison with France. Like Charles he hated the Dutch, but unlike Charles he was eager for war. He listened eagerly to the merchants' complaints, but his motives were not primarily commercial. As Clarendon wrote:

"Having been even from his childhood in the command of armies and in his nature inclined to the most difficult and dangerous enterprises, he was already weary of having so little to do and too impatiently longed for any war, in which he knew he could not but have the chief command."

His servants eagerly encouraged such thoughts, hoping for lucrative commissions and fat profits from prizes and the like. James did not disdain such considerations, but his main motives were a lust for glory and frustrated patriotism. "All the world rides us and I think we shall never ride anybody," he exclaimed. His eagerness for war even overcame his love of France. When the French threatened to enter the war on the Dutch side, James told the French ambassadors that England would not reduce her demands even if she had to fight France as well. When they reminded him that he was half French, he replied: "It is true, but the English are stubborn whether they are right or wrong . . . so your arguments can make no impression on me."[37]

Neither Charles nor Clarendon wanted war, as they believed that the royal finances could not support it. James complained bitterly at Clarendon's opposing him in a matter "upon which he knew his heart was so much set and of which everyone took so much notice". For once, Parliament was on James's side and the war began early in 1665. Despite the opposition of his wife, brother and mother, James insisted on commanding the fleet. He won a hard-fought victory off Lowestoft, but when he returned to shore he was reluctantly persuaded not to risk his life again. There was even a move to oust him from the direction of naval affairs. Although it failed, his interest in the conduct of the war during 1666 was somewhat spasmodic. He did, however, strongly oppose the fateful decision not to send out the fleet in 1667.[38]

The navy was not James's only interest. The restored monarchy naturally feared that those who had held power in the 1650s would try to recover what they had lost, and a series of plots and petty risings in the early 1660s gave some colour to these fears. The Dutch war and a small rising in Scotland in 1666 made the court acutely conscious of the smallness of the army, scattered as it was in garrisons all over the country. There were numerous proposals to strengthen this army and many were associated with James. In a way, this was odd, since Monk (now Duke of Albemarle) was the commander in chief and James held no official position in the army. In 1661, after Venner's rising, James persuaded Charles to raise a few extra regiments. At the end of that year, it was proposed in Parliament that a new army should be raised under James's command, but MPs had had enough of armies and nothing came of the proposal. There was more talk of James's commanding the army in the North late in 1665 and in 1666 Pepys noted that he was eager to lead the army against the Scots rebels. In 1667 there were more rumours that Charles would raise a large army: "the design is, and the Duke of York . . . is hot for it, to have a land army and so make the government like that of France; but our princes have not brains, or at least care and foresight to do that." James now clearly had a reputation as a hard man. Once when he expressed fears for Charles's safety, Charles replied, "They will never kill a lamb to have a lion rule over them."[39] If James was eager to command the army, however, his motives were probably less sinister than his contemporaries assumed. To them, an army was by definition an instrument of absolutism. To James, an army offered both added safeguards against republican insurrection and a chance to resume the military life he missed so much.

* * *

On 13th June, 1667, a Dutch fleet sailed up the Medway and burned or carried off some of the Navy's finest ships. This humiliating episode showed starkly the cumulative effect of seven years of indolent and incompetent government. To quote Sir Allen Broderick, a courtier:

"Of 800 men in constant pay at the storehouses there [Chatham], four men and no more were at work, 796 either never hired, never paid, discharged or wandering whither they pleased .. . . The castle at Upnor made a place for entertainment of the commissioners of the Navy. No ammunition there, little elsewhere, the powder bad to such a degree as made it scarce serviceable. . . . In all places the same face of supine security. Had the Dutch come on they had without resistance fired all the shipping to London Bridge."[40]

The court was in a panic. Scapegoats had to be found and the obvious choice, the man with most enemies, was Clarendon.

His enemies were of two types: the men (and women) of pleasure, led by the royal mistress, Lady Castlemaine, who wanted to get the King to themselves, and the men of business (notably Coventry) who thought they could do Clarendon's job better. Between the two came the amphibious Bennet, now Earl of Arlington, who was at home in either world. Clarendon was now old and weary, crippled by gout every winter. His old ally, Lord Treasurer Southampton, had just died. Years of vilification and mockery had undermined the Chancellor's monumental self-confidence. Outwardly he was calm, confident of his innocence. He had, after all, always opposed the war. "Yet," noted Broderick, "he is railed at with the same vehemence as if he alone had managed the affairs." The courtiers argued that only Clarendon's dismissal could assuage Parliament's wrath. On 24th August Charles agreed and sent James to persuade Clarendon to resign. He refused, so on the 30th Charles resolved to dismiss him, whereupon Baptist May told him that he was now king for the first time.[41]

James's position was very embarrassing. Many of those who helped push Clarendon out were past or present members of his household, such as Coventry (who resigned), May and Lord Berkeley. James dismissed Henry Brouncker for saying "he wondered why His Royal Highness should appear so much for the Chancellor and go about to hector the King out of his resolution." If he ever wavered in his loyalty to his father-in-law, it was not for long.[42] But Clarendon's dismissal did not bring the affair to an end. Coventry and Arlington had got what he wanted, but the Chancellor's more violent enemies had not. Prominent among these was the Duke of Buckingham, of whom Burnet wrote:

> "He was never true either to things or persons, but forsakes every man and departs from every maxim, sometimes out of levity and an unsettledness of fancy and sometimes out of downright falsehood; he could never fix himself to business but had a perpetual unsteadiness about him. He is revengeful to all degrees and is, I think, one of the worst men alive, both as to his personal deportment and as to the public."

Vicious and irresponsible Buckingham might be, but Charles found his raillery and malevolent wit irresistible.[43] He now saw a golden chance to use his power over the King to destroy Clarendon, drive his followers out of office and gain supreme power for himself. As James was so closely identified with Clarendon, the growth of Buckingham's influence was highly ominous.

By early September there was talk of Monmouth's being declared legitimate and the Queen's being sent to a nunnery. When Parliament met on 10th October James's embarrassment and anxiety increased. Charles insisted that Parliament should thank him for dismissing Clarendon. He allowed James to stay away when the vote was taken, but Buckingham remarked gleefully that James's humiliations were only just starting. He and his allies told Charles that James had opposed him (presumably through his allies and dependents) and that James lived more like a monarch than he did. Buckingham and Berkeley hinted that it was dangerous to allow James to keep his guards near Whitehall, since there was no knowing what Clarendon and Anne might persuade him to do. Buckingham argued that the Commons would give no money while Clarendon remained unpunished and that Charles could not be safe while the Chancellor was alive. On 20th October Charles agreed that he should be impeached on charges of high treason. "It is certain," wrote Lord Conway, "that that [sic] poor Lord Chancellor [is] destined for death and that the King is to be the chief witness against him." Charles made his intentions clear by commanding his servants not to oppose his wishes.[44]

It was now clear that Buckingham and his friends aimed to destroy James's power along with that of Clarendon. Conway feared "that either a bill of divorce is to follow or a bill to affirm that the King was married to the Duke of Monmouth's mother." Pepys thought that James believed his enemies would not stop because they feared that he would avenge Clarendon's disgrace. His behaviour in the Lords was closely watched and any sign of opposition to Charles's will was seized on and magnified. Then, on 7th November he was saved further embarrassment by going down with smallpox, which kept him in his room for almost five weeks. While he was ill, the Lords and Commons wrangled over the impeachment until Clarendon fled to France on 29th November. Although James had written, on Charles's orders, advising him to leave, Clarendon's main reason for going was fear that Charles would dismiss Parliament and set up a court of twenty-four peers to try him. With Charles in his present mood, there could be no doubting the outcome.[45]

Clarendon's fall marked the end of an era. His position as "prime minister" may have been illusory, but not even the illusion could be preserved in future. Moreover, his fall showed that Charles's ministers could not rely on him to protect them against Parliament. Not that Parliament had been responsible for his dismissal or his expulsion: the initiative for both came from within the court and neither House shared Buckingham's enthusiasm for the impeachment. The real lesson of Clarendon's fall was that Charles could be persuaded to allow court politicians to use Parliament in their vendettas with their rivals. Even so, the fact that Parliament had been used on this occasion made the Commons more confident and ministers more wary of offending it. As James wrote in 1681, "His Majesty's calling for the help of his Parliament to destroy the late Earl of Clarendon has proved [fatal] to his ministers; for you see they have still fallen on most of them since and claim it as a right to do so."[46] Such consequences lay well in the future, however. More immediately, Clarendon's flight enabled his enemies to turn their attention to his allies and followers. For the next eighteen months James's position was to be very precarious indeed.

CHAPTER FIVE

Conversion (1668–72)

The court politics of the period after Clarendon's fall were perhaps the most confused of Charles's reign. Intrigues, reconciliations and backstabbings followed one another in a bewildering kaleidoscope of shifting alliances. Yet some coherent underlying themes do emerge. In particular, Arlington and Buckingham sought to capitalize on Clarendon's disgrace and to prevent his return. They had persuaded Charles that the Commons would vote him money only if the Chancellor were totally ruined. Now they argued that it was also necessary to demolish the whole "Clarendonian" system. First, Clarendon's followers had to be removed from office because (it was alleged) Parliament held them responsible for the mishandling of the recent war. Secondly, Clarendon's system of managing the Commons had to be overhauled. He had met informally with a few leading MPs (mostly backbenchers respected by their colleagues) to co-ordinate tactics. Arlington had already argued the need for more systematic methods, including promises of rewards to those who supported the court. Now Buckingham, who had convinced both the King and himself that he could do as he wished with Parliament, appointed Sir Robert Howard and others of his friends to manage the King's business in the Commons. Thirdly, whereas Clarendon had urged Charles to comply with the intolerant majority in the Commons, Buckingham claimed that the Dissenters were so powerful, especially in the business community, that Charles should grant a measure of comprehension or toleration.[1]

Put to the test in 1668, these new policies failed lamentably. Howard and his friends lacked the respect of most MPs and their undertaking to manage the House was seen as a threat to the independence of the Commons. In reply to Charles's suggestion of a toleration, the Commons brought in a new bill against Nonconformist meetings or conventicles. As one MP remarked, "The King if he pleases may take a right measure of our temper by this and leave off crediting the undertakers who persuade him that the generality of the kingdom and of our House too is inclined to a toleration." Buckingham and Arlington claimed that such intransigence showed the continued influence of Clarendon. To overcome it, Charles should dismiss the rest of Clarendon's followers from office, dissolve Parliament and call a new one, containing more Dissenters. Charles was reluctant to take such extreme measures, but agreed to prorogue Parliament from May 1668 to October 1669. During the recess

Buckingham and Arlington were to do all they could to secure a dissolution and to break the last vestiges of Clarendon's following.[2]

With Clarendon gone, many of his former followers looked to James for leadership. This and the conviction that James would be out for revenge led Arlington and Buckingham to seek to destroy his influence. James disliked the two men on both personal and political grounds. He thought it was scandalous to press Charles to dismiss trusted servants like Ormond on the pretext that Parliament would demand their removal if he did not. It was doubly scandalous to make such demands when Buckingham favoured quite openly notorious republicans, like the old Leveller, John Wildman. James complained bitterly that Buckingham consorted so much "with the fanatics and other enemies of monarchy and that he owed his influence with the King to the credit he was said to have with all these factious people." Similarly, he was strongly opposed to toleration for Dissenters. He told Colbert de Croissy, the French Ambassador

"that nothing was more pernicious to the King's service than to support the Presbyterians and sectaries, as these gentlemen [Buckingham and Arlington] planned to do; that they were trying to make the King believe that they made up the greatest and most considerable part of the kingdom and that it was necessary for the good of his affairs to give them satisfaction; but that in fact the Episcopalians or Anglicans, joined with the Catholics, were far more numerous and powerful and that as they were all very well affected towards the monarchy, it was prudent and politic to support them as much as possible and cast down the others."[3]

Whatever his feelings, James had to express them with caution, for his position was far from impregnable. Charles had been irritated by James's refusal to join in the attack on Clarendon and James's own servants were often eager to report—and misrepresent—anything he might say or do. Although there was at this time little talk of a divorce or of Monmouth's legitimation, James's conduct of naval affairs came in for severe scrutiny, for the navy and its administration contained many lucrative places which were held by "Clarendonians". Moreover, James's naval patronage was one major source of his still considerable political influence. Thus in attacking his conduct of naval affairs, his enemies sought both profitable places for themselves and their allies and the destruction of James's influence at court and in Parliament. James felt too insecure to show his resentment at this interference in his own especial preserve, so he concentrated on putting the navy's affairs in order before others could do so, while showing the greatest respect and submission towards his brother. He knew only too well that he could not compete with Buckingham. As his secretary told Pepys: "There is no way to rule the King but by briskness, which the Duke of Buckingham hath above all men; and that the Duke of York having it not, the best way is what he practises, that is to say a good temper till the Duke of Buckingham and the Lord Arlington fall out, which cannot be long."[4]

For a long time it looked as if such a strategy would not work. James was given no say in the appointment of two new treasurers of the navy, who at once set out to find evidence of mismanagement and corruption. Buckingham tried yet again to make Charles fearful of James's military power. He even travelled with an armed escort, claiming that James planned to have him killed. Charles, when tackled, denied in December 1668 that he had any thought of altering the succession: "He loved James [Monmouth] well, but for his brother the crown was his right and he knew none more worthy of it." Despite such assurances, James's anxieties continued. Ormond and Coventry were dismissed from their offices early in 1669, while Buckingham pressed Albemarle to seek the post of lord admiral. By May, however, the worst seemed to be over. James was reconciled to Charles and Pepys found him confident that he could now withstand any criticism of his conduct of naval affairs.[5]

His worries were not entirely at an end. If there were no more challenges to his position as admiral, the question of divorce still cropped up occasionally. In June 1669 the Queen miscarried (although Charles allowed himself to be convinced that she had not been pregnant), and Buckingham argued that Charles should divorce her: he claimed, indeed, that he was morally obliged to do so. The issue revived in March 1670 with the case of Lord Roos, son and heir to the Earl of Rutland. Lady Roos, who had little time for her morose, drunken husband, had gone off to London and returned pregnant with a child whom she named Ignotus (after the father). In 1667 a private Act of Parliament had debarred little Ignotus from inheriting his father's titles and property. Now Lord Roos sought another Act to divorce him from his wife and enable him to remarry. Many thought that Roos's divorce could act as a precedent for the King's and Buckingham hinted that Parliament could dissolve marriages for reasons other than adultery. James, Anne and the Queen intrigued busily at court to hinder the bill's passage and James deployed his considerable influence among the bishops and other peers. Charles, however, began to attend the debates in person and his presence helped push the bill through by the narrowest of margins. Despite Charles's interest and Buckingham's hopes, however, Roos's divorce did not have the consequences which James feared. However much Charles might have relished the prospect of a younger and more fruitful wife, he consistently rejected proposals that he should divorce the Queen.[6]

By the summer of 1670 the storms which began with Clarendon's fall were really over. James survived partly because Charles trusted in his loyalty, partly because Buckingham and Arlington distrusted each other too much to work together satisfactorily and partly because he had acquired an unlikely ally at court. Lady Castlemaine may have hated Clarendon, but she had no wish to see Charles remarried or Monmouth preferred before her own children. Early in 1668 she was reconciled to James and Anne and more than once it was her influence which reconciled Charles to his brother.[7] There was still to be friction at times between the two brothers, but not until the Exclusion Crisis was there to be such a systematic attempt to destroy James's credit with the King and then the main impetus came more from Parliament than from court. For James it had been a thoroughly uncomfortable time and also a rather strange one. For while he had been fighting for his political life, two remarkable things had happened. James had been converted to Catholicism and Charles had announced his intention to declare himself a Catholic.

*   *   *

Following his father's wishes, James had been brought up as a member of the Church of England. His tutors and chaplains had followed Laud in laying great stress on order and seemliness in worship. Some, like Dr Stuart, had taught him to believe in a "real but inconceivable" presence in the eucharist, a teaching which James thought differed little from that of the Catholic Church. He recalled that his mentors took care to give him a distorted picture of Catholicism but that they were more concerned to prejudice him against Presbyterianism. In the process they stressed the Church of England's claims to authority, claims based on the apostolic succession, by which the apostles' authority had been transmitted through generations of bishops to the present episcopate. As the Catholic Church had had such a continuous existence over the centuries, High Anglicans regarded it as a "true church", although they regarded some of its practices as flawed and corrupt. The Presbyterians and sectaries, however, had no such claims to authority and originated (it was argued) in human pride, ignorance and greed. They should therefore be made to see the error of their ways, by force if need be.

James's upbringing, then, predisposed him to look more favourably on Catholicism than on Protestant Dissent. As a young man he does not seem to have questioned what he had been taught, although he was impressed by the seemliness and devotion with which Catholics worshipped. On the whole, however, he was more preoccupied with love and war, but when he returned to England he began to think more deeply about religion. It struck him that the arguments used by High Anglicans to support the authority of their church would apply much more strongly to the Church of Rome. How, he wondered, could the Church of England condemn the sects for denying its authority and separating from it when it had itself separated from the Catholic Church? James's mind was not equipped to grasp subtle distinctions. He thought in simple, black and white terms: good and evil, obedience and disobedience, loyalty and rebellion. As he saw it, either separation could be justified or it could not. If it could be justified, all authority and order in religious matters would disappear and anarchy would prevail. If it could not be justified, the Church of England's claims to authority were unfounded and only the Church of Rome could claim infallibility. The more he thought about it, the more convinced he became that the Catholic Church's claims to authority "could not be denied without overturning the very foundations of Christianity. And once I was satisfied on that point (which is the principal point to consider) all the rest fell into place." When tackled on various points of doctrine, he returned always to the question of the Church's authority which, he claimed, rendered other more recondite points of controversy irrelevant. He found confirmation for his views in the passage in St Matthew so often quoted by Catholics: "Thou art Peter and upon this rock I shall build my church." He found confirmation, too, in the history of the English Reformation. He read and reread Heylin and

Hooker, but could find no justification for the English church's separation from Rome.[8]

There were, of course, political overtones to his attachment to Catholicism. His reading of history strengthened his conviction that Protestantism was often associated with sedition and rebellion. It would, however, be quite wrong to suggest that James saw his religion purely in political terms or became a Catholic because he thought Catholicism the best support for royal authority. He was well aware of the Church of England's stress on the subject's duty of passive obedience and if anything placed too much reliance upon it.[9] James certainly found the Catholic Church's claims to authority satisfying, but for reasons which were more psychological than political. In this he was very different from Charles. Charles saw Catholicism as a useful social and political cement, but was too sceptical, inquiring and fond of novelty to submit his mind to another's direction, least of all to that of a priest. James's mind was much less perceptive and questioning. One reason why he had fitted so well into the military life was that it provided a clear structure of authority. Orders were given and obeyed. Officers—even lieutenant generals—exercised their initiative along lines set out by standing orders and regulations and within limits set by their superiors' commands. James expected his inferiors to obey him but did not hesitate to obey those (like Charles or Turenne) whose authority he accepted. In the army, James had known where he stood; his actions were either right or wrong. The Catholic Church offered the same sort of incontestable, infallible authority, the same sort of detailed rules to guide his conduct. Having once accepted the legitimacy of its authority, James was happy to submit to it. It provided the reassuring certainty which his tidy mind craved and which it had failed to find in the Church of England. He proceeded to follow Catholic observances with an enthusiasm which he had never shown for those of the Church of England. Unlike Charles, James found routine practices comforting rather than boring and he clearly *believed* in those of the Catholic Church.[10]

For James the step from High Anglicanism to Catholicism was not great, but it still had to be taken and its timing requires explanation. The uncertainty of his political position in 1668 may have led him to contemplate a future as a "private person" and the state of his eternal soul. After considerable thought, by the beginning of 1669 he was convinced that no salvation could be found outside the Catholic Church, a conviction which may have been strengthened by Turenne's conversion late in 1668. He told a Jesuit, Fr Simons, of his desire to be reconciled and asked if the Pope would grant a dispensation allowing him to continue to attend Anglican services. Simons said that he would not and this was confirmed when James wrote to Rome. This placed James in an embarrassing position. He was eager to own his faith publicly by ceasing to attend Anglican services, but as Charles had also promised to declare himself a Catholic, James was reluctant to announce his conversion before his brother and to expose himself alone to the odium which it would incur. By January 1670 he was impatient to declare himself, and was now under added pressure from his wife. She too had been raised as a High Anglican, even practising secret con-

fession. Won over by James's arguments from Heylin and elsewhere, she stopped taking Anglican communion late in 1669. James was in a more conspicuous
position, and despite Anne's pressure he still hesitated. He was received into the
Catholic Church just before he left to command the fleet early in 1672. He had
not taken the sacrament at Easter in 1671, although he still accompanied
Charles to chapel. Not until the spring of 1676 did he cease to attend Anglican
services; by then his Catholicism was so notorious that his avowing it openly
could do him little further harm.[11]

One can only guess at James's frustration in the years after his conversion.
He had decided to commit himself in the expectation that he and Charles
would declare their conversion together, only to find Charles receding further
and further from his undertaking. As one who disliked subterfuge and con-
cealment, James longed to own his new faith and to help others to see the truth
as he had seen it. He found success with his wife, but Charles would not let
him put any pressure on their daughters and entrusted their education to Protestant tutors. Other, more unexpected frustrations were to follow from his
conversion. For the first time he felt guilty about his sexual adventures. At
first he made a real effort to reform. Croissy wrote that "his devotion has withdrawn him entirely from the pleasure of women." But James's sexuality was
too powerful to be mastered. As he could not show it openly, it was driven
underground, into furtive affairs with unattractive women, whom Burnet
malevolently suggested had been given him by his priests as a penance. James
told Burnet, who tackled him about these affairs, "that a man might have a
persuasion of his duty to God so as to restrain him from dissembling with
God and man and professing him to be of another religion than that which
he believed was true, though it did not yet restrain all his appetites." If James
found spiritual certainty in his conversion, it left him with considerable political
and emotional problems.[12]

*   *   *

In the latter part of 1668, as James's inclination towards Catholicism hardened into certainty, he found that Charles shared his views. In December
Charles expressed a desire to be instructed in the Catholic faith and to discuss
the question with Lord Arundell of Wardour, Sir Thomas Clifford and Arlington. They met on 25th January, 1669, the feast of the conversion of St Paul.
Charles talked of his sorrow in being unable to profess his faith openly and
asked them to consider how best to settle the Catholic religion in his three
kingdoms. With tears in his eyes, he said that he knew there would be difficulties, but that he preferred to act now, while he and James were still young
and vigorous. After much discussion, it was agreed that the best course would
be to seek the help of Louis XIV.

This was an extraordinary conference. Charles's choice of confidants was
odd. Only Arlington was a leading minister, and he remained nominally an
Anglican until the very end of his life. Clifford was a rapidly rising politician
who was soon to become a Catholic, but showed no sign of changing his
religion before August 1669. Arundell was an elderly and politically inex-

perienced Catholic peer, whom Charles was to send to negotiate with Louis in 1669. Yet even if one allows for the possible unreliability of the evidence,[13] the fact remains that Charles announced his intention to declare himself a Catholic. He was not remarkable for the depth of his religious faith and in exile he had firmly resisted his mother's pressure to turn Catholic. Now that he was firmly established as the king of a strongly anti-Catholic country, the idea of his turning Catholic would seem bizarre to the point of lunacy. In an effort to make sense of his decision, one must consider the context in which it was made.

In July 1667 the treaty of Breda brought the second Anglo–Dutch war to an end. The Dutch were prepared to offer reasonable terms because they were becoming afraid of Louis XIV, who was using various legal pretexts to annexe pieces of territory in the Spanish Netherlands. Charles's ministers, notably Arlington, were also worried by Louis' behaviour and the English, Dutch and Swedes formed a Triple Alliance early in 1668 which effectively brought Louis' annexations to a halt. Louis was displeased and sought to detach Charles from the Triple Alliance. Charles expressed a willingness to be detached so when Croissy came over in July 1668 his first priority was to establish a close liaison between Charles and Louis, which would lead (Louis hoped) to a joint attack on the Dutch. He soon found that Charles was difficult to pin down. He made it clear that he would put nothing in writing. He and Arlington stressed how unpopular a French alliance would be in England and argued that its unpopularity could be reduced if the French made certain concessions. "Nothing could assure or strengthen the King's authority but the affection of his subjects," Arlington told Croissy. He talked especially of the need for a commercial treaty to satisfy the merchant community, while Charles talked anxiously of France's growing naval power. Both these themes recurred in Charles's letters to his sister Henrietta (known as Madame, because her husband, Louis' brother, was called "Monsieur"). It is uncertain whether Charles was really concerned to protect English commercial and naval interests, or whether he feared the public reaction if he failed to do so, for his ministers stressed to him the political harm it would do at home if his foreign policy were too openly pro-French. Whatever Charles's motives in demanding these concessions, however, Louis gave no indication that he would agree to them.[14]

This, then, was the situation in December 1668 when Charles told James that he wished to become a Catholic. James can have known little or nothing of the negotiations with Croissy. He had scarcely spoken to him, and through most of 1668 was on such bad terms with Charles and Arlington that they were most unlikely to have taken him into their confidence. Charles announced his intention to declare his conversion during a brief reconciliation with James and it is just possible that he allowed himself to be swept along by James's enthusiasm. Even if his professions of conversion were insincere, Charles may have got the idea from James. It may be significant that on 14th December he began to use a cipher in his letters to Madame, which implies that he had something very secret to tell her.[15] This however raises a still more difficult question.

If Charles was not sincere—and I believe that he was not—what was he trying to achieve by his strange behaviour?

To answer this question, one must imagine the position in which Charles found himself in December 1668. On one hand, the eight years since the Restoration had been turbulent enough for him to feel far from secure, especially as his army was derisorily small. Moreover, the recent war had increased his dislike of the Dutch and he was eager to avenge the Medway disaster. For security at home and revenge abroad, therefore, he needed Louis' friendship. On the other hand, there were good reasons to maintain the Triple Alliance. The English, like the Dutch, did not want an overmighty neighbour in Flanders, nor did they want France to replace Holland as their leading commercial rival. Whether or not Charles shared such anxieties, he had to take them into account. Moreover, however much Charles wanted a war with the Dutch, he could not afford one. His finances were in tatters and Parliament, after the mishandling of the last war, was in no mood to vote money for another. Ideally, Charles wanted the best of both worlds. On one hand, he needed to placate his subjects and safeguard England's continental interests by maintaining the Triple Alliance. On the other, he wished to secure his position at home by means of a close union with France, but without paying the price which Louis demanded—an all-out war against the Dutch. If, in addition, he could secure concessions on commercial and naval matters, so much the better.

It seems to me, then, that although Charles's promise to declare himself a Catholic *may* at first have been sincere, it soon became a clever—almost over-clever—bargaining device. It provided both an added reason for Louis to join with Charles (the advancement of their religion) and a reason to delay England's attack on the Dutch. Charles claimed that his conscience would allow no delay and that he would have to suppress any opposition which might arise at home before he could think of making war abroad. By making it a matter of conscience he hoped to make it hard for Louis to disagree with him. This can be seen most clearly in the negotiations with Croissy at the end of 1669. Charles's first proposals included an insistence that his declaration of Catholicism should precede the war against the Dutch, stringent safeguards against Louis' attacking the Spanish Netherlands and a huge French subsidy of £800,000. These and other conditions led Croissy to complain that Charles was making war against the Dutch impossible. His suspicions of Charles's integrity were increased by his raising other difficulties and his increasingly obvious reluctance to announce his conversion. Even so, the difficulties were at last overcome. A surprisingly harmonious session of Parliament early in 1670 produced a substantial grant of money and Madame came over to use her influence on her brother. The treaty was signed at Dover on 22nd May, 1670. Although it stated that Charles's declaration of Catholicism should precede the war, Charles had promised his sister that the war should come first.[16]

Thus it seems that Charles's eagerness to announce his conversion waned as his improved financial position made a war against Holland feasible. But if Charles's ardour cooled, James's did not. He was eager for Charles to avow his conversion so that he could do the same, but Charles would not let James dictate his foreign policy. For two months after the conference of 25th January, 1669, James was told nothing of Charles's negotiations with Croissy. Not until April did he talk seriously with the Ambassador about a possible alliance. When Croissy was eventually told, six months later, of Charles's plans to declare himself a Catholic, he found that James raised far fewer difficulties than Charles and Arlington, but added that he was so zealous that little notice was taken of his opinion.[17] When Madame came to Dover to press Charles to give the Dutch war priority over his declaration, James was ordered to spend successive week-ends in London, to prevent disturbances after the latest Conventicle Act. When he returned to Dover after Whitsun, he found the treaty signed and Charles committed to make war on the Dutch. If he had hoped to change Charles's mind after Madame left, he was prevented from doing so by an illness which lasted three months. By the time he recovered, preparations for the war were well under way.[18]

*　　*　　*

In the two years after the signing of the Secret Treaty of Dover, James pursued two main objectives: to persuade Charles to announce his conversion and to prosecute the war as effectively as possible. His influence at court was still less than he would have wished. If he was one of the King's inner circle of advisers, his influence was much smaller than Arlington's. He lacked Arlington's courtly and diplomatic skills and his religious zeal soon came to embarrass Charles. James's one firm ally was Clifford, who shared his enthusiasm for Catholicism and became lord treasurer late in 1672. When Arlington and Charles suggested negotiations with Rome about possible terms of reconciliation, they aimed to provide a pretext to delay Charles's declaration of Catholicism. James and Clifford took the move seriously, however, and Clifford eagerly drafted the instructions of Charles's envoy.[19] As James's impatience grew, he showed obvious signs of his conversion, hoping to persuade Charles to declare his. In 1671 he asked Croissy to tell Charles that he could no longer take the Anglican sacrament and in 1672 he went to the fleet at Easter to avoid attending the royal chapel and taking communion. Far from forcing Charles's hand, such demonstrations of zeal made him more reluctant than ever to declare himself.[20]

Eventually even James came to understand that Charles's main concern was the war. As Charles and Arlington said that Charles would declare his conversion after the war, a quick and complete victory seemed necessary in every way, and James threw himself energetically into preparing the fleet. He began to hope also that the war might strengthen the monarchy, by giving Charles a chance to enlarge his army. Parliament's conduct in the spring of 1671 clearly annoyed him. There was some carping criticism of Charles's ministers and demands for tougher measures against the Catholics. James told Croissy in July that Charles should not call Parliament again until after the war had started,

"adding in confidence that affairs are at present here in such a state as to make one believe that a king and a Parliament can no longer subsist together;

that they must now think only of the war against the Dutch, using the means [money] which they now have, without further recourse to Parliament, to which they should not resort until after a happy outcome to the war and to [the King's declaration of] Catholicity, when they would be in a position to obtain by strength what they cannot have by gentleness."

At first this passage seems a clear statement of hostility to parliaments in general, an impression increased by the use of the French word *force*, which can be translated as either "force" or "strength". Considered in the context of the dispatch as a whole, its meaning is rather different. Both James and Buckingham had criticized Arlington for advising Charles to prorogue Parliament too soon and thus losing some extra import duties which they claimed would have been granted had Charles waited a little longer. They argued that it would now be disastrous for Charles to ask for more money. With his preparations so far advanced, Charles would be in an exceptionally weak position and the Commons could attach to their grant whatever conditions they chose. A successful campaign would greatly strengthen the crown's bargaining position: indeed, in the autumn of 1672 James was eager for Parliament to meet even though that summer's campaign had not been a great success.[21] No doubt James often found Parliament irritatingly dilatory, inquisitive and bloody-minded. But it was a fact of political life and his influence in both Houses was still considerable. Apart from this single ambiguous reference, there is no evidence of James's urging the use of military force against Parliament.

As part of his preparations for the war, Charles issued a Declaration of Indulgence in March 1672, which allowed Dissenters to worship publicly (under certain conditions) and Catholics to worship unmolested in their homes. All Charles's leading ministers approved the declaration, but for different reasons. To Arlington it was a security measure, "made in favour of the Nonconformists, that we might keep all quiet at home whilst we are busy abroad". Buckingham and Lord Ashley saw in it the toleration for Dissenters which they had advocated for so long. Clifford supported it as the first step towards removing the laws against Catholicism.[22] There is no direct evidence of James's attitude. Like Clifford he later opposed the revocation of the declaration and presumably he welcomed the liberty granted to Catholics. There is little in his past record, however, to suggest that he would have approved the much greater liberty granted to Dissenters. His upbringing, his father's execution, Charles's dealings with the Scots and his own association with the "Clarendonians" must all have inclined him to dislike Protestant Dissent on both religious and political grounds. His conversion, however, radically altered his position and was bound to lead him, sooner or later, to reconsider his views. The old Cavaliers who had been his allies hated Popery as much as Dissent. Having thrown in his lot with a minority sect, James was eventually to realize that logic dictated that he should work with the other, Protestant sects to try to secure liberty for Catholics within the context of a general liberty of conscience.

It took some time for James to appreciate this logic. Emotionally, politically and socially he had far more in common with the Anglicans than with Baptists or Quakers. He does seem always to have been tolerant towards Dissenters as individuals. He told Pepys that he did not object to his clerk Tom Hayter's being a Baptist so long as he served the Navy Office well, and there were other examples of his kindness to individual ministers or Quakers.[23] More generally, he told Burnet often that he was against persecution for conscience's sake. Burnet assumed that he meant that he was against the persecution of Catholics and doubted whether his priests would let him allow the same liberty to others. It is certainly hard to reconcile James's remarks with his opposition to toleration for Dissenters in 1668–69, unless he saw the Dissenters' offence as political rather than religious and their conventicles as centres of republicanism and sedition. Whatever James's doubts about the doctrines of the Church of England, he had none about its political usefulness: "he always thought it the interest of the monarchy to preserve the Church of England as by law established."[24] His first instinct was thus to maintain his links with the Anglicans who dominated both Houses of Parliament and who (he believed) had much in common with the Catholics. Only occasionally did the Anglicans' hostility to Popery drive him to throw in his lot with Dissent, as in 1675–76 or 1687–88. There is no evidence that he showed any sympathy with Dissent in 1672. It is much more likely that he expected that his and Charles's conversions would spark off a mass movement from the Church of England to the Church of Rome.

In April 1672 James went to command the combined Anglo-French fleet for the summer's campaign. On 28th May the fleet had just taken on provisions in Southwold Bay when the Dutch took it by surprise. James was in the thick of the fighting and twice had to change his flagship. The battle was confused and inconclusive. The losses of the two sides were about the same, and fog prevented the English from pursuing the enemy. News of the battle was not well received in England. The war had been unpopular even before it started: "even the Cavaliers dread a war and ominate ill." Popular fear of the French was immeasurably increased when Louis invaded the Dutch republic and overran five of its seven provinces in a matter of weeks. Compared with such triumphs, an inconclusive sea-fight was just not good enough. James's leadership was questioned (he had let himself be taken by surprise) and the relative inactivity of the French contingent was bitterly criticized. Charles resisted the clamour to put Rupert in James's place, not because of any concern for James's reputation but because he thought James would be more likely than Rupert to maintain good relations with the French. The rest of the campaign passed inconclusively and James returned to shore in September with his lust for glory unfulfilled.[25]

By the summer of 1672 James's conversion was more or less common knowledge and his zeal was clouding what little political judgment he had once possessed. When Buckingham, in one of his fits and fancies, expressed a desire to turn Catholic, James told him of Charles's decision to announce his conversion. Knowing Buckingham's notorious unreliability, this was an incredibly foolish thing to do.[26] James's conversion greatly increased the suspicions of Charles's intentions created by his alliance with Louis, the epitome of Catholic absolutism, and the Declaration of Indulgence, which rested on the prerogative and gave liberty to Papists. Such suspicions were found even at court, where such unlikely patriots as "Bab" May said that the war was intended to destroy the Protestant religion. By the autumn, Charles knew that he would have to call Parliament for money to continue the war. He begged James to still the rumours by taking the Anglican communion at Christmas, but James said that his conscience would not allow it. With news of his conversion all over the City, the court had every reason to expect a difficult session.[27]

CHAPTER SIX

"A Popish Successor"
(1673–79)

Between the session of Parliament which ended in April 1671 and the one which began in February 1673, there was a major change in the political atmosphere. "Hitherto," wrote Burnet, "the reign of King Charles was pretty serene and calm at home. A nation weary of a long civil war was not easily brought into fears and jealousies which . . . might end in new confusions and troubles." The Parliament elected in 1661 was known, with good reason, as "the Cavalier Parliament" and believed in the traditional Cavalier values: in "Church and King" above all, but also in cheap and effective government and in proper rewards for loyal service. As one MP grumbled in 1673: "The King's conscientious good friends are (as they have always been) little regarded, both in themselves and the principles they own; . . . undoubtedly if such men and their principles were but at this day regarded, all would speedily do well." On the rare occasions when Charles had sought to placate the old Cavaliers, it had proved very successful. Early in 1670 his making known that he would approve new measures against conventicles so enraptured the Commons that they voted him substantial duties on wines for eight years, and Andrew Marvell commented sourly that Charles "was never since his coming in, nay all things considered no king since the conquest, so absolutely powerful at home as he is at present".[1]

Between 1670 and 1673 the composition of the Commons scarcely changed, but its behaviour changed greatly because (as Burnet put it) "the court had now given such broad intimations of an ill design both on our religion and the civil constitution." For at least fifteen years from 1673 the fear of "Popery and arbitrary government" was to be the dominant theme of English politics. The connexion of Catholicism with absolutism was seen as axiomatic. With its stress on the Church's unquestionable authority, Catholicism was seen as the natural corollary of absolute monarchies like that of Louis XIV. James's conversion and the French alliance helped create fears of the court's intentions, in church and state, which had not existed in the 1660s. In particular, James's conversion and the Queen's childlessness together raised the prospect of the first Catholic monarch in England since Mary. English Protestants' reading of *Foxe's Book of Martyrs* and other histories led them to believe that Catholic rulers spared no cruelty in their efforts to force their Protestant subjects to become Catholics, a belief strengthened by Louis XIV's treatment of the Huguenots.[2]

If James's contemporaries assumed that he would try to change England's religion and government, the growing might of Louis XIV threatened to provide him with the means to do so. In 1672 Louis had overrun most of the Dutch republic and, had he not demanded excessively humiliating terms, might well have established a puppet regime at The Hague. Even after the young William III had emerged to repel the invaders, the danger remained that Louis would conquer most of the Southern Netherlands, and there were many in Holland and England who believed that he wanted to seize the whole of the Low Countries. If he did, he would be able to destroy the trade of both Holland and England, while control of the Dutch and Flemish ports would make an invasion of England much easier. In fact, Louis' main concern was not to conquer the Netherlands or England, but to strengthen his northern frontier. His contemporaries, however, could not know his inmost thoughts and had to try to guess at his intentions from his actions, which suggested that he aimed to bring all Europe under his sway.[3]

Thus the main underlying theme of domestic politics in 1673–78 was anxiety about the prospect of "a Popish successor", while the dominant theme in foreign affairs was the fear that Louis would conquer all the Spanish Netherlands. Home and foreign affairs were linked by fears that, having conquered the Low Countries, Louis might turn his attention to England and that when James became king (or even before) he might use a French army to impose Catholicism on his subjects. These fears were exploited by the Dutch and Spanish ambassadors in London who spared no effort to convince Members of Parliament that the only way to save the Netherlands was for England to make peace with the Dutch and then join in the war against France. Lack of money forced Charles to abandon his French ally in 1674, but it was another four years before he began to prepare for war.

Thus it was fear of change at home and abroad and not a desire for change which motivated the Parliamentary opposition of the 1670s. If respect for the royal family inhibited MPs from doing much about the threat of a "Popish successor", they could and did press Charles to adopt a more acceptable foreign policy. James might believe that the opposition threatened the monarchy, but SirWilliam Temple saw things more clearly. He toldWilliam III that

"the crown of England stood upon surer foundations than ever it had done in former times and the more for what had passed in the last reign and that I believed the people would be found better subjects than perhaps the King himself believed them. That it was, however, in his power to be as well with them as he pleased and to make as short turns to such an end; if not, yet with the help of a little good husbandry he might pass his reign in peace, though not perhaps with so much ease at home or glory abroad as if he fell into the vein of his people."[4]

Such a paradoxical argument—that a king of England was strongest when he followed the wishes of his subjects—was beyond James's comprehension.

He thought of government in simple terms of authority and obedience. The constraints he recognized were imposed by the law of the land, not by the need to retain the political goodwill of independent country gentlemen. While he shared the outlook and prejudices of those gentlemen, his attitude made good political sense. When he told Charles to reward his loyal servants and not to "take off" those who opposed him in Parliament, many backbenchers would have agreed with him. When he urged Charles to rule consistently and firmly and not to dither or stagger from expedient to expedient, many back-benchers would again have agreed with him. Indeed, both these criticisms of Charles's kingship were voiced by the Earl of Danby, who became Charles's leading minister in 1674. Danby stressed the need to pursue the policies which the old Cavaliers wanted and to reward them properly for their services. There was much in such a strategy to appeal to James. Temperamentally he had a great deal in common with Danby and the old Cavaliers. However, he could not support Danby wholeheartedly because one of Danby's major policies was the repression of Catholicism. When this became apparent early in 1675, James had to face up to the fact that his conversion had estranged him from the men whose political attitudes he shared. He accepted the logic of this change to the point of allying temporarily with the Dissenters, but he never really accepted that, while the old Cavaliers respected him as the King's brother, they hated his religion. To James the transition from Anglicanism to Catholicism had been so easy and natural that he could not understand why others should not find it equally easy and natural. He could not understand either why stolid Anglican gentlemen clung to their image of Catholicism as cruel and intellectually dishonest, an image which to James was manifestly false. He could not accept that their anti-Catholicism was too deep rooted to be removed by any amount of argument. He preferred to blame individuals for misleading them rather than accept anti-Catholicism for what it was: such a dominant feature of the English political scene that James's dreams of a Catholic England were doomed to failure from the start.

*　　*　　*

When Parliament met on 4th February, 1673, the court was full of trepidation. The Commons were to be asked to vote money for a war about which they had not been consulted and to acquiesce in a wide-ranging measure of toleration three years after passing a new Conventicle Act. In fact, there was little criticism of the war and the Commons soon agreed in principle to vote over a million pounds to carry it on. MPs made it clear, however, that they disliked the in-dulgence on both constitutional and religious grounds. They feared that if the King were allowed to suspend, on his own authority, laws imposing penalties for religious offences, he might claim a right to suspend other laws as well. They showed that they were more afraid of Catholics than of Dissenters by bringing in a bill to grant a limited toleration to the latter, although this toleration was soon severely restricted by provisoes and conditions.

If the Commons behaved more moderately than many had expected, the House still insisted that the indulgence should be revoked. Some of those who demanded this most loudly were courtiers, including members of James's household. Some of the cabinet council urged Charles to abandon his declaration but Shaftesbury, Clifford, Buckingham and Lauderdale all pressed him to maintain it. Arlington alone of the leading ministers argued that the war was the first priority and that it was worth sacrificing the declaration to get the necessary money from Parliament. The debate raged in the cabinet council for over three weeks. At last on 7th March Arlington got his way, helped by Louis' insistence that Charles should continue the war at all costs. Charles broke the seal on the declaration, rendering it null and void.[5]

James had naturally opposed the cancellation of the declaration and had advised Charles to dissolve Parliament rather than capitulate to its demands. Privately he complained that Charles was ruining all by his weakness. Charles paid little heed to James's advice. Indeed, he believed that much of the Commons' opposition stemmed from the fears aroused by James's refusal to hide his conversion. Members of both Houses hinted that Charles's successor might be of another religion. Anxious to exclude Catholics from positions of power, the Commons brought in a bill requiring office-holders to subscribe a "Test" denouncing the Catholic doctrine of transubstantiation. James tried to have his servants and a number of Catholic army officers exempted from the Test, but without success. Clifford attacked the bill forthrightly in the Lords and claimed later that it needed only a dozen men like himself to open the eyes of the nation to the bill's iniquity. James warmly approved the speech, but the Commons talked of proceeding against Clifford as a Papist. The Test bill passed both Houses; Charles gave his assent and received the money he needed to continue the war.[6]

On 29th March Charles adjourned Parliament until October. For Arlington, interested only in the supply bill, the session had been an unexpected success. For James, it had been a disaster. The indulgence had been revoked and, as his conscience would not let him take the Test, he would soon have to resign all his offices, with a consequent reduction in both his influence and his income. Clifford, his closest ally, would also have to resign his post. (He retired from public life and died a few months later.) In resigning his offices, James gave further confirmation of his conversion and strengthened the hand of his enemies at court, who stressed to Charles that James's Catholicism was the main cause of his troubles. The old arguments for a divorce were reiterated more insistently than ever. It had seemed in February that a divorce might not be needed, as the Queen was very ill. By March she was recovering and several MPs told Charles that Parliament would gladly pass a bill annulling his marriage. James suspected that such suggestions originated within the court and there were certainly many there who were eager to destroy his influence and his hopes of becoming king. As before, the projects of divorce foundered on the King's hostility. Perhaps Charles thought it was unjust in itself or that it was no business of Parliament's, perhaps it was just that when Charles had last sounded MPs on the subject, in 1667, it was clear that the majority was against a divorce. Nevertheless, Arlington still thought that Charles would not be sorry to find some pretext to annul his marriage and pressed him to do so, but the leading advocate of the divorce was now the Earl of Shaftesbury.[7]

Anthony Ashley Cooper, Baron Ashley and first Earl of Shaftesbury had been Chancellor of the Exchequer (not then an office of the first rank) since 1661 and had shown considerable ability as an administrator. He did not emerge as a major political figure until he was made lord chancellor, and an earl, in 1672. He had supported the indulgence because of the relief it gave to Dissenters, but had spoken strongly in the Lords for the Test bill. He had never been on particularly good terms with James, whose open avowal of Catholicism completed the breach between them. Like many others, Shaftesbury saw the "Popish successor" as a real threat to the Ancient Constitution and the Protestant religion, but he was much more prepared than most to do something to prevent it: indeed, its prevention became his dominant concern, even his obsession. He suggested that Charles should divorce the Queen and remarry, that Monmouth should be declared legitimate or that James should be excluded from the succession. He pursued those objectives while still in office, and after his dismissal early in 1674 he became the leader of the opposition to James inside and outside Parliament. His enemies stressed his ambition for power, which was considerable, but he wanted that power to save England's religion and liberties from ruin under a Catholic king and he was not prepared to accept office on conditions that would inhibit his pursuing that objective.[8]

Rumours that Charles would divorce the Queen or declare Monmouth legitimate recurred during the summer of 1673. The Queen was pressed to retire to a convent but was dissuaded by the Portuguese Ambassador and one of the priests at court. Even more alarming to James were reports that Parliament would exclude him from the succession, at which Charles was very concerned.[9] As James's conversion became common knowledge, Dutch and Spanish propaganda alleged that Charles and Louis aimed to impose absolutism in England and to establish French dominance over Europe. The army raised for the war was sullen and mutinous but was regarded with the deepest suspicion. Even the godless Buckingham was suspected of being a Papist because of his association with the court: "His Grace of Bucks hath taken great pains and the sacrament almost in all the churches of his lieutenancy of Yorkshire . . . but the people hearken as little to his devotion as (I believe) Heaven to his prayers." The King's ministers all tried to dissociate themselves from James, while Charles again tried to persuade him to conform to the Church of England.[10]

James was not easily cowed. He refused to abandon his religion and pressed Charles to preserve the alliance with France, no doubt feeling that he might need Louis' help. Although he laid down his offices and ceased to attend the privy council, he still directed all admiralty business and attended the two more informal and confidential bodies, the cabinet council and the committee for foreign affairs. Thus he retained a considerable voice in policy making, despite his exclusion from office. Moreover, he hoped to command the expeditionary force which Charles planned to send to Flanders that summer. He suggested that he could get round the Test Act by producing his commission only after he had left England. According to the Venetian resident, James planned to use the army to coerce Parliament if it refused to vote the King money. Whether or not that was true, if James was at the head of an army he would be in a much stronger position to resist any attempt to exclude him from the succession. Charles, however, was reluctant to let James go, and was given an excuse to refuse his request when the judges ruled that to grant him a commission would violate the Test Act.[11] Having failed to secure command of the army, James looked forward to the coming session of Parliament with great anxiety. He feared that Bab May and others in Charles's household would badger him to give Parliament whatever it wanted if it would only grant him money. He was already violently unpopular: "It is not to be writ the horrid discourses that passes now upon His Royal Highness's surrendering," wrote one observer in June. By the time Parliament met his unpopularity had been increased still further by his second marriage, to a Catholic princess who (rumour had it) was the Pope's daughter.[12]

* * *

Anne Hyde had died on 31st March, 1671. Although still in her early thirties, she was grotesquely overweight. Her almost incessant pregnancies had undermined her health and she suffered from cancer of the breasts. She died in great pain, and told James "death is very terrible." She refused to take the sacrament according to the Anglican rite, but if the last rites of the Catholic Church were administered to her, it was done very secretly. James showed little sorrow at her death. She had been a strong-minded woman and had exercised considerable influence over him, but the passion of ten years before had long since evaporated. As Evelyn remarked sadly: "None remembered her after one week, none sorry for her; she was tossed and flung about and everyone did what they would with the stately carcase."[13]

Within days of her death, discussions began about James's remarrying. Always impulsive, he was most attracted to those who were nearest to hand, especially Lady Bellasis, to whom (despite her Protestantism) he gave a written promise of marriage. Charles said angrily that he could not have believed that James would be such a fool a second time; he managed, fortunately, to recover his promise. Charles was quite determined that this time James's marriage should be properly arranged and that the maximum of diplomatic benefit should be extracted from it. This meant that James must find a foreign wife. As there was no suitable French princess available and Charles's ties with Louis were already close, Charles considered the two branches of the House of Habsburg, Spanish and Austrian. A Habsburg marriage could help to dissuade Spain and Austria from helping the Dutch in the coming war. Accordingly, negotiations were started at Madrid and Vienna for the hand of the Archduchess of Innsbruck.[14]

Ever the dutiful brother, James accepted that Charles should have a major say in his choice of a wife. He made it very clear, however, that he was impatient to remarry and that his wife must be beautiful. Having decided from her portrait that the Archduchess was indeed beautiful, James soon convinced himself that he loved her madly, brushed aside Charles's reservations and pestered him to start the negotiations. Neither the Spaniards nor the Emperor were in any hurry however. The discussions proceeded on their leisurely way through 1672 and into 1673, until they were brought to an abrupt halt by the death of the Empress. The Emperor promptly announced that he would marry the Archduchess himself and offered James his sister instead. James replied gallantly that he would not marry the sister of his rival. It was now March 1673. James's impatience was now increased by the need to marry before Parliament reconvened in October, for he feared that it might try to make him marry a Protestant.[15]

The negotiations of the next few months showed many of the characteristics of farce. In a frenzy of impulsive impatience, James changed his mind with bewildering rapidity as new reports or rumours reached him and new arguments or snags were suggested to him. Information and instructions passed back and forth between London and Paris, Rome, Vienna and elsewhere, much of it out of date by the time it arrived. As he received a stream of contradictory orders James's agent, the Earl of Peterborough, started, stopped and changed direction like a demented chessman. In April Richard Talbot and others persuaded James to seek a wife associated with France, since he might need Louis' help in the near future. As there was no suitable member of the French royal family, James considered various princesses from families linked (or subordinated) diplomatically to France. Everyone at court argued the merits of a different lady, extolling her charms and belittling those of her rivals. Bombarded with conflicting information, often second- or third-hand and of dubious validity, James vacillated in a fury of anxiety and unrequited passion, while the weeks passed and October moved inexorably nearer. Louis wished him to choose the Princess of Neuburg, but Peterborough reported that she was plain, blonde and dumpy. Charles argued that beauty did not matter and that one could get used to any face within a week, but James insisted that good looks were essential. He much preferred the sound of the Princess of Wurttemberg, but Charles disliked Germans and would not allow the Princess's mother near his court, as she was a notorious intriguer. At last, on 15th July, Louis ordered Croissy to propose either the sister or daughter of the Duchess of Modena, adding that he would provide either of them with a dowry of £90,000.[16]

James had already considered and rejected the two Princesses of Modena, first because he still hoped for the Archduchess of Innsbruck and then because Modena was so far away and time was short. When Louis' offer arrived, however, all other possibilities seemed to have been exhausted. Peterborough was ordered to proceed to Modena, while Louis stressed to the Duchess the desirability of the marriage and the need for haste. James still had doubts. He heard that Mary Beatrice, the younger princess, was red haired, ugly and too delicate to bear children, while her aunt was thirty and perhaps already past child-bearing. Moreover, it transpired that Mary Beatrice had no wish to marry and had long planned to enter a convent. Discouraged by this information, James sent to Peterborough to return. On 15th September Croissy reported that Charles now thought that James would have to wait until after Parliament had met. But James's orders to Peterborough reached him too late, for the men on the spot were making considerable progress despite the reservations of both the Duchess and the Pope. In the eyes of the Church, James was not a Catholic because he still attended Protestant services. Moreover, both the Duchess and the Vatican wanted assurances that the Princess would be free to practise her religion in England.[17]

These obstacles were by no means easy to overcome. Louis's agents at Modena and Rome stressed the strong evidence for James's conversion and promised that, although the situation in England would not allow the Princess to have her own chapel, Louis gave his personal assurance that she would not be molested. The Pope was sufficiently impressed to write to the Duchess and the young Princess, pressing them in general terms to agree to the marriage for the good of the Church. In the eyes of the Vatican this did not, however, amount to permission for the marriage to proceed. A dispensation would still be needed and before that could be granted the lawyers of the curia wanted more concrete assurances of James's Catholicism and of the arrangements for his future wife's devotions. To procure such assurances would take time, and it was already early September. Louis' agents therefore concentrated their efforts at Modena. They argued that the Pope's letter amounted to a licence to proceed, that the dispensation was the merest of formalities and that the Duchess could ask for no better guarantee for her daughter's freedom of worship than the promise of the Most Christian King. Finally, Peterborough threatened to go home unless she agreed at once. On 20th September the marriage ceremony was performed, with Peterborough as James's proxy.[18]

On 22nd September James received Louis's rather premature assurances that the marriage would take place, and exclaimed that "God had concluded it, contrary to the expectations of those who thought they had spoiled it." In fact, the difficulties surrounding the marriage were by no means over. The Pope and his nephew were furious that it had been completed without all the "forms prescribed by the sacred canons used by the Church". While aged canon lawyers tried to puzzle out how to grant retrospectively the dispensation which should have preceded the marriage, the Pope multiplied the conditions which had to be met before he would grant the dispensation. He wanted a formal guarantee from Louis of the new Duchess's freedom of worship. He wanted a formal promise that the children of the marriage would be raised as Catholics. He wanted the Duchess of Modena to confess her fault and to petition for absolution. He wanted James and Mary Beatrice to send a formal, submissive request for the dispensation. Such cavils were irritating, but had little practical effect, for Mary Beatrice was already on her way to England. Nevertheless, James's understandable failure to observe the formalities in his marriage soured his relations with the Holy See for some years. Not until 1676, when James assured the Pope that he would stop attending Anglican services, was the dispensation finally issued.[19]

In general James was crude and tactless in his dealings with Rome. He and

Mary Beatrice failed to perform the little courtesies or send the letters of compliment which the Pope and cardinals expected. He failed to understand the curia's pedantic legalism or the intricacies of Italian politics. As a prince and a zealous convert, he expected the Pope to grant whatever he asked, and set his heart especially on a cardinal's hat for his wife's uncle, Rinaldo D'Este. Rinaldo was a singularly unsuitable choice: apart from family rivalries and his association with France (which did not endear him to a pro-Habsburg curia), he refused to take full priest's orders because he hoped to succeed his nephew as Duke of Modena (which, eventually, he did). Apart from making such unreasonable demands, James weakened his credit at Rome still further by ignoring or antagonizing the only Englishman who possessed any influence there, Cardinal Philip Howard.

Initially the most serious threat to the marriage came not from Rome but from Parliament. When it met on 20th October Mary Beatrice had not arrived and Charles decided to prorogue it for a week. Shaftesbury, as lord chancellor, deliberately delayed summoning the Commons, which used the time to draw up an address demanding that the marriage should not be consummated. When the House met again, it protested once more about the marriage, expressed great anxiety about the army and resolved to vote no more money until the nation's fears of Popery and Popish counsellors had been removed. The court was in utter disarray and Charles, sceptic though he was, even consulted an astrologer about the most propitious time to address the Commons. The Commons, however, were so unmanageable that Charles prorogued Parliament until after Christmas to give passions a chance to cool.[20]

The prorogation offered only a brief respite and the court's fears continued, amidst wild talk of another civil war. Panic-stricken ministers thought only of saving themselves while Charles dithered in miserable indecision: "The King calls a cabinet council for the purpose of not listening to it and the ministers hold forth in it so as not to be understood." Charles was under more pressure than ever to divorce the Queen and send James away from court. James alone remained resolute. He refused to leave court unless Charles positively commanded it and pressed his brother to dissolve Parliament, call a new one and continue the war. He advised him, too, to dismiss from their offices all who had opposed his wishes in Parliament, while rewarding those who had served him well. Charles did agree that Shaftesbury's opposition had been so blatant that he had to be dismissed, but for the rest Charles just did not know what to do: while James advised firmness, most of his other courtiers begged him to make concessions. In this situation, with the court bitterly divided and her husband's future in jeopardy, the new Duchess of York arrived at Dover on 21st November.[21]

With James's position so precarious, few dared accompany him to greet his bride. After three days at Dover, they came to London to meet a mixed reception. Some church bells rang all night, but an effigy of the Pope costing £50 was burned at Southwark. There were problems of protocol. The Queen's English ladies "humped" and walked out when the Duchess of Modena was allowed to sit in the Queen's presence. The Duchess was also very annoyed that her daughter was not to have a public chapel and soon returned to Italy, whereupon her daughter cried for days. It was hardly surprising. She was only fifteen and had been brought up in a sheltered, Catholic environment. Now she found herself in a cold and barbarous country, where they burned the head of her church in effigy, where she could worship only in secret and where they treated her mother with studied discourtesy. Her husband was forty—old enough to be her father—tall, hard-faced, cadaverous and full of crude sexual aggression. She wrote sorrowfully that she saw the married state as her cross and that her only consolation lay in James's piety and kindness.[22]

There were thus many reasons to expect that the marriage would prove a failure: the haste with which it had been arranged, the bitter hostility it provoked in England, the great differences in age and background between James and his spouse. Yet despite these inauspicious circumstances, the marriage proved a conspicuous success. Bonds of love and affection grew up between James and Mary Beatrice far more lasting than the ephemeral passion of his first marriage. It no doubt helped that James was now older, but it was more important that, unlike Anne, Mary Beatrice was, and remained, beautiful. "She was tall and admirably shaped," wrote Peterborough, "her complexion was of the last fairness, her hair black as jet, so were her eyebrows and her eyes," but the latter so full of light and sweetness as they did dazzle and charm too." Others were less effusive, but still favourably impressed. "She hath very good eyes, very good features and a very good complexion," wrote Conway, "but she wants the air which should set off all this and having been bred in a monastery knows not how to set one foot in front of another with any gracefulness." Such social accomplishments were to come with maturity; meanwhile, many were charmed by her innocence and lack of affectation. Once she had got over her shyness, she showed a childlike exuberance, revelling in toboggan rides and pelting her husband with snowballs. She was only four years older than his daughter Mary, and they soon became close friends. After the initial furore caused by her marriage, she became more popular than her husband. She kept out of politics (at least until she became queen), was obliging and gracious to all and "gave herself up to an innocent cheerfulness". She learned to speak English fluently and showed that she possessed a lucid mind and a sound grasp of detail. It was her charm and beauty, however, which captured James's heart. Like Anne, she was almost constantly pregnant. Within nine years she produced five children, all of whom died young, and suffered several miscarriages. Unlike Anne, she kept both her figure and her looks. Having an attractive wife did not cure James of his infidelities, but he was more discreet than in the past and apparently felt considerable guilt about his inability to control his passions. By the standards of his age, such peccadilloes were less reprehensible in princes than in ordinary men. In most respects, James proved a devoted husband and father, while Mary Beatrice's love and companionship were to prove a great comfort to him in the tribulations which lay ahead.[23]

* * *

When Charles prorogued Parliament in November 1673 he delayed for a while the crisis provoked by James's conversion and marriage, but he was desperate for money and had to meet Parliament in January 1674 as arranged. Even James now agreed that the war could be carried on no longer, but peace and the disbanding of the army were insufficient to calm the Commons. Even the most moderate wished to "be secured in religion and freed from other apprehensions," and some were far from moderate. A little clique of peers, led by Shaftesbury and Holles, harrassed James mercilessly in the Lords. They argued, for example, that James should not sit on the King's left hand, in the chair customarily reserved for the Prince of Wales, but on a bench with the other dukes. The Commons drafted bills to ensure that if James became King he would have to call Parliament at his accession and respect the independence of the judiciary. A committee of the Lords recommended measures to ensure that children of the royal family should be educated as Protestants. Finally, Carlisle argued that all such restrictions on a future Catholic king would prove futile and that Protestantism could be safe only if Catholics were debarred from the throne. This was far too radical for the great majority of the peers, however, and the House accepted James's motion to let the matter drop.[24] Faced with such open challenges, James begged Charles to dissolve Parliament, but it was not until 24th February that Charles prorogued it until November, amid rumours that James was to be accused of treason. His ministers were taken by surprise, but for James at least it offered a welcome respite. He now had some nine months in which to rebuild his political position before Parliament met again.

The political scene at court had changed dramatically since the start of 1673. Clifford was dead, Shaftesbury and Buckingham had gone into opposition. This left only Lauderdale and Arlington from that notorious quintet of ministers whose initials had formed the word "Cabal", and Lauderdale was still concerned mainly with Scotland. Arlington, however, was a great survivor, the smoothest and most adaptable of courtiers, "absolutely the best bred and courtly person His Majesty has about him". His dominance was challenged in 1674 by a very different character. Clifford's successor as lord treasurer, Thomas Osborne, Earl of Danby, was a forthright Yorkshireman who relied more on force of personality and weight of argument than on making his advice seem agreeable. His first priority was to reorganize Charles's finances so that he could survive without Parliamentary grants if need arose. As Charles's ordinary revenue was swollen by the boom in overseas trade in the 1670s, Danby might well have succeeded, but for the burden of interest on past debts and Charles's wilful refusal to economize. In politics, Danby hoped to return to the days before the French alliance and the prospect of a Catholic king had soured the relationship of king and Parliament. Parliament, he wrote, "must be gratified by executing the laws against Popery and Nonconformity and withdrawing apparently from the French interest."[25]

Danby's views on religion and foreign policy thus differed radically from James's. This made lasting co-operation between them unlikely, but they could and did work together in the short term. In 1674 they agreed in disliking Arlington and his approach to the management of Parliament. In Danby James at last found a minister who advised Charles to lead rather than follow the Commons, to reward those who served him well and punish those who did not. Thus James joined Danby in condemning Arlington's attempts to prepare for the next session by wooing those who had taken the lead in opposing the court in the last. They also co-operated in pressing Charles to postpone meeting Parliament until 1675 and were delighted when they got their way, overcoming by sheer determination both Charles's own preference for the line of least resistance and the nagging of his courtiers.[26]

At this stage James may not have been fully aware of Danby's intended political strategy. He must, however, have had some inkling of his plans, or perhaps he was unwilling to trust anybody too far, for in 1674 he began to seek political support from two new and very different quarters. First, he tried to obtain large sums of money from abroad, so that Charles would not need to call Parliament. His confidential secretary, Edward Coleman, approached the papal internuncio at Brussels and Louis XIV's confessor, Ferrier, in the hope that the House of Habsburg, the Pope or the French King would provide the necessary money. To the internuncio he stressed the harm that was likely to befall the Catholics if Parliament met, to Ferrier he alleged that it would try to force Charles to make war on France. It was soon apparent that he would get nothing from Rome, but the French at first seemed more interested. Once James and Danby had had the session postponed, however, Louis saw no further reason to continue the negotiation. James knew of both negotiations and was actively involved in the approach to Ferrier, which was apparently intended to by-pass the new French ambassador in London, Ruvigny, who was a Protestant. He did, however, ask Ruvigny twice whether Louis would lend Charles four or five hundred thousand pounds to have the session delayed.[27]

Meanwhile a very different source of support offered itself, from among the Protestant Dissenters. Since the indulgence had been withdrawn, their legal position had been precarious. The council allowed them a tacit toleration but, as the old laws were once again in force, it could do little to restrain zealous Anglican JPs who wished to persecute them. Conscious of their vulnerability, some Dissenting leaders offered Charles money, in March 1674, to dissolve Parliament in the hope that a new one would be less rigidly Anglican. In July leading Presbyterians approached James. It is possible that they got the idea of doing so from Sir John Baber, one of the King's physicians who had long been a leading advocate at court of the Presbyterians' cause and was also closely associated with Lord Holles, the leading Presbyterian peer. Holles had been one of James's most vigorous critics in the spring session, but he had changed his mind by the start of 1675. As Baber was later closely associated with James, it seems likely that Baber brought James and Holles together. James, for his part, felt sufficiently insecure in July 1674 not to reject the Presbyterians' overtures, but he made little positive response and privately continued to distrust the Dissenters.[28]

In November his attitude began to change. As part of their preparations for the next session of Parliament, Danby and Lauderdale (who now began to show an interest in English affairs) asked the bishops to consider how best to calm the Commons' religious anxieties. James must have suspected that Danby planned new measures against Catholics and Dissenters, for when the Presbyterians renewed their approach, James received it much more favourably. He began to talk of the desirability of a general liberty of conscience and secured pardons for a number of Dissenters convicted under the Conventicle Act. He also pressed Charles to issue a general pardon to all those convicted of religious offences. The Presbyterians, meanwhile, offered to press for his restoration to his offices when Parliament met. Early in January 1675 James approached many of his erstwhile opponents in the Lords and declared that he was willing to promote laws to secure the rights, religion and liberties of the nation. Those he approached, however, doubted his sincerity and suspected that he did not really want Parliament to meet at all. They may have been right. James again asked Ruvigny if Louis would lend Charles enough money to enable him to dissolve Parliament, but one should remember that a dissolution would have been welcomed by the Dissenters.[29]

From November 1674 to January 1675, then, it seems that James was hedging his bets, cultivating the Presbyterians and attempting to propitiate his leading critics while he waited to see what Danby and the bishops would do. Then, early in February, the bishops proposed that the laws against both Catholics and Dissenters should be enforced to the full. James had accepted the need to make a gesture towards enforcing the laws, but had expected nothing so rigorous. Danby and Lauderdale told him that they had not wanted such severity, but James soon found that this was untrue. James now felt more inclined than ever to throw in his lot with the Presbyterians and Danby's other opponents, especially as they renewed their offers to have him reinstated as lord admiral if he procured a toleration. He began to argue that the rigid Anglicans constituted too narrow a basis of support for the government, since (he believed) three-quarters of the population were nonconformists of one sort or another. Two considerations, however, prevented him from aligning himself unreservedly with the opposition. First, most of those who offered their support demanded that James should agree to abandon the French alliance and this he would not do. Secondly, however much he hated Danby, James was too loyal to Charles to attack his chief minister openly, or to oppose directly those measures of Danby's which Charles wished to pass. James was prepared to advocate measures of which Danby disapproved (like liberty of conscience) but not to vote or use his influence directly against the King's wishes.[30]

The conflict between James's personal inclinations and his duty towards his brother was seen in the debates on "Danby's Test". A bill was brought into the Lords which required office-holders to swear not to attempt to alter the government in church or state. This would have excluded both Catholics and Dissenters from office and most of the Catholic peers voted against it, but Charles made it quite clear that he wanted the bill to pass so James felt that he had no choice but to support it. (The bill was not put before the Commons, presumably because it would not have passed.) James did make a hesitant reference to the benefits of toleration in the debates upon the King's speech, but the session was soon brought to a standstill by a fierce jurisdictional dispute between the Houses, in the case of *Shirley vs Fagg*. Shaftesbury and his friends did all they could to embitter the dispute, hoping to force Charles to dissolve Parliament. Charles and Danby preferred to prorogue it until October.[31]

James's views on the session must have been mixed. On one hand, he had not been attacked at all and no new measures had been taken against the Catholics. On the other hand, he had preferred not to let his supporters suggest his restoration to office, probably because he feared that the proposal would be rejected. Moreover, he still believed that a new, less Anglican, House of Commons would be better disposed towards both the Catholics and himself. He was thus torn between the attractions of a dissolution and his hopes of deriving some benefit from the present Parliament. This uncertainty helps explain his inconsistent behaviour during the summer. Danby's credit with the King seemed unassailable and James was scarcely consulted. When Parliament was prorogued in June, Coleman declared that it ought to be dissolved and James apparently agreed. He welcomed an approach from Shaftesbury (whose main aim was to have Parliament dissolved) and apparently supported his efforts to regain Charles's favour. By late July, however, James was said to be eager for Parliament to meet. He renewed his contacts with the Dissenters and Coleman asked Ruvigny if Louis could supply him with some £20,000 to pay to MPs in James's name. Clearly Coleman believed that James could expect the support of something approaching a majority in the Commons. There is no direct evidence that James authorized Coleman's approach, but he may well have done so. Danby used the treasury's extensive patronage to reward his supporters and James may well have felt that he needed money to compete with Danby at his own game.[32]

The autumn session proved brief and unproductive. *Shirley vs Fagg* again helped Danby's enemies to obstruct government business. With little hope of securing either liberty of conscience or his own restoration to office, James added his support to the growing demand for a dissolution. On 20th November he supported a motion to prepare an address requesting the King to dissolve Parliament. The motion was narrowly defeated, but James's open separation from Danby's interests earned him a message of compliment from Shaftesbury. The motion proved counter-productive. Two days later Charles prorogued Parliament for fifteen months.[33]

Charles was able to do without Parliament for so long because Louis had promised him a modest subsidy in return for not calling it. James fully supported his brother in this. He now believed that he could hope for nothing from the present House of Commons and that Charles should either dissolve Parliament or delay its next meeting for as long as possible. He believed too that the French alliance was more necessary than ever and that Louis was "the only support remaining to [the King] against the ill will of the majority of his subjects".

On almost every point, James's advice was directly opposed to Danby's, and the two of them quarrelled bitterly at Newmarket in 1676. James argued that further persecution of Dissenters and Catholics would do Charles great political harm. Danby argued that exclusive Anglicanism was the only sure basis for monarchy and organized a religious census which showed that Dissenters and Catholics made up only a small fraction of the population.[34] James argued that Parliament should be dissolved or delayed. Danby argued that a new House of Commons would be less loyal than the present one, as it would contain more Presbyterians, and that the existing House would be in a better temper when it met again. James argued that the French alliance should be preserved; Danby claimed that unless Charles prevented Louis from conquering more of Flanders Parliament would become unmanageable. More worrying still from James's point of view was the vendetta against him pursued by Danby and Henry Compton, Bishop of London, and their insinuations to the King that James's conversion was the cause of all his difficulties with Parliament. Compton persuaded Charles to order James to let him prepare his daughter, Mary, for confirmation. Compton and Danby also persuaded the King to order James to dismiss Coleman from his post as secretary to Mary Beatrice. Typically, James recalled Coleman and he continued unofficially to perform much the same functions as before. When James ceased to attend Anglican services, Danby pressed Charles to dissociate himself from his brother by sending him away from court. As usual, James refused to leave voluntarily and Charles refused to order him to go. Even so, Danby's arguments had made sufficient impression for Charles to say repeatedly to Courtin, the new French Ambassador, that James's conversion was the source of all his problems.[35]

All James's arguments that Charles's complaisance for Parliament's prejudices against France and Catholicism would ruin the monarchy made little impression. By October 1676, James accepted that Parliament had to meet and that something must be done to allay the fears provoked by Louis' latest conquests in the Low Countries. Both he and Charles told Courtin that Louis should agree to peace terms which would leave the Spanish Netherlands sufficiently defensible to act as an effective barrier between France and the Dutch republic. If he did not, they alleged that they risked a revolt in England—unless they did something to halt Louis' progress. They were probably being unduly melodramatic in order to persuade Louis to make peace, but Courtin took their fears of a revolt seriously. Seeing James as the only one at court who was now friendly to France, Courtin tried to play on his fears that Danby would sacrifice him to Parliament in order to persuade him to do all he could to ensure that Parliament should not meet. When James said that he could not prevent its meeting, Courtin urged him to sow division between the Houses or place himself at the head of Danby's enemies. James rejected both proposals, as contrary to the duty he owed to his brother.[36]

James probably suspected (rightly) that Courtin was exaggerating his peril for his own ends. He expressed confidence that Charles would not abandon him to his enemies, and added "that he would give his consent to the precautions which were proposed to assure the Protestant religion because, if he succeeded to the throne, by the laws of England he would not be committed to anything." Such disingenuous reflections did not stop James from worrying that there might be a move to exclude him from the throne or from cautiously renewing his contacts with his allies of the last session. Holles told him of a plan to argue that Parliament was legally dissolved, using medieval precedents to show that it should meet at least once every twelve months. James refused to commit himself, somewhat to Holles' irritation, but in general his negotiations left him fairly confident.[37]

His confidence was not misplaced. He had to agree to support a measure of Danby's, limiting a Catholic king's control over appointments in the Church of England. In the end, in fact, he opposed it because it also included provisions to raise all children of the royal family as Protestants. Fortunately for James, the bill failed to pass the Commons. Little else occurred to upset him and, indeed, two things happened which presaged the end of his estrangement from Danby. First, four peers claimed that Parliament was legally dissolved. James joined with the majority of the Lords in sending them to the Tower for their presumption. He was annoyed not only because their claim challenged the King's prerogative of summoning Parliaments at will, but also because a pamphlet, *Considerations on the Question whether the Parliament is Dissolved*, included a claim that Parliament had the right to regulate the succession. Although Shaftesbury and his friends denied responsibility for the offending passage, the damage was done. All James's old suspicion of Dissent and fear of republicanism came flooding back. He abandoned his allies of the last two years and, in so doing, took the first step towards a rapprochement with Danby.[38]

Secondly, James became more and more disturbed by the reaction in England to Louis' continued successes in the Low Countries. In London a German was beaten up by a crowd of women who thought he was a Frenchman; when they discovered that he was a German, they apologized and kissed him. Like Charles, James was irritated by Louis' refusal to be satisfied with moderate gains and to heed Charles's plaintive reminders of the damage his conquests were doing to Charles's affairs at home. It was some time before James accepted Danby's argument that Charles had to break with France. As Danby saw it, since Charles could not survive financially without Parliament, he had to "fall into the humour of his people", at least on foreign policy. He added, "I could never see what useful help we can receive from France when the peace shall be made." It took some time to cure James of his belief that the security of the English monarchy depended ultimately on the French army, but another of Danby's arguments offered a viable alternative which James was eventually to embrace. Danby argued that once Charles had raised an army for the war, he could "speak boldly" to Parliament and insist on its paying his debts before he would disband his army. By May James was using similar arguments to Courtin, while assuring him that Charles did not really intend to make war, but to use the threat of war as a pretext to secure the money for an army. Even so, James continued to argue that Charles should not meet Parliament until

well into 1678 and that he should preserve the French alliance. Danby meanwhile, continued to tell Charles that James's conversion was to blame for
Parliament's obstreperousness. By August, however, there were signs that
James and Danby were prepared to work together and their reconciliation was
completed in the following months, which saw James's daughter Mary marrying William of Orange and Charles preparing for war against France.[39]

* * *

For some years William's relations with his uncles, Charles and James, had
been less than cordial. After William's father died in 1650, his enemies (who
feared that he wished to turn the Dutch republic into a monarchy) had tried
to restrict drastically the powers of future heads of the House of Orange.
William was formally excluded from the offices held by his ancestors, the
positions of stadholder of five of the seven provinces and captain general of the
union. Charles had shown some interest in having his nephew restored to what
many regarded as his rightful place in Dutch public life, but he clearly expected
William to obey him, as head of the family, and so (in effect) turn the republic
into an English satellite. William, however, proved much more uncompro-
misingly Dutch than his uncles expected. When in 1672 a popular revolution
impelled him to power in the aftermath of the French invasion, he became a
head of state in his own right. Although he was not quite twenty-two, his
organizing ability and ruthless singleness of purpose soon made him a major
European figure. His uncles were slow to appreciate this change. They continued
to treat him with a certain condescension, while he regarded himself as their
equal.

There were two points on which Charles particularly disapproved of
William's behaviour. First, he strongly suspected William of secretly stirring
up the English Parliament to attack the French alliance in 1673–74, thus
indirectly forcing Charles to make peace with the Dutch. Secondly, Charles
regarded as foolhardy William's determination to continue the war against
France, whatever the cost to the Dutch and their allies. He considered that
William's demand that Louis should hand back the bulk of his conquests was
quite unrealistic and that by prolonging the war William was merely allowing
Louis to conquer more of the Spanish Netherlands. He argued that William
should make peace at once, on terms that were less than ideal, rather than be
be forced to accept worse terms later. Unlike William, Charles did not believe
that Louis wished to conquer all the Spanish Netherlands and so he thought
that the details of the peace mattered less than bringing the war to an end, for
he did not believe that Louis would renew it at a later date. Charles, it is true,
had strong reasons of his own for wanting William to make peace and thus
forestall Parliament's demands for war. Nevertheless Charles's was a pragmatic
and reasonable view and one which had many supporters in the Dutch republic.
William's attitude towards France left no room for pragmatism, however.
To him, Louis' power was already too great and had to be reduced, whatever
the cost, before it engulfed all Europe.[40]

In his efforts to persuade William to make peace, Charles had one great inducement to offer: the hand of James's elder daughter. While the Queen had no children and Mary Beatrice had no sons, Mary was the second heir to the throne, after James. By marrying her, William could move a little closer to the English throne, but not much, for Mary's chance of succeeding was not great. By 1677 Mary Beatrice had produced two children, and there seemed every prospect that in due course she would produce a healthy son. The most immediate advantage which William saw in marriage to Mary was that it would bring him closer to his uncles and (he hoped) enable him to influence their foreign policy. If they could only be persuaded to send an army to Flanders, the allies might yet drive out the French. Thus while Charles saw the marriage as a step towards peace, William saw it as a means of continuing the war.

There had been talk of a marriage of William and Mary as early as 1674. James had been opposed to the idea, mainly because he hoped (quite unrealistically) that Mary would marry the Dauphin. William, meanwhile, had said that his position was not yet secure enough for him to think seriously of marriage. He added that Mary was too young and that he knew nothing about her[14]. By early 1676, however, William's position within Holland was sufficiently uncomfortable to give him second thoughts. Each campaign saw him struggling to co-ordinate a motley group of armies and to overcome the ineptitude and eccentricity of his fellow generals. The Dutch opposition to the House of Orange, shaken by the violent events of 1672, began to recover heart and to argue that William was squandering the republic's resources to carry on a hopeless war from which only he could benefit. William therefore asked Sir William Temple, Charles's ambassador at the Hague, whether he would find Mary an agreeable wife and whether, if he married her and became associated with the court, he would alienate all his friends in England. Temple reassured him on both points and William decided to ask Charles's permission to come to England at the end of the summer's campaign. His failures in the field that year, especially his failure to take Maastricht, made it more necessary than ever that he should persuade Charles to enter the war. Charles, however, was offended at William's repeated refusals to heed his advice and denied him permission to come over, while James was furious that William had approached Charles without telling him. As so often, William's lack of tact did him no good. His uncles, meanwhile, told Courtin how pleased they were that their upstart nephew had been taught a lesson at Maastricht.[42]

By the summer of 1677 the situation had changed. Charles and James's anxieties about the possible consequences of Louis's conquests in Flanders made them more eager to persuade William to make peace while William approached them much more tactfully. In June he sent over his most trusted servant, Bentinck, who paid assiduous court to both Charles and James. He returned with a very kind letter from James to William and permission from Charles to come over at the end of the campaign, provided Parliament was not in session. Courtin was not told of this and his successor, Barrillon, did not hear until September that William was coming. James told Barrillon that he did not know the purpose of William's visit, but Barrillon got the impression that James would not be averse to William's marrying his daughter. Others noted that James spoke very favourably of William and James wrote to William that he looked forward to talking with him about current affairs.[43]

William reached the court, then at Newmarket, on 9th October, and was careful to attend James's *coucher* and *lever*. James found him correct, but a little over-formal. On the 14th the court returned to London and serious negotiations began between Charles and William, in which James played little part. On the 17th, without any preliminaries, William suddenly asked James for Mary's hand. Charles tried to persuade him to agree first on terms for a peace, but on the 20th William sent Temple to tell Charles that he would go home unless Charles gave his consent at once. Charles, who had by now decided that William would be "reasonable" about the peace terms, agreed and told Temple to tell James what had been resolved. It seems likely that Charles had decided to agree to the marriage before William sent his ultimatum, but he may not have told James of his decision. Temple thought that James seemed surprised but he said, "The King shall be obeyed." He told the council that his consenting to the marriage showed clearly his desire to "preserve the peace and unity of the kingdom" and to maintain the established order in church and state.[44]

James clearly hoped that the marriage would help to reduce the unpopularity and suspicion caused by his conversion. But had he given his consent willingly? Barrillon thought that he had merely submitted to Charles's commands and reported that James had stressed that Mary Beatrice was pregnant and was young enough to bear him several sons. However, James had been less than frank to Barrillon in September about the object of William's visit and he may well, like Charles, have been making every effort to play down his role in a step which he knew Louis would dislike. James also apologized to the Pope for the marriage, but he would have found it hard to justify in terms which the Pope would accept. Danby also thought that the marriage had been made against James's will, but Danby greatly exaggerated his own part in bringing it about.[45] Against this one should set Barrillon's reports in September and October that James did not seem averse to the idea of the marriage. If he seemed taken aback on the 20th, this was perhaps because he had not expected Charles to consent before agreement had been reached about possible peace terms.[46]

Moreover, if one considers certain gradual changes in James's attitudes during 1677, it seems very possible that he may have welcomed the marriage. In mid-October Barrillon noted for the first time that James was working closely with Danby and that he respected the treasurer's firmness and skill. Danby's influence can be seen both in James's expectation that the marriage would make him more popular and in his remark in November that "the Presbyterians and other malcontents . . . feared a peace because they saw well that it would deprive them of the means of making trouble." Clearly, James no longer had any time for his former allies. Moreover, even before his reconciliation with Danby, James had expressed irritation at Louis' reluctance to disgorge his conquests in the interests of peace. It seems, then, that for both James and Charles the marriage and the rapprochement with Holland were the products of a genuine, if temporary, disillusionment with France, which James was to express much more forcefully than Charles.[47]

The wedding itself was hardly a jolly affair. When Mary heard of her fate, she wept for a day and a half. William was twelve years older and four inches shorter than his bride. Hook-nosed, solemn and asthmatic, "he had a constant deep cough . . . spoke little and very slowly and most commonly with a disgusting dryness." He was also slightly hunchbacked, very unfashionably dressed and had forgotten much of the English he had learned from his mother. The wedding took place on 4th November, without Mary's sister Anne, who had smallpox, and Mary Beatrice, who was about to give birth to a son who, had he lived, would have destroyed Mary's hopes of succeeding to the throne. William was anxious to return to Holland, for he feared (rightly) that his marriage to a Stuart princess would be seen as evidence of monarchical ambitions. The marriage also reduced his popularity in England. Rumours spread that he was a Papist. On 5th November an effigy of the Pope was burned with a string of oranges around its neck. Mary was heartbroken at leaving her family, especially Mary Beatrice, to go into a strange land with a husband she hardly knew. As with James's second marriage, however, a match hastily arranged for political and diplomatic reasons proved a lasting success. As William's cold reserve gradually thawed, Mary came to love him for his kindness and thoughtfulness and to respect his ability and integrity. Her unquestioning devotion helped sustain him through seventeen years of difficulties and uncertainties. When she died, in 1694, he was so distraught that it took him months to recover.[48]

Before he left, William and Charles agreed on a set of proposals which Lord Feversham carried to Louis. Under them, Louis would have ceded rather more of his conquests than he had so far seemed willing to do. Charles hoped that Louis would accept the terms or at least use them as a basis for negotiation. When Louis rejected them, Charles was in an awkward position. He was not prepared for war, but he had gone too far to back down and needed anyway to recover Parliament's goodwill quickly, for the wine duties granted in 1670 would expire in the autumn of 1678. Reluctantly, therefore, Charles allowed Danby and the "hawks" at court to push him towards war.[49]

Rather surprisingly, perhaps, James emerged as a leader of these "hawks". At first he had expected Louis to accept the Feversham proposals and had told Barrillon that if Louis rejected them, all England would rebel. When Louis' rejection arrived, however, James suddenly became eager for war. He told the Venetian resident that too much success had made Louis arrogant. Barrillon argued in vain that the Commons would demand new measures against James and the Catholics in return for voting money. James now had the bit between his teeth. His eagerness doubtless owed much to his hopes of recovering his lost popularity and more to his hopes of commanding either the army or the fleet.[50] Predictably, his bellicosity put his relationship with Barrillon under strain, although he tried to play down his personal eagerness for war by arguing that Charles had no choice but to make war, in order to satisfy his subjects. It also brought him into conflict with Charles, who was less impulsive and saw far more clearly than James the snags involved in making war without the wholehearted co-operation of Parliament.[51]

There can be little doubt that James and Danby wanted war both because it was politically necessary and because it would provide an opportunity to enlarge the army. Barrillon wrote in April:

"The Duke of York believes that he is lost, because of his religion, unless he takes advantage of this chance to subjugate England. . . . I believe that he has been persuaded that it will be easier to carry through this design in time of war than in peacetime."

Barrillon reported several times that James wished to use the army to restore the monarchy's power and that many people feared that he intended to use it to impose absolutism. But did he? Barrillon was now on bad terms with James and was working closely with his enemies, so his interpretation of James's motives inevitably reflected their fears and suspicions.[52] It is worth noting also that Barrillon never reported James as saying that he wished to use the army to alter the constitution. On the contrary, James argued that the King needed an army in order to *preserve* the existing order. He told Barrillon that Charles had allowed the royal authority to be dangerously eroded. His anxieties grew as the Commons expressed distrust of the army, demanded sterner measures against the Catholics and refused to vote money for the war which it had earlier demanded. James saw this as clear proof that the House's main aim was to whittle away the King's power. As a result, he was almost relieved that, by May 1678, the threat of English intervention seemed to have persuaded Louis to make peace. He wrote to William:

"Now the ill men in the House strike directly at the King's authority and should we have been engaged in a war now, they would have so imposed upon the King as to leave him nothing but the empty name of a king and no more power than a duke of Venice and how long they would have let him have that name the Lord knows; I am sure it would not have been long."[53]

James's conviction that the opposition in the Commons was inspired by republicanism was indicative both of his misreading of the history of the civil wars and of his insensitivity to the feelings of others. He was quite unable to appreciate the fears aroused in the minds of Protestant gentlemen by the prospect of a Catholic king and by the raising of a large army. He could not understand how such fears could drive loyal monarchists to interfere in areas which traditionally and legally were the King's undoubted preserve: the Church, foreign policy and the direction of the armed forces. What James saw as a concerted and ideologically motivated attack on the monarchy, they saw as simple self-preservation. Conversely, the average MP would have been bewildered and offended that James thought him a republican. As he did not share James's fears of rebellion, he was quite unable to understand the true reason why James wanted a larger army. Traditionally Englishmen associated standing armies with tyrannical regimes, like those of Cromwell or Louis XIV, and so they assumed that James must want an army to establish a similar tyranny.

James's motives were, however, like those of the Commons, essentially defensive. As he told Barrillon many times, if the government had to face a rebellion it would be far more likely to survive if it possessed a substantial army.[54]

As James and Monmouth struggled to raise and organize the army, the war on the continent drew to a close. For a while peace seemed certain and then, in June, Louis refused to implement the agreed terms unless his Swedish allies received full satisfaction. The court's bellicosity revived but was soon rendered obsolete by events abroad. The Dutch made a separate peace with France, which left their allies little option but to follow suit. The hope that the war would continue had led Charles to spend on keeping the army in being the money which Parliament had voted to pay it off. With a large, bored and ill-disciplined army quartered around the Home Counties, Parliament was liable to be tetchy and anxious when it met in October. Money was even more short than usual and Charles could no longer hope for any help from Louis, who had not forgiven his defection to the allies. James's conversion was as much of a political liability as ever and the Commons' recent conduct suggested that Danby's much-vaunted system of Parliamentary management was under great strain. For the court, it was a nervy, edgy summer recess. Charles had quite enough on his mind without bothering overmuch about a dotty clergyman called Israel Tonge, who came to court in August with a long and implausible story of a Catholic plot against Charles's life, a story which Tonge had been told by one Titus Oates.

* * *

It emerged later that Oates had a thoroughly unsavoury past. Expelled from two Cambridge colleges, he had failed to make a career as either an Anglican clergyman or a Jesuit novice. His unlovely exterior reflected accurately his unlovely personality. He was habitually dishonest, totally unscrupulous and aggressively homosexual. His patron, Tonge, was comparatively harmless but was obsessed with the Jesuits and thought they were trying to kill him. For this reason, no one at court took Tonge's allegations very seriously, but, as no king could ignore a threat of assassination, Danby was ordered to investigate. For some weeks, Tonge shuttled between Danby and Oates, who gradually added to his story. In an effort to add greater authenticity, Oates sent some clumsily forged letters to James's confessor. This was the first James had heard of the matter and he insisted that it should be investigated. On 28th September the council read the letters and heard a statement from James. It agreed that the letters appeared to be forgeries. Satisfied, James followed Charles to Newmarket, no doubt believing that he had cleared the matter up as far as it affected him. Nobody took Tonge seriously and no one had had time to plough through the eighty-one articles which Oates had sworn the previous day before the London JP Sir Edmund Berry Godfrey. Thus when Oates first appeared before the council the afternoon that James left London, what he had to say came as a shattering surprise to all present.[55]

For hour after hour Oates reeled out names, dates and places until the councillors were dizzy with mingled amazement and admiration. "If he be a liar he is the greatest and adroitest I ever saw," remarked secretary of state Henry Coventry. As yet, however, Oates's testimony did not seem to threaten James. He had accused some of James's Catholic friends, like Bellasis and Arundell of Wardour, but had stressed that the Jesuits who had allegedly plotted Charles's death thought that James was too loyal to his brother to be allowed to live.* He did, however, mention in passing that if Coleman's papers were seized, some highly incriminating material would be found. The council duly sent a messenger to take them. The order cannot have come as a surprise to Coleman. Two days earlier Godfrey had told Coleman that Oates had mentioned him in his allegations and James had advised him to destroy any letters which might prove compromising. But either Coleman had forgotten that he possessed any such letters or he did not regard them as incriminating. He let his papers be seized, surrendered himself and even handed over the keys to his ciphers. As the council was still busy with Oates, it was not until 4th October that it began to read Coleman's correspondence.⁵⁶

The councillors were shocked by what they read. The letters dated from 1674 to 1676 and were addressed (among others) to Louis XIV's confessors, the internuncio at Brussels and Cardinal Howard. Many talked of money to bribe MPs, or to remove the need for Charles to call Parliament. Much of the language was obscure or allusive, which made the letters appear more sinister than they were, but it was clear that some of the letters had been written at James's command. Indeed, in one letter Coleman wrote that James had been

> "converted to such a degree of zeal and piety as not to regard anything in the world in comparison with God's Almighty glory, the salvation of his soul and the conversion of our kingdom which has a long time been oppressed and miserably harrassed with heresy and schism."

Whatever the precise content of Coleman's intrigues—and from the letters it was often far from clear—such passages were bound to have an enormous impact. First, they seemed to provide independent and authentic confirmation, if not of Oates's story itself, at least of the sort of designs which he had described. Secondly, after Oates had been careful to keep James out of the Plot, Coleman's letters placed him squarely in the centre of it.⁵⁷

James's feelings when he learned that Coleman had failed to destroy his letters can only be imagined. To make matters worse, Coleman insisted that James had authorized the bulk of his correspondence, apparently under the misapprehension that anything commanded by the King's brother could not be treasonable. James saw at once that he had no alternative, if he wished to preserve his claim to the throne, but to deny point blank that he knew of all but an unimportant fraction of the correspondence. Coleman was doomed anyway, and James's only thought was to avoid being dragged down with him. Fortunately, when James swore on his honour as a prince that Coleman was

---

* Oates did hint once at James's involvement, but he did not follow the hint up. (*CSPD 1678*, p432.)

lying, both the Lords and the council were predisposed to believe him, especially when Oates himself declared that James had known nothing of the letters. The Commons were less easily convinced. On 4th November some MPs proposed that he should be kept away from the King's person and a few hinted that he should be excluded from the succession. Coleman was hastily tried, convicted and executed before he could harm James any further, but there was no way to undo the damage which he had already done. By now Oates's story had been linked in the popular mind, however loosely and illogically, with the fears of "Popery and arbitrary government" which had existed since James's conversion and which had recently been reinforced by the raising of the army. Coleman's letters made the connexion more concrete and more explicit. From the investigation of the Plot it was now to be a natural progression to propose James's exclusion from the throne. For over five years fears of "a Popish successor" had contaminated the political atmosphere, but men had been restrained from expressing those fears openly by respect for James and for the royal family. Oates's allegations and Coleman's letters intensified those fears to a point where many no longer felt so restrained.[58]

James's influence in Parliament was too strong to be destroyed overnight. The Lords rejected Shaftesbury's demand that James should be sent away from court and he could still muster enough support in both Houses to secure exemption from a bill excluding Catholics from Parliament (which removed the Catholic peers from the Lords). On the other hand, Charles ordered him to stop attending the admiralty board and the committee for foreign affairs and he was unable to dissuade Charles from proposing much more severe measures against the Catholics. More ominously, late in November Oates and a new witness, Bedloe, accused the Queen of complicity in the Plot. Neither the King nor the majority of the Lords believed their allegations, but they gave added strength to a renewed clamour for a divorce. Meanwhile, Monmouth ostentatiously dissociated himself from James and was soon being talked of in London as a possible "Protestant successor". Despite sharing his interest in things military, James had always been suspicious of Monmouth's ambition and concerned at Charles's fondness for his son. Monmouth's open break with James doubtless encouraged the witnesses to edge towards accusing James of complicity in the Plot. Oates could hardly do so, having exonerated James unequivocally, but Bedloe had been more cautious. He now alleged that someone, who might have been James, had been present when the Queen agreed to Charles's assassination. It was clear that, given suitable encouragement, he would accuse James directly and others were to do the same early in 1679.[59]

The Plot ended James's co-operation with Danby. To Danby it offered an excellent opportunity to pose as the defender of Protestantism and to repress the Catholics. Many suspected, too, that he would use it as an excuse to keep up the army. James naturally opposed the persecution of Catholics, nor could he accept the political necessity of allowing the judicial murder of innocent men, merely because they were popularly believed to be guilty. Others were well aware of the rift between James and Danby and exploited it. Shaftesbury and

Halifax continued to attack James, but others saw Danby as the more dangerous of the two, especially as his control of treasury patronage gave him so much influence over the Commons. Holles and the Presbyterians promised to leave the Catholics alone if James would abandon Danby and agree to disband the army. They were supported by Barrillon, whose orders were to protect James, to ruin Danby and above all to get rid of the army. Barrillon therefore did all he could to strengthen the prevailing suspicion that the army had been raised, not for a war against France, but to establish absolutism at home. James was reluctant to abandon the army, however, for he feared that without it the monarchy would be defenceless. Bewildered and fearful, he did not know what to do or whom to trust. In his anxiety he went out of his way to justify himself, where a more perceptive man would have maintained an aloof and dignified silence.[60]

James's greatest fear was that Charles would not stand by him. He was only too aware of his brother's "ductile spirit", his habit of taking the line of least resistance. As Bab May had once remarked, "they need but opiniatre the matter and he was sure the King would yield at last." Charles was as bewildered and anxious as James. He accepted Danby's advice to tell James to withdraw from all policy-making bodies, to propose severe measures against the Catholics and to allow Parliament to investigate the Plot. But on other points he stood firm. He made it clear that he would not agree to any changes to the lawful succession and he refused to allow the Commons to pass a bill mobilizing the militia, saying that by law control of the militia was vested solely in the crown. The Commons had passed the bill because it wanted the militia—an amateur force, officered by country gentlemen—to protect law-abiding Protestant citizens against both the Papists and the army. To Charles, however, the bill seemed designed to allow his subjects to arm against him, at the very time that those same subjects were trying to deprive him of his army. He re-read the history of 1641-42 and asked Barrillon for money to keep up part of his army. Barrillon refused so Charles, reluctantly, had to disband it, a process delayed by the difficulty of borrowing the necessary money.[61]

Charles, then, had to sacrifice the Catholics and, more reluctantly, the army in order to appease the Commons and to preserve the prerogative and James's right to succeed him. This forced him to trust far more than James would have wished to the essential loyalty of his subjects and, as it turned out, that trust was amply justified. For the time being, however, things went from bad to worse. In December Ralph Montagu, formerly Charles's ambassador in Paris, revealed to the Commons some letters he had received from Danby, empowering him to ask Louis for money in return for Charles's proroguing Parliament. The letters gave Danby's enemies the chance they had been waiting for. They seemed to carry on the designs in Coleman's correspondence and it did Charles's credit no good that he had countersigned them. The Commons were so incensed against Danby that Charles had to prorogue Parliament in order to save him.

At the end of 1678, therefore, both Danby and James felt that they could hope for nothing from the present Parliament. Together they persuaded Charles to dissolve it and call a new one. Thus the House of Commons elected in a flush of enthusiasm in 1661 ended in bitterness and recrimination, thanks very largely to James's conversion. The elections produced a House which was likely to be rather more suspicious of the court and more difficult to manage, but less bad than many had feared. The election results merely strengthened Danby's conviction that if he were to save himself, he had to remove James from the court. While he remained, it would be easy to allege that Charles was influenced by "Popish counsels". Charles therefore tried to persuade James either to conform to the Church of England or to leave the court. He sent Sancroft, the Archbishop of Canterbury, with the Bishop of Winchester to try to convince James of the errors and iniquities of Popery. James, predictably, was unconvinced, and he also refused to leave the court without a positive order from Charles. Charles finally sent him such an order on 28th February, in a letter drafted by Danby, which told him that he must leave not only the court but the country. James had no choice but to obey, but feared that, once he was abroad and unable to protect his own interests, Charles would be persuaded to abandon his rights in order to save himself. This, James believed, would merely accelerate the destruction of the monarchy. James was reassured a little by Charles's formal declaration to the council that he had never been married to anyone but the Queen, but not much. On 3rd March he and Mary Beatrice set sail sadly for Holland. It was the start of a period of exile which was to last, intermittently, for almost three years. During that time, James had to watch from a distance, impotent and frustrated, the attempts to exclude him from the throne.[62]

CHAPTER SEVEN

Brussels and Edinburgh
(1679–82)

James's departure did little to diminish the fear and hatred with which he was generally regarded. Charles's apparently miraculous escape had forced people to consider what would have happened had the Plot succeeded. The prospect of a Catholic successor had hitherto seemed somewhat hypothetical. Charles was only three years older than James and seemed very healthy. The Plot made the prospect of a Popish king seem far more immediate and there was no short-age of pamphlets to remind the English what they could expect under such a ruler:

"Fancy, that amongst the distracted crowd you behold troops of Papists, ravishing your wives and your daughters, dashing your little children's brains out against the walls, plundering your houses and cutting your own throats by the name of heretic dogs. . . . When he (as all other Popish kings do) governs by an army, what will all your laws signify? You will not then have Parliaments to appeal to; he and his council will levy his arbitrary taxes and his army shall gather them for him."[1]

Given such assumptions about the behaviour of Papists in power, James's exlusion was the only logical remedy. Mere restrictions on his power would be ineffectual, since it was widely believed that Catholics did not feel themselves bound by any promises made to "heretics". Not all accepted the logic or justice of exclusion, however. As part of the reaction to the upheavals of the Inter-regnum, the sacred character of monarchy had been more heavily stressed and had become more widely accepted. As the principle of the hereditary suc-cession was an integral feature of both the English monarchy and the Ancient Constitution, there were many (especially among the Anglican clergy) who regarded it as sacrosanct. They argued that subjects were obliged, like the primitive Christians, to suffer patiently whatever a Popish king might do to them and not to attempt to alter the constitution.

In the highly-charged atmosphere of 1679, such scruples and passivity found comparatively few supporters. For most, fear of the "Popish successor" weighed far more heavily than attachment to the hereditary principle, as was shown clearly by the Exclusionists' sweeping victories in the three general elections of 1679–81. The Exclusionists (or "Whigs", as they came to be called) thus controlled the Commons, but to pass the legislation they wanted they needed the consent of the Lords and the King. As the Lords usually followed the King's wishes, his attitude was crucial. He said consistently that he would not agree to James's outright exclusion, but would consider any scheme to limit his powers. The Whigs were adamant that such limitations would not work, so Charles's refusal to countenance exclusion forced them into more and more radical measures. Often that radicalism was the product of particular situations and of the fear, anger or frustration which those situations engendered. Fear of the army had already led the Commons to challenge the King's right to direct the militia, which had been reaffirmed by the Militia Act of 1661. The King's right to nominate office holders was challenged when the Commons demanded the dismissal of all those associated with James, especially in the armed forces. Again, fear of a military coup (together, perhaps, with avidity for office) was the main motive. Moreover, the Whigs in the Commons came to demand the dismissal of any minister whom they suspected of giving advice which they disliked. When the Lords rejected the exclusion bill in 1680, some MPs argued that the Lords should not reject measures which the Commons thought were in the national interest. The Commons thus came to challenge both the King's traditional right to direct the executive and the Lords' traditional position in the legislature, arguing that both should conform to the wishes of the House of Commons. Such radical arguments were ultimately, however, means to an end, and that end was the preservation of England's religion and constitution against the threat posed, now and in the future, by James.

Despite Charles's public insistence that he would never agree to exclusion, there were many who were reluctant to take his rebuttals as final. Many courtiers alleged that he would not risk all to save James, but that to put a better appearance on his abandoning him, Charles wished to make it look as if he had been forced into it. There was doubtless much wishful thinking and self-interest behind such allegations. James had many enemies at court and most courtiers wished to see Charles reconciled to Parliament so that he could obtain the money to pay them. However, the fact that so many at court believed that Charles would eventually yield encouraged those outside to press him harder to do so. Similarly, many both inside and outside the court chose to ignore Charles's repeated statements that he would never designate Monmouth as his successor. In their efforts to break down Charles's resistance, the Whigs sought to create the impression of an irresistible demand for exclusion, with the implied threat of a national rebellion if it were refused. To this end, they conducted a vigorous campaign of petitions and propaganda, while behaving truculently and extravagantly in the Commons. If in their excitement they produced rhetoric whose implications were more extreme than they intended, that did not trouble them unduly, since their main aim was to frighten the King into compliance.

There can be no doubt that the radicalism of the Whigs' behaviour really worried the King. It also worried those who came to be known as Tories, who saw in the Exclusion crisis unpleasant echoes of the events of 1640–42. Again, there were ambitious politicians (like Shaftesbury) who sought to exploit the situation in order to gain office. Again the Commons were challenging the

King's most basic powers—his right to control the armed forces, choose his own advisers and formulate policy. Again the bishops and clergy were attacked, for defending the hereditary principle. In time, more and more of those who believed that "forty-one is here again" came to see in the Whigs' behaviour a greater and more immediate threat to the Ancient Constitution and the Church of England than could be posed by the possible behaviour of a "Popish successor". James might never become king. Even if he did, he might behave far less badly than the Whigs expected. As the Tories began to criticize the Whigs' methods, the Whigs turned against them the venom which hitherto they had concentrated on the Papists. In the Commons the Whigs had a large enough majority to expel or silence Tories who dared to criticize them, but in the press the Tories, led by the redoubtable Roger L'Estrange, more than held their own in both reasoned argument and abuse. The Whigs' tactics were meant to create the impression of a nation unanimous in its demand for exclusion. In fact, they divided the political nation more deeply and more bitterly than at any time since the Restoration.

Charles II is often credited with great political skill in handling the Exclusion crisis, but I suspect that such credit is undeserved. His secrecy and dissimulation make it impossible to be certain, but there is considerable evidence that he showed less clearsightedness or constancy of purpose than many historians claim. In July 1681 he told Barrillon that he would have agreed to James's exclusion if Parliament had granted him money and not tried to limit his prerogative in other ways. He added, in explanation, that he did not believe that an act of exclusion could have prevented James from succeeding to the throne.[2] Thus Charles opposed exclusion mainly because he saw it as part of a much wider attempt to reduce the king to a mere figurehead. Throughout 1679 and 1680 Charles, like many others, feared a general rebellion. Halifax, for example, asked his friend Reresby how many of his neighbours he could rely on if there were a civil war.[3] Charles's first instinct, therefore, was to buy time by granting concessions. He allowed Parliament to investigate the Plot and authorized the trial and execution of those accused of plotting his death. He took the initiative in suggesting new measures against the Papists, hoping to relieve the tensions created by the Plot. He appointed leading Exclusionists to office, notably on the reconstituted privy council. On the other hand, he was careful neither to sacrifice any of the crown's essential prerogatives, nor to give the new Whig office-holders any real power.

Such delaying tactics came naturally to Charles and, as it happened, they worked well. Few as yet doubted the veracity of the Plot, but many came to believe that it had been fully investigated, that the guilty had been punished and that it was no longer a cause for anxiety. The new witnesses who came forward were less assured and credible than the old and were managed increasingly blatantly by Shaftesbury and the Whigs. This merely strengthened the Tories' conviction that, as in 1641, anti-Catholicism was being used as a smokescreen to cover an attack on Church and monarchy. By 1680 the nascent Tory reaction against the Whigs' radicalism was apparent, but Charles hesitated to throw all his weight behind the Tories, despite James's urging. Many of his other advisers still claimed that a few well-chosen concessions could placate Parliament and secure a much needed grant of money, and Charles found such a possibility very alluring. The session of October 1680 to January 1681 should have made it clear that his hopes of compromise were illusory, but he still found it hard to face up to the retrenchments and austerity which would be needed if he were to live without money from Parliament. Against all the evidence, he let himself be persuaded that the Parliament which was to meet at Oxford in March 1681 would prove more amenable. Only after that failed did he set out to exploit the Tory reaction systematically and with great success.

It could be argued that Charles survived the Exclusion crisis not because of his political skill but because his position was much stronger than most people realized. In making their comparisons with 1641 the Tories were unduly alarmist. Charles I had been forced to call the Long Parliament by his need for money to repel an invasion from Scotland. In the Exclusion crisis a small Scottish rising in 1679 was quickly crushed and Charles II was never so short of money that he could not survive without grants from Parliament. In 1641 the need to suppress the Irish rebellion had raised in an acute form the question of who should control the army. In the Exclusion crisis Ireland remained quiet. In 1641 Parliament's fears had been of the likely behaviour of the present king. In the Exclusion crisis the fears were of the possible behaviour of the present king's possible successor. The dangers of 1680 were more hypothetical and less immediate than those of 1641.

There was a more subtle sense in which the comparison with 1641 was misleading, for it rested on an incorrect analysis of the origins of the civil war. The Tories saw it as a "great rebellion"—a deliberate revolt designed to achieve certain definite ends. In fact the Parliamentarians had fought in self-defence, because Charles I was preparing to make war on them. Nevertheless, in a sense the Exclusionist Whigs did have much in common with the Commons' leaders in 1641, but not in the way the Tories thought. Neither Pym and his friends nor the Whigs had any intention of rebelling against the King. The aims of both were defensive and conservative—the preservation of the Ancient Constitution and the Protestant religion—but both were forced by circumstances and by their fear and distrust to use radical means in order to achieve these conservative ends. Both mobilized popular support in order to put pressure on the King and the Lords. Neither developed a coherent constitutional theory to underpin their actions. They defended particular claims on the basis of the right of self preservation or sheer necessity: the phrase "*salus populi suprema lex*" appeared frequently. Yet they tried to fit such essentially pragmatic and political arguments into an essentially historical and legalistic view of the constitution. Their radical demands were fitted, uncomfortably, into a basically conservative ideology because, in the last resort, their aims were fundamentally conservative.

The Whigs, then, were not revolutionaries any more than Parliament's leaders in 1641–42 had been revolutionaries. Indeed, the very fact that there had been a civil war in 1642 made civil war less likely in 1679: men knew how much they stood to lose. On the other hand, this very fact encouraged the Whigs to exaggerate the danger of civil war in order to frighten the King. Yet in fact the intensity of feeling was far less than in 1641, as was shown clearly by the almost total absence of violence during the Exclusion crisis. In 1641–42 angry and violent crowds took to the streets repeatedly, demanding Strafford's execution or the bishops' exclusion from the Lords. There were massive demonstrations in the Exclusion crisis: some of the ceremonies where the Pope was burned in effigy were said to have attracted two hundred thousand people. But these demonstrations were essentially peaceful and good natured. When Barrillon attended one in 1679 he was amazed that "no manner of mischief was done, not so much as a head broke, but in three or four hours the streets were all quiet as at other times. It would not have been so at Paris," he said.⁴ The civil wars and Charles I's execution had given the English a reputation for rebelliousness and radicalism which they did not really deserve. The fact that they were not inclined to rebellion helps explain why Charles II survived the Exclusion crisis. The fact that so many Tories believed that the English *were* inclined to rebellion helped to create the backlash which Charles was to exploit so effectively in the years that followed.

* * *

After a brief visit to William and Mary, James took up residence at Brussels. He was pleased to meet again some of those he had known twenty years before, but soon became bored and frustrated. There was little to do, except pay visits and take the air, and when summer came the city emptied rapidly. James and Mary Beatrice received some visitors from England and her mother came for a while, but as it became apparent that their exile would be a long one their court began to dwindle. Money was short, since James's household had to bear its share of the economies recently ordered by the King. As James waited anxiously for each letter from England, he hunted ferociously to relieve his boredom.

The dissolution of the Cavalier Parliament and Danby's resignation soon afterwards removed the dominant landmarks from the political scene. Left to his own devices, Charles reverted to his old habit of "taking off" members of the opposition, but in a somewhat original manner. On 21st April he appointed an entirely new privy council, consisting mostly of the court's erstwhile opponents, with Shaftesbury as lord president. Shaftesbury still insisted on James's exclusion and began to work closely with Monmouth, but two other new councillors proved more tractable. The Earl of Essex came of an impeccably Royalist family. Much respected for his integrity, he had opposed the court (and especially Danby) for reasons of principle, but with moderation and caution. The Earl of Halifax's opposition had been much more extreme than his later reputation for moderation would suggest. In 1674 he had been one of the few peers to support Carlisle's proposal for James's exclusion from the throne. Intensely ambitious and eager to direct affairs, he lacked the mental toughness needed for success in the ruthless world of Restoration politics. The "trimming" between extremes which he later elevated into a political philosophy looked, during the Exclusion crisis, uncomfortably like an unprincipled attempt to keep in with both sides. In the process, he sometimes showed an unpleasant cynicism,[5] which perhaps helps to explain his remaining with the court while the less gifted but more straightforward Essex reverted to opposition.

James would find little comfort in Charles's placing his trust in such men as Essex and Halifax, but a third new adviser was rather more to James's liking. Robert Spencer, Earl of Sunderland had served on several diplomatic missions and in February 1679 was made a secretary of state. His record included no hint of opposition to the court, nor did it indicate the extraordinary mixture of qualities which he was to show over the next decade. Time was to show that Sunderland possessed a ferocious appetite for responsibility but lacked the application to detail which should have gone with it. He had a penetrating but narrow political intelligence: he was able to anticipate the wishes of first Charles and then James and to plan his political strategy accordingly, but having once embarked on a line of action he carried it to its logical conclusion, regardless of changing circumstances. Like James he was so used to the court that he was insensitive to the fears and principles of the squires who ran local government and filled the back benches of the Commons. Unlike James, he was financially reckless, a compulsive gambler for whom office was a financial necessity. He owed his success at court to sheer force of personality above all else. If even the fearsome Judge Jeffreys cringed before Sunderland's withering sarcasm, it is not surprising that the lesser men at James's court proved quite unable to compete with him. Despite his stubbornness James was easily dominated by confident, strong minded men and, although Sunderland was highly strung and impulsive, there was no doubting the strength of his will.[6]

As yet, Sunderland's close relationship with James lay in the future. In the spring of 1679 James's cause seemed doomed and, as an aspiring politician, Sunderland pinned his hopes elsewhere. Having discovered that Shaftesbury and Monmouth were unwilling to share power with anyone and were irrevocably committed to exclusion, he turned to Essex and Halifax, with whom he agreed on two key points. First, they pressed Charles to enter into a close alliance with the Spaniards and Dutch. They claimed that the French alliance had done as much as anything to poison his relations with Parliament and that, for political reasons, it was vital to prevent Louis from undertaking any further actions in the Low Countries. Secondly, they advised Charles to do all he could to remove Parliament's fears of the Catholics, allowing the Commons to investigate the Plot. Above all, they claimed, James should not return to England, or there would be a general rebellion. Charles was the readier to believe such allegations because his spies told him that such a rising was imminent. As all three leading politicians agreed that James was a political liability and feared his influence over the King, he remained in Brussels, exchanging visits with dull Flemings and solemn Spaniards and sending his son in law long gloomy letters about the perils facing the English monarchy.[7]

Events in England soon redoubled his anxiety. When Parliament met the

Commons brought in and passed an exclusion bill, while both the Commons and the new privy council pressed Charles to dismiss magistrates and officers who they alleged to be "creatures of the Duke", "arbitrary Protestants" or "favourers of Popery". Charles did not openly resist such demands, but found frivolous pretexts to keep in office those he regarded as loyal, saying (for example) that one JP kept good foxhounds. Such levity was unlikely to reassure James, who was particularly concerned at the attempt to purge the officer corps of the army and navy: "If His Majesty make any further concessions, he is gone, for if once they get the navy, purge the guards and garrisons and put new men in, they will be absolute masters."[8]

As James saw it, the demand for his exclusion was only the opening move in a campaign by the Presbyterians and republicans to reduce the King to a cipher and then destroy the monarchy: "they that would go so far would never think themselves safe so long as [the King] were alive, remember Edward II, Richard II and the King my father."[9] Such an interpretation, although inaccurate, was logical, given Royalist assumptions about the causes of the civil war, and it was one shared by Charles and William. The three leading members of the royal family agreed about the nature of the problems which Charles faced but disagreed about the best way to tackle them. Charles had been convinced by his new ministers that he could win Parliament over by a strong line against France and against the Catholics. William came to take a broadly similar view. Anxious to use England's influence to prevent further French aggression in Flanders, his main concern was that Charles should be on good terms with Parliament: otherwise his foreign policy would be hamstrung by lack of money. William's views on English affairs were influenced increasingly by Sunderland and by Sunderland's uncle, Henry Sidney, Charles's ambassador at the Hague. In time they convinced William that Charles could re-establish good relations with Parliament provided he sacrificed James's interests. Sidney claimed that William regarded James's exclusion as inevitable, although it should be added that Sidney had a certain capacity for self-deception and that William said several times that Charles should not agree to exclusion. At the same time, William still hoped that Charles and Parliament could reach agreement, although he was rather vague about how this was to be achieved.[10]

James thought that Charles's compliance was dangerous and William's attitude was incomprehensible and disloyal. As he saw it, the royal family stood or fell together and he expected William, as its most junior member, to follow the lead of his seniors. In June he wrote to William in some irritation that he did not agree with him that Parliament should soon meet again, and thereafter his letters became shorter and less confidential, but still friendly. To Charles he wrote that he must not let his opponents meddle with the armed forces or with the government of Scotland or Ireland. If there was to be a rebellion—a prospect which did not seem greatly to distress James—it was essential that Charles should be able to rely on the armies of all three kingdoms. As the Tory reaction began to gather momentum late in 1679, James talked less of rebellion. He did not doubt his enemies' malevolence but now believed that his friends would prove strong enough to defeat them. Thereafter his message to Charles became consistent to the point of tedium: he must make no concessions or the monarchy would be destroyed; instead of relying on men like Halifax, with dubious records, he should place his trust in the tried loyal servants of the crown, the old Cavaliers and Church of England men.[11]

In the spring and early summer of 1679, James's self-confidence reached its nadir. "It is a great satisfaction to me to know that anyone wants me," he wrote with a rare touch of self-pity. He was relieved that Charles had blocked the exclusion bill by proroguing Parliament, but Sunderland and his colleagues still insisted that James should not be allowed to return. James's friends again advised him to turn Protestant, again he refused: "if occasion were I hope God would give me His grace to suffer death for the true Catholic religion as well as banishment," he wrote.[12] Even when Charles dissolved Parliament in July, he wrote to James that he feared that he would be prosecuted, on the evidence of Coleman's letters, if he returned to England. James sent to England for his foxhounds and settled down for a long, boring winter, but relief was at hand. On 22nd August Charles fell seriously ill. Sunderland wrote to inform James and Feversham advised him to come over at once. James set out immediately with only two companions and reached Whitehall on 2nd September.[13]

*   *   *

Charles's sudden illness had thrown the court into a panic. Essex, Halifax, Sunderland and the King's mistress, the Duchess of Portsmouth, all feared that if Charles died Shaftesbury and Monmouth would seize power and wreak a bloody revenge on their enemies. Only James was of sufficient standing to foil them, so the ministers had sent word to him secretly, while denying to all and sundry that they had done so. Whatever its circumstances, James's return proved a triumph. After months of dire warnings that James's return would provoke an immediate rebellion, his arrival caused no disturbance whatever. James was told that, had Charles died, the Lord Mayor of London would have proclaimed him king. The Mayor and aldermen certainly waited on James, and all but one kissed his hand. The courtiers, too, rushed to greet him: "It's believed for three days last passed [there] has been more kneeling within these walls than in four months before."[14] Charles's illness was the main reason for this enthusiasm. Many saw James as the only man who could save the nation from civil war if Charles died, while others simply took care to keep in with the heir presumptive. James was quick to exploit such a favourable situation. Although he had little time for Essex and Halifax he had never doubted Sunderland's loyalty. Sunderland, for his part, was quick to sense the improvement in James's fortunes and soon convinced James of his devotion to his interests. In the next few months Sunderland's credit grew while Essex resigned and Halifax withdrew sulkily to Nottinghamshire to plant carrots and cucumbers. Meanwhile, James steered his young brother-in-law, Lawrence Hyde, (Clarendon's younger son), towards a position of power. In November he replaced Essex as first commissioner of the treasury. Outside the court, too, James gathered all the support he could. Anxious old Cavaliers and bishops assured him of their loyalty to his interests. James received their assurances with all the graciousness he could muster and promised the bishops that, if he ever became king, he would not try to establish Catholicism by force.[15]

Once the ministers' first panic had passed and Charles was on the mend, they found James's presence an embarrassment. Again they argued that James should leave the country, but James was far from willing to go and it was by no means easy to make him go now that his position was so much stronger. In order to persuade him, Charles agreed that he should go to Edinburgh rather than Brussels and that Monmouth should leave England at the same time. Monmouth left for Holland the day before James left to bring Mary Beatrice back from Brussels, but he did not stay away for long. Late in November Monmouth returned to London to wild popular acclaim: there were sixty bonfires between Temple Bar and Charing Cross. Charles, however, forbade Monmouth to come to court and stripped him of his offices. In June 1680 James persuaded Charles to declare once again in council that he had never been married to Monmouth's mother, but there were still many who convinced themselves that Charles was not really angry and that, in his heart, he loved his son better than he loved his brother. James himself still had anxieties on this score and did all he could to discountenance Monmouth's pretensions.[16]

Nevertheless, when James left for Brussels on 25th September, after over three weeks in England, he had every cause for satisfaction. Eighteen peers accompanied him to his ship: the people of London might shout for Monmouth but the men of wealth and influence were rallying to James. He was no longer a friendless exile but the head of a large and growing body of "Tories".* Even if he had to go away again, he would in Scotland be able to perform a useful task and to build up support for himself (notably by strengthening the Scots army, which might well prove invaluable if civil war broke out in England). He returned to England within a fortnight and enjoyed a further triumph. Shaftesbury, as lord president, convened the council on his own authority and tried to discuss the question of James's going to Scotland. Furious at his presumption, Charles dismissed him from his post on 14th October, James's birthday. A week later James dined in the City with the Honourable Artillery Company, a gentlemen's militia of which he was colonel. Despite posters on the doors proclaiming that all who attended were betrayers of the Protestant religion, there was a good turnout. Oates and Bedloe watched from a balcony and cried out, "a pope, a pope," until one of James's guards threatened them with a pistol, whereupon they changed their cry to "no pope, no pope, God bless his highness," and sneaked away. After all the rumours about the City's hostility to James, it was reassuring for him to spend a convivial evening there and suffer nothing worse than a few catcalls. As he smugly remarked, "this was pretty well for a poor banished man so little time since."[17]

James had hoped to be allowed to stay in London, using an illness of his

---

* A tory was a type of Catholic Irish bandit. The term was first applied to "Church and King" men at the end of 1680. (I am grateful to Mr Peter Taylor for this information.)

wife's as a pretext. Charles, however, insisted that he should go, but added that it should not be for long. James left for Scotland on 27th October. On his way he met with a mixed reception. The Earl of Salisbury took care to be away from Hatfield when he called, the civic authorities in York treated him with cool discourtesy and in some towns far fewer gentlemen than expected turned out to greet the King's brother. At Stamford, however, the gentry were present in force, thanks to the influence of the Earl of Lindsey. Lindsey advised James to rely on the old Cavaliers; James assured him that that was exactly what he intended to do. A succession of other peers waited on him on his way north: the Earl of Ailesbury, the Earl of Derby, the Duke of Newcastle, the Earl of Strafford, the Archbishop of York. As James entered Yorkshire Reresby was one of fifty gentlemen waiting to greet him. His journey, in fact, gave James a chance to show himself to his supporters, and they in turn showed their support for him. Some who could not come in person wrote to offer their services and James replied as graciously as his stilted prose would permit. Despite occasional affronts his overall feeling must have been one of satisfaction: the monarchy's "old friends" were rallying to him.[18]

James reached Edinburgh on 24th November. There was some difficulty about his sitting on the Scottish privy council without taking the oath of allegiance. James argued that, as the King's brother, he did not need to take it, for it was directed against rebels and fanatics. He soon got his way. In general, he approached Scottish affairs with caution, preserving a benevolent neutrality among the various aristocratic factions. Significantly, perhaps, one of the few subjects in which he took an active interest was the militia which, under an act of 1668, could be sent to England if need arose. As James saw it, his main task was to gather information about Scottish affairs in order to advise his brother. In January 1680 Charles wrote that he could now return to England and he reached London late the following month.[19]

Charles's leading advisers were now Sunderland, Hyde and the young Sidney Godolphin, with Portsmouth lurking in the background. They still hoped to reconcile King and Commons and had taken advantage of James's absence to enforce the laws against Catholics much more rigorously. James was furious, especially with Hyde, but was told that such measures were politically essential. More to James's taste was the removal of JPs thought to be supporters of Exclusion and their replacement by loyal men. In April James wrote with satisfaction that the judges reported a great increase in the strength of the "Cavalier or Church party" all over the country. The key to the ministers' strategy, however, lay in foreign policy. Still convinced that it was vital to prevent further French incursions into the Spanish Netherlands and that the nation would unite if the King made war against France, the ministers sought alliances with the Dutch and Spaniards. Some perceptive observers doubted whether the Commons would be impressed by such measures and Charles, too, needed to be convinced. Although negotiations for a French subsidy had broken down in December, Barrillon still argued that his interests could best be served by renewing his liaison with France. When James returned, therefore, Charles was being pressed to choose between a Dutch and a French alliance and both sides believed that James's support could tip the scales in their favour. James continued to assure Barrillon that his interests and Louis' were inseparable, but Barrillon soon became convinced that his assurances were insincere and that he really supported the Dutch alliance. This impression is confirmed by James's letters to William, which expressed bewilderment and irritation at Louis' conduct in the Low Countries. In fact, the uncertain state of English affairs made the cautious Dutch unwilling to enter into any engagement with Charles. The only result of much diplomatic effort was a treaty with Spain which later proved an embarrassment.[20]

After dissolving Parliament in July 1679 Charles had ordered a general election, which produced a House of Commons which was likely to be still more committed to exclusion. Charles therefore delayed meeting Parliament, hoping that its members' ardour would cool and that his ministers could find ways to appease them. Angry at being deprived of the main vehicle for their efforts, the Exclusionists produced numerous petitions that Parliament should meet. To anxious Tories, these petitions raised further echoes of 1640–42. Meanwhile, Charles (as usual) negotiated with the opposition leaders, hoping to find an expedient other than exclusion which would satisfy them. James seems to have played some part in these negotiations, which predictably failed. By June James accepted that Parliament would have to meet that autumn, but expected it to be so unruly that Charles would be forced to dissolve it within a week. He was now convinced that the Exclusionists were a noisy but unrepresentative minority and that most of the nobility and gentry were opposed to exclusion. He believed that the reaction against extremism was gathering strength and so that once this Parliament had been dissolved, the next election would produce a much more moderate House of Commons.[21]

James was over-optimistic. The Exclusionists were far from a spent force. They showed their strength in June when the Middlesex grand jury would have indicted James as a Popish recusant and Portsmouth as a common whore, but for the judges' quickwittedness in dismissing the court. The propaganda effect of the move was considerable and it frightened Portsmouth so much that she resolved to sacrifice James's interests in order to save herself. Hitherto she and James had been on friendly terms. Now she joined Sunderland and Godolphin in urging Charles to send James back to Scotland before Parliament met and in arguing that, as James's Popery was the cause of Charles's troubles, all would be well if he abandoned him. They soon convinced themselves that Charles would agree to exclusion, a conviction which Charles's inscrutability did nothing to dispel. "His conduct is so secret and impenetrable," wrote Barrillon, "that even the most skilful observers are misled. The King has secret dealings and contacts with all the factions and those who are most opposed to his interests flatter themselves that they will win him over to their side."*

---

* It is noteworthy that although both Sunderland and Sidney usually claimed that Charles would agree to exclusion, on occasion each of them expressed the opinion that he would not (Sidney, I 243–4; Prinsterer, V 430–1).

Charles's behaviour may well have reflected genuine irresolution, but James found it infuriating. His anxiety grew: by September he feared that he would be impeached and likened himself to a stag at bay.[22]

By the beginning of September Sunderland and Portsmouth had persuaded Charles that James should go away, but it was quite another matter to persuade James that it was in his interest to do so. He was bitterly angry with Sunderland and Godolphin for "betraying" him and for advising him to leave. As usual, he said he would go only if Charles ordered him to. Charles eventually did so even though a majority of the council thought that James should stay. Charles told his brother that he could not protect him if he stayed and that he feared Parliament would send him to the Tower. All his ministers now claimed that there was a real danger of rebellion. James was bitterly depressed. Those he had trusted had deserted him. Only Hyde was loyal and he could do little on his own. James knew Charles well enough to suspect that Charles would soon bow to his ministers' importunity and sacrifice him, once James was no longer there to stiffen his resolution. He was still convinced that any serious concession would lead inevitably to the ruin of the monarchy. All the ebullient confidence of the past year collapsed in a matter of days and James and his duchess prepared gloomily for the long journey to Scotland. They left London on 20th October. The next day, the Parliament assembled which was to decide whether James should ever be king of England.[23]

* * *

The Commons wasted little time in passing another exclusion bill which was sent up to the Lords on 15th November. The City of London petitioned the King to agree with the Commons. Charles told the petitioners to mind their own business and set out to make it clear to the Lords that he wanted the bill to be rejected on its first reading. The debate lasted the whole day. Charles was present throughout and left no doubt where his sympathies lay, sneering when Monmouth expressed concern for his safety. Charles's firmness ensured the bill's rejection. Contemporaries laid great stress on Halifax's eloquent arguments against it, but they probably made little difference. Almost a week before, Conway had predicted that only thirty peers would support the bill, which proved exactly correct. Sixty-three voted against it.[24] The Commons were so stunned that they undertook no business the next day. Sunderland and Portsmouth, their whole strategy in ruins, could only argue that in his heart Charles still wished to be forced to agree to exclusion. The Whig leaders in the Commons proceeded on the same assumption and made more and more extreme demands, including the dismissal of all judges, JPs and army officers obnoxious to Parliament. Such demands merely strengthened Charles's conviction that exclusion was merely a preliminary to the total emasculation of the monarchy. MPs talked openly of the possibility of civil war: "Let it be so if there be no other way to prevent Popery," said one. The Commons threatened to impeach those ministers who were known to oppose exclusion, notably Hyde and Halifax. Halifax talked of retiring from business but Hyde was made of sterner stuff. He persuaded Charles to prorogue and then dissolve Parliament in January 1681, without consulting the council.[25]

James watched these events from Edinburgh with an anxiety increased by the knowledge that the news he received was almost a week old. He was delighted when the Lords rejected the exclusion bill, but thought Halifax's proposals for stringent limitations on the powers of a Catholic king even worse than exclusion. As usual, he warned his brother that concessions would bring disaster. As usual, he refused to give up his religion, but he was careful to remind his Anglican supporters that "I have ever stuck to them and shall continue to do so." Although he had great faith in Hyde and was delighted that Sunderland was dismissed from office in January, he still distrusted Halifax and blamed him for Charles's decision to call a Parliament at Oxford in March, which gave James's enemies at court an excellent pretext to keep him in Scotland.[26]

For some time Hyde and the other treasury commissioners had argued that Charles could now survive financially without Parliament. A few days before the Oxford Parliament met his financial independence was assured by a treaty with France guaranteeing him a modest subsidy. He was thus able to face the Oxford Parliament more confidently. It proved even more extreme than its predecessors and Charles dissolved it after a week, this time with no mention of calling another. Convinced at last that there was no hope of agreement with Parliament, Charles took Hyde's advice and threw his full weight behind the Tories. He issued a declaration, to be read in every parish church, comparing the Oxford Parliament's behaviour with that of the Long Parliament in 1640–42. Already he had started to dismiss Whiggish JPs. Now the council began to harrass the writers and publishers of Whig newspapers while their Tory rivals grew in confidence and abusiveness. After saying for many months that he would "stand by his old friends", Charles at last suited his action to his words.[27]

James was delighted that Charles had seen sense at last and hoped that he would now be allowed to return to court. Hyde would certainly have been glad to have him back, as would his ally Edward Seymour, but others wished him to remain in Scotland. Portsmouth feared that James would not forgive her supporting exclusion, while Halifax, alone of Charles's ministers, still hoped to reconcile him to Parliament. Various reasons were advanced why James should stay in Scotland: that he should finish the good work he was doing there or that he should not come until the end of a series of trials of leading English Whigs. The most important arguments, however, related to the unsettled state of affairs on the continent. The Treaty of Nijmegen of 1678 had tried to define the new frontier between France and the Spanish Netherlands, but its provisions were open to various interpretations. A conference was called to resolve these ambiguities, but Louis decided to use his army to enforce his interpretation of the treaty, which included a claim to sovereignty over all the territories which had ever "depended" on his new acquisitions. As these included most of the lands around Luxemburg, Louis occupied them, blockaded the city and demanded that the Spaniards should cede it to him.[28]

Louis' action renewed William's fears that the French planned to devour the whole of the Spanish Netherlands. He pressed Charles to seek a reconciliation with Parliament so that the English could join with the Dutch to stop Louis before it was too late. Charles and James were both annoyed at William's presuming to advise them on their domestic affairs, especially as he was quite unable to suggest how this reconciliation should be achieved. William agreed that exclusion was unjust, limitations would reduce the King to a cipher and that Charles had been quite right not to surrender his control of the militia and of appointments to office. He still insisted, however, that, unless King and Parliament could agree, Louis would conquer the whole of the Netherlands. He added limply that he understood little of English domestic affairs. Charles replied sharply that much needed to be done to restore his position at home before he could think of intervening abroad. William's visit to London in July 1681 only made matters worse, and showed how far his relations with his uncles had deteriorated since 1677–78. William was annoyed by Charles's refusal to recognize the menace from France, Charles was annoyed by William's contacts with the London Whigs and the two parted on thoroughly bad terms. They were never to meet again.[29]

Charles's advisers agreed that further French gains in the Netherlands could have serious political repercussions in England, but only Halifax claimed that, if Charles called Parliament, the nation would unite against France. Hyde and Charles did all they could to limit Louis' gains, but their bargaining position was pitifully weak. Louis knew that if Charles called a Parliament he was most unlikely to persuade it to co–operate. Nevertheless, Charles rashly promised the Dutch that he would call Parliament if Luxemburg fell and then pleaded with Louis to save him from his embarrassment by refraining from starving the city into surrender. Faced with the prospect of being forced to call Parliament, it seemed best to Charles that James should remain in Scotland.

* * *

Compared with England Scotland was a backward country. Much of its soil was boggy, rocky and unfertile and the bulk of the peasantry was desperately poor. Edinburgh had maybe thirty thousand inhabitants—as much as any English town other than London—but was cramped and squalid and as yet showed little sign of its eighteenth-century elegance. Politically, too, Scotland was backward. The nobility possessed a dominance over lesser landowners and peasants which had long since disappeared in England. In the Highlands the crown owed what little authority it possessed to its ability to influence the clan chiefs and to exploit their rivalries. The Lowlands were more settled and orderly, the lesser landowners and townsmen counted for more, but there too the crown could not ignore the power of the great nobility. The art of governing Scotland lay in balancing aristocratic interests and harnessing the nobles' territorial power for the King's benefit. Unlike England, in Scotland violence lurked just below the surface of politics and the government used armed force to repress disorders with a frequency and severity which would have been unthinkable in England.

The most divisive issue in Scottish politics under Charles II was religion, or rather church government. Before 1638 the prevailing system had combined clerical self-government with episcopal authority: each diocese was organized on a presbyterian basis, but with the bishop as president of the diocesan synod. In 1638, however, this system was destroyed as part of the Covenanters' reaction to Charles I's attempts to impose Laud's liturgy and Laudian episcopacy on Scotland. The next two decades saw the emergence of two main groups in the Scottish church. A radical minority, the "Protestors", argued that Presbyterianism was the only divinely approved form of church government, that episcopacy in any form was intolerable and that the rulers of the state should follow the direction of the clergy. The "Resolutioners" were more numerous and more moderate. They disliked the theocracy and bloodthirsty extremism of the Protestors, and most would have been happy to return to the compromise of James VI's reign—a predominantly presbyterian system tempered by episcopacy. Such a system would have commanded wide support and would have proved the most stable basis for the Scottish church under Charles II. But it was not to be. At the Restoration a small group of Scottish peers convinced the King that a much more episcopalian system was both desirable and feasible. The bishops were given much more extensive powers and the clergy were required to seek ordination from them. Many Resolutioners, as well as Protestors, found such changes intolerable and so the government was faced with a massive problem of religious dissent.

From 1663 to 1679 Charles's chief minister for Scotland was Lauderdale, a strange, contradictory character. Coarse-featured and slobbering, he was often irascible and brutal and had an insatiably avaricious wife, yet he was also a man of learning and sensibility, well versed in Greek and Hebrew. A former Resolutioner, he disliked the brand of episcopacy imposed at the Restoration, but his lust for power overcame his ecclesiastical scruples and for fifteen years he tried to enforce an essentially unworkable system. The bishops advocated repression, to break rather than contain dissent, but dissent was too widespread to be suppressed. The use of force was liable to provoke a violent reaction from the Dissenters while the amount of force required was likely to provoke opposition from the nobility. On the other hand a toleration, tacit or open, would not work either. The more moderate Dissenters might enjoy their liberty quietly, but the radicals would be satisfied only when they had rooted out episcopacy and remodelled church and state according to their will. Moreover, the bishops condemned any indulgence to dissenters as a betrayal of the Church. Lauderdale was in an impossible position. Whether he tried repression or indulgence, he was liable to provoke disorder, or criticism, or both, which would call his competence into question and give his rivals a pretext to attack him. Lauderdale therefore oscillated uncomfortably between a limited indulgence and outright repression, and often tried to combine the two. As time went on, repression came to predominate, eliciting ever louder protests from Lauderdale's enemies among the nobility.[30]

Except in 1675–76 when he was at odds with Lauderdale about English affairs, James seems to have supported his policies consistently.[31] By 1679, however, Lauderdale's memory was failing and his enemies closed in for the kill. A brief rebellion gave them their chance. Monmouth suppressed the rising at the skirmish of Bothwell Brig, but allowed most of the rebels to go home. He also proclaimed a limited toleration, allowing Dissenters to worship in their houses, hoping that this would discourage them from attending the large "field conventicles" which the government regarded with such suspicion. The decision to send James to Scotland removed the need to dismiss Lauderdale. James ascribed his good reception there to Lauderdale's influence but, while he treated Lauderdale's friends well, he took care to avoid identification with any faction: "I live here as cautiously as I can and am careful to give offence to none and to have no partialities and preach to them laying aside all private animosities and serving the King his own way." Even Burnet admitted that his conduct was amiable and moderate.[32]

On his first visit James approached the religious question with some caution. He wrote that "the best men" were troubled by the indulgence with which Monmouth had treated the rebels, but thought that it should not be revoked until they did something to forfeit it. Meanwhile he advised that the government should continue to allow house conventicles. In fact, the Bothwell Brig rising made it possible both to isolate the most radical Dissenters and to treat their offence as political rather than religious. The rising had begun as a field conventicle and its leaders had denied Charles's right to rule. Such radicalism alienated the more moderate Dissenters and frightened them into greater conformity, so that they worshipped in their houses rather than in the fields. Many moderate Dissenters were prepared to support the government's vindictive pursuit of those involved in the rebellion, in which the laws were stretched well beyond their normal limits. A few "Cameronians", the most militant section of the Protestors, had remained in arms, but were scattered at Airds Moss in July 1680 and some of the stragglers were taken while James was in Scotland. The treatment of these unfortunates, and the use on them of the torture of "the boots", is often cited as evidence of James's cruelty and fondness for religious persecution. James felt nothing but loathing and contempt for these people and he was certainly not squeamish, but two points should be made. First, torture, though abandoned in England, was used quite often in Scotland although its legality was questionable. Secondly, whatever the Cameronians claimed, James saw their offence as political and not religious and he was justified in doing so. These were not mild and inoffensive non-conformists but the successors of the fanatical ministers of the 1640s and 1650s who had spoken far more of God's wrath than of His love and whose bloodthirstiness had sickened hardened soldiers. Had they managed to seize power, they would have repaid with interest the Episcopalians' brutality. It is worth noting, too, that when James saw that torture and the fear of death made no impression on them, he said "Take them away, else they will say what will hang themselves" and had them banished or imprisoned instead.[33]

The combination of a restricted toleration of moderate Dissenters and the stern repression of extremists continued Lauderdale's strategy, if with greater success. James stressed to the Scottish Parliament the need to suppress the political manifestations of dissent—seditious conventicles and "extravagant and horrid doctrines"—but saw the remaining Bothwell Brig rebels as only part of the problem. The rebellion had shown the need firstly, to strengthen the powers of the crown and secondly, to identify the potentially disaffected, not among the poor and weak but among the nobility. With the King on the defensive in England, it seemed doubly necessary to be sure of Scotland. These preoccupations appeared when in the summer of 1681, James summoned the Scottish Parliament. This was a feeble body compared with that of England. Usually it merely ratified the decisions of the lords of the articles, a steering committee of peers and officials under the presidency of the King's commissioner (on this occasion, James himself). James found little difficulty in pushing through the measures he wanted. He secured additional taxation to support the army and an act guaranteeing his succession to the Scottish crown (which was separate from that of England). The most contentious new measure was the Test, which in many ways resembled "Danby's Test" of 1675. It was to be taken by all office holders, beneficed clergymen and MPs and included promises to adhere to the Protestant religion, to defend the King's rights and prerogatives and to attempt no alteration in church or state.[34]

The Test was rushed through with little debate and some strange anomalies went unnoticed. James was eager to secure an oath of non-resistance, however, for there were two peers whose loyalty he particularly wished to try. The first was the Duke of Hamilton, who had opposed Lauderdale for years. His territory around Lanarkshire was a centre of radical dissent, although his own religious views seem to have been adaptable. For a long time Hamilton wriggled, making great professions of loyalty and sending his son to plead his case at court. He finally took the Test in March 1682, to avoid losing his offices. The second noble in whom James was interested was the Earl of Argyll. He was no religious radical either and although he had opposed Lauderdale's use of force against Dissenters, he was generally regarded as Lauderdale's ally. James showed little sign of hostility to Argyll—if anything, the reverse—until the autumn of 1681 when some associates of Lauderdale and Argyll were dismissed from office. Argyll had many enemies among the Highland nobility who were eager to convince James that he could not be trusted. His reaction to the Test was awaited with interest, since most of the nobility had taken it without demur. In November Argyll produced a paper of his reasons for being unwilling to swear not to alter the government of church or state. James was scandalized: had he either taken the Test or refused it "nothing would have been said to him." Argyll's enemies quickly exploited James's anger. Scots law was even more unfavourable than English law to those accused of political offences. Argyll was accused of various offences, including treason, and convicted.[35]

James denied that he wished to have Argyll executed. His aim, he said, was to destroy Argyll's excessive territorial power and, especially, to deprive him of his "superiorities", whereby his tenants were obliged to follow wherever he commanded them. Argyll was not to know this. He escaped in his daughter's clothes, whereupon sentence was pronounced against him. James hoped to divide Argyll's lands among his local rivals and so create a more even balance of power in the Western Highlands, but Charles was persuaded to let them pass intact to Argyll's son. James was criticized for his severity in this case, but this was probably unfair. As James said, Argyll knew the law well enough to know what would happen to him. It seems, indeed, that James had protected Argyll against an attack by his enemies the previous summer.[36] Although later historians (especially Scots Presbyterians) depicted James's period in Scotland as a reign of terror, that was not how it seemed at the time, in either Scotland or England. He managed the difficult feat of persuading many of the prickly and cantankerous Scottish nobles to work together and avoided too deep an involvement in their feuds. The repression of the Cameronians was accepted as necessary and even desirable by many moderate Presbyterians as well as by episcopalians. The English Tories, meanwhile, saw his conduct in Scotland as evidence of the truth of his repeated assurances that he would support the Church of England against its enemies. The Whigs might disagree, but it was the Tories whose support James wanted in 1681–82.

*　　*　　*

By the start of 1682 James felt that his work in Scotland was done. The resistance of Bothwell Brig was well-nigh eradicated and the bulk of the nobility and clergy had taken the Test. Meanwhile, in his efforts to secure his recall to England, James had acquired a powerful new ally. Portsmouth was eager to be reconciled, because she hoped that James could grant her £5,000 a year from the post office revenue. James did nothing to discourage her, although he knew that the money could be granted away only by Act of Parliament. Portsmouth now joined Hyde in pressing Charles to let James return. Halifax continued to argue that it would be unwise to recall him when Charles might be forced to call a Parliament by the crisis at Luxemburg. At last, late in February James heard that he would be allowed to come, although it was said at court that he would not stay for long. James received a rapturous welcome at Yarmouth and Norwich, but was careful not to overplay his hand when he joined Charles at Newmarket, claiming that he had no wish to meddle in any affairs but those of Scotland. This modest approach pleased Charles who, against Halifax's advice, decided to take James back to London with him. There too he was received better than most expected and thoroughly enjoyed the Artillery Company's feast.[37]

By now Charles had agreed that James could return permanently. Louis had now withdrawn from Luxemburg, so there seemed no danger of a continental war. On 3rd May James set sail for Scotland, to fetch his wife. He had a narrow escape when his ship sank, with the loss of perhaps a hundred and fifty lives. James himself escaped with difficulty and his servants had to stand with drawn swords to prevent the seamen from piling into his lifeboat and sinking it. This sad accident apart, the future looked bright. The sound and fury of the Exclusion crisis had passed, James had defied the malice of his enemies and they were now retreating in disarray. Soon Shaftesbury was to flee to Holland, where he died in 1683. There was no certainty that James would soon succeed to the throne or, indeed, that he would ever do so. Charles was still only fifty-two and very active. Nevertheless, James could look forward at last to a period of calm, untroubled by Parliaments. He and his wife would be able to enjoy the pleasures of the court, the city and the hunting field. They could travel freely to Newmarket, Windsor or Winchester. They could practise their devotions discreetly, without fear of criticism or molestation. After four years and more of alarms and anxieties, such a calm would be a welcome change.[38]

CHAPTER EIGHT

The Tory Revenge (1682–85)

After the Exclusion crisis Charles made it clear that he would rely on his "old friends", the Tories. The Tories, for their part, magnified the King's authority even more vehemently than at the Restoration. Then there had been an element of consensus among the ruling elite. Most agreed on the need to return to normality, while the yearning for revenge of both Royalists and moderate Parliamentarians was satisfied, in part at least, by the execution of the surviving regicides. No such consensus existed in the early 1680s. The fears and rancours of the Exclusion crisis left the political nation deeply divided. The Whigs had used their dominance of the Commons to abuse and harass the Tories and to undermine the authority of the Church. The ferocity of the party battle left scars which would not heal easily and the Tories thirsted for revenge. To get that revenge and to prevent what they saw as the real danger of another "great rebellion", the Tories looked to the power of the King.

Both Charles and James were eager to gratify them. James may have advocated liberty of conscience in 1675–76, but the Dissenters' support for exclusion completed his return to his earlier view that Protestant Dissent was inseparable from republicanism. His alliance with the bishops, renewed in 1679, grew stronger in the next few years. The chief patrons of the High Church clergy were Lawrence Hyde (created Earl of Rochester in 1682) and his elder brother, Henry, second Earl of Clarendon. As Anne Hyde's brothers, their links with James were personal as well as political. Rochester was a leading member of the committee for ecclesiastical promotions, which between 1681 and 1684 established many clerics friendly to James in the upper levels of the hierarchy. James's leading Anglican chaplain, Francis Turner, for example, became within three years first dean of Windsor, then bishop of Rochester and finally bishop of Ely. Any anxieties which the High Churchmen may have had about James's treatment of the Church if he became king were removed by his conduct in Scotland. In England, too, the laws against Dissenters were enforced more vigorously than at any time since the Restoration; there was even one attempt to dragoon them into conformity. Meanwhile, the laws against Catholicism continued to be enforced. At last, Charles was giving the old Cavaliers the policy of religious repression which they had always wanted.[1]

Besides persecuting the Dissenters, the Tories were eager to break the Whigs as a political force. A few were tried for treason or other offences. Others were prosecuted by individual Tories on actions of *scandalum magnatum* (defaming a peer of the realm). James initiated such an action against Oates and was awarded damages of £100,000, with the rather superfluous addition of £1 costs. Such prosecutions were made easier by the fact that the legal profession was as deeply divided politically as the rest of the nation, so that Charles was able to appoint a strongly Tory bench of judges. Law and politics were never separate in the seventeenth century. The crown's powers were defined in legal terms. The King appointed and promoted the judges and they saw themselves as his servants. Their charges to grand juries at quarter sessions could be thinly disguised government propaganda and they were often asked to report on public opinion or the workings of government in the localities. They usually saw maintaining the security of the state as one of their main responsibilities, especially in treason trials. In the early 1680s, treason—and the administration of justice generally—became a thoroughly partisan business. Whig sheriffs chose Whig juries which gave verdicts in favour of Whigs. Tory judges did all they could to secure the conviction of Whigs and Dissenters and, as the Tories came to dominate local government, they were helped by Tory juries. As one diarist remarked, "If anything of Whig or Tory comes into question, it is ruled according to the interests of the party." The judges of the 1680s have often been accused of subservience to the crown, but this presupposes that they were not acting out of principle. In fact, the perversions of justice in these years sprang, not from judicial subservience, but from the fact that both Whigs and Tories subordinated justice to politics.[2]

The Tories' stranglehold on the legal system made possible the most remarkable development of the early 1680s: the establishment of Tory control over the parliamentary boroughs. The great majority of MPs sat for borough constituencies and during Charles's reign there was considerable friction between the rulers of such boroughs and the neighbouring peers and gentry. The local landowners often expected a borough, especially a small borough, to elect their nominees as its MPs, whereas the leading burghers often had their own ideas about whom they wished to elect. Moreover, in many boroughs the dominant families were Dissenters while in the countryside the strength of High Anglicanism among the gentry and clergy increased markedly. Thus a religious divide opened up between town and country which had scarcely existed before the civil war.

The struggle to control the boroughs and the religious and political antagonisms between town and country were brought to a head by the Exclusion crisis. In many towns, Dissenting magistrates resisted the pressure of the Tory gentry and elected Whig MPs. After the Oxford Parliament, the Tories counterattacked. The Corporation Act of 1661 had required municipal office holders to take the sacrament according to the Anglican rite. Its aim was to exclude Dissenters from municipal office, but it largely failed, partly because many municipalities had failed to enforce it, partly because many Dissenters thought "that it is a madness to lose an office for a bit of bread and a cup of wine." Something more drastic was required, therefore, and from 1682 the Tory minorities in several towns petitioned the King to confiscate their borough's charter and to issue a new one, so drafted as to ensure Tory dominance in both municipal affairs and parliamentary elections. They based their suggestions on the precedent of London. The City's Whig sheriffs returned juries which acquitted Shaftesbury and other leading Whigs, so legal pretexts were found to challenge its charter. The Tory judges declared the charter forfeit and the King gradually extended his authority over the City government and the livery companies. As London had failed to save its charter, lesser boroughs usually surrendered theirs at the first hint of a challenge. The new charters usually gave the King power either to nominate officials or to veto the election of anyone he disliked. Some also restricted the franchise, usually to members of the corporation. Thus the King gained greater control than ever before over the internal affairs of very many boroughs, a control which he used in 1685 to influence the composition of the Commons to an unprecedented extent. The crown, in fact, could now pack Parliament.[3]

Although the crown benefited from the campaign against the borough charters, the initial impetus came from the Tories. In Bristol the belligerent Sir John Knight suggested that the charter should be confiscated. In Yarmouth it was "the loyal party", in Norwich "a very small but angry body of men". As Charles did not intend to call a Parliament, he showed no haste to confiscate old charters or to issue new ones. Only fourteen charters were issued in 1682–83. In the latter part of 1684 the tempo increased, reaching a peak in March 1685 as James prepared to hold his first general election: seventy-six charters were now issued within nine months. The impetus now clearly came from the government and considerable pressure was put on some boroughs to surrender their charters.[4] The Tories had little real quarrel with such methods, however, as the election results of 1685 clearly indicated. Nevertheless, there were tacit conditions underlying both their defence of royal authority and their participation in the campaign to bring the boroughs to heel. If the Tories talked mostly of the dangers from Whiggery and Dissent, this did not mean that they no longer disliked Popery and arbitrary government. It was just that, at present, the main threat to the established order seemed to come from Dissent rather than Popery, from below rather than above. They exalted the monarchy because they believed that the monarchy alone could prevent the overthrow of the constitution and the Church. They assumed that James would respect and defend both of them, a perfectly reasonable assumption in view of his recent record. Events were to show that it was mistaken.

* * *

Charles's love of ease grew with age. After the anxieties of the Exclusion Crisis, he was glad to subside into comfortable indolence. As his appetite for women waned, his relationship with Portsmouth became one of cosy domesticity. He was happy to spend his days "in fishing or walking in the park". At Newmarket, "he let himself down from majesty to the very degree of a country gentleman. He mixed himself amongst the crowd, . . . went a-hawking in mornings, to cock matches in afternoons (if there were no horse races) and to plays in the evenings, acted in a barn and by very ordinary Bartholomew fair comedians." Such a life might bore the younger courtiers, but it pleased the ageing King.[5]

Such a lethargic approach to government did not appeal to James. He was eager to exploit the Tory reaction, to build up the power of the crown and wreak revenge on his enemies. First, however, he had to re-establish his position at court. For years, successive ministers had impressed on Charles that the main causes of his difficulties with Parliament were James's religion and the influence which he was believed to have on policy and appointments. Charles therefore feared that if James were restored to an obvious position of power it might provoke unrest and disorder. He also, perhaps, disliked the thought of being dominated by his more diligent and single-minded brother. Whatever the reason, Charles was very reluctant to allow James to play a leading role in his government.

In James's struggle for power he had three main allies. Rochester had supported James's interests since 1679. His skilful direction of the royal finances made him indispensable, although Charles had little personal fondness for him. He was arrogant, tended to drink too much and his insistence on severe economies made him many enemies among the "men of pleasure", who still had considerable influence with the King. Portsmouth's influence over Charles, however, was entirely personal. She had not always been on good terms with James, but whatever James thought of her reasons for seeking a reconciliation, she was too powerful at court for him to spurn her offer. He took good care to maintain a good understanding with her and supported her moves to bring Sunderland back into office, accepting that he repented his error in supporting exclusion. Sunderland resumed his place of secretary of state in January 1683 and joined James and Portsmouth in pressing Charles to readmit James to the cabinet council, the privy council and the admiralty. Sunderland and Rochester both wished to increase James's power in the hope that he would use that power to their advantage. They were well aware, too, that he might one day become king and so they were prepared to support his policies without reserve in order to retain his favour.[6]

Most of the other leading men at court supported James's interests, but not unreservedly. Seymour, Conway, Ormond and Lord Keeper Guilford had all strongly opposed exclusion. They urged Charles to use all legal means to break the Whigs and agreed that James, as heir apparent, should take a prominent part in government. On the other hand, they expected Charles to keep within the law and to continue to support the Church against its enemies, whereas James hoped to halt the persecution of Catholics. So long as James did nothing to forfeit their confidence, however, he could rely on the support (or at least the benevolent neutrality) of the leading Tories. Only one man at court was firmly opposed to his interests. Halifax was never a Tory, nor did he revel in the persecution of Whigs and Dissenters. He alone urged Charles to call a Parliament and argued that it would do as he wished. He alone urged strong action, with the Spaniards and Dutch, to stop Louis from making further inroads into the Spanish Netherlands. He alone had consistently opposed James's return from Scotland and did all he could to weaken James's influence. Some of his demands were unrealistic: Charles had no intention of calling Parliament and without it he could not pursue a vigorous foreign policy. He therefore suffered one humiliating defeat after another. He threatened to resign if James returned to England or if Sunderland were restored to office, yet still he clung to office, either because he could not bear to relinquish his tenuous grasp on power, or because he still hoped to win the King over to his viewpoint. He complained endlessly "of the unsteadiness of the king's temper", but in fact, even if Charles did not take Halifax's advice, he still supported him despite all the efforts of his enemies to remove him. Halifax, for his part, played skilfully on Charles's fears of being dominated and became almost a symbol of Charles's independence and freedom of action. His power, however, was often more symbolic than real.[7]

Charles thus tried to avoid giving James and his allies a monopoly of power and attempted to maintain a balance between the competing ministers. When Sunderland was received again at court, Halifax was compensated by being made lord privy seal and a marquis. Puffed up with these marks of favour, he overplayed his hand. Filled with vain hopes of becoming lord treasurer, he attacked Rochester's conduct of the financial administration, making a variety of allegations of malpractices and errors of judgment, most of which seem to have been quite unfounded. On the other hand, Charles rejected James and Portsmouth's suggestions that Rochester should be promoted from first commissioner of the treasury to lord treasurer. Thus a year after James's return from Scotland James had failed to add more than marginally to his strength at court. Then came the Rye House Plot.[8]

Harassed by the authorities and with no prospect of a Parliament to revive their flagging fortunes, some of the Whigs had turned to conspiracy. A few of the most radical, some of them republicans, plotted to kill Charles and James on their way from Newmarket to London but their plan misfired. Others, fired by drink or frustration, had talked vaguely of encouraging the King's guards to revolt and demand a Parliament. Such designs did not involve any attack on the King's person and were only "embryos of things that were never likely to have any effect". Charles, however, could see little difference between plotting a rebellion and plotting his assassination and chose to treat the various conspiracies as part of an integrated plot. Thoroughly frightened that a rebellion might begin at any time, he stepped up the repression of Whigs and Dissenters. Many weapons were confiscated from men suspected of "disaffection" and some Nonconformist preachers were imprisoned. Those implicated in the plot were tried and condemned. Although treason trials were always weighted heavily against the accused, there is little doubt that most of those condemned had plotted against the King's life and only in one case, that of Algernon Sidney, was the definition of treason stretched far beyond any reasonable limits. Those convicted were shown little mercy. Charles, thoroughly frightened, was if anything even more implacable than his brother and, unlike James, was unwilling even to consider a pardon for Lord Russell.[9]

When the plot came to light, in June 1683, Charles restored James to the cabinet council, remarking that since their enemies had wished to kill both of them, he wished to have the benefit of his brother's advice. James played some part in the interrogation of the witnesses, although he said far less than Charles did. He saw in the plot a chance to crush the enemies of monarchy, once and for all. It also seemed to destroy the last vestiges of Charles's fondness for Monmouth. A number of Monmouth's former political associates were implicated, but he sent to assure Charles that he had not been involved in it. Charles replied that if he kept such company, he was bound to be suspected of complicity.[10] As Charles seemed adamant, on 24th November Monmouth came to Whitehall, threw himself at Charles's and James's feet and begged their forgiveness. Charles was delighted and pardoned his erring son, but his delight was short lived. When the *Gazette* announced that Monmouth's confession had confirmed the truth of the plot, his Whig friends proclaimed that it was untrue. Pressed to put the substance of his earlier verbal confession into writing, Monmouth hesitated, complied and then recanted. Charles was furious, both at his son's duplicity and at the damage which his recantation had done to the credibility of the plot. In an effort to restore that credibility, Charles ordered the execution of Algernon Sidney. James, Rochester and Sunderland were relieved. Halifax had done much to persuade Monmouth to surrender himself and to smooth the path to his reconciliation with his father. Like Shaftesbury, Halifax had hoped to manipulate the King through Monmouth. While it looked as if his design might succeed, James had had a few anxious days. By 7th December, however, he could write smugly that he was sure that Charles would never again believe anything Monmouth said.[11] Although Monmouth could not be prosecuted because of his pardon, the council's harassment drove him into exile early in 1684, where he was soon to be the cause of yet more trouble.

Since the Exclusion crisis Charles's relations with William had gone from bad to worse. William continued to fret about Louis' activities on the southern fringes of the Spanish Netherlands, where the assault on Luxemburg resumed in earnest in 1683. William saw this as a direct threat to the Dutch republic but few Dutchmen agreed with him: Luxemburg was a hundred miles away from their frontier. Charles too showed little sympathy with William's anxieties. He believed that even if Louis conquered all the Netherlands he would still pose no real threat to England. In fact, however, he did not believe that Louis wished to conquer all the Netherlands and thought that Louis would be satisfied if the Spaniards conceded what he saw as his "rights" under the Treaty of Nijmegen. He added pragmatically that the Spaniards could not resist the French and the Dutch were unwilling to help them, so William, instead of encouraging the Spaniards' resistance, should advise them to cut their losses and give Louis what he wanted. Again and again, Charles and James stressed that they had to avoid war abroad because of the unsettled political situation at home.

There was thus a total lack of understanding between William and his uncles, stemming from their different views of Louis' intentions and of the international situation. Monmouth's arrival in Holland added a further cause of misunderstanding. For some reason, William got it into his head that Charles was really still very fond of Monmouth and so would be grateful if William treated him kindly. He may have got this impression from the Whig exiles in Holland, or the fact that Charles had pardoned his son may have persuaded William that he was innocent of complicity in the plot. There was also a story that Charles had told William that any letter from him which did not bear a certain seal did not represent his true feelings and that his letters telling William to show no countenance to Monmouth did not bear that seal. Whatever the reason, William treated Monmouth with elaborate courtesy while Charles lived but sent him away at once when Charles died, which would suggest very strongly indeed that William believed that such courtesies and kindness would be welcome to the King. James and Charles were furious that William blandly ignored their complaints and their insistence that Monmouth really had been implicated in the plot. James appealed both to William's sense of family solidarity and to his self-interest. "Let the Prince flatter himself as he pleases," he wrote to Mary, "the Duke of Monmouth will do his part to have a push with him for the crown if he . . . outlive the King and me." James and Charles were so angry that they talked of recalling the British regiments in the service of the States General, but William remained sublimely confident that Charles really approved of his conduct. Only Charles's death was to remove this misunderstanding and make possible a fresh start in Anglo-Dutch relations.[12]

While James's relationship with William worsened, he improved his political position at home. In May 1684 he took his place on the privy council for the first time in eleven years and resumed the direction of admiralty business. In October Charles agreed to release from prison any Catholic recusant whose family had served Charles I in the civil wars. Such a change was unwelcome to the Tories on both religious and legal grounds, and Guilford opposed it strongly. James and his allies were now in the ascendant, however, and this was seen most clearly in Irish affairs. Since 1677 the Lord Lieutenant had again been Ormond, the last of the old generation of Cavaliers. At the time of the Rye House Plot, his Irish enemies had alleged that many JPs and army officers in Ireland were Dissenters or had served the Cromwellian regime. The following year Richard Talbot returned to court after a long absence and Sunderland became the secretary responsible for Irish affairs. For months Talbot and his allies, by their allegations and insinuations, slowly eroded Charles's trust in his oldest servant. It was said that Ormond was too old, that he sold commissions in the army to the highest bidder, that he appointed disloyal men to office. At last, in October, Charles wrote and told him that he was to be replaced by Rochester. As Ormond's son wrote from London, "I find that great reformation is intended both as to civil and military affairs and therefore Lord Rochester, who fears no odium, is chosen for that purpose." Barrillon wrote that Rochester was to put the army into the hands of men who could be relied on in case of any disturbance in any of the three kingdoms. He added that James was especially eager that this should be done and that some of the new officers would be Catholics.[13]

Ormond's recall was a triumph for James, Sunderland and their Irish Catholic allies. It signalled the imminent end of James's reliance on the Tories and the beginning of a more openly pro-Catholic policy. It also brought into the open a rift within James's trio of allies. Rochester, despite his brash exterior and administrative competence, was thin-skinned and had been deeply wounded by Halifax's attack on him in 1683. He began to threaten to resign, hoping that Charles would make him lord treasurer and so give him sole control of his finances. Charles was always wary of overmighty servants, however, and Halifax played skilfully on his fears that Rochester wanted a monopoly of power. Rochester, meanwhile, became more edgy and paranoid. In August 1684 he at last offered his resignation. To his surprise, Charles accepted it, compensating him with the modest post of lord president of the council, with a promise of the much more lucrative and prestigious post of lord lieutenant of Ireland when Ormond retired. James was embarrassed by Rochester's conduct and would have preferred him to remain at the treasury. However, he was satisfied with Godolphin as Rochester's successor and set out to hasten Ormond's retirement so that Rochester could be sent to purge the Irish army of its "disaffected" officers.[14]

Rochester had no objection to going to Ireland. In March Ormond had been very ill and Barrillon reported that Rochester coveted the lord lieutenancy and wished to consolidate his fortune. But once Rochester's appointment was decided, Sunderland's relentless ambition became apparent. Having lost his power base in the treasury to Sunderland's ally Godolphin, Rochester was in no position to resist as Sunderland stripped him of his powers. He persuaded Charles to agree that military commissions should be issued, not by the lord lieutenant but by the secretary of state in London: Rochester was to do Sunderland's bidding in Dublin while Sunderland ruled the roost at Whitehall. Charles, tired of Rochester's behaving like a spoiled prima donna, willingly acquiesced in his humiliation. James deeply resented it, but there was little he could do. Sunderland had made himself as administratively indispensable as Rochester had once been. With Rochester's power broken, Sunderland and Portsmouth turned to finish off Halifax, who shrugged off defeats with a doggedness which Rochester must have envied. On this, at least, James agreed with Sunderland and by January 1685 it seemed that Halifax's fall was only a matter of time.[15]

On 2nd February Charles suffered a stroke while shaving. He recovered somewhat, but was subjected to the full gamut of seventeenth-century medical treatment—emetics and enemas, bleeding and blistering—which were intended to draw the "evil humours" out of his body, but instead weakened it further. On the 4th he seemed out of danger, but suffered a relapse next day. James knelt constantly at his bedside, administering whatever the doctors prescribed. The bedchamber was crowded with courtiers, physicians and divines: dying, for a king, was a very public business. When Charles refused to take the sacrament from the bishops, James asked him, in a whisper, if he would like him to fetch a priest. Charles replied that he would, but the only priest who could be found who spoke English was John Huddleston, an aged Benedictine who had helped to save Charles's life after the battle of Worcester. Huddleston was a simple man and was taken aback to be asked to receive his King into the Church, but performed his task well enough. James had the room cleared of all the Protestants except Feversham and the Earl of Bath, and Huddleston was smuggled up the backstairs. Charles confessed and received the sacrament and extreme unction, and the peers and bishops were allowed back. Charles acknowledged that James had always been a loyal and loving brother and asked him to take care of Portsmouth, Nell Gwynn and his "poor children". It was noted that he did not mention Monmouth or (as Evelyn remarked) his people or the Church. At nine o'clock on Friday 6th February, Charles II lost the power of speech and shortly before noon he died. After a quarter of a century as his brother's first subject, James became king.[16]

CHAPTER NINE

The New King

During Charles's brief illness, the council had closed the ports and deployed soldiers around London, but such precautions proved unnecessary. James was proclaimed king without the slightest disturbance and there were many reports of spontaneous popular rejoicing.[1] James, indeed, seemed to go out of his way to reassure the Tories. Immediately after Charles died, James declared to the council that it was untrue that he was "a man for arbitrary power":

"I shall make it my endeavour to preserve this government both in church and state as it is by law established. I know the principles of the Church of England are for monarchy and the members of it have shown themselves good and loyal subjects; therefore I shall always take care to defend and support it. I know too that the laws of England are sufficient to make the king as great a monarch as I can wish; and as I shall never depart from the rights and prerogative of the crown, so I shall never invade any man's property."

At the council's request, James agreed to have the speech printed. The next day he repeated these assurances to Sancroft and Bishop Turner, adding that "he would never give any sort of countenance to Dissenters, knowing it must needs be faction and not religion if men could not be content to meet five besides their own family, which the law dispenses with."[2] Such expressions helped to remove any lingering anxieties which the Tories may have had about the prospect of a Catholic king. Loyal addresses rolled in from all over the country, congratulating James on his accession. Many of them specifically mentioned his promises to preserve the established order in church and state.

James's first measures, in general, showed no sign of a radical break with the policies of Charles's last years. The suitors who thronged the court, expecting a major change of office holders, were disappointed. James confirmed all Charles's officers in their places and in the next few weeks made only a few changes, promoting trusted personal servants, like Dartmouth and Churchill, to places in the royal household. Even Halifax, tottering on the brink of dismissal when Charles died, was retained, but in the less powerful and profitable place of lord president. James told him that he would forget the past, except for Halifax's opposition to exclusion. Former exclusionists were told that James would forgive them if they showed, by their actions, that they now saw the error of their ways. Only a few were refused permission to kiss the King's hand. In general, James showed a magnanimous willingness to bury the past and rejected a proposal that supporters of exclusion should be debarred from sitting in Parliament.[3] His reluctance to make changes reflected his belief that those who held places of profit under the crown would be obliged by both self-interest and duty to serve the king well, and that, as long as they did so, the king should uphold their actions and preserve them in their employments.[4] His instinct was to keep his servants rather than to change them, therefore, and most of the officials whom he inherited from his brother had served the crown well. If he later dismissed very many of these officials, this was mainly because his objectives had changed and with them his criteria of loyalty.

The one major change was the rehabilitation of Rochester. James had not wished Rochester to be shipped off to Ireland and soon created him lord treasurer. His conscientious but less able brother, Clarendon, succeeded Halifax as lord privy seal. The changes made it clear that Rochester was to be James's chief minister. Those who had congratulated themselves on his eclipse in the weeks before Charles's death now had to reckon with the hostility of both the new king and the new treasurer. Portsmouth's influence was hardly of a kind to be transferred from one king to another and she ceased to exercise any influence. Sunderland was more tenacious. Like Halifax, he was given the benefit of the doubt for the time being, but he was well aware that he would have to fight to recover the power which had been within his grasp only weeks before.

James's care to reassure the Tories probably owed much to Rochester's influence. Other changes in the style of government reflected James's own character. He was far more diligent than Charles had been and devoted more time to business. He was also more careful and scrupulous in money matters. He kept a close check on his revenue and expenditure (of which he received a weekly account from the Exchequer) and cut down on his household expenses. One of his main concerns was to repay his brother's debts. This was a matter of both principle and common sense, since it helped to maintain the crown's credit with the London bankers and reduced the burden of interest payments. During his short reign James devoted nearly a million pounds (about half his average annual revenue) to debt repayments.[5] He also did what he could to reduce waste and corruption in the administration. He paid his servants punctually and warned Exchequer officials against peculation. He announced his intention to suppress useless offices and to prevent the sale of employments. As he regarded public and private morality as inseparable, he declared that he would not employ drunkards, blasphemers, gamblers and men who did not pay their debts. He warned that anyone who came to court drunk would lose his place and admonished husbands to be faithful to their wives and sons to obey their fathers. He also followed Louis XIV in trying to suppress the fashionable practice of duelling.[6]

The effectiveness of some of these declarations of intent may be doubted. Duels continued and James employed men who were notorious for their gambling (Sunderland) or their fondness for the bottle (Rochester and Jeffreys). Nevertheless, James's accession brought a dramatic change to the character of the court. James was more of a stickler for ceremony than Charles, but he was still more accessible than most monarchs and still met foreign ambassadors in the Queen's apartments after dinner. Charles's court had been notorious for its licence. Courtiers had outraged decent society by their drunken japes, their whoring and obscenity, their blasphemy and casual violence. Charles, who alone had the authority to discipline such men, had been more inclined to be amused than outraged by such escapades. Even if they angered him, his anger seldom lasted for long. James, however, had never had much time for the "men of pleasure". They had helped to hound Clarendon into exile and, in the 1670s, had pressed Charles to sacrifice his brother to Parliament. Temperament-ally, too, James had little in common with them. Never very quick witted or an inspired conversationalist, he was unable to keep up with their jests and did not share their frivolous and self-indulgent approach to life. James was a man of simple tastes. He told Pepys of his "universal sauce", which he ate with fish, flesh or fowl, "made of some parsley and a dry toast beat in a mortar, together with vinegar, salt and a little pepper". He drank little and with age became increasingly intolerant towards alcohol, arguing in 1685 that the Commons should place further duties on wine. "Who obliges people to make themselves drunk?" he asked.[7]

James's natural puritanism was increased by his conversion. It was, indeed, not only a conversion to Catholicism but a conversion from habitual but empty conformity to active and devout piety. In trying to put his principles into prac-tice, James had to wrestle with his own extremely powerful sexuality. He might embarrass Charles and Portsmouth by commending Louis for sending his mistress away from court, but he still had women smuggled up the backstairs to his apartments. After his conversion he no longer pursued women openly, but his appetites were little diminished: he remarked that he envied Louis his self control. He concealed his amours as best he could and tried to expiate his guilt by the intensity of his devotions. When he became king he sent away his chief mistress, Catherine Sedley, but she soon returned and a scandal erupted in 1686 when James created her Countess of Dorchester. This time the Queen's tears convinced James that Sedley had to leave court, but James still saw her and there were other, more obscure, women whom he saw in a little secret apartment at Whitehall or on occasional hurried visits to St James's.

This secrecy might have been undignified but it helped prevent friction between James and his jealous wife. Her unaffected charm and her keeping out of politics had won her many friends, but when she became Queen "her outward affability" was "much changed to stateliness". She became haughty and was drawn by the competing factions at court to use her influence with James for political ends. As she was a zealous Catholic and knew little of England outside the closed world of the court, the policies she espoused were not always politic-ally wise. Much less robust than James, she was seriously ill in 1685 and after yet another miscarriage in 1686 she was convinced that she was fated never to bear a child who would survive infancy. Apart from her devotions, her main pastime was playing cards with her ladies. James, however, was still furiously energetic. Despite occasional minor injuries and his wife's pleas to be more careful, he continued to hunt ferociously, partly because he loved it, partly because his doctors told him his health depended on it. His health, in fact, continued excellent; when he had a touch of gout, he refused to believe it, although he could not get his boot on. His other great pleasure was his army. Dressed in a red uniform, carrying his general's baton, he thoroughly enjoyed putting his soldiers through their paces, especially in mock battles: the more noise there was, the better James liked it. In the camp at Hounslow Heath each summer he found some compensation for the military career for which he was admirably suited, but which he had been destined never to pursue.

In theory, there were good reasons to expect, in February 1685, that James's reign would prove rather more stable and successful than his brother's. He possessed solid virtues which Charles had lacked: a willingness to work hard at the minutiae of government and high standards of personal conduct, which he tried to apply in both his government and his court. Yet his reign was a disastrous failure. One reason was that his kingship shared much of the weakness of that of Charles II. Chancellor Clarendon had written many years before that, although James seemed more fixed and determined than Charles, "it was rather from an obstinacy in his will, which he defended by aversion from the debate, than by the constancy of his judgment, which was more subject to persons than to arguments and so as changeable at least as the King's." All his efforts to assimilate information and his determination to be positive and decisive could not compensate for his basic lack of intelligence and, above all, his inability to appreciate what was, or was not, politically feasible. As a result, he was easily manipulated by cleverer men. Like Charles, he refused to reach decisions on the basis of debates in the privy council, or even the more informal cabinet council, because he feared being misled by his top civil servants. But his preference for informal decision making merely made it easier for his most favoured courtiers to convince him of the truth of what he wished to believe. As Burnet wrote, "He had no true judgment and was soon determined by those whom he trusted; but he was obstinate against all other advices." Once he had been persuaded to accept a particular analysis of a problem, James stubbornly ignored all arguments which contradicted that analysis. When pressed to change his mind on a minor point connected with an embassy to Constantinople, James remarked tetchily, "Let the reasons be what they will, I am resolved not to do it." His obstinacy was that of a slow and unintelligent man who was always fearful that abler men would get the better of him. Just as in religious matters he avoided disputes on details and put his faith in the infallible authority of the Church, so in political matters he placed his trust in the judgment of men who managed to convince him of their loyalty and good intentions. Unfortunately, his trust was to prove sadly misplaced.[8]

Even these weaknesses, however, might have proved much less than fatal. The system of hereditary monarchy was bound to produce some inept monarchs and the Stuart dynasty, whether for reasons of genetics or environment, produced more than its share of politically incompetent rulers. However, the English in the later seventeenth century were a docile and peaceable people, doubly so for having recently experienced a civil war. The danger of rebellion was virtually non-existent, Scotland and Ireland were quiet and the sea largely isolated England from the dynastic power politics of the continent. Once James's first Parliament had granted him an adequate revenue, he had little real need to call another, so there was little real danger of serious disputes there with his subjects. The Tories were still vociferously loyal. The Whigs, shattered and demoralized, lay low or crept to make their peace with the new King. James's position was thus so secure that he could make all kinds of mistakes without placing his regime in serious jeopardy.

Yet within four years James was forced to flee into exile. The explanation for the deterioration of his fortunes involves a whole complex of factors, of accidents, miscalculations and misunderstandings, but two major ones can be picked out. The first was Sunderland's influence. Inordinately ambitious, his career had been shattered once by his error in supporting exclusion and was nearly wrecked a second time by Charles's death. He fought his way back; having convinced James of his zeal for his interests, he had the strength of character to dominate James's affairs. Unencumbered by principles of his own, Sunderland committed himself to and tried to anticipate the wishes of the King. He thus encouraged James to believe in the feasibility of the ambition which was dear to his heart and which proved the second major cause of his downfall—the ambition to advance the interests of Catholicism. Having embarked on this strategy and convinced James that his objectives could be attained, Sunderland was trapped. He could not tell James that his plans would not suceed and that they were provoking a dangerous amount of distrust and resentment, at home and abroad, for that would have meant the end of his influence and his power. He therefore pressed on, as slowly as he dared, from one impossible expedient to another, hoping that everything would turn out well in the end. For Sunderland, eventually, it did and he returned to serve William III from 1692. For James, however, it did not.[9]

* * *

James saw monarchy as a sacred institution. Its powers and the principle of hereditary succession were, he believed, divinely ordained. He shared this view with most of his English predecessors and most of his European contemporaries. It had been elaborated by James I, who stressed the divine attributes of kingship and claimed that all laws originated in the will of past kings, but went on to stress that a king was bound to answer to God for his conduct and to observe the laws of the land. Continental theorists, too, distinguished sharply between despotism, in which a king did whatever he wished, and absolutism, in which the king exercised an unfettered power to make decisions and to formulate policy within the limits imposed by both the particular and the "fundamental" laws of the country.[10] The English constitution differed from that of France in two important respects. The French king could legislate and levy taxation without the consent of any representative body. The English king could not. None the less, with the approval of his judges the English king could exploit imprecisions and ambiguities in the law and interpret his powers more widely than had been conventional in the past: both Charles I and James II did this. Charles had done so mainly to raise money, but James did not and indeed repeatedly stressed his respect for his subjects' right to enjoy their property in peace.

If the Stuarts laid great stress on ruling within the letter of the law and on respecting their subjects' legal rights, they expected their subjects, for their part, not to interfere in the conduct of government. James I had stressed that his observing the laws was a voluntary choice on his part, not something which his subjects had the right to compel him to do. "I will not be content," he said, "that my power be disputed upon, but I shall ever be willing to make the reason appear of all my doings and rule my actions according to my laws." Parliament could advise the king but he was free to accept or reject its advice and, in the last analysis, he was answerable to God alone. James II lacked his grandfather's philosophical mind, but shared his basic assumptions: "I thank God [that the monarchy] yet has had no dependency on Parliament, nor on nothing but God alone, nor ever can be and be a monarchy." James's conception of monarchy was by no means devoid of benevolence or of a sense of responsibility towards his subjects. Indeed, he was only too aware of the responsibilities imposed on him by the office of king and of the need to account to God for his stewardship.[11] His view of kingship, however, left no room for any sharing of power or for the delegation to subjects of decisions which were properly the king's. Moreover, James's conceptual rigidity and his intolerance of the opinions of others left little room for the constructive exchange of views between king and subjects, at court, in the council or in Parliament. Government for James was a one-way process: the king commanded, the subject obeyed. The king had a sacred duty to use responsibly the powers granted to him by law. His subjects had an equally sacred duty to do as he commanded. He could not accept that they had any right to question either his judgment or his interpretation of his powers. But irrespective of whether James believed his subjects had any right to question his government, they did so, and their opinions could not be ignored, for there were occasions on which he might need their co-operation. He would need it if he wanted either legislation or money from Parliament and he would need it if he ever had to cope with a rebellion or an invasion.

James thus saw the office of king as a sacred trust to be used for God's service and, for James, God's service meant the advancement of Catholicism. He saw the promotion of his new religion as a sacred duty, a belief strengthened by his strong sense of the workings of God's Providence in the fifteen years before his accession. He had known the risks involved in becoming a Catholic: "What I have done was not hastily but upon mature consideration and foreseeing all and more than has yet happened to me," he wrote in 1679.[12] The fact that he survived the assaults of the exclusionists and lived to triumph over his enemies strengthened his conviction of divine favour and his belief that God would make use of him to promote the cause of His Church. The conviction that God was with him, indeed, became so deep-rooted that it led James to believe that the designs which he saw as God's were bound to succeed, regardless of all objective evidence to the contrary. James's faith was such that it transcended mere human reasonings.

What precisely were James's objectives? He said repeatedly that he wished to "establish" or "re-establish" Catholicism in England. His Protestant subjects assumed that Catholicism could be "established" only by violence and brutality, but that was not, apparently, James's intention. In 1691 he wrote to Cardinal Howard of his hopes of being restored and seeing "Catholic religion established again as it was in my time in all my dominions". He told Barrillon in 1688 that "he hoped God would grant him His favour and help him to accomplish his aims, which were designed above all to establish the Catholic religion in England so that those who professed it could live as Catholics in complete security." For James, the "establishment" of Catholicism did not mean making Catholicism the dominant religion, but putting Catholics on an equal footing with Protestants, by allowing them to worship freely and to hold public office. James claimed very consistently that he was against persecution for conscience's sake: "he desired nothing but to follow his own conscience which he imposed on nobody else." He wrote to Charles in 1680 that "though he wished all men alike in his religion, yet thought it unlawful to force any man, much less a kingdom, to embrace it." When he advocated the persecution of Dissenters, it was always on political grounds, although it should be added that at times he treated as axiomatic the connexion between religious nonconformity and political disaffection. He never raised any objection, however, to Dissenters' worshipping quietly in their homes.[13]

It seems, then, that James did not believe in imposing his religious views on others by force. Even if he had wished to do so, it would have been quite impractical. It was generally realized that the Catholics were few, perhaps only one per cent of the population. James's army was small and the great majority of its members were Protestants.[14] An even stronger reason why the forcible imposition of Catholicism was impossible was that James had no Catholic heir. After eleven years of marriage to Mary Beatrice, she had not borne him one child who had lived beyond the age of four. His heir presumptive was Mary and for most of his reign James proceeded on the assumption that he would be succeeded by his Protestant daughter and her Protestant husband. There were suggestions that he should alter the succession in favour of a Catholic, but this James's attachment to the hereditary principle would not allow. He wrote in 1687:

> "Not only could it never enter my head to think of changing [the succession] but I know full well that it is not in my power to do it, even if a pope and a parliament joined with me. For where the crown is hereditary (as it is in these kingdoms, thanks be to God) His Almighty power alone can dispose of it, not only the hearts of kings but their crowns being in His hands."[15]

James's hopes of advancing Catholicism before Mary succeeded him depended, therefore, not on compulsion but on making willing converts. James was convinced that the rightness of Catholicism must seem as blindingly obvious to others as it was to him. "Did others enquire into the religion as I have done, without prejudice or prepossession or partial affection, they would be of the same mind in point of religion as I am." He had especially high hopes of winning converts from the Church of England. "He flatters himself," wrote Barrillon, "that the Anglican Church is so little removed from the Catholic that it should not be difficult to bring the majority of them to declare themselves openly. He has told me several times that they are Roman Catholics without knowing it."[16] These potential converts could be won over, he believed, provided the "prejudice" and "partial affection" he mentioned could be removed. To this end he pursued two main objectives. First, knowing how Catholic beliefs and practices had been misrepresented by Protestant polemicists, he wished to remove the penal laws which prohibited Catholic worship and evangelism. He was sure that if the Catholic clergy could compete with the Protestants on equal terms, the number of Catholics would increase rapidly. Secondly, he thought most people were reluctant to turn Catholic for reasons of self-interest: he once remarked that most Anglicans had no religion at all. Clergymen feared to lose their livelihood, landowners feared to lose the monastic lands confiscated by Henry VIII. James tried to reassure them on these points. More insidious was the exclusion of Catholics from offices and from Parliament by the Test Acts of 1673 and 1678. To James these Acts were doubly iniquitous. They demanded a denunciation of transubstantiation, in which James fervently believed, and they denied the king the services of a loyal and deserving group of subjects, leaving Catholics as second-class citizens and so deterring would-be converts from showing the courage of their convictions. He told Barrillon that "the possibility of holding offices and employments will make more Catholics than permission to say Mass publicly."[17]

James's aim, then, was to have the penal laws and Test Acts repealed. If that were done, he believed that Catholics would become so numerous that his successors would have to allow them a measure of toleration. He even told the papal agent in London, D'Adda, that once the laws no longer held people in fear England would be Catholic within two years.[18] But these aims, which seemed so just and reasonable to James, seemed far less so to his Protestant subjects. Many believed that Catholicism was too erroneous to be tolerated. Even those who were prepared to remove the penal laws mostly drew the line at removing the Test Acts, fearing the restless ambition which they traditionally ascribed to Catholics. They believed that if a Catholic king could admit Catholics to employments and to Parliament, they would soon gain a monopoly of power and use it to extirpate Protestantism.

James regarded such fears as wicked and irrational but they were a fact of life and he had to overcome them if he wished to repeal the penal laws and Test Acts. If the repeal was to carry any legal weight, it would have to comply with the forms of law. As the 1678 Test Act excluded Catholics from Parliament, the laws had to be repealed by a Parliament composed of Protestants. In 1685 James naturally relied on the Anglicans who had supported his cause so consistently since 1679 and who had proclaimed so loudly the subject's duty of passive obedience. However, the strongly Anglican Parliament elected in 1685 made it clear that it would do nothing to favour the Catholics. For over a year James tried to overcome their resistance to repealing the laws against Catholicism and was bitter at their obstinacy. "I must tell you," he said in 1687, "that in the King my father's time the Church of England's men and the Catholics loved each other and were, as 'twere, all one; but now there is gotten a new spirit among you which is quite contrary."[19] Hesitantly and reluctantly, James abandoned the Anglicans and appealed to the Dissenters.

It was not the first time that he had done this; he had done much the same in 1675-76. It was, however, a reversal of his alignments of the last decade and it involved a controversial extension of the royal prerogative. He had already dispensed some Catholics from taking the Test, thus allowing them to hold offices. He now suspended the penal laws altogether, pending their repeal by Parliament. This meant that both Catholics and Dissenters (who had been persecuted until 1686) could worship freely and hold office. Meanwhile, James prepared to hold a general election which, he hoped, would produce a Parliament of Dissenters who would repeal the penal laws and Test Acts. His preparations involved a purge of office holders even greater than that of the early 1680s and a growing measure of pressure and legal chicanery.

James's English subjects (and many later historians) equated "Popery" with "arbitrary government" and assumed that James aimed to establish absolutism as well as Catholicism. James was certainly authoritarian by nature and, after twenty-five years' waiting, revelled a little in his power as king. But that did not mean that he wished to overthrow the laws and constitution and establish an absolutism like that of Louis XIV. While he told Barrillon with monotonous regularity that he wished to promote Catholicism he never said that he wished to make England's government like that of France. He assumed that William would succeed him and saw no reason to strengthen the monarchy for William's benefit. He did, however, wish to leave the Catholics strong enough to escape extirpation under his successor. He wanted, in Lauderdale's phrase, to "shine in a red letter after he is dead".[20] If James stretched his powers beyond conventional limits, he did so because he could not achieve his objectives without doing so. In accusing him of trying to establish absolutism, his contemporaries and later historians confused means with ends, treating James's abuses of power as a central rather than an incidental feature of his rule. Such abuses of power were highly selective; all were geared to allowing Catholics to worship freely and hold office. James stressed, quite rightly, that he always respected his subjects' property. Yet even if the dispensing and suspending powers were means to an end and not ends in themselves, they were still novel and alarming extensions of royal power. Technically, perhaps, they could be justified. Politically, they could not. Whatever James, his propagandists and his judges might say, his subjects feared to see such powers being used by a Catholic king, who seemed to be closely allied to Louis XIV. In the last resort, James failed because he failed to heed the political and religious prejudices of his subjects.

* * *

James's fate was not to be determined only by his own actions or by events within England. Much depended too on what happened abroad and especially on the actions of Louis XIV and William III. At James's accession, Louis seemed at the height of his power. At home the nobility and the parlements had been brought to heel and Louis was preparing for a final assault on the Huguenots. Paris was the cultural capital of Europe and the new palace at Versailles was only the most monumental expression of an unprecedented cult of kingship. Abroad Louis had enjoyed two decades of almost uninterrupted military and diplomatic success. He had even occasionally taken part himself in a "campaign", which was little more than a stately progress from one short-lived siege to the next.

Yet behind the glittering façade there were serious weaknesses. At the top all might be diligence, efficiency and smooth routine. In the provinces, administration was a bewildering labyrinth, with innumerable local and regional variations of laws and institutions, currencies and taxes, weights and measures. The practice of selling offices to raise money had merely added to the size and complexity of the administration and created an ever-growing number of people with a vested interest in maintaining the existing confusion. Moreover, the larger and more complex the bureaucracy became, the greater was the share of taxation which it devoured and the harder it became to control. Louis and his ministers did what they could to impose order on this leviathan, but his wars and his palaces had to be paid for, in the last resort, by imposing a greater and greater fiscal burden on the peasantry. By 1685, however, there were signs that there were limits to how far the peasants could be squeezed. Crippling taxation during the war of 1672–78 had provoked several peasant revolts and Louis seems to have accepted, after the Peace of Nijmegen, that France could not afford another protracted war.

Louis' foreign policy was never fully understood by his contemporaries, who tried, from his actions, to guess at the motives behind them. They saw the legal trickery used to establish claims to territories in Flanders or Alsace. They saw the unprovoked attack on the Dutch in 1672. They saw the gratuitous brutality of the bombardment of Genoa and Louis' obvious joy in humiliating his enemies. They noted his conspicuous failure to help defend Christendom against the Turks. From these observations, they drew the logical conclusion: that Louis was an insatiable and unprincipled aggressor, who would not rest until he had brought all Europe under his sway.

Yet this picture was only partly accurate. Aggressive, ambitious and brutal Louis certainly was, but beneath his foreign policy lay a nagging undercurrent of fear. The Habsburgs (especially the Spanish branch) might wield only a fraction of their former power, but they still possessed many territories, some of them in sensitive positions on France's frontiers. The Spaniards held Franche Comté, the Southern Netherlands and various territories in north Italy. The Emperor possessed a confused variety of territorial rights in Alsace and Lorraine which the Treaty of Westphalia (1648) had done little to clarify. Louis was only too aware of the weakness of his northern frontier. In 1636 and again during the Frondes, Spanish armies had swept across the plains of northern

France towards Paris. Apart from the lack of geographical obstacles, the frontier was a jagged muddle, with Spanish and French towns intermingled. Louis' military advisers stressed the need for a rational, clearly defined linear frontier, which could be fortified and then properly defended. This linear frontier was Louis' main objective in the War of Devolution (1666–68) and the Dutch War (1672–78). At Nijmegen he achieved almost all that he wanted, adding the great fortress of Luxemburg and a few minor scraps of territory over the next six years.

From 1678 Louis turned his attention more to his eastern frontier, which was better protected by nature but where there were still "gates", through which an enemy could attack. Louis gained Franche Comté at Nijmegen and tried to close the other gates in the next few years, using a mixture of legal chicanery and highly concentrated armed force. He got away with such conduct mainly because the Emperor, Leopold II, was preoccupied with his war against the Turks, who besieged Vienna in 1683. The following year Leopold and Louis signed a truce at Ratisbon, guaranteeing Louis possession of his recent annexations for twenty years. In return, Louis promised to forgo further prosecution of his "rights". In the next few years, Louis' anxiety mounted. Leopold won one crushing victory after another, driving the Turks back through Hungary. In August 1688 he took Belgrade. Leopold's conquests greatly increased both his prestige and his resources; Louis became convinced that as soon as he had finished with the Turks, Leopold would turn to attack France. To guard against this, Louis ordered a series of fortifications along the eastern frontier, including some on the eastern bank of the Rhine, which the Germans saw as an infraction of the truce. The fact that Louis extended his fortifications rather than enlarged his army showed, however, that his intentions were primarily defensive. To complicate matters further, there was the problem of the Spanish succession. King Carlos II was sickly, mentally deficient and genetically unsound. He had no children—perhaps fortunately—and by 1685 his death had been regarded as imminent for almost twenty years. Both the Habsburgs and the Bourbons advanced claims to Carlos' vast territories in Europe and the Americas. If either dynasty gained the whole Spanish empire, it would wreck any semblance of a balance of power. The prospect that the Austrian Habsburgs might gain a large part of this massive inheritance was yet another reason for Louis to look to his defences.[21]

It is in this context that one should see Louis' policy towards James. Experience had shown him that England was an unreliable ally. As they had to ask Parliament for money to fight a war, the Stuarts were not masters of their own diplomacy. Convinced by Charles's making a separate peace in 1674 that all Parliaments were likely to prove hostile to his interests, Louis concentrated on securing Charles's neutrality. Sometimes he encouraged the opposition in Parliament, more often he paid Charles a subsidy so that he would not need to call it. Charles in turn did Louis what small diplomatic favours were within his power, while trying to dissuade him from seeking further conquests in the Southern Netherlands.

By the time James became king, the truce of Ratisbon had given Louis all that he could expect for the time being and he concentrated on fortifying his eastern frontier. There was therefore little that he wished James to do for him, other than preserve the status quo (which included making no new alliances with Louis' enemies). Once he saw that James's Parliament had given him an adequate revenue, Louis refused to continue the subsidy which he had paid to Charles. He assumed that James needed no particular inducement to remain on good terms with him, as it was (he thought) in James's own interests to do so. James's plans to promote Catholicism in England could succeed only if there was peace on the continent. His interests were thus quite incompatible with those of William who (Louis believed) was bitterly opposed to the progress of Catholicism and was eager to start another war against France.

Louis' confidence in his analysis of James's position was shaken in 1685 when James renewed Charles's treaties with the Dutch, but in the long run it proved substantially correct. For most of James's reign, therefore, Louis acted on the assumption that James needed him far more than he needed James. He treated with disdain James's interventions on behalf of English men and women caught up in the persecution of the Huguenots. He tried, unsuccessfully, to take advantage of James's weakness by demanding commercial and colonial concessions. In 1688, as war loomed nearer, Louis began to demand more tangible services from James and offered to pay for them—albeit as little as possible. Louis often expressed interest in James's measures to promote Catholicism and talked frequently of his friendship for James, yet he made it clear that this was a somewhat one-sided friendship. The onus was on James to earn Louis' goodwill, by subordinating his interests to those of France. When Louis was eventually moved to offer James some tangible assistance, it was too late.

*   *   *

William III's domestic position was far less secure. The Dutch republic was a federation of seven provinces which had won independence from Spain after eighty years' struggle. The provinces' economies and social structure varied greatly and each had its own provincial assembly or States. One major cause of the revolt had been Philip II's attempts to overcome the provinces' particularism and to integrate them into a unitary state. Each province sent a delegation to the States General of the United Provinces, but sovereignty lay with the States of each province so all major decisions in the States General required the approval of all seven provinces. Moreover, the same localism operated within each province. In the States of Holland, for example, decisions on many issues required the agreement of all the delegates, so one great town, like Amsterdam, could block a resolution approved by all the other towns and provinces.[22]

A federal constitution which placed local above provincial or "national" interests might seem a recipe for chaos. In fact, the system usually worked fairly adequately, for three main reasons. First, there was the dominance of the province of Holland, which contained most of the commercial and industrial towns. Controlling much of the wealth of the republic and contributing almost three-fifths of its taxation, it was far more influential than any other province.

Moreover, fear of being dominated by Holland drove the other provinces to band together to protect their interests, so there were often two—rather than seven—main blocs in the States General. Secondly, there was the civic pride, talent and political responsibility of the regents, the rulers of the great towns of Holland. Although not elected by the ordinary citizens, the regents showed a concern for their well being which was much more than merely self-interested. They were also sensitive to the political opinions of the ordinary townsmen, partly because they lived in such close proximity to them, partly because the republic had the freest and most vigorous political press in Europe. Thus, while the regents were fiercely attached to the principle of local self-government, they were also prepared, if need be, to subordinate parochial interests to the common good.

A third reason why the republic's cumbersome constitution worked tolerably well was the unifying role of the Princes of Orange. In many countries local representative bodies or estates disappeared or were reduced to impotence because they could not provide the decisive leadership required for war. The Dutch rebels became well aware of this during the revolt against Spain and looked to their greatest noble family, the House of Orange. In the seventeenth century it became accepted that each Prince of Orange would be appointed stadholder (or lieutenant) of five of the seven provinces and captain general and admiral general of the union. This system worked well enough until the Princes became ambitious to put their power on a more permanent basis, to turn the republic into a monarchy. The behaviour of William II in particular highlighted the tension between the old Netherlandish tradition of local self-government (institutionalized in the federal constitution) and the newer centralized monarchies, which experience suggested offered the best means of mobilizing a state's resources for war. When William II died in 1650, his opponents, the States party, reasserted the old federalist and republican values and did all they could to ensure that his son, William III, should not inherit his family's traditional offices.

Even after the revolution of 1672 impelled William into the offices of his ancestors, the States party remained fearful of his supposedly monarchical ambitions. It saw his stubborn insistence on continuing the war against France as a pretext to perpetuate the army and so his own power. The States General made peace without William's approval in 1678, but his fear and hatred of Louis continued, sharpened by Louis' vindictive attacks on his property in France, especially the little principality of Orange. As Louis again began to nibble at the Spanish Netherlands after 1678, William implored the States General to stop him, but the regents of Holland, especially those of Amsterdam, were weary of war and wished to rebuild their trade after six years' disruption. They accused William of over-reacting and even of irresponsible warmongering. Their suspicions that William wanted a war because he wanted an army to strengthen his position at home were, in fact, mistaken, but they were plausible and were skilfully fed by Louis' ambassador at the Hague, the Comte d'Avaux. Between 1678 and 1685 William suffered successive humiliations. The Dutch military budget was substantially reduced, while the truce of Ratisbon guaranteed to Louis twenty years' enjoyment of his ill-gotten gains.

William's position when James became king was a thoroughly unhappy one. Never a patient or tolerant man, he raged at the myopic parochialism (to say no worse) of the regents of Holland. He could not understand why they did not share his obsession with the danger from France, or how they could accept d'Avaux's assurances that Louis would not attack the republic. He could see little prospect of improving his position at home. He could usually count on the votes of five of the seven provinces and of the nobility and some of the smaller towns in Holland, but most of the great towns remained opposed to him. In one or two, like Dordrecht and Leiden, he was to place his own nominees in office by fomenting divisions among the regents or by rigging the electoral system. He could also do something to manipulate the proceedings of the States General and the States of Holland through his ally Gaspar Fagel, grand pensionary of Holland, who was adept at exploiting procedural uncertainties and ambiguities. But Amsterdam remained obdurate and its obduracy could be overcome only if its rulers came to share William's views of the international situation. There was little sign of their doing so in 1685, but in three years their attitude was transformed. Fear of an Anglo-French alliance and of Catholicism overcame their constitutional scruples and they acquiesced in William's programme of rearmament.

When Charles died, William made a real effort to be reconciled to James. He knew that James, like Charles, had shown little sympathy for his fears of Louis, but hoped that he could now make James appreciate the threat which French ambitions posed to the Netherlands, to Europe and to England. At first it seemed that James might prove amenable, but it was not to last. Misunderstandings and suspicions multiplied. James was angry at the States General's refusal to expel the English and Scots political refugees from the republic. William feared that James might cut Mary and himself out of the succession. Although personally tolerant of Catholics, William strongly disliked the political manifestations of Catholicism and feared that the Catholics at James's court might persuade him to forget all legality and honesty. He feared too that James's measures might provoke a rebellion, which would also threaten Mary's chance of succeeding to the English throne and William's chance of bringing England's resources into his great struggle against France.

These misunderstandings and suspicions owed much to poor information. D'Avaux sent Barrillon news and gossip which was designed to embitter James against William and which was also exploited by Sunderland and the Catholics and supporters of France in the English court. William's sources of information were even less reliable. Citters, the Dutch ambassador in London, was thoroughly inconsistent, sometimes alarming the States General with fears of war and then remarking placidly that war was quite impossible. His reports were also often factually inaccurate, perhaps because many of his contacts were ill-informed about affairs at court but also because his negotiations were conducted in French, a language in which he was not very proficient.[23] Apart from Citters, William's main sources of information were first, letters from his contacts in England and second, the English exiles in Holland. The former varied enormously in reliability, the latter were naturally extremely hostile to James and his measures. The most important of these exiles was Burnet, whose knowledge of events in England was far from accurate, as is clearly shown by his *History of My Own Time*. His personal animus against James also grew as James tried to have him extradited to Scotland, to face trumped-up charges of treason. Even so, William clearly regarded Burnet as an authority on English affairs and continued to consult him even after James had persuaded him to send the combative Scotsman away from his court. Moreover, in his conversations with Mary, Burnet imprinted on her mind his interpretation of events since the Restoration.[24] From men like Burnet and from his own prejudices against France and Catholicism, William became more and more convinced that his and Mary's claims to the crown were in severe jeopardy. Being an active and determined man, he decided to do something about it.

CHAPTER TEN

King and Parliament
(February to November 1685)

Three days after Charles died, James announced his intention to summon a
Parliament. He also announced that he would continue to collect the revenues
voted to Charles for life and that he had no doubt that Parliament would vote
the same to him. Some thought this very irregular. It was normal for a new
king to collect the customs before his first Parliament met, but Charles II
had been the first king to be granted the excise, so there were no precedents
for its collection at a new king's accession. For this reason, a new contract for
the collection of the excise had been sealed the day before Charles died and the
judges ruled (by a majority of eight to four) that the contract was valid. On
16th February James issued a proclamation publicizing this ruling and, despite
a few grumbles, found little difficulty in collecting Charles's revenues.[1]

These proceedings reflected not contempt for the laws, but uncertainty about
how Parliament would behave. The last Parliament had been almost hysteric-
ally exclusionist. Since then the Tories had been given a monopoly of local
and municipal office, but until the elections were held and Parliament met,
James could not know what its mood would be. He feared that it would either
grant his revenues only for a limited period or attach unacceptable conditions
to its grant (for example, new measures against Catholics).[2] To meet this danger
and to strengthen his financial position, James and his ministers asked Louis for
a subsidy, claiming that Louis had not yet paid over all that he had promised
to Charles. Louis eventually agreed to pay these arrears, but James, Rochester
and Sunderland used every possible argument to persuade Barrillon that Louis
should pay more. They pleaded, they wheedled, they grovelled. Barrillon
passed on their argument, adding that he thought a further subsidy would fix
James inviolably in Louis' interests, but that if Louis refused, he did not know
what James's pique might lead him to do. Louis sent him about £150,000, but
with strict orders not to pay it over until he saw how Parliament behaved.[3]

From James's point of view, the elections were very successful. Burnet
claimed that "in all England it would not have been easy to have found five
hundred men so weak, so poor and so devoted to the court as these were."
Burnet, however, was the last man to welcome a solidly Tory House of
Commons and the Tories were naturally delighted: "Such a landed Parliament
was never seen," wrote Ailesbury smugly. The Tories had seen little cause
for anxiety in the first three months of James's reign. True, James had insisted

on going openly to Mass, arguing that it would be timid and dishonest to hide his beliefs; some Tories, like Evelyn, agreed with him. More worrying, perhaps, were his attempts to persuade his ministers to accompany him to his devotions at Easter. Sunderland went as far as the chapel door, but Rochester chose to go into the country for the holiday.[4] More worrying still were hints that James might regard his promises to the Church of England as conditional. At the beginning of March, he had summoned Sancroft and some of his colleagues and complained that the Anglican clergy were preaching violently against Catholicism and the Pope and were expressing fears for the survival of Protestantism. James told them:

"I will keep my word and undertake nothing against the religion which is established by law, unless you first break your word to me. But if you do not do your duty towards me, do not expect that I shall protect you. You may be sure that I shall find means to do my business without you."

Some Catholics at court, indeed, were arguing that James should establish a general toleration. James rejected their advice, preferring to rely on his "old friends" of the Church of England. Nevertheless, his warning to the bishops must have created some anxiety among the Tory MPs who gathered at Westminster in May. This was especially true of those, like Reresby, who had been told by their Catholic neighbours that James wished them to remove the laws prohibiting Catholic worship and debarring them from office.[5]

In his opening speech, James reiterated his assurances that he would defend and support the Church, while making it clear that he expected its members to continue to be loyal to him. He made it clear, too, that he would strongly resent any proposal to vote for only a term of years revenues which had been voted to Charles for life. He stressed "that this would be a very improper method to take with me and that the best way to engage me to meet you often is always to use me well". It was a vigorous speech, James read it well, and the Houses cheered at every pause. At the end James announced that the rebel Earl of Argyll had landed in Scotland, news which was met with loud shouts of "Long live the King". James's advisers had prepared their ground carefully. Ailesbury had addressed a meeting of two hundred and fifty members on the need to vote James his ordinary revenue for life. On 26th May a bill to that effect passed the Commons with scarcely a word said in opposition, except by Seymour, who called for an investigation of the conduct of the general election. He found few supporters. No sooner had James given his assent to this bill than a second money bill was brought in, to raise by additional customs duties a fund to pay off Charles's debts and to refurbish the fleet. A month later a third supply bill granted James extra duties on linen, silk and spirits for five years, this time to meet the cost of suppressing Monmouth's rebellion.[6]

The speed with which these revenues were granted led both contemporaries and historians to accuse this Parliament of weakness and subservience, in granting James a large revenue which he was to use to support a standing army. But, as Professor Chandaman has shown, this accusation was unfair and failed to distinguish between the King's ordinary and extraordinary revenue. The ordinary revenue—voted for life—was the same as Charles II's, which for most of his reign had been thoroughly inadequate. What the Commons did not know, and did not trouble to investigate, was the present yield of that revenue: by 1685 it was yielding appreciably more than even the most optimistic estimates of the early 1660s (whereas for most of Charles's reign it had yielded less). The two extraordinary grants were temporary and for specific purposes. The first seems indeed to have been used to pay Charles's debts and to fit out the fleet. If James needed to spend only a fraction of the money from the second grant, this was hardly the fault of Parliament, which could not have known how easy it would prove to put down the rebellion. The Parliament of 1685 behaved very much like the Cavalier Parliament, voting the King a revenue which was intended to be sufficient to enable him to live of his own and then granting additional, extraordinary revenue as need arose. It erred only in failing to investigate fully the current yield of the ordinary revenue.[7]

On the question of money, then, the first session of James's Parliament showed itself generous, but not recklessly so. Its members believed in monarchy, but one which operated within the Ancient Constitution. Moreover, the Tories were attached to the Church as well as the monarchy, as they soon made clear. On 26th May the committee on religion resolved to petition James to enforce the laws against all types of religious nonconformity. Hearing of his, James summoned some leading MPs and reproved them severely for such an offensive resolution (which asked him, in effect, to persecute the Catholics). Next day, the matter was debated by the whole House of Commons, which voted against putting the question whether to agree with the committee. It resolved instead to present an address saying that the House was satisfied with his promise to secure the Church of England, which was dearer to them than their lives. The Commons thus avoided adopting a resolution which would have angered James, but it had made its point. It did so again later in the session. A bill was brought in extending the definition of treason to cover written or spoken words "to incite or stir up the people to hatred or dislike of the person of his majesty or the established government." Much to James's annoyance, the Commons added a proviso that it should be lawful to defend the Church of England's doctrine and worship against "Popery or any other different or dissenting opinions". James preferred not to let the bill pass with this clause in it and Barrillon thought that the incident hastened the end of the session.[8]

From James's point of view, the session had been much less bad than he had feared but less good than he had hoped. He now had an adequate revenue and could begin to reduce the burden of interest-bearing debt. He could start, too, to repair the damage done to the navy by the enforced financial stringency of Charles's last years. On the other hand, he had not dared to propose the repeal of the penal laws, let alone the Test Acts. The Tories had made it clear that they would support his regime loyally, even enthusiastically, provided he respected the constitution and upheld the dominance of the Church. It was soon to become clear that James would not observe these conditions.

*   *   *

When the news of Charles's death reached the Hague, William and Mary were entertaining Monmouth royally, convinced (apparently) that this was what Charles wanted. On hearing the news William at once sent Monmouth away from his court and sent his kinsman Ouwerkerck to assure James that William repented of his conduct towards him and asked what he could do to make amends. William declared that he was ready to submit entirely to James's will. James, clearly pleased to see William so penitent, prescribed three conditions. First, William should have no further dealings with Monmouth. Secondly, he should dismiss from the three English and three Scottish regiments in the States General's service those officers whom James thought unreliable. Thirdly, he should follow James's directions in his dealings with his neighbours —which meant Louis. William agreed to the first two without demur; to the third, he gave a general assurance to do nothing contrary to James's interests. James made it clear that he wanted William to show less obvious hostility towards France, but on the whole seemed well satisfied. He decided to replace his present Ambassador at the Hague, Chudleigh (whom William loathed), with Bevil Skelton, whom William disliked less. He promised to keep William fully informed of his foreign policy, so that "for the time to come the same confidence will be established between us as our near relation and the good of our family requires."[9]

William continued to try hard to convince James of his good intentions. He was persuaded not to stipulate that he would do nothing against the interests of his religion, and wrote to ask Rochester what else he could do to win James's friendship. He told Skelton that he would follow James's wishes in foreign policy if James gave his reasons in writing, promoted officers whom he disked when James recommended them and promised to report on Monmouth's movements (while still doubting that Monmouth intended James any harm).[10] His eagerness to please probably owed more to fear than love. He shared the normal Protestant belief that Catholics would stop at nothing and feared that James might exclude him from the succession. He feared, too, that unless James were appeased he might establish closer links with France. James was probably more sincere. For some years he had been annoyed with William and had believed that he needed Louis' friendship but he was also well aware that Louis and Barrillon had, at times, paid money to opposition MPs.[11] Moreover, James had a strong sense of family solidarity: the phrase "our family" appears often in his letters to William. As king and head of the family, however, James expected William to obey him, just as he had obeyed the King, his brother. In the spring of 1685 William seemed to be showing the necessary obedience and James, in return, showed him a limited measure of consideration, nominating few new officers to the British regiments and often seeking William's opinion of those he suggested. Encouraged by Rochester and perhaps still afraid that Louis planned a new enterprise in Flanders, James received three ambassadors from the States General very kindly, although he made it clear that he could not think of serious negotiations until Parliament had met.[12]

He was soon given a chance to put to the test the friendship professed by

William and the States General. Early in May Argyll sailed from Holland for Scotland with three ships laden with arms. In a similar incident four weeks later, Monmouth set out for England with four ships, again full of arms. Naturally, James wished to know how these two rebel leaders had managed to load up and sail at a time when William and the States General were trying to establish good relations with him. Admittedly, there were practical difficulties in finding and stopping the ships. They were anchored near the Texel, in the mouth of the Zuyder Zee, some fifty miles from Amsterdam where the relevant admiralty authorities were based. There they were outside the jurisdiction of the admiralty of Amsterdam, which could act there only with a special order from the States General. Moreover, it took time to assemble the force needed to tackle ships filled with armed men and more to find them amidst the channels and islands between Amsterdam and the open sea. Nevertheless, such difficulties were not insuperable, and everyone blamed someone else for allowing the ships to escape. Skelton was clearly slow and negligent, especially on the second occasion. When he heard that the ships were being loaded, he sent to the Amsterdam authorities, instead of applying at once to the States General. He must have known by 23rd May that he needed a special order but did not obtain it until the 28th. Even then, the order referred only to one ship, the *Helderenbergh*, although he had been told from the outset that there were four. In extenuation, one can suggest only that Skelton was preoccupied with persuading the States General to send their three Scots regiments to help deal with Argyll. When the order reached Amsterdam, there were further delays as the English consul there (as on the first occasion) could not provide full details of the ships' whereabouts. The admiralty sent a yacht, which took off the pilot of the *Helderenbergh*, but refused to interfere with the other ships without an order. By the time a frigate arrived next day, the vessels had gone.[13]

Whatever the responsibility of Skelton and the consul, it suited almost everyone to blame the authorities at Amsterdam. Skelton knew that James was on good terms with William and (according to d'Avaux) was paying court to William, hoping for a post in Mary's household. William was naturally glad to blame his enemies from Amsterdam, but he seems to have been genuinely afraid that these incidents might harm his good relations with James. He offered to send the three Scots regiments (which pleased James) and took pains to persuade the States General to let them go; the only opposition, predictably, came from Amsterdam. When James asked for the three English regiments, to serve against Monmouth, William again did all he could to give James satisfaction. He now declared angrily that Monmouth had lied to him and sent Bentinck to offer James his services, adding that (if James wished) he would bring over the English regiments in person.[14]

How sincere were William's denunciations of Monmouth and offers of help? The French argued that William was really in cahoots with Monmouth and d'Avaux produced various implausible reasons why this should have been so. Bentinck may (as d'Avaux claimed) have maintained contact with Monmouth and William was certainly reluctant to believe that, after all Monmouth's solemn oaths, he would do anything drastic against James. Once William saw that Monmouth intended to overthrow James, his conduct was quite consistent. He did not wish to have his chances of the succession destroyed by a usurper and remained anxious until Monmouth had been routed. Moreover, he asked Bentinck to find out if (once the rebellion was over) he could expect military help from James should his enemies within the republic drive him to extremities.[15] The men of Amsterdam, meanwhile, clearly sympathized with Monmouth. The admiralty justified itself at length, but it had clearly shown no eagerness to apprehend the ships, while Argyll's followers had found the authorities very affable. Even d'Avaux, strongly prejudiced in favour of Amsterdam, admitted that the authorities there had interpreted their powers as narrowly as possible.[16]

It seems, then, that the Amsterdam authorities were happy to see Monmouth and Argyll depart and that William was not. James was clearly convinced of William's sincerity: James knew enough of Dutch affairs to know that he had little authority in Amsterdam. He declared himself satisfied with the efforts of William and the States General and displeased with Amsterdam.[17] Moreover, William's prompt measures to send over the Scots and English regiments contrasted sharply with Louis' decision to refuse James a subsidy, a decision reached while the campaign against Monmouth was still going on. Louis, unlike William, did not take Monmouth's forces seriously.[18] Once the rebellion had been defeated, James showed his satisfaction with the Dutch by renewing his brother's treaties with the States General, much to Louis' annoyance. The renewal committed James to nothing new but was a significant gesture of friendship which hinted at possible new liaisons.

By the autumn of the 1685 there were a few hints of friction and distrust between James and William. William feared that James might ask him to employ more Catholics in the British regiments, which might cause a political row in the republic. William was embarrassed at James's naming the totally inexperienced Earl of Pembroke to command the regiments. When the *Helderenbergh* returned to Amsterdam, James was annoyed that the authorities used various pretexts to avoid handing it over to him. James was also displeased that some soldiers in the British regiments had shown sympathy for Monmouth and demanded rather more extensive changes than before to remove "disaffected" officers. However, he still declared himself willing to heed William's advice.[19] Such minor irritations apart, however, when James prepared to meet his Parliament for the second time in November, his relations with William were still much more cordial than would have seemed possible twelve months before.

*   *   *

Argyll's rising caused James little anxiety: he landed in a remote part of Scotland and was soon defeated. Monmouth, however, landed in south-west England, which had shown considerable support for him at the time of the Exclusion crisis. James's regular army numbered less than ten thousand and was scattered in garrisons. It would take time to gather a sizeable force of trained men and to raise new regiments. Meanwhile, James was reluctant to trust the militia in combat, even against a force of poorly armed peasants. His reluctance was confirmed when some of the Somerset militia went over to the enemy. James therefore decided to take no chances and not to risk a battle until he was sure of winning. As yet none of the gentry had joined Monmouth, but if James suffered even a small defeat, Monmouth's prestige and forces were likely to increase dramatically. James therefore used the militia to shadow Monmouth and stop recruits coming in to him and had the bridge at Keynsham broken to prevent his advancing on Bristol. Meanwhile, Feversham, James's commander in chief, played a waiting game. Monmouth had landed on 11th June. On the 28th, as William fretted at the Hague, Feversham remarked placidly that he could have beaten Monmouth by now but wanted no unnecessary casualties. After marching to Keynsham via Taunton, Monmouth retreated to Bridge-water. On 5th July he attempted a night attack on Feversham's forces at Sedgemoor. Despite the advantage of surprise, the attack was bungled. Once Feversham's regular troops rallied themselves, Monmouth's ill-trained, ill-armed followers stood little chance. Most fled, except for "some particular obstinate scythemen and clubmen, most of which died for it, as all did, until the soldiers were weary of killing".[20]

Monmouth was taken on the morning of the 8th, disguised as a shepherd. He wrote desperate, submissive letters to James and the Queen. He threw himself at James's feet and begged for his life. He claimed that he had been tricked into issuing the declaration in which he proclaimed himself king and accused James of having Charles poisoned. James dismissed his pleas of innocence as dishonest and had little but contempt for his fear of death. Such conduct, he told William, was unworthy of one who had taken it upon himself to be king. Parliament had already passed an act of attainder, declaring Monmouth guilty of treason, so he was executed, clumsily, on 15th July.[21]

After the rebellion came the reprisals, the notorious "Bloody Assizes". On 1st July, before Monmouth had been defeated, Sunderland wrote that James had been told by his ablest lawyers that those who had proclaimed Monmouth king could be hanged without trial, adding that James "would have some of them made an example of as a terror to the rest". In the weeks after Sedgemoor, luckless peasants were summarily and brutally killed, notably by the fearsome Colonel Kirke. Soon after, the judges, headed by Jeffreys, arrived on the western circuit. Jeffreys's temper was not improved by his being "tortured by the stone", but he was always ferociously hostile to any form of dissent. Most seventeenth-century judges thought it necessary to secure convictions whenever possible in treason trials, for the security of the state. Even so, Jeffreys and his colleagues stretched the law of treason even more than usual and Jeffreys's verbal violence was exceptional even by the robust standards of his day. Nobody knows how many were executed for their alleged complicity in the rebellion, but it is unlikely to have been much less than three hundred. Many others were transported, which meant that they were granted to courtiers who sold them into slavery in the colonies. The prisoners (Jeffreys wrote to

James) were worth ten to fifteen pounds each and he feared that "persons that have not suffered in your service will run away with the booty."[22]

The judges' severity and the courtiers' scramble for this human booty are repellent to modern eyes, but the sixteenth and seventeenth centuries saw exemplary punishments for rebels as vital for the maintenance of peace and order. In 1569, after the rebellion of the northern earls, 450 peasants were butchered under martial law, far fewer than Elizabeth's government had intended. Elizabeth's courtiers, like James's, competed eagerly for the rebels' forfeited property. In the 1650s Cromwell regularly had prisoners of war transported to the plantations. Most men of property, therefore, viewed the punishment of Monmouth's followers with either indifference or satisfaction. There was, it is true, some sign of a hostile reaction in the west country. In December a heavy defeat for a government candidate in a by-election at Bristol was seen as "a sort of revenge for ill treatment by my Lord Chancellor and the soldiers". On the other hand, one of the region's leading magnates, Edward Seymour, expressed nothing but satisfaction at the rebels' punishment.[23] James, too, clearly approved what Jeffreys had done. He was always severe by nature and had earlier refused to pardon fifteen criminals sentenced to death, even though the Queen had pleaded for them, because he believed that the law should take its course. While Jeffreys was on his "campaign" (James's word) he informed James fully of what he was doing and, when he returned, James made him lord chancellor.[24]

The defeat of the rebellions greatly strengthened James's position at home. He still believed that the republicans would rebel, given half a chance, but he could now ensure that he was better able to deal with them. Monmouth's rebellion made James very aware of his military weakness: even at Sedgemoor Feversham had only two thousand foot and eight hundred horse. James decided to keep most of the forces he had raised for the emergency, thus doubling the size of his standing army, which increased to almost nineteen thousand officers and men. By contrast, the militia's poor showing convinced James that it was useless and dangerous. He hoped that Parliament would allow him to use the militia money to help maintain the army. When he failed to persuade Parliament to do so, he simply ignored the militia, ordering that it should no longer muster. Meanwhile, James spent much of his time in the summer and autumn of 1685 organizing and disciplining his army.[25]

Never one to underestimate the strength of his enemies, James saw his triumph over the rebellions as a great deliverance, a sign that God approved of his regime and wished him to advance the Catholic cause:

"Unless Thou defendest the city, the guard watches in vain. We know and our own experience tells us, unless Thou reachest forth Thy hand, we are presently in danger of sinking; sometimes, O Lord, Thy all wise Providence seems to sleep and permits the storm to grow high and loud, yet never fails to relieve Thy servants who faithfully call upon Thee in the day of trouble."[26]

His faith fortified, James resolved to press on with renewed determination to make the Catholics' position safe for all time. While enlarging his army he had commissioned nearly a hundred Catholic officers. As a strictly temporary measure this was probably legal. As officers were obliged to take the Test within three months of being commissioned, they could technically serve for up to three months without taking it. Ignoring the arguments of Halifax and Guilford that it was illegal to employ them, James said that he was determined to do so, as good officers were in short supply. He added that it was up to his law officers to find expedients acceptable to the laws.[27] The English, however, always disliked standing armies, and one which contained Catholic officers seemed even more sinister. It was soon to appear more sinister still. On 8th October Louis issued the Edict of Fontainebleau, revoking the last vestiges of the toleration granted to the Huguenots by the Edict of Nantes, almost a century before.

*   *   *

In both England and the Dutch republic, the news of the persecution which followed was greeted with horror. Many of the stories brought by Huguenot refugees were untrue or exaggerated, but the reality was disturbing enough. Louis claimed that the measures which he took to save his subjects' souls were no business of anyone else, but others disagreed and there were cases where it was debatable whether those who were being harassed were in fact Louis' subjects. Louis claimed that all Dutch and English Protestants who had been naturalized had become his subjects and so had their wives and children, whether they had been naturalized or not. Moreover, although he assured James and the States General that those who had remained English or Dutch citizens would be free to leave France, with their property, such assurances were not always respected by Louis' officials. Moreover, if their wives were French, the wives and children had to stay. Many members of the English and Dutch merchant communities were thus affected by the persecution, as friends or relatives were maltreated and trade was interrupted.

In Holland the persecution brought the first hint of rapprochement between William and Amsterdam. Amsterdam's merchants were particularly deeply involved in the French trade and the city's Protestant clergy, like those elsewhere, talked loudly of the perils facing European Protestantism. The regents of Amsterdam did not stop opposing William, but they agreed to open up channels of communication through which William was able gradually to undermine their resistance. Louis had expected such a reaction:

"I see clearly . . . that the Prince of Orange and his adherents will make use of the good success which God is giving to my efforts to convert my subjects to turn the States General against my interests, but the benefit which will result from this is so great that (whatever the effect it may produce where you are) it will not make me weaken in my determination to perfect the work."

He was sure that the rulers of Amsterdam would soon get over their excitement and see again that their true interest lay in close friendship with France, which alone could protect their liberties against William.[28]

The persecution also had a second, less obvious, effect on Dutch opinion.

The conduct of the Catholic King of France made the Dutch look more anxiously at the conduct of the Catholic King of England. The Dutch Ambassadors might report James's professions of friendship towards the States General, but d'Avaux reported that at the Hague many believed that James was much more friendly to Louis than to William.[29] Such suspicions were soon strengthened by a series of petty incidents. They led William and the States General to treat James more coolly, which in turn helped make James suspicious and hostile towards the Dutch.

In England the news of the persecution had a less obvious impact, not least because the press was firmly under government control. The *Gazette* made no mention of what was happening in France, a fact which provoked some comment, as news filtered through during October and November. English Protestants read with anxiety a speech by the Bishop of Valence urging Louis and James to join in extirpating heresy in their dominions. Faced with such news, even the most loyal Tory was bound to feel threatened by James's enlarged army and to fear that it would soon be filled with Papists. More than ever the Tories wer concerned to preserve the Test, the "great guard and security to our church". "Never was there a more devoted Parliament," remarked one observer, "but you know the point of religion is a tender point."[30]

James's subjects mostly assumed that, as a Catholic, he must approve of Louis' persecution of the Huguenots. In fact, James's attitude is not easy to determine. Barrillon wrote often that James had expressed admiration for Louis' heroic efforts to root out heresy and that he had apologized for authorizing a collection in aid of the Huguenot refugees in England, saying in extenuation that English opinion was so agitated that he had no choice. Such letters need not be taken at face value. Barrillon knew that this was a matter dear to Louis' heart and may have embellished or even invented James's remarks to please his master. Even if James really said these things, it does not mean that he was sincere. James often larded his remarks to Barrillon with unctuous flattery of Louis and seldom said anything to Barrillon which he thought would displease the French King; if he did, Barrillon failed to report it. When undertaking some action which he thought Louis might not like (such as asking the States General for the three Scots regiments) James failed to mention it. Moreover, against the remarks reported by Barrillon one can set others—to Citters, to the Spanish Ambassador Ronquillo, to William himself—in which James condemned the persecution as impolitic and un-Christian.[31]

Any analysis of James's attitude should therefore be based on his actions, not his words, but here too there are contradictions. James ordered the collection for the refugees as soon as it was requested, but it was five months before the necessary authorization was issued and it included the condition that the money was to go only to those who used the liturgy of the Church of England. One reason for this delay was Barrillon's insistence that the letters for the collection should contain no expressions offensive to Louis. Barrillon also persuaded James to suppress a book about the persecution by one of the refugees. James gave as his reason the obligation of kings to defend each other against insults, but it was naturally seen as implying approval of Louis' conduct. Such beliefs were confirmed by James's allowing French officials to search English ships for fugitives in French ports.[32] On the other hand, James's ambassador in Paris, Sir William Trumbull, did all he could to help English and Scots caught up in the persecution. Although James and Sunderland reprimanded Trumbull occasionally for some rather indecorous expressions, he was clearly carrying out James's orders. In June 1686, for example, Trumbull was told that the French Protestant servants who had come with him from England would not be allowed to leave France. James at once ordered Trumbull to return to England and to bring his Huguenot servants with him. Louis expressed surprise, remarking that he thought a king of James's religious zeal would not have concerned himself with such matters. But James was adamant, so Louis eventually let Trumbull take his servants with him.[33]

It is not easy to see a consistent pattern in James's behaviour, but I think it is possible. Despite his remarks to Barrillon, I suspect that James genuinely disapproved of the violent methods Louis used to convert the Huguenots. He seems to have disliked religious persecution on principle and was only too aware of how much more difficult Louis' actions made his task in England. If he hesitated to show his disapproval openly or to make representations to Louis to change his policies, this can be explained in three ways. First, James may have realized that Louis' mind was made up and there was no point in trying to change it. Secondly, he seems to have accepted Louis' argument that it was an internal matter and concerned himself only with marginal cases: British subjects who had not been naturalized, or Trumbull's Huguenot servants. Thirdly, as 1686 wore on, James came to regard Louis' friendship as vital to the success of his Catholicizing measures at home. He was therefore reluctant to push Louis too hard on matters which he knew were disagreeable to him. Louis was well aware of this reluctance and knew that if he refused James's requests, James could do little about it. When he did make a modest concession, he stressed his own magnanimity and expected James to respond with suitably fulsome expressions of thanks.

James's treatment of the Huguenots within England reflected a tension between different principles or emotions. On one hand, James sympathized with them as victims of persecution and saw that it would create a very bad impression if he did nothing for them. On the other hand, he distrusted them on political grounds. As early as July 1685 he suspected that the Huguenots had been mixed up with Monmouth's rebellion and these suspicions were carefully nurtured by the French. James's experience of Dissenters in England and Scotland had prejudiced him strongly against Calvinists, whom he regarded as enemies of monarchy. Moreover, at this time James was still seeking the co-operation of the Tories, many of whom looked with distaste on non-episcopal Protestant churches. Seen in this context, James's slowness in providing for the refugees and his insistence that they use the Anglican liturgy becomes comprehensible, if hardly creditable.[34]

* * *

The expansion of the army, the employment of Catholic officers and the persecution in France all contributed to a growing unease as the meeting of Parliament approached, so James decided that he must at least be sure of his own servants. Halifax had criticized both the employment of Catholic officers and the persecution in France. James therefore resolved to ask him point blank whether he would support the repeal of the Test Acts and the Habeas Corpus Act. (The latter, passed in 1679, prevented the government from imprisoning anyone without showing due cause.) Halifax said he would not, so James dismissed him from office, and from the council. To ram the point home, James told the other councillors that he would place no confidence in anyone whose principles and sentiments were opposed to his. Already, the spectrum of political and religious opinion at court was narrowing. Halifax, meanwhile, freed of the constraints of office, prepared to attack James's measures in the coming session.[35]

Despite James's efforts to discipline his servants, the court approached the session in some disarray. Some argued that James, to propitiate the Commons, should not insist on keeping the Catholic officers. Others claimed that any sign of weakness would be fatal and that if the Commons were not kept firmly in their place they would try to rule all. The Catholics too were divided. The wealthy lay Catholics feared reprisals against their estates after James's death if he went too far and were ready to settle for a mere toleration, by connivance if need be. The priests and zealots, however, argued that only the repeal of the penal laws and Test Acts could ensure the survival of Catholicism. Whatever the wisdom of the arguments for moderation, the arguments for firmness appealed to James's religious enthusiasm and his authoritarian temperament. The zealots got their way. James's opening speech, on 9th November, stressed the militia's poor showing against Monmouth. "There is nothing but a good force of well-disciplined troops in constant pay that can defend us from such as, either at home or abroad, are disposed to disturb us." James therefore asked for money to support the army. As for the Catholic officers, he was well satisfied of their loyalty. After availing himself of their service, "I will neither expose them to disgrace, nor myself to the want of them, if there be another rebellion to make them necessary for me." Unlike his speech in the previous session, this one ended without repeating James's assurances to the Church of England.[36]

The combative tone of James's speech needled the Commons. On the 12th the House resolved to bring in a supply bill, but refused to specify that it was "for the support of the additional forces". Moreover, it resolved to bring in another bill to make the militia more useful. One speaker after another stressed the militia's virtues and claimed that "a standing army is destructive to the country." Next day the House resolved, by a majority of one, to consider the question of the Catholic officers before that of the supply; the motion was supported by a number of officials and army officers, much to James's annoyance.[37] Worse was to come. On the 14th the Commons resolved to present an address which, in a cautious and circumlocutory manner, informed the king that the House regarded the employment of Papists as illegal. Various compromises were suggested, mostly designed to give some sort of satisfaction to these officers while ensuring that no more should be employed. James, however, would have none of it. He told the Commons that he had not expected such an address, after warning them against unnecessary fears and jealousies and stressing the need for a good understanding between them.[38]

This sharp reproof seemed bound to antagonize the Commons. One MP exclaimed "We are all Englishmen and we ought not to be frighted out of our duty by a few high words." This "was looked upon as so undecent an expression to the King (though the House generally liked the motion) . . . that they sent that member to the Tower and left that business *sine die.*" Chastened, the House returned to the question of supply. It had voted to raise £400,000 by extending for five more years (from 1690) the customs duties voted the previous session and to raise £300,000 over ten years from new duties on French wines. Thus while in theory voting James an extraordinary grant of £700,000, the yield for the first few years would be only £30,000 a year. James was most displeased. Meanwhile, on the 19th, the Lords debated the question of the Catholic officers. James was present, while one peer after another stressed the need to preserve the laws against Popery and some said "horrible things" of the Catholics. What he heard removed any lingering inclination which James may have had to keep the Parliament in being. The following day he prorogued it for three months after a session lasting less than a fortnight. It was never to meet again.[39]

CHAPTER ELEVEN

The King and the Judges (November 1685 to April 1687)

The prorogation of Parliament was as significant as it was unexpected. It marked, after just nine months of James's reign, a break with the Tories who had supported him since 1680. The House of Commons elected in 1685 may have been "the most devoted and the most resigned to the service of the crown that ever was or ever will be chosen", but its members were not subservient nonentities, ready to do whatever the King's ministers commanded. Most were country gentlemen with minds of their own, who had upheld the crown's authority for what had seemed to them sound religious and political reasons. James's conduct had reminded them that Church and constitution could be threatened from above as well as from below, by "Popery and arbitrary government" as well as by Dissent and republicanism. Loyal the Tories might be, but their sense of self-preservation made them reluctant to provide the money to pay a standing army, still less one which contained Catholic officers. Their steadfastness and a sense of common danger led to a mending of political fences. From London and Bristol it was reported that "Whig and Tory seem quite laid by and now nothing talked of but whether a Protestant or a Papist" . . . "as if it were high time for Protestants of all sorts to be friends."[1]

At court, the prorogation marked a crucial point in Sunderland's campaign to supplant Rochester as James's chief minister. Sunderland started off with some grave disadvantages. Rochester had been James's brother-in-law, and he had supported James's interests unswervingly, whereas Sunderland had supported exclusion and had angered James late in 1684 by trying to pack Rochester off to Ireland. Rochester had inherited and extended his father's connexions with the Anglican nobility and gentry and with the High Church clergy, many of whom he had helped to advance. Sunderland had no such power base outside the court and his churchmanship was so minimal that he had few friends among the clergy. At court, however, he was an experienced and unscrupulous operator. Moreover, as he was relatively unencumbered by principles or pre-existing obligations, he was free to seek allies where he could and to adopt whichever policies seemed most advantageous. He therefore turned to the one group at court whom Rochester could never gain (the Catholics) and to the one policy which Rochester could never advocate—the advancement of Catholicism.

At his accession James had set up an unofficial council of Catholics to advise him on religious matters, to which he admitted Sunderland once he was convinced of Sunderland's zeal for the Catholic cause. Sunderland used this council to extend his power. Rochester, naturally, did not attend and the rest of its members could not compete with Sunderland in either ability or experience. Sunderland therefore dominated it and extended the scope of its proceedings, drawing more and more business into its orbit. For some time, the role of the privy council had been mainly formal; now the same fate befell the smaller cabinet council, which consisted of the King's leading officers (who, in 1685, were all Protestants). The Catholic council, meanwhile, became the most important advisory body.[2]

Sunderland thus used the Catholic council to mould the Catholics' views and then used the Catholics to influence the King, but it was not the sole basis of his power. Sunderland possessed the experience of administration and diplomacy which most of his other courtiers conspicuously lacked and made it his business to cultivate and use others whom James trusted. Hitherto Mary Beatrice had kept out of politics. Now Sunderland exploited her influence over her husband, playing on her religious zeal and ignorance of English affairs, so that she became convinced that only if Sunderland directed affairs could the Catholic cause prosper. Two other allies proved more difficult to handle, for they were also potential rivals. Richard Talbot (created Earl of Tyrconnell in 1685) was regarded by some as a ranting buffoon, but behind the explosions of rage and dyspeptic inconsistency lay an acute political brain. He was an ambitious man with a clear idea of what he wanted and of how to get it. He was doubly formidable in that, alone of James's courtiers, he had the personality to outface Sunderland in an argument before the King. Fortunately for Sunderland, Tyrconnell's ambitions were focused on Ireland, but he was never an easy ally, partly because of his fiery personality, partly because the changes which he wanted in Ireland were likely to have serious political repercussions in England.[3]

If historians have often underestimated Tyrconnell, they have probably overestimated the influence of the Jesuit, Edward Petre. Although he was never James's confessor, contemporaries agreed, from the end of 1685, that his credit with James was very great. He must have possessed considerable charm or personality, for his standing at court owed nothing to his standing in the English Province of the Society of Jesus, which was lowly, or to his abilities, which were limited. His main interest seems to have been his own advancement. He persuaded James to pester the Pope to make him either a bishop or a cardinal and was furious when the Pope refused. Sunderland soon saw that Petre's credit with James could be useful to him and used the Jesuit to support his arguments about what needed to be done. He paid for Petre's services by pandering to his considerable vanity. In time, the exhilaration of dabbling in politics went to Petre's head. He slipped from Sunderland's control and fell in with Catholic extremists, like Melfort. There is little evidence that he had any serious ideas of his own, outside the purely ecclesiastical sphere, but his influence and lack of political sense made him a powerful if unreliable instrument which could be manipulated by cleverer men.

The final ally whom Sunderland used was Barrillon. The image we have of the Ambassador is unattractive: massaging his fat thighs, pulling hairs out of his nose, picking his ears and cutting his nails in public, arguing by hints and insinuations rather than directly. He knew the court well, having been in London since 1677, and had worked closely with Sunderland during Charles's last years. James allowed Barrillon more frequent access than any other ambassador and talked to him of his affairs at great length, if not always with total sincerity. As secretary of state, Sunderland was well placed to dominate James's foreign policy. Although there was a second secretary (the Earl of Middleton) Sunderland ensured that the English ambassadors in Middleton's province (which included Holland) carried on a purely routine correspondence with Middleton, while communicating on more confidential matters with Sunderland or James. Moreover, after the subsidy negotiations of 1685 (in which Rochester was involved) Sunderland was the only minister to whom Barrillon spoke at all frequently. In June 1686 Barrillon remarked that he hardly knew Petre, who had by then been a major figure at court for over six months. Thus much of Barrillon's information about events at court came from Sunderland, and should therefore be treated with some circumspection. However, Barrillon worked with Sunderland only because he believed they shared the same objectives. Louis often stressed to Barrillon that he hoped that James would succeed in strengthening English Catholicism, which was the goal which Sunderland claimed to pursue. He also agreed with Sunderland that this goal could be achieved only if there were a close understanding between James and Louis. More cynically, Barrillon calculated that if James's policies caused divisions and disorders at home, he would be unable to rally his subjects for a war against France. Like Tyrconnell but unlike Petre, Barrillon was too astute to be a mere tool of Sunderland's. He helped Sunderland because he thought it in Louis' interests to do so.[4]

Sunderland's influence depended only partly on his ability to manipulate the King and others. He also offered policies which were designed to appeal to James. Before the fatal session of Parliament in November 1685, James usually followed Rochester's advice. Abroad, he sought good relations with William and the States General. At home, he continued to rely on the Tories. James found a way to stop the persecution of Catholics while continuing to persecute Dissenters, by granting relief to those whose families had served Charles I in the civil wars: most Catholics had done so, most Dissenters had not. He thus discriminated between Catholics and Dissenters on political, not religious grounds. This cessation of persecution provoked virtually no opposition and some Catholics thought it was the most they could hope for. Only too well aware that James had no Catholic heir, they feared that if the Catholics tried to gain too much during James's lifetime they would suffer for it when William and Mary came to power. Rochester agreed: he argued that the Tories offered the only viable basis of support for James's regime and that it would be unwise to alienate them by demanding too much for the Catholics.

Such timid arguments were not congenial to James. His sense of divine mission made him eager to do more for the Catholics than merely allow toleration by connivance. His authoritarianism led him to discount the opinions of his subjects when they differed from his own. He listened eagerly to suggestions that the half-hearted, "trimming" arguments of Rochester and the moderate Catholics were not only unnecessarily cautious, but also self-interested and even dishonest. It was easy to argue that, as Mary's uncle, Rochester was concerned to preserve his interest with the heir presumptive and that, as a Protestant, he was fundamentally opposed to the advancement of Catholicism. Rochester could not argue that it was undesirable to do more for the Catholics, but he did argue that it was not politically possible. Sunderland and the Catholics contested this and insinuated that Rochester was misleading James for his own ends. If James would only be firm, they claimed, his subjects would eventually comply with his wishes, while any sign of fear would merely encourage them to be obstinate. Louis' letters to Barrillon harped on similar themes and Barrillon doubtless passed his master's views on to James.

Such arguments appealed to James for they assured him of the truth of what he wished to believe. They were based, however, on some fallacious assumptions. They placed more weight on Tory professions of non-resistance than was wise and treated Tory objections to Catholicism as being based on fear, ignorance and self-interest rather than principle. When James took a firm line with Parliament it worked badly, but Sunderland and his allies soon persuaded James to see the prorogation as a triumph. James expressed pride in his firmness in not having sacrificed an essential part of his prerogative to the "malcontents". He congratulated himself on having been too clever to be fooled by the Commons' offers of money. Sunderland had had little hope that Parliament would do as James wished. Now he and the Catholics argued that James should not call another until he was quite sure of success. They pointed to the courtiers and office-holders who had opposed James's wishes in the last session and argued that Parliament would never become more amenable while such men retained their places. James should therefore dismiss his unreliable servants—which meant, in effect, Rochester and his Tory followers.[5]

Sunderland wanted a purge of office-holders in order to fill the court, the administration and the armed forces with men who depended on him, including perhaps some of his Catholic allies. James, however, never liked dismissing trusted servants. He dismissed from office a few MPs who had opposed his wishes in the Commons, but not nearly as many as Sunderland wished. Rochester remained in office. In March 1686 Barrillon reported that James trusted the treasurer in all his affairs except those of religion. His credit was not harmed, either, by Sunderland's overplaying his hand. He accused Rochester of trying to set up Catherine Sedley, now Lady Dorchester, as an official royal mistress, with a position and influence similar to Portsmouth's. The accusation seems to have been quite untrue, and when Sunderland and his Catholic friends tried to remonstrate with James about his mistress, they received a crushing snub.[6]

In the long run, however, Sunderland was bound to get his way. He was prepared to commit himself to James's religious objectives in a way which

Rochester was not and to advise measures which Rochester could not support. His assault on Rochester had to be a war of attrition. As 1686 wore on, Rochester suffered one defeat after another. His relatives were dismissed from high office: Queensberry, the Lord Treasurer of Scotland, and Archbishop Boyle, Lord Chancellor of Ireland. His brother Clarendon, as Lord Lieutenant of Ireland, was ordered to implement measures in favour of the Catholics of which he clearly disapproved. Meanwhile, Tyrconnell's friends at court claimed that Clarendon was obstructing the execution of these measures. When the Scots Parliament, usually so amenable, refused to grant freedom of worship to Catholics, many at court blamed "the cabal of the Prince of Orange" and more particularly Rochester and Queensberry. Even in his own little empire, the treasury, Rochester was forced to reinstate Sir Nicholas Butler, one of the customs commissioners, who had been dismissed after a quarrel. Butler had immediately become a Catholic, which doubtless explains his reinstatement.[7]

Despite such pressures, James continued to trust Rochester, whose financial expertise seemed to make him indispensable. Indeed, he concentrated more and more on treasury business, partly because James consulted him less and less on other matters, partly because Rochester did not wish to be associated with some of James's measures. The spring and summer of 1686 saw two important changes of policy. First, having failed to obtain what he wanted from Parliament, James resorted to prerogative action to grant relief to the Catholics until such relief could be granted by a Parliament. Secondly, he began to consider abandoning the Anglicans and throwing in his lot with the Dissenters.

* * *

In undertaking both these changes of direction James made some use of his position as supreme governor of the Church of England. That position, as Catholic head of a Protestant church, was anomalous and it might have seemed logical for James to submit to the Pope and divest himself of his authority over the Anglican Church. But James had no intention of doing either. In September 1685 he decided to establish diplomatic relations with Rome. He picked as his ambassador the Earl of Castlemaine, a man of great religious enthusiasm, little common sense and no diplomatic experience. Barrillon remarked acidly that it was strange to choose a man whose main claim to fame was that his wife had been Charles II's mistress. In November 1685 Ferdinando D'Adda arrived at court as the Pope's envoy, although it was not until the spring of 1687 that the Pope allowed him to assume the character of papal nuncio.[8]

If James thus reopened formal contacts with the Vatican, his attitude was by no means one of unqualified submission. His instructions to Castlemaine stressed

"That we are extremely sensible of the great providence of God in preserving us from so many dangers and difficulties which have attended us for embracing the Catholic religion and that having suffered for it we do not doubt but his Holiness will be persuaded of our sincere intentions to maintain it and by all lawful means to endeavour the propagation of the same."

James therefore expected to "have all the power as to the nomination of bishops

... possessed by any time by our royal ancestors or which any other prince has in his [dominions]," for:

"whereas by reason of a long interruption of church government we may have acquired new rights or a just claim to peculiar methods ... you are not to be diverted by precedents and practices of other kingdoms from prosecuting such means, though unusual, as we shall think fit to prescribe and suggest towards the attaining of our ends. ... When any of our demands meet with difficulty, you may represent to the Pope how much the interests of the Catholic religion are concerned therein and that our desires should be granted."[9]

Such instructions were hard to reconcile with James's repeated professions of filial obedience and submission to the Holy See. Both the aggressive tone and the insistence on royal control of the church were reminiscent of Louis XIV, with whom Innocent XI had a series of bitter disputes. Moreover, the Pope soon came to share the general belief that a close liaison existed between James and Louis. In fact, there was little friction between James and the Pope over the internal needs of the English church, but in Ireland trouble arose over James's claim to nominate not only the Catholic bishops but deans and other ecclesiastics. His legal right to do so was highly questionable. In most Catholic countries (apart from France and Spain, whose rulers had obtained special privileges) the lay ruler had no positive right to appoint bishops, even if the Pope often appointed the ruler's nominees. Moreover, even the Spanish and French kings had no right to appoint to deaneries and other lesser benefices. James, however, insisted that these rights had been established by Henry VIII and used by Mary. He continued to try to exercise them well into the 1690s, much to the Pope's irritation. As Cardinal Howard remarked in 1693: "I was sorry to see that few or none of our English churchmen have studied or had the practice of these things, much less the lay people, both of whom so very wrongly informed his majesty therein."[10]

The greatest friction between James and the Pope arose on questions which had little to do with the well-being of the English or Irish Catholics. James assumed that his heroic struggle to promote the Catholic religion placed the Pope under a moral obligation to grant whatever James and his Queen thought reasonable. He renewed his demand that the Queen's uncle, Rinaldo D'Este, should be made a cardinal. Despite Rinaldo's manifest unsuitability, the Pope finally agreed, in order to soften the blow of his refusing a second demand, that he should make Petre a bishop. Innocent XI strongly disliked Jesuits and was determined to uphold the clause in the Society's statutes which declared its members ineligible for high ecclesiastical preferments. James at last accepted that the Pope would not make Petre a bishop, so asked him to make him a cardinal instead. Again and again the Pope gave Castlemaine his reasons and D'Adda repeated them to James and Sunderland. Again and again James refused to accept that the refusal was final, claiming that Castlemaine had led him to expect the Pope to change his mind. Petre and his friends, meanwhile, accused D'Adda, Howard and eventually even Sunderland of misinforming the Pope and prejudicing him against Petre. James was persuaded to take the direction of English affairs at Rome out of Howard's hands and to entrust them to Rinaldo. He thus replaced a man who was both knowledgeable and respected with one who was neither and whose sole claim to eminence was his kinship with the Queen. The story of James's relations with Rome is one of ignorance, arrogance and irrelevant self-gratification. Even when James offered to mediate between Louis and the Pope, he hoped that in return the Pope would at last make Petre a cardinal.[11]

James was thus unwilling to restore to the Pope the powers over the English church which the crown had acquired at the Reformation. He believed, not only that these powers were rightfully his, but also that they were needed for the advancement of Catholicism. Two aspects of the royal supremacy were particularly relevant: first, the 'ower to maintain discipline among the Anglican clergy and secondly that part of the king's dispensing power which could be used for ecclesiastical purposes.

In the first weeks of his reign, James had ordered Sancroft and his colleagues to forbid their clergy to preach seditious sermons, warning that if the sermons continued he might reconsider his promises to the Church. Anti-Catholic sermons continued, however, some reflecting openly on the King.[12] In February 1686 James again summoned Sancroft and some other bishops and complained of such anti-Catholicism, mentioning especially the Sunday afternoon lectures and catechizing. He was persuaded not to demand the suppression of these exercises, on condition that Sancroft reissued the directions to preachers issued in 1662. These ordered the clergy to avoid controversy and "abstruse and speculative notions" and to concentrate on practical, moral divinity.[13] Still the sermons continued and anti-Catholic tracts poured from the press. A few bishops tried hard to enforce James's orders, but others were clearly unsympathetic. James replaced bishops who died with more compliant men (like Parker at Oxford and Cartwright at Chester), but such changes could alter the character of the episcopate only very gradually. Meanwhile, even prelates who had been closely associated with James, like Turner or Sancroft, proved less co-operative than he expected. Others were openly hostile. Compton had long been on bad terms with James. In the November session of Parliament he criticized strongly James's employing Catholic officers, for which he was dismissed from the privy council. In May 1686 John Sharp, rector of St Giles in the Fields, preached a sermon which James thought offensively anti-Catholic. He ordered Compton to suspend Sharp. Compton refused, which brought to a head the problem of James's inability to control the Anglican clergy. As he could not rely on the bishops to execute the disciplinary powers which the King, as supreme governor, had vested in them, he decided to delegate those powers to someone else. On 8th July he issued a warrant to establish an ecclesiastical commission, which was to exercise the King's powers to visit and discipline ecclesiastical persons and institutions, including the universities.[14]

Most contemporaries saw this as a revival of the Court of High Commission abolished by Parliament in 1641, and assumed, therefore, that it was illegal.

As Ogg has shown, this was not strictly correct. The commission claimed to exercise only those of the King's powers of ecclesiastical jurisdiction which had not been declared illegal by the Acts of 1641 and 1661. Unlike High Commission, it never called itself a court, nor did it impose fines or imprisonment. It claimed jurisdiction only over ecclesiastics and imposed only the purely ecclesiastical penalties of suspension and deprivation.[15] Although many questioned its legality, the most offensive aspect of the commission was perhaps the use to which it was put. It was used, first, to stop the Anglican clergy from warning their flocks against the dangers from Popery and secondly, to force the universities to admit non-Anglican students and teachers.

The corollary of James's disillusionment with the Anglicans was a softening of his hostility towards Protestant Dissenters. At first, this hostility had been reinforced by the support which some Dissenters gave to Monmouth, but after the November session of Parliament he began, for the first time, to doubt the Anglicans' loyalty. He was still reluctant to believe that (given time, and a degree of firmness on his part) the Tories would not see the error of their ways. He still saw them as the natural supporters of monarchy. Nevertheless, he knew that if (as he saw it) the Anglicans abandoned him, the obvious alternative was to offer a general toleration and seek support among the Dissenters. During 1686, as the Tory gentry remained opposed to toleration for Catholics and the Anglican clergy insulted his religion, James began to criticize the Church of England, not only for opposing his wishes but also for persecuting Dissenters. He came to believe that the Dissenters had been forced into their disloyal behaviour by religious persecution and so that, once the persecution was ended, the Dissenters would become loyal subjects of the crown. Thus the political arguments for relying on the Anglicans and for repressing Dissent were gradually weakening.

It is easy to see James's conversion to toleration as opportunistic and insincere. He certainly turned to the Dissenters only after failing to get his way with the Anglicans. Yet his change of heart was slow and complex. On one hand, he was never a tolerant man in the sense of being able to appreciate views which differed from his own. On the other hand, he had always claimed to be against religious persecution as such, and had justified the persecution of Dissenters, in England and Scotland, on political grounds. By 1686, however, the simple equation of Dissent and disloyalty seemed far less obvious than in 1681–85. Slowly and painfully, James had to rethink his position. He came to see a general religious liberty as not only feasible but right in itself. It took time to rid himself of the hope that his "old friends", the Tories, would forget their aversion to Catholicism; it took time to overcome his reservations about the Dissenters' political leanings. Once he had done so, his lifelong opposition to religious persecution could develop into a positive commitment to liberty of conscience, which he upheld in 1687–88 with every sign of sincerity.

In overcoming his prejudices in favour of Anglicans and against Dissenters, James received considerable help from his courtiers. Sunderland and his Catholic allies argued that Rochester and the Tories would always obstruct James's religious measures and that he should therefore dismiss them and cease to rely on their support. A more upright adviser was the Quaker, William Penn. In 1673 James had told Penn, "that he looked upon us [the Quakers] as a quiet industrious people and though he was not of our judgment, yet he liked our good lives." Although Penn had supported Exclusion, he returned to court in 1685. James told him that he did not wish peaceable people to be troubled for their religion, but he still distrusted the Quakers in general, while expressing confidence in particular individuals. In 1686 Penn's influence grew. In March James suspended all legal proceedings against Quakers and by August other Dissenters could meet freely, if they petitioned the King for relief. James granted such petitions and expatiated on the cruelty of the Church of England, declaring his willingness to end persecution for conscience's sake. He sounded the various types of Dissenters, to see "whether if liberty and impunity could be granted by law, the Dissenters would, in a body, signify their thankful acceptance thereof." By the beginning of 1687 the persecution of Dissenters had virtually stopped.[16]

If James had been content simply not to enforce the laws penalizing Catholic and Dissenting worship, there was little to stop him. James, however, wanted the penal laws and Test Acts formally and permanently removed. As he came to accept that the Tory Parliament of 1685 would not do so, he realized that he would have to call another. While the Tories dominated the shires and boroughs, however, a general election would produce another strongly Tory House of Commons. Before he could secure a Dissenting House of Commons, he would have to replace the Tory office-holders in the constituencies with Dissenters and Catholics. Under the Test and Corporation Acts, Dissenters and Catholics were excluded from such offices. Therefore, in order to employ them (and, he hoped, to encourage converts to come forward) James had to use his prerogative, his dispensing and suspending powers.

After proroguing Parliament in November, James granted some seventy Catholic army officers a pardon for having accepted commissions without taking the Test. The judges assured him that he had the power to grant the pardon, but were divided (one writer said seven to five) about his power to dispense them from taking the Test and oaths (of allegiance and supremacy) in the future. James therefore merely recommissioned the officers, since he could employ them for up to three months without their being asked to take the Test. He toyed with the idea of publishing the decision of the majority of the judges in favour of his dispensing power, but decided against it as the decision had not been unanimous. He resolved instead to establish its legality by means of a test case.[17]

If this case were to have the desired outcome, James had to be sure of the judges. In February he dismissed two for refusing to acknowledge his dispensing power and four others were dismissed in April. James could now bring his test case with every prospect of success. Sir Edward Hales, a Catholic officer was prosecuted for holding office contrary to law, but pleaded the King's dispensation. Lord Chief Justice Herbert found a pretext to call in all the judges and eleven of the twelve ruled that "'tis an inseparable prerogative of the kings of England to dispense with penal laws in particular cases and upon particular necessary reasons" and "that of those reasons and those necessities the king himself is sole judge."[18]

This ruling provoked considerable controversy. Nobody denied that the king possessed a dispensing power, by which he could allow an individual to disobey a statute. There were many precedents for such a power, which had been extended into new areas by the assertion of the royal supremacy, whereby the king assumed the pope's power to dispense with ecclesiastical regulations. What was at issue was less the dispensing power as such than the way in which it was used. Tudor writers declared that it should be used "where equity requireth a moderation to be had". It had been agreed, too, that it could be used only in cases of transgressions against the law of men (*mala prohibita*), not transgressions against the law of God (*mala in se*). The offence created by the Test clearly fell into the former category. It could also be argued that the king could dispense with any statute which took away "any prerogative which is sole and inseparable to his person". The Test Act could be seen as coming into that category.*[19]

Technically James had a reasonable case in claiming a dispensing power. He was no lawyer, as he freely admitted: "I am obliged to think what my judges do is according to law." He expected his legal advisers to preserve his rights, but distrusted lawyers and remarked that the law was used as a pretext for many injustices. Impatient with the law's subtleties and technicalities, James stuck to simpler, more clear-cut concepts like the laws of God and nature. These (he claimed) gave the king an inalienable right to his subjects' service and imposed on those subjects an inviolable duty to obey their king. Any statute which deprived the king of his subjects' service or debarred them from serving him was (in the eyes of both James and Penn) unjust in itself. Moreover, it was far from improper to dismiss judges who obstinately refused to recognize the injustice of such laws.[20]

James's subjects did not see matters in this way. They did not share his view of the law and resented the appearance of duress given by the judges' dismissal. They had resented the uses to which James had already put the dispensing power, admitting Catholics to the army and allowing converts to Catholicism to retain their college fellowships (the latter by virtue of the ecclesiastical part of the dispensing power). The judges' ruling in the Hales case opened the way to the admission of Catholics to civilian offices and perhaps (they feared) to benefices in the Church and seats in the House of Commons. Meanwhile, in Ireland Tyrconnell was busy filling the army and the administration with Catholics. For the Tories in particular the future looked alarming indeed. James was treating them harshly but spoke kindly to the Dissenters, while Rochester's credit at court was clearly reduced. To make matters worse, James's

---

* In 1689 the dispensing power was declared illegal only "as it hath been assumed and exercised of late".

relations with the States General and with William had deteriorated seriously since the beginning of the year.

* * *

The worsening of James's relationship with William and the Dutch was a complex process, not least because of the continuing divisions within the republic. Much of the distrust which developed was the product of misunderstanding and of misinformation and rumour. Periods of nagging irritation alternated with spasms of panic, which soon evaporated but left an added residue of distrust. There were few real turning-points, but rather several longstanding causes of friction and ill feeling which were exacerbated by particular incidents (often trivial in themselves) and so gradually became more serious.

For James, the most serious cause for complaint was the Dutch authorities' failure to expel the English political and religious refugees who congregated in a number of Dutch towns. James thought the expulsion of these "rebels"

"a thing of the last consequence for the peace and quiet of my kingdoms . . . for when once removed from thence they can do no mischief, though the republican spirit increases every day amongst us here; but should they be but connived there, they would still be contriving new designs to disturb me, for that restless and rebellious party will never be quiet."

He could not understand how such men could be allowed to flaunt themselves in Amsterdam and elsewhere when they posed such an obvious threat to his security.[21] But the States General failed to hand them over, even though they were obliged to do so under various treaties, for two main reasons. First, the fragmentation of authority made it very difficult to reach overall agreement to expel the exiles. Even after the States General and States of Holland had resolved to order their expulsion, the States of the other provinces were slow to follow suit and individual towns were even slower to execute the States' resolutions. Secondly, many Dutchmen did not regard the exiles as criminals or traitors. Some alleged that they had fled from religious persecution. Others said that they would expel the exiles only if James sent witnesses to prove their guilt. At Amsterdam, the authorities said that they had always provided a refuge for people of all nations and hinted that many of the exiles had merely fallen foul of great men at court.[22]

The Dutch, therefore, took refuge in the intricacies of their constitution or claimed that those James named could not be found. James, however, suspected that they were simply unwilling to hand the exiles over. Certain particular cases increased James's anger or the Dutch authorities' reluctance to co-operate. In May 1686 Burnet arrived at the Hague. James's earlier friendship had long since turned to hatred and Burnet goaded him further with pamphlets attacking his measures in both England and Scotland. James had Burnet prosecuted for treason in Scotland and he was outlawed when he failed to appear. He then demanded that Burnet should be handed over as a proclaimed traitor, but the States General refused. On the other hand, as Skelton was about to leave for his new embassy in Paris late in 1686, some English army officers tried to kidnap one of the exiles, Sir Robert Peyton, and to send him to England in

Skelton's ship. The people of Rotterdam were outraged at such treatment of one of their fellow citizens and demanded a severe punishment for the officers. James disavowed their action but argued that they were only trying to serve their king. The States of Holland stripped them of their commissions and deported them, which James regarded as quite unnecessarily severe. Meanwhile, Peyton shocked the Dutch by revealing that Skelton had offered to secure him a pardon in return for one thousand pounds.[23]

The dubious legality of the proceedings against Burnet and Peyton strengthened the conviction in Holland that they were innocent of the crimes with which James charged them and made the authorities doubly reluctant to hand them over. There might seem little reason, however, for James to blame William for this. He knew that William's power was limited, especially in Amsterdam (perhaps the main refuge of the exiles). Nevertheless, James did come to hold William responsible. His ambassadors at the Hague (first Skelton, then Albeville) reported many anecdotes, true and false, showing William's sympathy with the exiles. When Skelton returned to England in October 1686 he was personally embittered against William and greatly increased James's resentment of William's conduct.[24] On some points, moreover, James was irritated by William's own actions. After a series of petty arguments about appointments in the British regiments, James announced petulantly in May that he would make no further nominations, as William paid so little heed to his wishes. Two months later he nominated the Earl of Carlingford, an Irish Catholic, as the regiments' commander. William argued that such an appointment would cause great controversy in the republic, but Sunderland replied blandly that there seemed no reason for this, as Catholics had often served in the Dutch army. When William finally refused, James, full of pique, refused to suggest another commander. His bitterness against William was soon increased by his patronage of Burnet (whom Albeville likened to Tartuffe). Eventually, he even allowed himself to be persuaded that William had tacitly encouraged Monmouth's invasion.[25]

If James's disillusionment with William developed gradually, William's distrust of James began to develop as the result of a particular incident. In 1680 Louis had occupied the principality of Orange. In 1685 he annexed it and stepped up the persecution of the local Protestants. That October James was asked to intercede with Louis on William's behalf. James agreed, partly out of a sense of family solidarity, partly because he believed that William's title to Orange was guaranteed by the Treaty of Nijmegen. Louis' secretary of state, Croissy, argued that the matter was none of James's business. Barrillon advised him not to ask something which Louis would have to refuse and complained of the forthright tone of Trumbull's representations. Sunderland, however, assured Trumbull that James fully approved of his conduct. Despite two outright refusals from Louis, James twice renewed his orders to Trumbull to press Louis to recognize William's rights.[26]

James thus persisted in seeking redress for William despite Louis' obvious irritation. He kept William fully informed of his negotiations and sought his advice. Barrillon claimed that James did not really care whether his representations succeeded, but his claim is not borne out by Sunderland's letters to Trumbull. At first, William was satisfied with James's efforts.[27] Then at the start of February 1686 William's tone changed. According to Burnet, James wrote to Mary "that he could do no more in that matter unless he should declare war upon it; which he could not think fit for a matter of so small importance." The latter phrase may have been an addition of Burnet's, but the remark about not making war was attributed at the time to both James and Sunderland. Sunderland himself wrote to William on 26th January, enclosing one of his letters to Trumbull, with the remark: "This the King commanded me to write as being fit, though he does not expect much from it." This might be realistic, but it was not tactful. William was furious. He could not agree, he wrote, that there was no more James could do. If James was so half-hearted, William wished he had never intervened at all. Surely he could have shown his resentment more forcefully and not allowed his nephew to be humiliated in the face of all Europe. For almost a year William had done all he could to convince James of his good intentions. Now he had asked James for help in a matter which touched him deeply and James had failed him. Worse, James had (as Mary said later) "preferred to join with the King of France against my husband". William's resentment of James's conduct on this occasion laid the foundation of suspicion of a secret liaison between James and Louis on which a whole crazy edifice of falsehoods and half truths was to be erected.[28]

The seed of suspicion sown in William's mind was soon nourished by events. At the end of 1685 a French special envoy, Usson de Bonrepaus, came to England for secret negotiations which were designed to end the sporadic hostilities between English and French settlers in North America. The Spaniards and Dutch did not know the purpose of Bonrepaus' visit and assumed that he was arranging a secret alliance between James and Louis to renew the war in Europe. Such allegations were the more easily believed because William and his henchmen were already giving out that Louis planned to renew the war that spring. Their claims were given credence by Louis' increased naval armament in the spring of 1686 and by an incident between Dutch and French ships off Cadiz, which caused a brief panic in Holland.[29]

Unlike William, James was quite convinced that Louis did not want war and that he lacked the resources to fight a war on the scale of that of 1672–78. He stressed especially that the exodus of Huguenots had left Louis very short of seamen. In this he was quite correct and in general he seems to have been well informed about the workings of the French court. Quite where he got his information is uncertain: it certainly did not come from his ambassadors in Paris.[30] James therefore saw little danger of Louis' upsetting the peace of Europe. Moreover, he came to identify his interests more and more closely with Louis', for two main reasons. First, Sunderland and the court Catholics argued that William and the Dutch would strive to frustrate his plans for the Catholics and that the success of those plans depended on a good understanding with Louis. Barrillon naturally supported such arguments, hoping to detach James from his embryonic liaison with the Dutch. He also passed on Louis' argument that both James's subjects and his neighbours would treat him with more respect if they believed he enjoyed a close understanding with France. Some of the Catholics, meanwhile, persuaded James to sound Bonrepaus about the possibility of military aid from France in an emergency.[31] Sunderland, for his part, was wholly committed to closer ties with France, partly because Rochester advised James to maintain good relations with the Dutch and partly because Sunderland had solicited a pension from the French.

The second reason why James now identified his interests more closely with Louis' was the result of a change in the European situation. William was slowly building up a network of alliances with Protestant powers, notably Brandenburg and Sweden. Meanwhile, a number of German princes banded together in the League of Augsburg to resist possible French aggression. Louis was concerned about these developments, especially in view of the Emperor's successes against the Turks. He stepped up the fortification of the eastern frontier, which confirmed his enemies' fears of his aggressive intentions. James was also worried, but for different reasons. As early as October 1685 he expressed fears of a Protestant league against England and France, masterminded by William and supported by Spain and Austria. His anxieties revived in 1686, especially as Louis assured him that William was bent on war. They were strengthened in 1687–88 by events and by Albeville's dispatches.[32]

If James identified his interests more closely with those of France, that does not mean that he slavishly followed Louis' wishes. He was at times highly critical of Louis' behaviour towards the Huguenots and the Pope: once he called him a bigot; on another occasion he said that too much adulation had made Louis forget the humility required of a Christian prince.[33] James's main priority in foreign policy was simply to avoid war. If a major war erupted, James would probably be drawn in. He would then have to call a Parliament to get the necessary money and Parliament might well grant it only on condition that he abandoned his plans to help the Catholics. Once James became convinced that William wanted war and that Louis could not or would not start a war, it was logical for him to co-operate with Louis in preserving the peace. Thus in Louis' disputes with Spain in 1686, James advised the Spaniards to concede what Louis demanded since they lacked the power to resist him. After the brush between the Dutch and French fleets, James hesitated to condemn the French, while his ministers told Citters that the States General would be wise to treat James as civilly as Louis did.[34]

Such remarks aroused suspicions which were greatly increased in July, when Citters wrote that James was fitting out a great fleet and that he and Louis would attack the Dutch the next spring. He alleged that James's courtiers (especially the Catholics) blamed the Dutch and the "rebels" whom they protected for obstructing James's designs. Although James assured him that he had no intention of making war, Citters reported that the French party and the Catholics pressed him to do so and on 6th August he sent over a document which was said to contain their arguments. This "Remonstrance" argued that

James should attack the Dutch now, while the Emperor was busy with the Turks. It alleged that James had both the right and the duty to alter the succession in favour of a Catholic and that, in order to secure French aid, James should (if need be) become Louis' vassal.[35]

James indignantly dismissed this "Remonstrance" as a ridiculous and malicious forgery, but Citters insisted that he had received it from someone highly placed at court and Barrillon admitted that it corresponded to what many Catholics were saying. Although it might seem incredible to expect the proud James to declare himself Louis' vassal, there were people at court who were foolish enough to believe almost anything. If it was a forgery, it was both clever and well informed. Moreover, for practical purposes its authenticity mattered far less than its impact in Holland. There it was accepted as genuine and printed under the title "Remonstrance to the King of England from his Privy Council". All James's angry disclaimers and solemn oaths could do little to remove the bad impression which the "Remonstrance" created, especially as James thought it beneath his dignity to issue an official disavowal. Indeed, Barrillon reported that James's reaction to the furore was somewhat ambivalent. On one hand, he disliked being misrepresented and feared that the States General really believed that he planned to attack them. On the other hand, he found the fear which the Dutch showed highly gratifying and hoped that fear would make them more co-operative. Although earlier his naval preparations had been much less extensive than Citters had claimed, James now decided to impress both his subjects and other powers by strengthening his fleet, which could prevent other states from interfering in English affairs. Rochester arranged a special loan of £400,000 for the purpose, the news of which revived the Dutch fears of a war the following spring.[36]

As 1686 neared its end, the political position in the Dutch republic seemed little changed. Amsterdam opposed William as steadfastly as ever and the States General were still unprepared for war. As Skelton remarked in October:

"The whole state seems to be in lethargy, for in the year and half that I have lived amongst them the States have not taken any one resolution. . . . They are in a great arrear to their army, their navy is rotting, their shipping being in so ill a condition that to build new ones the charge would not be much greater than to repair the old and all their magazines empty without any care being taken to recruit them."[37]

But beneath the surface were strong tensions and anxieties which had not been present eighteen months before. Amsterdam still opposed any enlargement of the army but its confidence in Louis had been badly shaken by the persecution of the Huguenots and by rumours of an Anglo-French attack on Dutch trade. Others less deeply hostile to William were becoming afraid that Louis would attack the republic and that James would join with him. They were worried, too, about the measures which James might take at home to propagate Catholicism.

William exploited such fears to the full. D'Avaux stressed that William and his supporters made all the political capital they could out of every rumour.

of war and claimed that often such rumours were started deliberately. He may well have been right. Only too aware of the republic's military and naval weakness, William spared no effort to persuade the States General and States of Holland to increase the military and naval budget. By the end of the year there were signs that the fleet would be increased at last. If the measures William used were often unscrupulous or dishonest, he believed that they were justified by the patriotism of his aims. To his long-held belief that Louis was planning another great assault on the republic were added new fears that James was allied to Louis and planned to impose Catholicism on England. Both these fears owed much to misinformation. Citters was simply erratic while others consistently misrepresented James, out of ignorance or malice. These included the exiles (notably Burnet) and many of William's contacts in England (like Lord Mordaunt). Such people gave not only William but many influential men in the republic a thoroughly distorted picture of what was happening in England and of James's intentions.[38]

* * *

William's anxieties were to be increased by events in England in the winter of 1686–87. Tyrconnell returned from Ireland in August, determined to have Clarendon dismissed from his post of lord lieutenant. He soon succeeded but it was not until December that James finally agreed to make Tyrconnell lord deputy in Clarendon's place.[39] His brother Rochester was harder to dislodge. His enemies told James incessantly that he could hope for nothing from Parliament while the court was divided and that Rochester's machinations were the cause of all James's difficulties. James, however, still hoped to persuade Rochester to fall in wholeheartedly with his plans. He gave him a chance to show his commitment to James's interests by declaring himself a Catholic (on the understanding that he would be dismissed if he refused). Sunderland and the Catholics were reluctant to give Rochester this chance to wriggle off the hook but James was sure that Rochester was honest enough not to feign conversion in order to keep his job. He was proved right. Rochester agreed to confer with Catholic priests and even paid court to Petre. James was kindness itself and the Catholics had to nag him ceaselessly to keep him from weakening. The climax came on 19th December. James told Rochester that no man should be at the head of his affairs who did not share his own opinions. He remarked that Rochester had advised against his going openly to Mass and employing Catholics, both of which had proved very much for his service. "Kings", he said, "were to look to the general good of their affairs and were not to have the natural affections which other men might." Dismissing him was thus a painful but unavoidable duty. Rochester did all he could to cling to office, but to no avail. On the 27th James decided that Rochester had to go and that the treasury should be administered by a commission.[40]

The hounding of Rochester and Clarendon out of office was part of a new and more vigorous phase in the campaign to secure the repeal of the penal laws and Test Acts. From November 1685 to October 1686 James did little to test or influence the opinions of the Parliament elected in 1685. In October 1686, however, James prorogued Parliament for four more months and told D'Adda that he intended to remove all those in the court, army and administration on whom he could not rely. Scores of "disaffected" JPs were dismissed and almost two-thirds of those who replaced them were Catholics. Sunderland declared that Parliament would do as James wished, provided the court was purged of all who were afraid of prejudicing themselves in the eyes of William and Mary —in other words, Rochester and the Tories. In December James began to question members of both Houses in his closet about their views, while the judges or trusted magnates sounded those who remained in the country.[41] Some asked time to consider, others argued that it was unconstitutional to ask them to commit themselves before they had heard the debates in Parliament, others said that their consciences would not let them support the repeal of the penal laws or Test Acts. James reacted to such answers with impatience and irritation. He claimed that the issue had been fully discussed already and that conscience did not come into it: he was not trying to force them to betray their principles, but merely finding out where they stood. James may have believed this, but in practice he subjected those he "closeted" to severe psychological pressure. Some found it hard to give an outright refusal (especially if they had recently received favours from the King), while others feared to lose their jobs, for they knew James was dismissing all who refused. James paid little heed to such considerations. He believed the penal laws and Test Acts were abominations, affronts to the monarchy which flouted the laws of God and nature. Those who wished to maintain such unjust laws must (he reasoned) be disaffected to his government and so deserved to lose their places. As his ends were so unimpeachable, the means he used were (to him) of only incidental importance.[42]

For James, the closeting campaign and the dismissal of those who refused to comply were to pave the way for a meeting of Parliament. For Sunderland and the Catholics, their main purpose was to drive Rochester and his followers out of office and make room for the employment of more Catholics. Sunderland was therefore far less upset than James at the campaign's lack of success. In mid-February James prorogued Parliament until April and began to offer bribes, which he had earlier refused to consider. Sunderland told Barrillon that this Parliament would never do as James wished, but that he could not advise James not to call it as he had assured him that all would go well once Rochester had been removed. In March James admitted defeat when Arthur Herbert, an old servant who was totally dependent on him, refused to do as he wished. On the 18th he prorogued Parliament until November. The closeting campaign continued into the summer, mainly to push more Tories out of office, but James had given up hope of getting what he wanted from the Anglicans. After months of hesitation, he decided to commit himself to an appeal to the Dissenters.[43]

James had already dispensed many individuals, Catholics and Dissenters, from the penalties imposed by the laws, but this was a cumbersome procedure, especially for the penal laws, as so many people were involved. It took time and a great deal of paperwork and the beneficiaries had to pay fees to those who wrote out the necessary documents. Moreover, some magistrates questioned the validity of the liberty thus granted. If non-Anglicans were to be wholly free to worship and hold office, the laws had to be abrogated or at least suspended. James does not seem to have asked the judges whether he possessed a power to suspend laws. He may have feared that their ruling would be unfavourable, but it seems more likely that he saw no need to consult them. As he saw it, if he could dispense individuals from the penalties of the laws, surely he could do the same for the entire population. He clearly saw his grant of toleration as resting on the dispensing power, whose legality had already been established by the courts. Barrillon gave no hint that he thought that, in issuing his toleration, James was claiming any extension to his authority. When the legality of the toleration was challenged in 1688, it was the use of the dispensing power which was questioned. The term "suspending power" was not used.* The Declaration of Indulgence of April 1687 was in fact vague about the authority by which it was issued. It stated that the execution of the penal laws was to be suspended and that it was against the law of nature for a king to be deprived of the service of any of his subjects. Therefore the King commanded that the oaths and test were not to be tendered to those admitted to office and that all those so admitted were to be granted dispensations.[44]

It seems, then, that James and the drafters of his declaration saw no real difference between the dispensing power and what was later called the "suspending power". Nevertheless, the two powers differed significantly in two ways. First, the purpose of the dispensing power was not to abrogate a law, but to temper justice with mercy where particular circumstances merited it. The proper way to abrogate a law was by Act of Parliament. Secondly, the use of the prerogative to suspend penal laws in religious matters had already twice been declared illegal by the Commons, in 1663 and 1673. Although a resolution of the Commons had no legal force, Charles had tacitly conceded the validity of the Commons' case in 1673 by cancelling his declaration. James's use of the dispensing power was clearly within the letter of the law, if not according to its spirit. The technical validity of the suspending power was more arguable and perhaps a case could be made for it, but there was no doubt that James used it in a manner quite contrary to the principles and spirit of English law.[45]

On 18th March James proclaimed his intention to grant a general liberty of conscience. He stressed that past attempts to enforce uniformity had failed and had divided the nation "as was sadly experienced by the horrid rebellion in the time of His Majesty's royal father"—a remarkable reversal of James's previous view of the causes of the civil wars, but one of which he made some play at this time. Liberty of conscience, the proclamation continued, bred peace and harmony, encouraged the immigration of economically useful citizens and so

---

* He told the Seven Bishops that he did not claim a power to suspend laws and that the indulgence rested on his dispensing power. BL, Egerton MS 2543, f 270.

stimulated trade and industry. These themes mostly reappeared in the De-claration of Indulgence, published on 4th April after consultation with leading Dissenters. Penn was said to have had a large part in drafting it and certainly it reflected his views. James now believed that the English wanted nothing more than toleration and that the Anglicans who opposed it were an unrepresentative minority. Once its benefits became apparent, he believed, Parliament would willingly make it permanent. Meanwhile, he exulted in the liberty which he had granted to the Catholics and was sure that many would now feel free to announce their conversion. He told D'Adda that he would continue on his chosen course without the slightest anxiety, leaving the rest to God. Whether or not his confidence was justified remained to be seen.[46]

CHAPTER TWELVE

The King and the Dissenters (April 1687 to June 1688)

Once James had chosen to take his stand on a general toleration, the tone and content of his government changed markedly. Hitherto he had put his trust in the Anglican clergy and Tory peers and squires whose strength lay mainly in the countryside, and so had upheld the landed interest. In 1685 he had stressed that he wanted the new taxes voted by Parliament to be placed on trade and not on land. The main strength of the Dissenters lay in the towns. They were concerned with trade and industry rather than agriculture. So, in 1687, besides stressing the natural equity of liberty of conscience, James also stressed its beneficial effects on trade. He began to advocate measures favoured by the advanced economic thinkers of the day, which might be expected to appeal particularly to the urban trading interest. He announced his support for a general naturalization of immigrants, in order to attract skilled craftsmen from abroad; as most religious refugees at this time were Calvinists, an influx of such immigrants would be especially unwelcome to the stricter Anglicans. He proposed a general land register, which would make land sales simpler and surer and reduce the lawyers' opportunities to make unnecessary profits. Such a register had been proposed in Parliament in 1685, but had received little support. James suggested improvements in the coinage: many coins were worn and clipped and so worth much less than their face value. The uncertainties which this created harmed both domestic and overseas trade, so James proposed that worn coins should be called in and reminted, a proposal eventually carried out under William III. James took steps to prevent the export of raw wool, which supplied England's competitors with a vital raw material, and forbade English mariners to serve on foreign ships. Finally, he proposed to abolish imprisonment for debt and to investigate the working of the system of poor relief.[1]

There is little evidence that James had advocated such measures before 1687, but he had been associated with people who had done so. These included William Penn, some of the Dissenters with whom James had worked in the mid-1670s and Thomas Sheridan, a servant of James's from about 1678.[2] Perhaps the most interesting figure to appear at court in the latter part of 1686 was the great economist and statistician, Sir William Petty. He had approached the court with some trepidation, but was pleasantly surprised to find James taking an interest in his disputes with foreign scholars and began to believe (like Penn) that he might persuade the King to adopt enlightened policies.

"I am starting the world again," he wrote, "and endeavour instead of quarrelling with the King's power to make him exert all he hath for the [use] of his subjects." At about this time he drew up a plan of economic reform which included a general toleration, a land register, a credit bank and a reform of the coinage, as well as other less feasible proposals like putting church property to more productive uses. Like Penn, Petty believed that the Catholic minority was too small to pose a threat to the Protestants and hoped therefore to make good use of James's unexpected conversion to a belief in toleration. Although there is no conclusive evidence that James was influenced by Petty, it is surely more than coincidence that James began to advocate, in 1687, measures which Petty had long supported. It is noteworthy, too, that after Petty's death, in 1688, James conferred a peerage on his widow which was to be inherited by their son.[3]

James's sudden commitment to progressive economic reforms might at first sight seem merely a propaganda exercise, but there was no inherent reason why James should have opposed such reforms, especially now that he no longer had any reason to protect the interests of Tory landowners. James had always taken a dilettante interest in trade and a more than dilettante interest in navigation. He was a substantial colonial proprietor and held shares in several trading companies: in 1687 he increased his holding of East India Company stock from £3,000 to £10,000. Moreover, his revenue depended in large measure on overseas trade so he had every reason to foster commercial expansion. For the same reason, he made it clear that he would maintain Ireland's "colonial" status and economic subordination to England.[4]

His concern for England's commercial interests can also be shown by his care to avoid concessions to the French. Bonrepaus was confident that James needed Louis' friendship so badly that he would have to concede whatever Louis demanded. In 1686–87, therefore, Bonrepaus pressed James to concede the claims of the French settlers around Hudson's Bay, to reduce the duties paid by French merchants in England and to allow them to trade as freely as Englishmen. But James and his ministers were adept at evasion and delay. Sometimes they contested the justice of the French demands, sometimes they agreed that the French had reason on their side, but argued that James dared not antagonize the English merchant community. After lengthy negotiations, the situation at Hudson's Bay and the position of French merchants in England remained as before, which (as Bonrepaus admitted) was to the advantage of the English. Annoyed by James's intransigence, Louis imposed fresh tariffs on English manufactures in 1688, which elicited further complaints from James. For domestic political reasons, James wished to retain Louis' friendship and so claimed that he was unable, rather than unwilling, to grant the concessions which Louis demanded. Such arguments were not, perhaps, very ingenuous, but James did manage to avoid sacrificing English commercial interests.[5]

Such measures to protect the trading interest followed logically from James's decision to abandon the Tories, whom he treated with greater and greater hostility. He expected that in time even the majority of Anglicans would come to appreciate the benefits of toleration, and was annoyed that so many of them refused to do so. The clergy greeted the indulgence with almost universal disapproval, although that disapproval took various forms. Some expressed pained resignation: "The concern that generally appears in good men's faces is ... the effect of pure grief, without any mixture of discontent. ... God grant we may all live up to our principles, both in doing and suffering." Others warned their congregations to prepare for bloody persecution and anti-Catholic preaching continued unabated.[6] Even passive acquiescence was not enough for James. Sunderland pressed the bishops to order their clergy to present an address thanking James for the indulgence. A few bishops responded eagerly, but most refused and so did the great majority of the lower clergy, who were supported in their refusal by the Anglican laity. A copy of the address was printed with various reasons against subscribing it, which reflected a suspicion that James might revoke the indulgence at any time. When the address was at last presented, James was far from satisfied, for it thanked him for his promises to uphold the rights of the Church and said nothing of the toleration for Dissenters.[7]

Such defiance made James increasingly vindictive towards the Church, which was seen most clearly in his treatment of the universities. By law, only those who took the oaths of allegiance and supremacy could matriculate, take degrees and hold college fellowships, which effectively excluded both Catholics and Dissenters. James regarded this Anglican monopoly of the universities as unjustifiable. Many colleges had been founded before the Reformation for the benefit of the Catholic Church and it seemed to James most improper that Catholics should not benefit from the endowments of their forefathers. The admission of Catholics to the universities thus seemed to James a matter of natural justice; it would also (he thought) hasten the triumph of Catholicism. The universities played a vital part in training the clergy and in forming the religious views of the sons of the nobility and gentry. If the Catholics could dispute freely there with Protestants, many would become convinced of the truth of the Catholics' arguments. James also believed that many dons and students were Catholics at heart and would declare themselves once they could do so without fear of the consequences. This belief received some support from a handful of conversions at Oxford in 1685–86.[8]

At first James merely dispensed dons or undergraduates from taking the oaths or attending prayers so that they could remain at the university despite becoming Catholics. In the summer of 1686, when the Dean of Christ Church died, James hesitated to put a Catholic in his place. By October he had overcome his hesitation. He appointed John Massey and dispensed him from performing the religious duties normally required of the dean. Massey may not have been a declared Catholic when he was appointed, but he was certainly regarded as a Catholic by early 1687. The same was true of Robert Charnock admitted, at James's command, to a fellowship at Magdalen College, Oxford, at the same time. Three months later James ordered the fellows of Sidney Sussex College, Cambridge, to admit another convert, Joshua Bassett, as their master, without tendering him the oaths. Sidney Sussex was an Elizabethan foundation and its statutes laid down that no Catholic should be admitted to the college. The fellows pointed out that it would be against their statutes to admit Bassett, but backed down when James insisted.[9]

Late in March 1687 news came of the death of the President of Magdalen, the richest college in Oxford. On 5th April James sent the fellows a *mandamus* to elect one Anthony Farmer as their new president. The sending of a royal order to elect particular men as fellows or heads of houses was a common practice, but Farmer was a very poor choice. Magdalen's statutes laid down that no one should be elected president unless he had held a fellowship there or at New College and Farmer had not. Moreover, his personal reputation was such that even the ecclesiastical commissioners described him as "a very bad man". Finally, although he had not declared himself a Catholic, it was believed that he was no longer an Anglican. The fellows informed the King of these objections, but James replied that he expected to be obeyed. On 15th April the fellows elected John Hough as their president and quickly admitted him to his office before an order not to do so arrived from Sunderland. They claimed that as the person named by the King was ineligible, they were entitled to elect someone else. They justified their haste by alleging that the time allowed for the election under the statutes had almost expired.[10]

Their arguments did not convince James or the ecclesiastical commission, which declared Hough's election void. The commission accepted that Farmer was ineligible, however, so James sent another *mandamus* to elect Samuel Parker, Bishop of Oxford. The fellows insisted that Hough's election was in accordance with their statutes and should therefore stand. They even defied James to his face when he came to Oxford in September, rendering him almost incoherent with rage:

"You have not dealt with me like gentlemen. You have done very uncivilly and undutifully. . . . Is this your Church of England loyalty? . . . Go home and show yourselves good members of the Church of England. Get you gone, know I am your king. I will be obeyed and I command you to be gone. Go and admit the Bishop of Oxford head, principal, what do you call it of the college, I mean president of the college. Let them that refuse it look to it; they shall feel the weight of their sovereign's displeasure."

Next day, he was calmer, exhorting the Oxonians to "love one another and practise charity: do as you would be done to, for that is the law and the prophets." He complained that some dons had charged his religion with idolatry, which he took as a personal insult, adding that he believed he had "no enemy . . . but among those who call themselves Church of England men". As the fellows remained obstinate, the ecclesiastical commission at length had Parker installed as president and some Catholics admitted as fellows, while most of the original fellows were deprived of their fellowships.[11]

It is easy to see why James was so annoyed by the fellows' conduct and especially by their pleas that their statutes obliged them to allow no dispensations from any authority. To James this was both disingenuous and bad law. It was disingenuous because their motives were less attachment to their statutes than dislike of James's religion: they had been quite ready to admit royal dispensations in the past when it suited them to do so. It was bad law to set local and particular statutes against the law of the land under which (as the judges had declared) the crown certainly possessed a dispensing power, a power which, moreover, it had exercised many times in the past. The fellows' refusal to admit Parker and to ask pardon thus seemed, to James, insolently and ostentatiously defiant.[12] But in his anger he stretched his authority, as delegated to the ecclesiastical commission, to unprecedented limits. Hitherto, ecclesiastics found guilty of misconduct had been suspended, but the commission not only deprived the fellows of Magdalen of their fellowships but declared them ineligible to hold any benefice in the Church. The moderate Catholics at court opposed this severity and so did Jeffreys and some of the other commissioners, but Petre, Sunderland and the other hardliners got their way.[13]

Although one could make a reasonable case for James's right to nominate heads of houses and dispense with college statutes, it would be much harder to justify the punishments which the commissioners imposed. In the last analysis, however, the issues raised by the affair were more political than legal. What mattered to James's Protestant subjects was less the legality of the powers which he claimed than the uses to which those powers were put. The Magdalen College affair offered stark proof of James's ill will towards the Church and strengthened the prevailing fears that he would fill the universities and even ecclesiastical benefices with Catholics. Already there were rumours that the vacant archbishopric of York was destined for Petre and that James had tried to admit two Catholic priests to livings in the diocese of Worcester. Moreover, James seemed (for the first time) to have used his prerogative to deprive subjects of their property, for the tenure of church benefices and college fellowships was seen as tantamount to freehold. Politically, then, the measures against the fellows of Magdalen were a serious mistake. Penn realized this and tried to mediate between the King and the fellows, but James was too angry and believed, as always, that it would be fatal to back down. By his rigidity and vindictiveness, he put himself in the wrong and completed the alienation of the Anglicans.[14]

With the Anglicans turning against him, it was vital that the indulgence should win the Dissenters' support, but the Dissenters were far from united and different sects and individuals reacted in different ways. The Presbyterians were the most numerous and wealthy but they too were divided. Traditionally they believed in a uniform national church, but exclusion from the narrowly Anglican Church re-established in 1662 forced them to rethink their position. Some pressed the Anglicans to modify their liturgy and requirements for ordination so that Presbyterians could become members of a broader, more comprehensive Church of England. Others, less willing to compromise, accepted sectarian status and demanded toleration, to be allowed to worship unmolested in their own way. This latter group was the more willing to take advantage of the indulgence and some London ministers organized an address thanking James for his declaration. Others, however, were on good terms with the Low

Churchmen among the Anglican clergy of the capital, who shared their desire for a more comprehensive church. They argued that the indulgence was of little use to them as they were prepared to attend Anglican services (provided, presumably, that those services were conducted by Low Churchmen). Despite pressure from their congregations, such moderate Presbyterians hesitated to hold meetings at the same time as Anglican services and complained at the toleration of the more radical sects, whom they regarded as dangerous heretics.[15]

The smaller sects (Independents, Baptists, Quakers) accepted the indulgence more eagerly and produced most of the early addresses thanking James for the declaration. But, as the Presbyterian Roger Morrice remarked, "It cannot be believed that, though these addresses give thanks for their liberty, that they will ever do anything to the establishing of Popery." Morrice's distrust of James's motives was shared by many other Dissenters. Although many took advantage of this unexpected liberty, their doing so did not imply any willingness to remove the penal laws, still less the Test Acts. James, however, argued that the liberty could not be secure while those laws remained on the statute book. His arguments were echoed in dozens of pamphlets, of which those by Penn were among the ablest. James also wished to show that "the generality of the nation" were "satisfied with" the indulgence and "at ease by it".[16] To this end, he had all the addresses he received printed in the *Gazette*, together with his replies. Moreover, he was careful to ensure that he received plenty of addresses and that they were couched in fulsome terms. As the supply of spontaneous addresses dried up, pressure was applied to the Dissenters as well as the Anglicans. In many counties Catholic sheriffs and gentlemen promoted addresses which were sent to London in the name of the grand jury or of the county as a whole. Jeffreys drew up an address from the City of London and pressed the Lord Mayor and aldermen to sign it. At Norwich Lord Yarmouth, a convert to Catholicism, told the Bishop, Mayor and aldermen that James would be deeply offended if they failed to address. The pressure continued into 1688: in May of that year, a particularly outspoken address from Carlisle (which described the penal laws and Test Acts as the laws of cannibals) was said to have been obtained by quartering dragoons on the town.[17]

It seems clear that the addresses which trickled in did not reflect the nation's reaction to the indulgence. Some Anglican clergymen reported that it had had no effect on the size of their congregations; elsewhere the fall in church attendance was perceptible but not disastrous. James, however, was now firmly convinced that the Church of England had survived only through persecution and that the Dissenters would therefore welcome the indulgence and be glad to make it permanent by repealing the penal laws and Test Acts. This conviction was confirmed by the addresses he received, even though he must have known that some were far from spontaneous and even though many carefully avoided any endorsement of the dispensing power or commitment to repeal the penal laws and Test Acts. Most of James's subjects were so afraid of his Catholicism that they paid little heed to the addresses, but James was so eager to believe that the Dissenters welcomed the indulgence that he was one of the few who was influenced by his own propaganda.[18]

His conviction that the Dissenters had welcomed his declaration was strengthened during his tour of the West Midlands in 1687. He left the Queen at Bath to take the waters, travelled northwards to Chester, returning to Bath on 6th September after a detour to berate the fellows of Magdalen. The aim of his journey was both to test and to influence opinion and to promote the repeal of the penal laws and Test Acts. He was generally satisfied with his reception. He told Barrillon that there had been rumours at Chester that he would force everyone to go to Mass and that people had been surprised that he allowed everyone to worship in his own way. He found that many were surprised that a Catholic king looked like a normal human being, having been led to believe that he was some kind of monster. Others thought, however, that the welcome which James had received was misleading. His servants had taken care to order the nobility and gentry to wait upon him as he passed, so many had appeared more out of duty than enthusiasm. There were also some untoward incidents: at Shrewsbury Penn was howled down when he tried to preach. Barrillon concluded: "Little reliance can be placed upon the external respect shown to the King should the question arise of taking measures which people believe will benefit the Catholics."[19]

Nevertheless, James was sufficiently heartened by his reception to begin preparing for a new Parliament. He had dissolved the old one in July, convinced at last that it would give him no satisfaction. The moderate Catholics had tried to dissuade him from so irrevocable a step, but the zealots had played on James's religious enthusiasm and had won the day. Sunderland was worried by James's decision. The Anglicans, he told D'Adda, had always supported the monarchy and the Dissenters had always opposed it. Moreover, the Dissenters hated the Catholics as much as the Anglicans did, and Sunderland feared that the army might prove unreliable in a crisis.[20]

It was the first time that Sunderland had expressed anxiety about the outcome of James's policies, but if he was sufficiently perceptive to worry about the future, most of James's other advisers were not and for this Sunderland himself was largely to blame. In his struggle against Rochester and his followers, he had driven many of the Protestant nobility away from court. When Trumbull, newly returned from Paris, attended James's *lever*, he was shocked to find him "in his nightgown at the fireside with a company of Irish and unknown faces, so that the only person in the room I had ever seen was my old Lord Craven." The closeting campaign had removed some of the Protestant office holders at court (Lords Maynard and Newport, for example), leaving only James's old servants (Dartmouth, Feversham, Churchill, Mulgrave) and largely apolitical civil servants (Godolphin, Pepys, Ernle) who got on with their jobs and did not try to advise the King on matters of policy. Others simply stayed away from court. Ormond, still lord steward, was old, tired and disillusioned. Early in 1687 he withdrew to the country, remarking sadly, "I had rather live and die in Carolina than in Ireland." Some Tory privy councillors attended council meetings rarely or never in 1687–88. These included not only those who had lost their offices, like Rochester and Clarendon, but magnates with great territorial influence: the Duke of Beaufort, who dominated South Wales and the Southern Marches, the Duke of Newcastle, with vast estates in the North Midlands, the Earls of Bath and Lindsey, who wielded great local power in the South-west and Lincolnshire. All these men had rallied to James's cause in 1679–80 and all continued to serve him in their regions, but with decreasing enthusiasm and conviction. The absence of such men from the council left a majority of either compliant Protestants or Catholics. In the more informal consultations where the major decisions were made, the dominance of the Catholics was greater still. Some Catholics, it is true, like Bellasis or Powis, urged James not to proceed too far or too fast, fearing reprisals when William became king. But their advice was all too often ignored and James placed more reliance on Petre, Melfort and the extremists.[21]

The Catholic extremists' dominance at court had serious consequences. The court was the nerve centre of the government, where all major decisions were made. It was also a major political "point of contact", where the King could win the support and seek the advice of his most powerful subjects. The peers at court were a valuable link between centre and provinces. Local officials asked trusted magnates to put their suggestions and grievances to the King, who could also obtain valuable information from those magnates about political opinion and administrative problems in the localities. By driving such men from court, James made it harder to persuade them to use their territorial influence as he wished and deprived himself of vital political information. As Bonrepaus remarked in 1688: "The English court is very badly informed of what is happening abroad and is even ignorant of most of what happens in London and the provinces."[22] Moreover, even when James *did* receive reasonably accurate information of the hostility to his measures among his Protestant subjects, he chose not to believe it. Instead, he accepted the Catholic zealots' argument that such manifestations of hostility were either atypical or could be overcome if he showed sufficient firmness. Convinced by his own defective reasoning that the Dissenters ought to support his measures enthusiastically, James clutched at any evidence, however flimsy, which supported this conviction while dismissing any evidence, however substantial, which contradicted it.

Sunderland, alone among those James trusted, was acute enough to perceive this, but Sunderland was trapped by the means he had used to clamber to power. He had argued, in opposition to Rochester, that it was perfectly possible to secure the benefits which James wanted for the Catholics, provided the right measures were taken. He could not now tell James that such measures were bound to fail. He had built up the influence of Petre and the Catholic zealots and used them to drive Rochester out and gain supreme power at court. Now he found that he could no longer control them. They still advocated the policies which Sunderland had advocated in 1685–86 and were now powerful enough to drive him out of office if he changed his tune. Sunderland, therefore, had to continue along the path which he had laid down, even though he was increasingly convinced that it could lead only to disaster. He could not tell James that his cherished plans were impracticable, but missed no chance to press James to modify those plans and seized almost desperately on every pretext for delay. The strain under which he worked played havoc with his nerves. He became irascible and moody, with bouts of lunatic optimism and black despair.²³ The struggle to make James see reason was long and never hopeless. Sunderland had powerful allies in Penn and the moderate Catholics, men whom James trusted. In the last resort, however, James followed the advice of the extremists because he *wanted* to believe that their assurances of success were justified. He was not deprived of better advice but chose to disregard it.

*   *   *

While James was comprehensively alienating his Anglican subjects, his relations with William went from bad to worse. Hitherto they had disagreed mainly on affairs connected with the Dutch republic (the "rebels" and the British regiments) or with their respective relations with Louis. William had been careful to avoid any appearance of interfering in England's internal affairs. From the end of 1686, however, he was drawn into English politics for two main reasons. First, James tried to persuade him to support the repeal of the penal laws and Test Acts. In November 1686 he sent Penn to say that, if William gave satisfaction on this, James would enter into the closest understanding with him, at home and abroad. William replied that he disliked religious persecution but thought the Test Acts an essential safeguard for the Protestant religion, which no promises of James's could replace. When Dijkveld was sent to England by the States of Holland early in 1687, James tried to convince him that the removal of the Test Acts would be of great advantage to William and Mary and to the monarchy. He argued that the Catholics were the most loyal of subjects, that the Test contained statements disliked by many Protestants and that nobody could be a good subject if he could declare his king's religion idolatrous. Albeville used similar arguments at the Hague, but William insisted that he was prepared to allow Catholics to worship unmolested but not to admit them to public offices.²⁴

The second reason for William's intervening in English affairs was his growing fear that Mary's claim to the throne might be threatened, in one of two ways. First, there were rumours that James would be persuaded to disinherit Mary in favour of a Catholic. William could not tackle James directly about this, but James knew of the rumours, was very offended by them and gave William every assurance that they were quite unfounded.²⁵ Secondly, William feared that James's measures might provoke a rebellion which, like that of the 1640s, could lead to the establishment of a republic. Like all the Stuarts, William greatly exaggerated the strength of English republicanism and believed that the radicals who had fled to Holland were much more typical of English opinion than they really were. William tried, through Albeville, to warn James of the dangers that faced him. He told Albeville:

"that the Roman religion could not become dominant without the King's breaking the laws and his own promises and without (he feared) one day causing disorders which would imperil the monarchy; . . . that it would be better to assure the Catholics of a reasonable liberty, for the present and the future, than to expose them to persecution and perhaps to extirpation; as for himself . . . he would maintain the Catholics in an honest liberty, as they have in this country, but he could never agree or consent to allow them to become dominant."[26]

James reacted to such advice with a mixture of bewilderment and irritation. He argued that measures like the repeal of the Test Acts would strengthen the monarchy and that it was therefore in William's interest to support them. He was amazed that William criticized his using the term "absolute power" in his Scottish declaration of indulgence. He wrote to Albeville:

"Is it credible that the prince who, according to all appearances, will succeed me, can find fault with the words 'absolute power'? For they cannot be taken to mean either the usurping of my subjects' property or constraining anybody in matters of religion. For the first, nobody can accuse me of ever having done it and for the second, everyone can see . . . that it is not my intention. . . . And whoever God pleases to have to succeed me, he would be very mistaken if he did not follow the path which I have traced for the security and strengthening of the monarchy and for the greatness of the nation."*

He ascribed William's hostility to his measures to William's Protestantism and to Temple and Sidney's having given him a false picture of English affairs, aided and abetted by other English malcontents and by Citters. As William remained deaf to his arguments, James proclaimed angrily that he was the head of the family and expected to be obeyed. He was angry, too, that Dijkveld complained that the priests had too much power at court. Before Dijkveld returned to Holland, James ran through every possible argument for the repeal of the Test Acts and asked him to relay them to William. When William was still unimpressed, James complained of his refusal to take off laws which were "so very severe and hard upon all dissenters from the Church of England". His letters to William thereafter were brief and inconsequential.[27]

William's intervention in English affairs was not restricted to attempts to persuade James to change his policies. Dijkveld was also ordered to encourage the moderates at court and to assure all kinds of Protestants of William's steadfastness in his religion and of his good intentions towards them. The moderate Catholics had already let William know, through Penn, that they were pressing James to remain on good terms with him. Dijkveld made what use he could of Powis, Bellasis and their followers, but (as Barrillon remarked) these were not

---

* This is one of the few occasions after the first weeks of his reign when James said that he wished to *increase*, and not just *maintain*, the powers of the monarchy. In most cases where he did so, he was trying (as here) to play on William's authoritarianism, hoping thus to persuade William to support his policies. For another example, see Bonrepaus to Seignelay, 21st June, 1687, BT 170.

the men in most favour with James.[28] Dijkveld was more successful in his efforts to reassure the Protestants. Some Dissenters had feared that William would throw in his lot with the Anglicans and were relieved to hear that he would allow them freedom of worship. Anglican politicians were encouraged by news of William's steadfast opposition to the repeal of the Test Acts to resist James's pressure more forthrightly. Some, like Danby and Nottingham, began a correspondence with William, supplying him with news and opinions and, in time, acting as his agents within England. These contacts were extended some months later when William sent his cousin Zuylestein, ostensibly to offer condolences on the death of the Duchess of Modena, but also to find out whether Parliament was likely to meet. In November Bentinck received the first of a series of well-informed newsletters about events at court, which formed a most valuable supplement to Citters' dispatches. Meanwhile, a number of Englishmen, including Mordaunt and Sidney, visited William in Holland.[29]

James was quick to note that Dijkveld entertained a great deal and seemed fondest of those of whom the court disapproved. By May, James's advisers blamed Dijkveld for the failure of the closeting campaign. But despite such evidence of William's interference in English affairs, James did not give up hope of persuading him to change his mind. He sent Albeville a letter, which he read separately to William and Mary, urging them to support the repeal of the Test Acts. In November he sent Mary a long letter setting out his reasons for becoming a Catholic, and Albeville tried hard to convert her. Mary played him along for a while before declaring herself unconvinced by his arguments. Meanwhile, James tried a more indirect approach. A Scots Presbyterian lawyer called James Stewart struck up a correspondence with one of his brethren in Holland and then with Fagel. He argued that there was no danger in the Dissenters' accepting liberty on James's terms and that William was being unreasonably suspicious in opposing the repeal of the Test Acts, since the Catholics were too few to be dangerous. He claimed, too, that James would break with France if William complied. Fagel drafted a reply which William approved and sent to Burnet to translate into English. It was eventually printed and distributed in England at the start of 1688. The *Letter* stated unequivocally that William and Mary were prepared to grant toleration to Catholics and Dissenters but not to repeal the Test Acts. It thus assured the Dissenters that they could continue to worship freely under James's successor, without paying the price which James demanded, the repeal of the Test Acts, with the risk which that involved of allowing Catholics into positions of power. Already many pamphlets were circulating (some printed in England, others imported from Holland) which urged the Dissenters not to trust James. Fagel's *Letter* was different in that it was an authoritative statement of William and Mary's views. It invalidated the central theme of James's campaign to woo the Dissenters, the argument that if they did not support his measures, they risked a renewed persecution in the future. It added greatly to the already considerable difficulties which James was meeting in his attempt to secure an amenable Parliament.[30]

*　　*　　*

James's electoral strategy contained two main elements. First, there was a sustained propaganda campaign, extolling the benefits of liberty of conscience and arguing the case for the repeal of the Test Acts. Secondly, the methods used to procure a Tory House of Commons in 1685 were used again, but this time to obtain a House that would repeal the penal laws and Test Acts. The closeting campaign was renewed, using three standard questions, and its scope was extended. Office holders were asked whether they would vote for repeal if they were elected to Parliament and whether they would vote for candidates pledged to do so. These questions were tendered not only to MPs and those holding offices at court, but also to JPs, deputy lieutenants and a wide range of minor officials, members of the London livery companies and all those holding offices in the corporations. In Lancashire the questions were tendered to all the gentry and the Lord Lieutenant (a Catholic) apparently planned to question all the freeholders, but here he was probably exceeding his instructions.[31] Those who answered equivocally or in the negative were to be dismissed and replaced by others more amenable.

About half the lords lieutenant refused to tender the questions to the gentry of their counties and were dismissed. The Earl of Northampton told the Warwickshire JPs that he himself would answer in the negative. The Earl of Abingdon told James that "all this noise of persecution was like shearing of hogs, a great cry for little wool" and that he saw the penal laws and Test Acts as the bulwarks of his religion. The majority of JPs showed a similar hostility to the questions. It is hard to give precise figures, since many answers were qualified or evasive. Of 1,311 JPs in 32 English counties, 217 were either absent or had no answer returned and 203 were Catholics put into commission since the autumn of 1686. Of the rest, 180 answered clearly in the affirmative and 104 answered "yes" with various qualifications (usually that the Test Act should be preserved or other provision made for the security of the Church of England). On the other hand, 375 answered firmly in the negative, 132 said they could give no answer until the matter had been debated in Parliament and 100 were evasive or doubtful.[32]

Recently John Carswell used an analysis of the returns to suggest that the response was much less unfavourable than used to be supposed and his opinion was echoed by Professor JR Jones.[33] However, Carswell's figures were occasionally inaccurate (he gave 23 JPs for Oxfordshire instead of 41) and failed to distinguish between Protestants and Catholics among those giving affirmative answers (adding, for good measure, those Catholics who did not answer at all). He then produced figures of 26.7% affirmative, 27.3% negative, 28% doubtful and 18% absent, which would suggest a fairly even division. However, if one deducts the Catholics, one finds only 16.3% of Protestant JPs answering definitely in the affirmative as against 33.8% who answered a definite "no". It would be reasonable, too, to assume that the majority of conditional answers were really negative (especially those who said that they would not support the Test Acts). Some, indeed, were not asked the questions because it was known that they would answer in the negative.[34] In other words, only a small minority of the existing Protestant JPs were prepared to commit themselves to support James's measures.

This response cannot have come as a great surprise to James, for the commissions of the peace were still predominantly Tory. Those whose answers were considered unsatisfactory were put out of commission and replaced with Dissenters, plus any Catholics of suitable standing who had not been put in already. Even after these changes, however, James could have had little hope of securing the election of his candidates in more than a few counties. The county electorates were too large to be bribed or intimidated, the franchise was fixed by law and the electoral influence of the Tory gentry and clergy was extremely strong. James's main efforts were therefore concentrated in the boroughs, which returned some three-quarters of the Commons. There too those who answered the three questions in the negative were put out of office. Some 3,500 men were put out of the London livery companies between September 1687 and February 1688. All those employed in the various branches of the royal administration were also tendered the questions, so that James could expect that those who depended on him for their livelihood would vote as he wished. In many corporations James already had the power to appoint and dismiss magistrates, under the charters issued in 1682–86. Where he lacked such a power, steps were taken to induce the corporations to surrender their charters and some thirty new charters were issued when, in August 1688, James at last decided to summon Parliament.[35]

The decision to concentrate on the towns seemed to make sound electoral sense. The electorate of the boroughs was much smaller than that of the counties and was often very small indeed: in some boroughs, only members of the corporation had the vote. The borough electorate was therefore easier to canvass, manipulate and intimidate and there were to be many complaints of force and fraud during James's electoral preparations. Moreover, the rulers of the towns were often Dissenters who resented the attempts of the neighbouring Tory gentry to interfere in municipal affairs. James thus offered them not only toleration but a chance to escape the tutelage of the local landed aristocracy. In this he used both the strategy and many of the agents of the Exclusionists, including former followers of Monmouth. Such men were experienced electoral organizers and propagandists and, as Dissenters themselves, were more acceptable to the urban rulers than Catholics or Anglicans would have been. Anglican gentlemen might resent being pestered by such men and regard their conduct as ill bred. They seem, however, to have done their job diligently, disseminating James's propaganda, canvassing electors and candidates and reporting at length to their masters in London.[36]

Quite who these masters were is not always clear. From October 1687 there was a committee of the privy council responsible for regulating corporations and this committee (or the whole council) drew up lists of those to be put into or out of corporations. It seems clear, however, that the council merely ratified decisions reached elsewhere, by two more informal committees. First, there was a "Catholic" committee (Jeffreys, Sunderland, Castlemaine,

Powis, Petre and Butler) which met at least as early as November 1687. The most active members were Jeffreys, Sunderland and Butler and they were helped by a Catholic lawyer named Robert Brent. Long associated with the treasury, Brent in 1686 had helped Catholics to procure dispensations. His ability and avarice were both considerable: he "thinks more of gain than of his majesty's service". It was alleged that, when some of the exiles in Holland wished to come to serve James, Brent demanded large sums of money in return for securing their pardons. His vices apart, Brent played a key role in gathering information from the King's agents in the constituencies and sending them the committee's orders. By February 1688 there were references to a second committee, consisting mainly of Dissenters, which also prepared nominations for the council committee. Here again, Brent served as an intermediary. Most of the members of this committee seem to have been Baptists and they nominated "sober Dissenters" for municipal offices, while making clear that they would do nothing to bring in Popery.[37]

The electoral campaign seemed, then, to be competently organized and based on reasonable assumptions. But would it work? All depended on the attitude of the Dissenters. Most contemporaries thought that their attitude was hostile, especially after the publication of Fagel's *Letter*. These contemporary opinions may have owed something to wishful thinking and placed too much weight on the JPs' answers to the three questions, which were not really relevant to the vital question of the attitude of the boroughs. On the other hand, Barrillon was sure that those at court thought that the campaign was going badly. James, as usual, was sublimely confident that, once the disaffected had been removed from office, all would go well; he told Barrillon that the Dissenters were entirely in his interests, except perhaps for a few rigid Presbyterians. He believed too, as always, that God was with him.[38] Sunderland, however, was deeply pessimistic and begged James to modify his demands. Indeed, it was the fear of many at court that the campaign to pack Parliament would fail disastrously that generated many of the tensions of the first months of 1688. These tensions were increased by a new and unexpected development: in October 1687 the Queen began to believe that she was pregnant.

Mary Beatrice had last miscarried in May 1686 and many thought that she would never bear a healthy child. Still not quite thirty, she had been worn out by repeated pregnancies and miscarriages and had taken the waters at Bath as much to restore her general health as to regain her ability to conceive. Despite the ever-present fears of yet another miscarriage, the zealous Catholics saw her pregnancy as little less than miraculous. The longer it lasted, the more confident they became that God would bless James's designs with a son, who would displace Mary and Anne as heir presumptive. They proclaimed their confidence more loudly than was tactful, which led some Protestants to suspect either that the Queen was not really pregnant or that, whatever the sex of her child, a boy would be produced and passed off as hers. As far as James's policies were concerned, the pregnancy raised more questions than it answered. Should he call Parliament before the child was born, in case it was a daughter, or wait until afterwards, hoping it would be a son? If he had a son, would the prospect of a Catholic successor make his Protestant subjects more obedient or more obstinate? The fact that there were no easy answers to such questions made coherent policy making even more difficult than usual in the first months of 1688. Two things were certain. First, the prospect that the leading men at court would continue in power after James's death increased the stakes in the power struggles at court. Secondly, as Mary Beatrice was twenty-five years younger than her husband, it seemed likely that she would outlive him and so courtiers competed for her favour.

The court politics of early 1688 were thus dominated by uncertainty about the outcome of the Queen's pregnancy (which seemed to be going well) and of the campaign to pack Parliament (which seemed to be going badly). The Catholic zealots were fatuously confident that the Queen would have a son and that the elections would go well (provided James did not weaken). Castlemaine told D'Adda that Heaven would bless James's good cause and that success was not to be doubted. Petre, meanwhile, was becoming grotesquely over-confident of both James's favour and his own abilities, and criticized D'Adda and even Sunderland for obstructing his promotion to the cardinalate which (Petre thought) he so richly deserved. In an effort to placate him and make him appear more considerable, James made him a privy councillor. It made no difference to his power, which was exercised in the closet, not the council chamber, but was a public demonstration (to Protestants an unwelcome one) of the Jesuit's influence. Sunderland found his hold on Petre slipping and pinned his hopes on the Queen, but she fell under the sway of Melfort, James's Scottish secretary and a convert to Catholicism, who in 1688 emerged as one of the most extreme zealots and advocates of firmness. Once Melfort had won over the Queen, in June, Sunderland's days in power were numbered.[39]

In his struggle to make James see 'reason and disregard the advice of his own former allies, Sunderland's most valuable ally was Penn. James not only liked and respected Penn but paid special heed to his views on Nonconformist opinion. Penn plied James with newsletters which purported to set out the Dissenters' views and pressed him to settle for toleration without insisting on the removal of the Test Acts or, failing that, to offer some sort of "equivalent" for the Test to remove the Protestants' fears. He suggested that Catholics should be excluded forever from the Commons and that offices should be divided equally between Anglicans, Dissenters and Catholics. James did agree to exclude Catholics from the Commons, but seems to have meant by this that they should be excluded only from the next Parliament. He had been told by the judges that he could not dispense with the 1678 Test Act—only a Parliament could alter a measure dealing with its own composition—but once Parliament had repealed it James seems to have expected that Catholics would be free to sit in Parliament.[40] The court worked on various plans for an "equivalent", giving even more explicit guarantees for the security of Protestantism than the promises of the declaration of indulgence. A draft toleration bill of about May declared that Anglican churches should be reserved for those worshipping according to the rites of the Church of England. Protestants who heard of such proposals were sceptical. As one remarked of the Test, "'tis no ill sign of the value of it when we see it so much coveted."[41]

James was thus faced with a bewildering variety of advice. The Catholic zealots argued that he should call a Parliament and insist on its repealing the Test Acts as well as the penal laws. Penn said that he should call a Parliament but not try to remove the Test Acts. Sunderland argued that the time was not yet right to call a Parliament and that, when it met, he should either leave the Test Acts alone or offer an equivalent. Caught between such conflicting counsels James dithered and did nothing. At last, early in March, Sunderland convinced him that further preparations were needed before Parliament met and that it would be very unwise to call Parliament unless he was quite sure that it would do as he wished.[42] James, however, was annoyed and perplexed by his subjects' reluctance to take this chance to secure liberty of conscience for ever, with all the benefits which went with it. He could only assume that they had been misled or that he had not made his benevolent intentions sufficiently clear. He ordered the judges to repeat, in their charges at the various assizes, his earlier assurances that he would dismiss from office all who opposed the establishment of liberty of conscience. They were also to extol once more the benefits of toleration, while the electoral agents tried again to convince their fellow Dissenters of James's good faith. These moves were the preliminaries to a formal restatement of James's intentions. On 27th April, a few days after the judges returned from their circuits, James reissued the declaration with a new preamble and postscript. This announced James's determination to call a Parliament by November at the latest and stressed James's desire to secure toleration and "the peace and greatness of our country". His sincerity, he said, was apparent from "the whole conduct of our government and by the condition of our fleet and of our armies, which with good management shall be constantly the same or greater if the safety or honour of the nation require it". He concluded smugly that "we have not appeared to be that prince our enemies would have made the world afraid of."[43]

Like James's other public pronouncements, this new postscript exuded naïve sincerity. Convinced of the purity of his intentions, James could not understand how his Protestant subjects could not be similarly convinced. Their fears, their suspicions were quite beyond his comprehension, just as they could not believe that James intended anything other than the destruction of Protestantism by fire and sword. They therefore could not understand why James had reissued his declaration. "It tells us . . . what it is the King designs, which we all pretty well knew before; he tells us that he has a pretty big army and will have a bigger if occasion require, which is a great comfort to us all." The declaration would have aroused little controversy had James not issued an order to the Anglican clergy, on 4th May, to read it in their churches, on two successive Sundays. By demanding, in effect, that they should endorse his grant of toleration, James provoked a confrontation with the Church's leaders which was to have the most serious repercussions.[44]

*   *   *

In the spring and summer of 1687, although James's relations with William worsened, there was little change in James's relations with the States General. Some old causes of friction persisted (like the States' refusal to hand over Burnet), one or two new ones appeared. The old disputes between Dutch and English in the East Indies broke out anew and the States General complained angrily of James's allowing Algerian pirates to shelter in English ports. Yet although there was no major new source of tension, in June 1687 William's patient efforts to improve the republic's military and naval preparedness suddenly bore fruit. The States General agreed to a series of financial reforms, notably major changes in the method of collecting import and export duties, which were to provide enough money to build maybe thirty new ships and pay the sailors who were to man them. Since 1678 William's diplomacy had been hamstrung by lack of money; now some at least of the constraints on his foreign policy were being removed.[45]

One indication of the strengthening of William's position was the more aggressive line taken by James's ambassador at the Hague (although he may also have been expressing James's annoyance at William's opposition to the repeal of the Test Acts). Ignatius White, Marquis of Albeville, was an Irish Catholic, whose career in the twilight world on the fringes of legitimate diplomacy went back to the 1650s. He had considerable experience of both the Spanish Netherlands and the Dutch republic and knew a number of Dutch politicians personally, notably Dijkveld. As he had little property of his own, he was regarded as easy to bribe, but although he accepted money from both Louis and William, he showed himself more competent, consistent and principled than Skelton.[46] Like James, Albeville was a zealous Catholic and feared that William was planning a Protestant crusade. Like James, he hoped in the spring of 1687 to reconcile James and William (much to d'Avaux's annoyance). By the end of June such hopes had evaporated. William's successes in the States General had put him in a much better position to thwart James's plans and to seize the English throne when James died. Albeville asked d'Avaux to press Louis to offer James aid in establishing Catholicism; Louis replied that, as James had not asked him for help, he assumed that James thought himself strong enough to achieve his ends unaided. Albeville also urged James to deal firmly with the States General or else they would show scant respect for his wishes. As it was, they believed his position at home was so precarious that he was incapable of undertaking any action abroad. When a strongly worded complaint about Dutch aggression in the East Indies had no effect, Albeville argued that James should give a more striking mark of his displeasure. When he returned to London in August, he began to press James to recall the English and Scots regiments from the Dutch service.[47]

Albeville had first suggested such a step in April. He laid great stress on William's commissioning men whom James regarded as disloyal and who would be quite willing to serve against him if William asked them to. James raised no objection in principle to recalling the regiments, but thought it best to wait until the Dutch gave him a pretext to do so. He was also reluctant to pay any more soldiers, since he already had as many as he needed. He therefore asked Louis to take the regiments into the French service. Louis refused, but offered to pay for their upkeep in England, adding that he would send James any help he needed, at any time, to maintain his authority. At first James remained set on having some British units in the French army, which he thought would give them an excellent training. By November, however, he had decided to accept Louis' offer and to recall the regiments, but still hesitated to put his decision into effect. Albeville, Petre and the Catholic zealots, supported by Sunderland, urged him to go ahead, the moderate Catholics advised caution. At last on 17th January, 1688, James sent to Albeville, now back at the Hague, to demand that the regiments should be sent back to England.[48]

The recall of the regiments revived the earlier fears that James intended to make war on the Dutch, fears which were strengthened by threatening remarks by James and his ministers.[49] James based his demands on specific treaties between England and the Dutch republic and on the right of a prince to the services of his subjects. To the first argument, the States General denied that any treaty then in force obliged them to send back the regiments in peacetime. To the second, they alleged that by the laws of nature and of nations, "he who is born free has the ability and the right to seek a living and to establish himself wherever he judges it to be most advantageous." They refused to send back the regiments in a body but they would (they said) allow individual officers to return. In fact, the States soon changed their mind and put every possible difficulty in the way of officers who wished to depart. They also refused to let either NCOs or private soldiers obey James's repeated commands to return. As a result, no more than sixty or seventy officers reached England.[50]

James was infuriated by the obstructionism and (as he saw it) duplicity of the States General. He was also irritated with Louis who, for a while, refused to pay the money he had promised on the grounds that his offer had presupposed that the regiments would be dispersed and made useless to William. Louis at last relented, but the Dutch did not. James made threatening noises and talked of war, but the States General did not take such threats seriously. "They say generally here", wrote Albeville, "that your majesty intends them no good and that you are in no capacity to do them harm." He wrote too that William planned to use the Dutch fleet to help the factious in England. The Catholic zealots urged James to make war on the Dutch, but he feared that if he did so he would have to call Parliament sooner than he had intended, which could ruin his plans for Catholicism. He told D'Adda that William was trying to provoke him into war, but that he was too clever to fall into such a trap. James might convince himself of this, but as Albeville handed in threatening memorials at the Hague while James assured Citters that he wanted peace, neutral observers could only wonder at such inconsistent conduct, which both irritated and emboldened the Dutch.[51]

Although James's conduct provoked raucous amusement in Holland, William became increasingly anxious. He received reports of force and fraud in James's electoral preparations. William feared that such methods might succeed, enabling James to establish Catholicism by force, or that they might provoke a rebellion. He received reports which said that the Queen was pregnant and others which alleged that she was not. Either way, there were dangers: if she had, or pretended to have a son, either that son would cut Mary' out of the succession or his birth would be the signal for a general revolt. There were still reports that James planned to alter the succession in favour of a Catholic, reports which William apparently believed. There were reports of a closer liaison than ever between James and Louis; Citters' dispatches stressed the close understanding between James and Barrillon. Behind all these particular fears lay a single recurrent nightmare. Since 1678 William had expected Louis to mount another great attack on the republic and on the other Protestant states of Europe. Amid the frustrations of the last decade, his difficulties with Amsterdam and other towns, he had been able to comfort himself with the confidence that, one day, he would be able to bring England's resources into the struggle against Louis which dominated his life. Now that confidence was greatly shaken and William feared that James might join with Louis against him, as Charles had done in 1672. By 1688 he no longer heeded James's assurances that he would not alter the succession and that he did not want war. He was far more inclined to believe those of his English contacts who argued that if William did not act decisively all would be lost—Mary's chance of succeeding to the throne, the Protestant cause in England and Europe. James might purge the army of Protestants, he might call a Catholic Parliament. At the end of April, William told Arthur Herbert and others who came with letters from England that "if he was invited by some men of the best interest . . . to come and rescue the nation and the religion, he believed he could be ready by the end of September to come over." Desperate perils required desperate remedies, so William was prepared to resort to armed force to make his uncle see the error of his ways.[52]

*　　*　　*

While William began his preparations for an invasion, James awaited the Anglican clergy's reaction to his order to read the declaration in their churches. The great majority of the London clergy decided not to read it and, on 17th May, Sancroft and six of his colleagues drew up a petition, pointing out politely that the dispensing power on which the declaration rested had been declared illegal in Parliament, notably in 1663 and 1673. James received the petition next day with a mixture of astonishment and fury: "This is a standard of rebellion," he exclaimed several times, and went on:

> "Is that what I have deserved who have supported the Church of England and will support it? . . . I did not expect this from you . . . I will be obeyed in publishing my declaration . . . God hath given me this dispensing power and I will maintain it. I tell you there are seven thousand men, and of the Church of England too, that have not bowed the knee to Baal."

With that he dismissed them, and pondered what to do next.[53]

As news of the petition leaked out and copies were distributed all over the country, James's first reaction was that the bishops had played into his hands: such obstinate opposition to toleration could only drive a wedge between

Churchmen and Dissenters. He soon found that he was wrong and that many leading Dissenters openly supported the bishops' stand. This growing solidarity between the leaders of the various Protestant denominations made James all the more anxious to reassert his authority. His father, he told D'Adda, had been undone by weakness; the English had to be handled firmly, for they always attributed mildness to fear.[54] It was not easy to deal firmly with the bishops, however, as it was by no means clear that they had broken any law. Jeffreys and the ecclesiastical commission wanted nothing to do with their case, which led some at court to argue that it would be unwise to proceed against them. Sunderland (and apparently even Petre) argued that the best way to deal with such a challenge was to ignore it: any attempt at coercion would provoke more determined resistance. For a while James vacillated. A proclamation ordering the clergy to read the declaration or face severe penalties was sent several times to the press and then withdrawn. At last, on 1st June, faced with conflicting advice, James unerringly chose the course of action which combined moderation and severity in the worst possible way: he would proceed against the bishops according to law, reserving the option of showing them mercy after they had been convicted.[55] Accordingly, when the bishops refused to give sureties for good behaviour they were sent to the Tower, exulting in their martyrdom and blessing the crowds which watched them pass on their way to prison. James had now committed himself too far to back down without loss of face; he could only hope that the court would produce the right verdict.

Then on 10th June the Queen offered a way out of his dilemma by giving birth to a son. After all the fears of a miscarriage, the baby's arrival took everyone by surprise: the Queen had been playing cards until late the previous night. James was so overjoyed that he fell on his knees and cried for most of the night. The baby, he announced, would be called James Francis Edward. The priests asked openly what would happen to the Protestant religion now that there was a Catholic heir. The Protestants were less happy. Many muttered about the supposedly suspicious circumstances of the child's birth. Some said that the child was early, others that only Catholics had been present when he was born. Many suspected that a substitution had been planned if not actually carried out. Such suspicions were transmitted to Holland where they formed the basis of scurrilous pamphlets. In fact there is no real evidence that the child was not the Queen's and much that suggests that he was. James found it hard to believe how anybody could be so wicked as to doubt that the child was his. The main reason for such doubts, indeed, was simply that most Protestants did not *want* to believe that James now had a son. "Be it a true child or not, the people will never believe it," remarked one observer, adding cynically that people would believe that the child was genuine only if he died. In fact for some weeks the child seemed far from healthy, thanks mainly to the royal doctors' insistence that milk was bad for babies and that he should be fed on boiled bread or gruel, with such additions as canary wine and "Dr Goddard's drops". Both Louis and the Pope regarded this method of feeding as eccentric to the point of lunacy: a wet nurse would be far more natural. The royal doctors and the King and Queen were at last forced to agree, but only after the child had nearly died early in August. Once allowed to suckle, from a tiler's wife rather than the gentlewoman favoured by the doctors, the little Prince went from strength to strength.[56]

If James had wished to pardon the bishops, his son's birth offered an admirable pretext; but he did not. The night after the Prince was born, the cabinet council altered the charge in the bishops' indictment from "scandalous libel" to the more serious "seditious libel". In the days that followed, when James was not cooing over his son and organizing his household, he pressed on with the bishops' prosecution, remaining confident of a conviction even after the judges of King's Bench had allowed them bail. The panel of jurors chosen by the sheriff of London included several former Dissenters and some employed by the King in the navy or revenue administration. Perhaps because of this, perhaps because he was sure that the law was on his side, James was still confident when the trial began on 29th June.[57]

His confidence was not justified. Despite repeated purges of the bench, some of the judges had recently shown misgivings about the legality of the tasks they were asked to perform (especially on the ecclesiastical commission). Of the four judges who presided at the trial, two (Powell and Holloway) clearly favoured the bishops, Wright was (for him) unusually moderate and only the Catholic Allibone was consistently hostile. Moreover, the audience at the trial was large and ferociously partisan. When Sunderland (who had just compounded his unpopularity by becoming a Catholic) gave evidence, the crowd hissed so menacingly that he could hardly speak. Wright tried to concentrate on the fact of publication, arguing that anything intended to cause "a stir among the people" was a libel. Holloway and Powell, however, insisted on discussing the petition's contents. Both roundly condemned the dispensing power: "If this be once allowed of, there will need no Parliament; all the legislature will be in the King." Given such a lead from the bench, the jury (after a night's deliberation) found the bishops not guilty.[58]

The shouting and cheers in court lasted a good half hour. The news spread through the city. Soldiers at the camp on Hounslow Heath gave a great shout when they heard it. That night there were bonfires throughout London, far more than for the birth of the Prince of Wales. Church bells rang, there were candles in every window and a crowd burned an effigy of the Pope outside St James's Palace, while the guards looked on. In Somerset they went one better and burned an effigy of the Prince of Wales as well. Meanwhile, seven men met to draft an invitation to William to invade England. They included both Whigs and Tories, a bishop (Compton) and a former lord treasurer (Danby), but were (as a group) not particularly representative or influential. Nevertheless, they gave William the invitation he had asked for and, more important, assured him that the invasion would succeed. "Nineteen parts of twenty of the people . . . are desirous of a change." The army officers were "discontented", the soldiers "do daily show such an aversion to the Popish religion" that neither they nor the seamen would resist their liberators. Finally, the seven added, "we do much doubt whether this present state of things will not yet be much changed to the worse before another year." William needed no further encouragement.[59]

CHAPTER THIRTEEN

Invasion
(July to December 1688)

For James, the bishops' acquittal was a humiliation. What had been intended as a show trial, punishing the bishops' temerity and reaffirming the legality of the dispensing power, had ended with the bishops' action vindicated and the dispensing power seriously undermined. James tried to explain it away, saying that too little care had been taken in selecting the jury and that his law officers and the judges had handled the case badly. Powell and Holloway were dismissed from the bench. James made it clear, too, that he would not weaken. He ordered the ecclesiastical commission to summon all those of the clergy who had not obeyed his order to read the declaration of indulgence. It soon became clear that the vast majority had failed to read it; neither the commissioners nor the diocesan authorities showed any eagerness to identify defaulters and nothing was done. James also insisted that Parliament, when it met, should repeal the Test Acts as well as the penal laws, arguing that any sign of weakness on his part would make his opponents more obstinate. He therefore ordered that those who had lit bonfires to celebrate the bishops' acquittal should be punished.[1]

This attempt to reassert the government's authority backfired. Grand juries refused to find that those who had started the bonfires had any case to answer, even though the justices sent them out to reconsider their verdict. Soon after, the judges went on their circuits, with orders to proclaim that Parliament would soon meet and to urge the electorate to vote for candidates committed to liberty of conscience. Several judges also went out of their way to criticize the conduct of the seven bishops. They met with scant respect. At Northampton the grand jury responded to a diatribe against the bishops by refusing to find a true bill against those who had started bonfires. At Winchester, the grand jury refused to declare its abhorrence of the bishops' petition and tried instead to present Catholic JPs for holding office contrary to law.[2]

Such acts of defiance were too uncoordinated to pose a serious threat to law and order, but they showed how hitherto silent critics of James's measures had been emboldened by the bishops' acquittal. Such measures also called into question the government's ability to secure obedience—let alone willing co-operation—in implementing its policies. Whatever the Dutch thought, there was no hint of rebellion in England in the summer of 1688, but James's Protestant subjects were now so disgusted and fearful that they were unlikely to do much to help him if he were attacked. The foundation of popular acceptance, so necessary for a stable regime in early modern England, had been dangerously eroded. Even so, that regime could not be toppled without the use of force from outside. All depended on William's success in preparing for his invasion. James's fate was to be decided, not in England but in Paris and the Hague, on the Rhine and on the Danube.

* * *

At the beginning of 1688 there seemed little reason why Louis XIV should look forward to the coming year with undue anxiety. It seemed unlikely that the Emperor's war with the Turks would be over very soon. The fortification of the eastern frontier was proceeding well. The men of Amsterdam might be showing unwelcome signs of weakness, but Louis could not believe that they would so far forget their true interests as to let William ride roughshod over their privileges. Nevertheless, Louis was concerned enough about the threats from the Germans and Dutch to take steps to perpetuate his influence at Cologne. The Archbishop of Cologne held a string of other bishoprics which together straddled the southern and eastern frontiers of the Dutch republic and offered easy access into north Germany. The present archbishop was friendly to France, but he was old and frail and Louis wanted to be sure of his successor. He therefore had his client Fürstenberg elected as coadjutor (and by implication next archbishop) of Cologne. To be valid, the election needed to be confirmed by the Pope, who refused. Even so, all the signs suggested that Fürstenberg would be the next archbishop.[3]

In fact, however, the pillars of Louis' diplomatic strategy were beginning to crumble. Rent by internal dissensions, the Turks were losing both the will and the capacity to resist the Emperor. Moreover, Louis could no longer rely on the regents of Holland to obstruct William's foreign policy. They still feared William's monarchical ambitions, but were coming to fear Louis more. In addition, they were coming under increasing pressure from the ordinary citizens of their towns, who were usually ready to accept the oligarchs' leadership, but in times of crisis became restless and were liable to be stampeded into terrible outbreaks of violence, such as the assassination of the De Witts in 1672. By the spring of 1688, the shopkeepers and artisans were being roused by the preachers of the Dutch Reformed Church and the regents ignored their views at their peril. Pressed from above and below, by William and their fellow citizens, the regents' opposition buckled and collapsed. By the autumn of 1688 they had not only ceased to oppose William but were giving him almost wholehearted support, while seasoned observers remarked in wonderment that they had never seen the Dutch so united.

There were two main reasons for this transformation: religion and trade. Since 1685 the Dutch had become convinced that Louis and James planned to extirpate Protestantism, first in their own kingdoms, then in the rest of Europe. The revocation of the Edict of Nantes also disrupted Franco-Dutch trade, with the exodus of Huguenot merchants and the harassment of Dutch merchants living in France. In 1687 Louis imposed severe new restrictions on the import of salt herrings into France and introduced new and prohibitively high tariffs, which were designed to drive many foreign manufactures, especially textiles, off the French market. These restrictions and tariffs, imposed unilaterally in defiance of existing treaties, dealt a severe blow to the fishing and cloth industries, two of the republic's largest employers. One great argument for a pacific foreign policy had always been that war was bad for trade. Now many Dutch traders felt that war could not make their condition any worse than it was already.

By 1688 many Dutch merchants believed not only that they had nothing to lose by fighting but that they would soon have to fight for the republic's very survival. Many now shared William's belief that Louis would soon make war on them and that James would join with him. Such beliefs were unfounded, but they were widely held, which helps explain how William secured the money to expand the Dutch fleet in the winter of 1687–88. Louis, meanwhile, had long believed that William wanted to renew the war of 1672–78 and James had come to believe it too. Both therefore saw this Dutch naval armament as a threat to themselves. The steps which James and Louis took to counter this threat increased the fears of the Dutch, which led them to support William's proposals to expand the fleet further, to enlarge the army and to fortify the republic's frontiers. Thus 1688 saw an escalation of fear and mistrust which was eventually to lead to war.

The first step in this escalation came in February. Louis pressed James to follow the Dutch example and expand his fleet. He claimed that the Dutch might be planning either to foment trouble in England or to help the Swedes against the Danes, which could lead to a war that would engulf all Europe. James hesitated. He was willing in principle to fit out twenty or thirty extra warships but jibbed at the expense involved, preferring to concentrate his resources on his army which could protect him against disorders at home. He was also reluctant either to risk a clash with the Dutch fleet or to order Albeville to present a memorial warning the States General not to attack Denmark. A clear difference of approach was apparent. Louis saw threats and shows of force as means of preventing war. James and Sunderland feared that they might provoke war. Louis was irritated at their timidity, but was glad enough to see James on bad terms with the States General, provided that their antagonism did not lead to open war.[4]

By the end of April the danger of war in the Baltic had passed and Louis told Barrillon to press James no further. James, however, was now so worried by the growth of the Dutch fleet that he ordered the fitting out of twenty new ships. The dockyards, which had lain idle in April, sprang to life in May and June and James began to look to his coastal defences, improving the fortifications of Chatham and Portsmouth. He told Barrillon that if he had tried to call Parliament, the Dutch fleet would have cruised off the English coast to encourage his opponents.[5] Louis was glad to learn that James had belatedly seen the need for a larger fleet, but still doubted if James's fleet was large enough, so at the end of May offered to join sixteen of his own warships to the English fleet. He wanted no formal treaty with James: such treaties had always cost him money and there was nothing that he wanted James to do for him. His aim was partly to ensure that James could defend himself, but more to deter the Dutch from attacking James by showing that Louis would come to his aid if they did. He therefore suggested that James should make his offer public.[6]

Louis' offer was far from disinterested. The old Archbishop of Cologne had just died and Louis had ordered d'Avaux to warn the States General not to interfere in the election of his successor. The Dutch were not in fact very interested in Cologne, but two of the other bishoprics which the old Archbishop had held (Liège and Münster) were in very sensitive positions on the republic's frontier. The States General therefore refrained from interfering in the Cologne election, in which Fürstenberg unexpectedly failed to get the two thirds majority which he required. From June 1688, therefore, the disputed election at Cologne looked as if it would provide the spark to ignite into war the hostility between Louis and the German princes.[7]

James and Sunderland suspected that Louis, in offering the ships, was trying to exaggerate the closeness of his understanding with James in order to deter the States General from intervening at Cologne. The ships in question were in the Mediterranean and would take some time to sail to the Channel. James for his part was grateful for the offer and for Barrillon's assurance that Louis would help him against his enemies, at home or abroad, but saw no need to avail himself of the ships at present. On the other hand, he was careful not to rule out the possibility of such naval co-operation in the future. As for making the offer public, James's feelings were mixed. Such an indication of a closer liaison with France might make his subjects more compliant or it might make them more obstinate, it might deter the Dutch from attacking him or it might provoke them to enlarge their fleet still further. In the end, James did what he usually did when faced with a difficult decision, and sought a compromise. The news of the offer was allowed to leak out. The impression which it created of a close Anglo-French understanding was strengthened when Croissy told the Dutch Ambassador in Paris that if James were attacked Louis would come to his aid and by James's remark to Citters that in case of need he would not lack friends.[8]

Such remarks could only strengthen William's hand. When news reached the republic of Louis' offer of ships, William proposed to the States General that they should raise another nine thousand seamen for the fleet. Having made up his mind to invade England, two main obstacles stood in his way. First, he had to persuade the States General to endorse such a costly and risky scheme. This was made easier by the growing belief in a close Anglo-French alliance, but William still avoided taking the States General into his confidence until very late in his preparations. Secondly, he had to guard against an attack on the republic while he and a large part of the Dutch army and fleet were busy in England. William assumed that Louis would not allow such an opportunity to pass. He therefore built up the republic's defences, enlarging the army and fleet and strengthening the frontier fortresses. He also began to construct a network of alliances with German princes, designed partly to create a coalition (based on the League of Augsburg) strong enough to hold its own against France, partly to secure the services of some thousands of experienced mercenary soldiers. In constructing his alliances, William had two great pieces of luck. First, in April 1688 the pro-French Elector of Brandenburg died and his successor was far more sympathetic to the allies. Secondly, the disputed election at Cologne aroused fears of French military intervention in Germany and so helped to unite the German princes. It also gave William a pretext to enlarge the Dutch army and to arrange a great camp at Nijmegen during the summer.

Naturally there was speculation about the purpose of William's hectic activity. As early as May d'Avaux thought that William would send troops to England in case of a rebellion there. Louis was worried that James might be unable to repel such an assault and pestered Barrillon over the next few months for information about the size of James's army and fleet and the loyalty of his soldiers and sailors. On the latter point, Barrillon's replies were rather vague; one could not, after all, judge their loyalty until it had been put to the test. D'Avaux's information, meanwhile, was very inconsistent. Sometimes he wrote that the naval preparations were accelerating, sometimes that they were slackening, sometimes that William would invade England that year, sometimes that he would invade the next year, sometimes that he was preparing to intervene in the Cologne election. Such uncertainty appears less surprising when one realizes that as late as 19th August William was still not sure that he would be able to invade England that autumn. In July Louis was sure that William would not attack James that year. By mid-August d'Avaux was sure that William intended to attack England but Louis still suspected that he might use the army at Nijmegen to intervene at Cologne. He therefore told d'Avaux to warn the States General very strongly not to interfere in the election there. A week later, following suggestions from Skelton (now James's ambassador at Paris), Louis ordered d'Avaux to give in a second memorial, saying that if James were attacked the close "liaisons of friendship and alliance" between James and Louis would oblige Louis to come to James's aid.[9]

This memorial was a crude and desperate attempt to deter the States General from supporting William's invasion plans. Far away in Paris, Louis was sure that it would work. D'Avaux was much less sure—the Dutch, he said, were mad for war—but he did as he was told. The memorial failed to intimidate the States General—if anything the reverse—and added substance to the rumours of a secret Anglo-French alliance. By the end of September a pamphlet was circulating which claimed to give details of this alleged alliance. William treated it as an established fact and the general opinion was that war with France was inevitable.[10]

By now William's preparations were almost complete. He had a fleet ready to carry some fourteen thousand soldiers to England, with arms for many more. On 28th September he at last told the States General of his plan to invade England. He stressed James's alleged alliance with Louis and his hostility to the Dutch. He had been invited, he said, by James's subjects to save them from Popery and slavery. He aimed neither to conquer England nor to dethrone

James, but to secure a free Parliament which could remedy all grievances. He used similar arguments to the Emperor, to whom he stressed also that he had no wish to harm the English Catholics. The States General accepted William's arguments with alacrity. The Emperor was less sure, but he was far away and his neutrality was enough. The final obstacle to William's enterprise was removed in late September. Louis had been building up his army very rapidly and there was speculation that he might use it at Cologne or against the Spanish Netherlands. He did neither. In the end, the attack came a hundred miles south of Cologne, at Philippsburg, the only one of the three major fortresses in Alsace which Louis did not already control. In August he had heard from Constantinople that the Turks were about to make peace, which would leave the Emperor free to join in the war in the west. This made it essential, first to do something to encourage the Turks to keep fighting and second, to close the last "gate" on the eastern frontier. The attack on Philippsburg seemed to serve both purposes. It was intended as a small localized operation but marked the start of a European war which was to last nine years. It also removed the last constraint on William. It was now most unlikely that Louis could attack the republic or the Spanish Netherlands. Moreover, as the conflict on the Rhine intensified, it became increasingly unlikely that Louis would be able to come to James's aid. If James was to repel William's invasion, he would have to rely on his own resources.[11]

*   *   *

As the summer wore on, the French expressed amazement at James's "surprising lethargy" and his failure to prepare to defend himself. It was not that he doubted William's ill will. He had long been convinced that William was behind much of the opposition he met with in England. Even so, James was reluctant to believe that William would be so "unnatural" as to make war on his father-in-law, or that Mary would acquiesce in his doing so. His confidence was shaken when William stopped the prayers in his chapel for the Prince of Wales, which implied that he thought that the child was spurious. James was deeply offended and, after complaints from Albeville, the prayers were resumed, although much against Mary's wishes.[12] But even if James came to accept that William was wicked enough to want to attack him, he still found it hard to believe that he would be able to do so. Indeed, an invasion came to seem less likely as the summer progressed. First, the autumn was no time for naval expeditions: the weather was far too stormy. Secondly, James could not believe that the States General would let William go. He knew that William's power had grown, but even so it seemed incredible that he should be allowed to take away a large part of the Dutch army when war seemed imminent at Cologne.

Two other reasons could also be adduced for James's reluctance to believe that an invasion was imminent: the inconsistency of the information which he received from Holland and the fact that so much of it came from the French. Obsessed with the need to avoid war, James and Sunderland were deeply suspicious of any suggestion from Louis which could lead to war with the Dutch.

To serve his own ends, Louis exaggerated the degree of understanding and co-operation between James and himself, hoping in this way to deter the Dutch from attacking either of them. James and Sunderland feared that such demonstrations of an Anglo-French liaison could bring upon them the very consequences which they were designed to prevent. They therefore disavowed such demonstrations, which Louis regarded as foolish and ungentlemanly. The disavowals, indeed, ensured that James got the worst of both worlds. They did not destroy the widely held belief in an Anglo-French alliance but they weakened the fear which that belief might have engendered in Holland, by making it clear that James would not take advantage of Louis' offers of assistance.

Those offers of assistance were, in fact, less substantial than they seemed, although that was partly James's own fault. Louis had first offered the sixteen warships early in June. By 26th July Louis had virtually decided not to bring the ships up from the Mediterranean that year. Three weeks later James told Barrillon that he was still not sure whether he would need the ships but that he would like Louis to keep them ready at Brest, just in case. By now it was too late to bring the ships to the Channel, but Bonrepaus was sent to England, not only to report on James's forces, but also to sign a treaty for the junction of the French and English fleets. Louis soon told Bonrepaus not to promise James any naval help that year. While avoiding any positive commitment, Bonrepaus took care not to tell James point blank that he could not expect help from Louis, for in that way he could make James more deeply obliged to Louis for his offer, even though Louis had no intention of carrying it out. Bonrepaus did, however, advise James to rely on his own fleet.[13]

James had certainly been tempted by the thought of adding to his fleet at no cost to himself, but had hesitated to accept the offer for fear of the harm which the joining of the fleets would do to naval morale. He showed a similar uncertainty in his response to d'Avaux's memorial. At first he seemed pleased, hoping that its threats would make the Dutch think twice before invading England. Skelton was reprimanded for acting without orders, but not for the content of his proposals. A week later, however, James and Sunderland disavowed the memorial vigorously, having doubtless heard of the furore it had caused in Holland. The queen claimed that the French were trying to drag James into a war. James told Citters categorically that he had no formal treaty with France. Skelton was recalled and clapped in the Tower. The incident showed that the understanding between James and Louis was less close than was generally supposed, for James suspected (rightly) that Louis would support his interests only so long as they coincided with those of France.[14]

This was seen clearly in September as all Europe waited to see where Louis' army would strike. James made it clear that he hoped it would be near the Dutch republic, perhaps in Liège or Cologne. D'Avaux advised Louis to attack the republic, but Louis insisted that "the need to prevent the ill designs of the court of Vienna" left him no choice but to attack Philippsburg. James was filled with despair at the news:

"I no longer know what can be done. The French forces are mostly at

Philippsburg and the rest are going to Italy. What help or diversion can I expect from them? The vessels of the King your master could not be made ready for some time and anyway I should ruin my domestic affairs if a French fleet were joined to mine."

Many at the English court accused Louis of deserting James and Louis thought it wise to send a little money (some £22,000) towards James's military expenses, while warning Barrillon not to hand it over if James's cause seemed hopeless. James was effusively grateful and talked wildly of an Anglo-French alliance against the Dutch, but Louis doubted whether James could carry Parliament with him. Meanwhile, James suggested to the States General that they should form a close alliance to enforce the Treaty of Nijmegen, a proposal which was received with unconcealed disdain.[15] If James still expressed little resentment of Louis' failure to contribute positively to his security, this was not because he was satisfied with Louis' conduct, but because he hoped that Louis would provide a safe refuge for his family and himself if the worst came to the worst. In that, at least, he was not to be disappointed.

As James could not rely on French aid, direct or indirect, all depended on the preparedness, size and loyalty of his army and fleet. It was not until 21st August that James began to take seriously the possibility that William might be planning to invade rather than merely to use the Dutch fleet to foment trouble within England. On that day James ordered the fitting out of another thirty-five ships and ordered army officers to their regiments where they were to bring their companies up to strength. Nothing else was done to enlarge the army and James and his ministers were still clearly sceptical about the likelihood of a major invasion. Not until 17th September, when a letter arrived from Albeville saying that William would embark in a week's time, was James seriously worried. A few days later he issued commissions to raise the first of many new regiments. As he later admitted, he had left it rather late. Had the sailing of William's fleet not been substantially delayed by contrary winds, James would have been found much worse prepared than he was.[16]

In terms of size James's forces seem to have been superior rather than inferior to William's. The invasion fleet consisted mainly of unarmed transports, with an escort of some sixty warships, about as many as in James's fleet. James's army was much larger than William's, which numbered about fourteen thousand men, maybe less. James's army probably comprised at least twenty thousand officers and men by September and its paper strength doubled over the next two months (including some six thousand Scots and Irish). However, these new levies were often so ill-equipped, understrength and inexperienced that they were of little military value and some never really existed except on paper. The colonel of an older regiment wrote that some of his soldiers were so short of clothes that they could not appear on duty. It is worth noting, too, that some 2,500 "soldiers" were officers' servants.[17]

When all allowances are made, however, James's fleet was still about equal to William's and his army was about twice as large. James should, therefore, have been able to cope with the invasion, provided that his soldiers and sailors would fight. William had often been assured that they would not and there was much evidence to support this claim. In July there had almost been a mutiny in the fleet when a Catholic captain had had Mass said on his ship. James had to go in person to pacify the sailors with money and kind words. As for the army, the soldiers had cheered at the bishops' acquittal and there had been clashes between Catholic and Protestant, Irish and English. Although James had talked often of the need to purge the army of unreliable officers and to fill it with Catholics, it was still overwhelmingly Protestant and James feared that to introduce Catholics on a large scale would lose him the loyalty of the Protestants. He therefore resisted Louis' arguments that he should bring over Catholic regiments from Ireland, especially after seven officers in the Duke of Berwick's regiment at Portsmouth refused to take Irishmen into their companies. James would have liked to punish the officers severely, but was told that as the law stood he could only cashier them. Other officers from the same regiment resigned in sympathy. The incident not only damaged the army's morale but gave credence to the rumours that James wished to fill the army with Papists and Irish. In the last weeks of 1688, there were a host of rumours of the arrival of French or Irish troops, of Popish murders and massacres, which placed a greater strain than ever on the fragile loyalty of James's soldiers.[18]

James's problems, faced with William's invasion, were thus more political than military. Somehow he had to restore his subjects' confidence in him so that his soldiers, militiamen and magistrates would make a real effort to resist the invaders. To this end, he made a series of political concessions, some of them very substantial. On 24th August, a few days after he realized that invasion was a real possibility, he announced his intention to call a Parliament on 27th November. Professor Jones has claimed that this decision was carefully calculated and based on full information. Such claims, it seems to me, are difficult to sustain. Barrillon had no doubt of the reasons for the decision:

"The King of England and his ministers see this as necessary to keep all the Nonconformists in the good disposition which they show at present towards the royal party. The court believes that this proclamation of a Parliament will please the nation and render odious any enterprise which the Prince of Orange might undertake."[19]

Barrillon, then, saw the calling of Parliament as a political gesture and remarked that James would not feel obliged to meet it at the appointed time. This view is supported by other evidence which shows that James did not yet have sufficient information to show that he would succeed in securing the election of candidates whom he regarded as "right". The election agents had been touring the constituencies since July but made their reports on 11th September, over a fortnight after the decision to call Parliament. Similarly, while some official candidates were told that they were to stand some months before, others were approached only after 24th August. Letters were sent on 15th September to no less than forty-one candidates, telling them that they were to stand for election. Others were approached in the hectic few days after James's announcement that Parliament would meet—Reresby, for example.

The choice of Reresby suggests that James had not inquired very closely into the views of those whom he ordered to stand. Reresby had avoided being tendered the three questions. He was reluctant to offend the King by refusing to stand, but was determined, if elected, not to vote against his conscience. Reresby's case was far from unique. Of twenty-six candidates named for Yorkshire, five had refused to answer the three questions, one had said that he had no intention of standing for election and two had said they would decide when they heard the debates. Only one had given an unequivocal "yes". A similar pattern could be found elsewhere. Returns survive covering 215 seats, of which the agents were unsure or pessimistic about only 59. In 24 cases, the borough needed further regulation or a recommendation was required from a Tory magnate and no candidate was named for 33 seats. Of the 99 candidates described as (or implied to be) "right", 20 had given hostile or doubtful answers to the three questions. Others were assumed to be "right" because they were royal servants (like Reresby or John Cooke—one of James's most outspoken critics in 1685) or because they were Dissenters.[20]

The agents' reports thus contained a large element of woolly optimism and wishful thinking. Moreover, when James decided to call Parliament even the dubious information contained in the reports was not available to him. Small wonder, then, that observers of all shades of opinion agreed that James could not get his candidates elected without fraud and gerrymandering on a monstrous scale. Even if he succeeded, it was by no means certain that those who were elected would do as he wished. Sunderland had pressed James for some time not to insist on removing the Test Acts or to allow some "equivalent". At times James seemed to accept his arguments, but in the end he followed the Catholic zealots and insisted that the Tests had to go. Such obstinacy was wildly unrealistic. Sir John Baber, one of the court's leading contacts with the Presbyterians, told Bonrepaus categorically that James would not be able to have the Test Acts repealed. All the evidence suggests that he was right.[21]

By now Sunderland was only too aware of the problems which James faced. Since the time of the bishops' petition he had argued consistently that James should not lose all by trying to gain too much. The Catholic zealots bitterly criticized such advice and accused him of faintheartedness, even treason. Already Sunderland had had to declare himself a Catholic in order to retain James's trust, but by early September Bonrepaus reported that only his administrative expertise kept him in office. Sunderland became gloomy and defeatist: he feared, indeed, that he would lose his head if William conquered England. He therefore joined with the leading Tories at court—Jeffreys, Dartmouth and Godolphin—in pressing James to take steps to win back the support of the Church of England men. They argued that the Dissenters were weak and divided and that the Anglicans offered the only sure foundation for royal authority. Recently James had paid little attention to such arguments but in September, when invasion suddenly seemed certain, fear made him inclined to try anything. On the 21st, as he began to mobilize his army, he declared that he was willing that Catholics should be excluded from the Commons. Three days later he summoned the bishops to London to discuss the present situation. "Now, my Lord," he told Clarendon, "I shall see what the Church of England men will do."[22]

The next few days saw a desperate struggle at court. While panic reigned at Whitehall and James worked into the small hours preparing his forces, he was under constant pressure from two conflicting groups. The Catholic zealots claimed shrilly that any concessions would be fatal to the Catholic cause. The Tories argued that only with Anglican support could James resist William's invasion. At first, the Catholics seemed to get their way. James recalled the Parliamentary writs he had issued only eight days earlier and talked to the bishops only in general terms. Then the tide began to turn. Godolphin pressed the bishops to draw up a list of demands and James had a private interview with Sancroft. On 3rd October the bishops (at James's request) presented their demands. These included the removal of Catholics from office and from the universities, the restoration of confiscated borough charters, the suppression of the ecclesiastical commission and the calling of a free Parliament. James assured the Catholics that he would not sacrifice their interests and told D'Adda to reassure the pope on this point, but Barrillon predicted correctly that most of the bishops' demands would be met. The ecclesiastical commission was dissolved, the charter of the City of London was restored and the expelled fellows of Magdalen were reinstated. After some hesitation, on 17th October James annulled all proceedings against borough charters since 1679. Meanwhile, Catholics were gradually dismissed from the commissions of the peace and the militia and the old Tory JPs and deputy lieutenants were reinstated.[23]

It might seem, then, that James had given the Tories all they wanted, but he still had not met the most essential demand of all, that for a free Parliament which alone could secure and make permanent his other concessions. James argued that it was impossible to hold elections with an invasion imminent, but there were reasons to doubt his sincerity. No sooner had Sunderland and his Tory allies persuaded James to grant his concessions than the Catholic zealots counter-attacked. They played hard on James's nagging feeling that such a sacrifice of the Catholics' interests was dangerous and dishonourable, and portrayed Sunderland's conduct as unwise and disloyal. On 14th October James told Barrillon that Sunderland's lack of firmness was harming his affairs. Meanwhile, he ignored the advice of many Catholics and even the Queen to send Petre away from court and told D'Adda that he was a king and a gentleman and would sooner die a thousand deaths than do anything against his dignity. He feared the fainthearted at Whitehall, he said, more than his avowed enemies outside. He would concede not a jot more but would trust in God, who had brought him through so many tribulations, not to abandon him now.[24]

Such remarks reflected a real resurgence of confidence after the panic of late September. The invasion still had not come, the wind still blew from the west, keeping the Dutch fleet in port. Perhaps the special prayers and the exposing of the host which he had ordered had had their effect. Once more James could believe that God was with him and had given him time to prepare to defend himself against his wicked nephew and rebellious subjects. This belief was strengthened when William's fleet set sail on 20th October, only to be driven back by a terrible storm. Fortified by this news, James at last dismissed Sunderland, on the 26th. Middleton became senior secretary of state and Viscount Preston became second secretary. The Catholics complained at James's having two Protestant secretaries, but (as D'Adda remarked) there was no Catholic remotely suitable for the post.[25]

The burst of exuberant confidence which had nerved James to dismiss Sunderland soon evaporated. News came that the sailing of William's fleet would be delayed for only about a week. Meanwhile, signs of disaffection were everywhere. Few magnates offered James their services and ordinary people seemed indifferent to the peril facing their king. Some, indeed, prayed for the wind to veer to the east. James was desperately short of ready money to pay his sailors and was not helped by the interruption of trade and a run on the bankers. Rumours of all sorts flew thick and fast despite a proclamation against the spreading of false news. James tried to scotch one type of rumour by enrolling in Chancery solemn depositions about the birth of his son. But no solemn depositions could make people believe what they had chosen not to believe and (as Louis sagely observed) the publication of the depositions probably did more harm than good.[26]

At the end of October the first copies of William's declaration or manifesto were discovered. It catalogued the misdeeds into which James had been led by his evil counsellors and cast doubts on the legitimacy of the Prince of Wales. William stressed that he had been invited to invade and that his sole aim was "to have a free and lawful Parliament assembled as soon as possible". The declaration was a skilful compilation, setting out widely held grievances and offering a remedy on which Protestants of all sorts could agree. William had been reluctant to entrust his fate to a Parliament, but his English allies had assured him that it was essential. At first James tried to suppress the declaration, but copies still circulated and rumours of its contents proved even more damaging than the declaration itself, so eventually the government printed it, with suitably critical comments.[27]

When the declaration appeared, James questioned some bishops and lay peers about the invitation which William claimed to have received from "a great many lords both spiritual and temporal". None of them admitted to signing it, but the bishops found various pretexts to avoid formally declaring their abhorrence of the invasion. While these discussions were proceeding, James heard, on the night of 3rd November, that the Dutch fleet had passed Dover. His own fleet, under Dartmouth, was trapped in the Thames estuary by the same easterly wind which now blew William's armada down the Channel. By the time Dartmouth got out and sailed westwards he was too far behind to catch William who landed at Torbay on 5th November, already a special day in the Protestant calendar.

*   *   *

When William landed, James had two main preoccupations. The first was the security of his wife and son. For some years he had fortified Portsmouth to the landward as well as the seaward side. Always fearful of the rebellious spirit of his subjects, he had felt the need for a secure refuge in time of crisis and for an avenue of escape to France. As early as 11th October he had resolved to send the Queen and the Prince of Wales to Portsmouth if William landed. His reasons were simple: " 'Tis my son they aim at," he wrote, "and 'tis my son I must endeavour to preserve whatever becomes of me." On 3rd November, when he feared that William might land at Portsmouth, he sent extra forces to strengthen the garrison there, which was under the command of his son, Berwick. From the start, then, James was careful to keep the way open for a hasty retreat for his family and himself.[28]

His second concern, of course, was to defeat William's army. William had decided to land well away from London and, although some of his advisers had favoured the north, the wind took him to the south-west. James, meanwhile, had concentrated his forces in the south-east, so that he could quickly gather a large army to march against William wherever he landed. His primary concern was to maintain control of London, not only against William's army but also against its dissident citizens. Already in October there had been riots and other disturbances around Catholic chapels, some of which had had to close. It seemed vital therefore to keep several thousand soldiers quartered around London and Westminster to keep all quiet.[29]

This preoccupation with London shaped the whole of James's strategy. He was faced with two basic alternatives. In each case the disadvantages seemed to outweigh the advantages, for William had already broken through the first and most effective of James's lines of defence—the sea. One possibility was to remain in London, to concentrate on keeping control of the capital and to wait for William to march eastwards. This approach was recommended by both Petre and James's French military adviser, the Comte de Roye—the latter on military grounds, the former because he was afraid of what might happen to the Catholics if James left. The main disadvantage of this strategy was that it allowed William time to gather recruits and to sap the morale of James's soldiers. Although the gentry and nobility were at first slow to commit themselves to William's cause (which led him to threaten to go home), once a few had committed themselves, more and more others followed. Time was then on William's side and his military superiority became more and more marked.[30]

The second possibility was to seek out the enemy and give battle. This raised the problem of keeping order in London while James was away, but in fact his army was large enough for him to leave several thousand soldiers there and still put a larger force than William's into the field. As it turned out James's departure did not lead to a collapse of law and order in London, but there was a more serious objection to this strategy, which became apparent when James tried it. He could march towards William's army but he could not force it to fight. Moreover, it was far from easy to move a large army around the English countryside in the middle of winter. Roads which were seldom good even in summer became well-nigh impassable in winter. Wagons and artillery moved at a snail's pace through mud and slush. Provisions and forage were hard to come by, partly because of the inadequacies of James's military administration (which in winter was geared to supplying scattered garrisons, not large, moving bodies of troops) and partly because of the hostility of local people, who proved far more willing to supply William's army than James's.

James's war effort was hampered by two other problems. First, he lacked reliable information. His government did what it could to suppress unlicensed news and to disseminate its own version of events, but much Williamite propaganda still circulated, supplemented by a vast amount of rumour. Thus most of the news which reached London was likely to be distorted or fictitious. When James took the field, most of his scouts defected to the enemy, so he was forced to rely mainly on rumour, which led him to believe that William's army was nearer than it really was and that London was in a turmoil. The second problem stemmed from the deficiencies of James's leadership. He certainly did not lack application—indeed, he wore himself out with overwork—but he proved incapable of delegating even the pettiest details. He thus spent an inordinate amount of time on trivia but failed to reach positive decisions even on minor matters, let alone tackling the major problems of provisions and forage. The indecisiveness which had become increasingly apparent over the last year or two now seriously impeded his military leadership.[31]

James's first concern when he heard of William's landing was to confine him to Devon and Cornwall and to deprive him of support from elsewhere. He sent cavalry and dragoons to Salisbury, had the bridge at Keynsham broken and ordered a close watch on the roads to the south-west. Meanwhile, riots continued in London. On 12th November James's soldiers fired on the rioters for the first time, killing seven or eight. Despite this unrest and the arguments of Roye and Petre, James prepared to march westwards, but before he left there were two ominous incidents. On the 15th news came that three regiments had deserted to the enemy, on which James ordered the rest of the army to fall back. Next day, news came that many officers and soldiers from the three regiments had returned, and James ordered his army to resume its march. Even so, the evidence of disaffection was worrying and James was jittery and uneasy. He changed his mind three times in two days about sending his wife and son to Portsmouth. Then, on the morning of the 17th, he received a petition from nineteen peers asking him to call a free Parliament. The Protestants at court pressed him to agree, but James said that it would not be convenient to hold elections while the rebellion lasted. The petitioners included one of James's generals, the Duke of Grafton. James had already warned him not to subscribe any such petition, but Grafton had replied that James's army and fleet would desert him if he relied too much on the French or the Papists. Such utterances did not augur well for the army's conduct in the coming struggle.[32]

That afternoon James left London for Windsor, having made his will. On the evening of the 19th he reached Salisbury. His plan (he wrote later) was to push his cavalry forward to take a line of towns—Axminster, Chard, Langport

—which would make it possible to confine William to Cornwall, Devon and western Somerset. He abandoned this plan for three reasons. First, the terrain proved unsuitable for cavalry; secondly, faulty intelligence led him to believe that William's army was already on the march; thirdly, James feared that any regiment sent towards the west was liable to defect. Even a plan to visit his own advanced quarters at Warminster came to nothing. Worn out by weeks of overwork and insufficient sleep, James suffered a series of violent nosebleeds and took to his bed. He claimed later that these nosebleeds were a blessing in disguise and that there had been a plan to kidnap him at Warminster and carry him to William's army. Whether or not that was true, James's illness gave him a chance to take stock of his position. It was not encouraging. He had been warned already that it would be hard to keep his army supplied with food and forage and that it would be difficult to defend Warminster and Salisbury against a determined enemy. He could see now that these warnings had been well founded. Moreover, the morale of his officers—even the generals—left much to be desired, while petitions for a free Parliament circulated among the soldiers. Intelligence of William's movements proved very hard to come by. In fact, he did not leave Exeter until the 21st, having taken a fortnight to acquire enough cavalry horses and draught animals to begin his march and to persuade the Governor of Plymouth to take his side. Rumour, however, led James to believe that William was already at Axminster and a more accurate piece of news increased his anxieties: Lord Delamere had risen in Cheshire and declared for William.[33]

In these circumstances it seemed pointless, indeed dangerous, to remain at Salisbury. Churchill excepted, the generals advised James to retreat towards London. Reluctantly James agreed and on the 23rd the withdrawal began. James now decided to position his troops along the Thames, from Marlow to Chertsey, on the assumption that William would attack London from the south-west. However much James may have wished to preserve the appearance of an orderly withdrawal, it soon assumed the characteristics of a rout. The first night Grafton and Churchill defected to William, with a number of officers and men, followed the next night by Anne's husband, Prince George. James was especially angry about Churchill, whom he had raised from nothing and from whom he had therefore expected total loyalty. The desertions filled the army with unease. No one was willing to trust his neighbour. As one eye-witness recalled:

"I can never forget the confusion the court was in. . . . The King knew not whom to trust and the fright was so great that they were apt to believe an impossible report just then brought in that the Prince of Orange was come with twelve thousand horse between Warminster and Salisbury. . . . Everybody in this hurly-burly was thinking of himself and nobody minded the King, who came up to Dr Radcliffe and asked him what was good for the bleeding of his nose."[34]

Further disasters awaited James when he returned to London on the night of the 26th. He had already heard of risings in Yorkshire and Nottinghamshire by William's supporters. That morning he had heard, too, that his daughter Anne had gone off to the rebels. A stolid, unimaginative woman, Anne shared her sister Mary's stubborn Protestantism and doubts about the legitimacy of their stepbrother. She lived in constant fear that her father would try to convert her to Catholicism, although in fact he never did. After the birth of the Prince of Wales, she dissociated herself completely from James's measures and refused to try to influence him in any way. In this she was encouraged by her confidante, Lady Churchill, who helped to persuade her to flee from London. To James, her defection ranked alongside Churchill's in its unnatural ingratitude and dealt a further blow to his confidence. If he could not trust his own daughter, whom could he trust?[35]

The trickle of defections now became a flood. All over the country Tory lords lieutenant and militia officers either failed to do anything to oppose William or called out the militia and joined him. Even some who remained loyal, like Dartmouth and Beaufort, sent petitions for a free Parliament. Many Tories, despite their belief in non-resistance, saw William as a deliverer. As one of them wrote: "How these risings and associations can be justified, I see not; but yet it is very apparent had not the Prince come and these persons thus appeared our religion had been rooted out." Meanwhile, the rumours and alarums continued unabated. Citters reported that the Queen had ordered the Catholics of Lancashire to rise and attack the Protestants but that their plans had been thwarted by Delamere. London was racked with rumours that the Papists would fire the city and massacre the inhabitants. Elsewhere there were wild stories that the French had landed in Kent or Cornwall. Despite continued sporadic rioting, the army and the City authorities still maintained order in London, but fears were growing that the situation could get out of control.[36]

It is against this background that one should see James's actions in the two weeks after his return to London. His world seemed to be collapsing round him. His most trusted servants were deserting him. The country seemed to be dissolving into chaos. His own physical condition had deteriorated. He was exhausted and emaciated: "The King is much out of order, looks yellow and takes no natural rest." He slept only with the help of opiates. He pondered gloomily on the mutability of human fortune and recalled Christ's sufferings at the hand of his enemies: "Yes, O my God, Thine own selected nation conspired against Thee and with innumerable affronts most barbarously murdered Thee." But he still placed all his trust in God, at whose right hand were crowns, riches and greatness. It was thus with fatalism and resignation that he considered the intractable problems which now faced him.[37]

As usual, he received two different types of advice. The Tories, led by Clarendon, Dartmouth and some of the bishops (supported by Middleton and Preston), argued that he had no choice but to come to terms with William. They took at face value the promise in William's declaration that he had come only to secure a free Parliament, and urged James to meet this demand of his own volition. They accepted that James would have to make major concessions, but insisted that no harm could come to his person. The Catholic zealots, meanwhile, continued to argue that concessions would prove fatal to the Catholics, the monarchy and James himself. As Melfort argued, his enemies had shown no restraint in their attacks on the Prince of Wales and would show none in their dealing with James. The zealots urged him to withdraw to France, to preserve his rights intact and to wait to be restored as his brother had been, once his subjects had seen the error of their ways.[38]

Of these two courses of action, the first would be much the more acceptable to James's subjects, but it contained two serious snags. First, it assumed that William could be brought to agree terms with James. William stressed that he would abide by his declaration and denied that he wished to depose James. His main concern was to bring England into the war against France as soon as possible. William's Whig associates, however, had no wish to see a settlement arranged by the Tories which would leave the Tories in power, nor did they want a general election while the Tories dominated local government and many of the boroughs. They therefore sought to persuade William to delay the meeting of Parliament and to stipulate conditions which James would not accept. Their aim, as Burnet explained, was not to harm James—William would not stand for that—but to drive him out of the country. William occasionally overruled the Whigs' demands, but their influential position in his entourage made a moderate compromise difficult to achieve. Moreover, William had no intention of halting his march on London while he negotiated with James.[39]

The second weakness of the Tories' proposals stemmed from James's own attitude. He talked much of his father and of Richard II, whose cases did not offer hopeful precedents for a king forced to negotiate with his subjects from a position of weakness. He feared for his own life and still more for the lives of his wife and son. On the 29th he ordered Dartmouth to transport the baby from Portsmouth to France. Dartmouth refused, James had the child brought back to London and mother and child left for France on 9th December. Apart from physical fear, James could not bear the thought of the concessions which he would have to make. He would have to allow the persecution of Catholics, the powers of the crown would be drastically reduced and, worst of all, Parliament would insist on investigating his son's birth, with predictable results. As James saw it, then, there were only two alternatives, resistance and flight. As late as 3rd December, James was still uncertain which to choose (although he was already making plans to send away his wife and son). He now had almost no advisers whom he could trust. Sunderland, on whom he had leaned for so long, was a broken reed. Petre had fled, Melfort was about to follow. James seems now to have placed most trust in the Queen and D'Adda. He does not seem to have taken Barrillon into his confidence about either his plans to send away the Queen and the Prince of Wales or his own decision to depart, perhaps because Barrillon thought that Louis' interests could best be served if James remained and used whatever influence he still had to prevent a war against France. James's last thoughts of resistance ended on 3rd December, when Feversham told him that he could no longer answer for the army's loyalty.

James had already prepared to negotiate with William, but did not really expect or wish the negotiations to succeed. His only hope was that the negotiations might slow down William's march on London and so give him more time to arrange his escape to France.[40]

On 27th November, the day after he returned to London, James summoned all the peers in town to wait upon him. About forty appeared. Almost all stressed the need to open negotiations with William and to call a Parliament. These and other demands constituted a "bitter draught", but James had little choice but to swallow it. He sent out the writs for a general election and commissioned Halifax, Nottingham and Godolphin to negotiate with William on his behalf. After some confusion about papers, the commissioners duly appeared before William on 8th December. They had been instructed to tell William that James had summoned a Parliament for 15th January and to propose that William's army should remain forty miles from London. William was asked to suggest any measures which could assist this design. After much discussion among his followers, William set out his demands. These included the dismissal of all Papists from office, the recall of proclamations describing William's followers as rebels, adequate financial provision for William's army and the placing of the Tower, Portsmouth and Tilbury in safe hands. If James saw fit to be in London when Parliament met, William wished to be there too, with the same number of guards, while the two armies should remain forty miles away. Such demands were not unduly harsh and many saw them as a reasonable basis for a settlement. The commissioners received them on the morning of the 10th. They sent off a copy at once and then set off for London, to press James to agree to William's conditions.[41]

The first James heard of the progress of the negotiations was when he received, on the 9th, an account of the commissioners' first meeting with William, which made it clear that William was most unlikely to halt his march on London. James ordered D'Adda to leave and sent off the Queen that night, in the care of a Frenchman, the Comte de Lauzun. On the 10th he talked of going to inspect his forces at Uxbridge the next day, but that was merely a blind. He stopped the issue of the electoral writs and entrusted his papers and a large sum of money to the resident of the Grand Duke of Tuscany. At nine o'clock that evening he received the letter setting out William's demands. He announced that he would give his answer in the morning. Ailesbury, one of the lords of the bedchamber, had heard of his plan to fly and begged him to place more trust in his subjects. Again, James said he would talk of it next morning. Shortly after midnight, he slipped down the backstairs, accompanied only by two Catholics, Sir Edward Hales and Ralph Sheldon. They took a boat across the river to Vauxhall. There horses were waiting and they rode eastwards to find the boat which was to take them to France.[42]

*   *   *

With the news of James's flight, law and order in London finally broke down. On the night of the 11th the sky was red with the flames from Catholic chapels. The following night the confusion was still greater, as the citizens were terrified with rumours that the Irish units from James's army were on the rampage, burning and killing wherever they went. The confusion was compounded by the disintegration of James's army. James had ordered Feversham to undertake no further hostilities against William. Feversham read this order to the regiments at Uxbridge, some of which then broke up while others marched off to join William. He took little care to disarm those who dispersed, so that disbanded soldiers joined the anti-Catholic rioters while armed bands of Irish Catholics roamed the country looking for food and shelter.[43]

In an effort to reimpose order, a number of peers met at the Guildhall on the 11th. They secured the Tower and ordered army officers to regroup their companies and to use them to keep order in the city. They also called out the militia. By the 13th, order had more or less been restored, but the political dilemma which the peers faced was less easily resolved. Some already argued that, by his flight, James had forfeited his right to the crown. Those Whigs who had opposed a reconciliation were overjoyed at James's departure and William was clearly pleased. He decided to march to London at once, ostensibly to restore order.[44] The peers at the Guildhall were deeply divided. The majority were loyalist Tories, who had wanted a negotiated settlement based on a free Parliament. James's flight was a bitter and incomprehensible blow, but they were still determined to do what they could to preserve James's rights. Led by Clarendon, Rochester and their allies among the bishops, the Tories failed to persuade their colleagues to include in their declaration an explicit assertion of James's prerogatives, but prevented the inclusion of a clause inviting William to come to London. The City authorities were less inhibited and their invitation served to legitimate the decision which William had already taken to resume his march. Nevertheless, the events of the 11th and 12th showed that James still had many supporters, if he chose to make use of them.[45]

James, meanwhile, was suffering still further humiliations. In the early hours of the 11th he and his companions rode through Kent, avoiding the main roads. The county was in a turmoil. Armed bands of peasants and seamen questioned travellers, looking for priests and other suspicious persons. Several towns had been taken over by the inhabitants, who regarded the municipal authorities as insufficiently vigilant and zealous. Everywhere, as in London, there were rumours and fears of the Irish, who were said to be looting and killing wherever they went. Somehow James's little party reached the Isle of Sheppey, where a custom house boat was waiting for them. It took some time to take on ballast and it was only towards midnight that they were ready to sail. Just then three small boats arrived, laden with seamen from Faversham looking for priests. At once they recognized Hales, who was a local man, but James was disguised in "a short black wig [and] a patch on his upper lip on the left side". Most of the seamen assumed that he was a Jesuit. Their leader, Amis, persuaded the fugitives to entrust their valuables to him, but the other seamen insisted on searching them again, removing James's breeches and searching "even to his privities". They took away a crucifix containing a fragment of the true cross, at which James was most distressed, but missed some small pieces of jewellery which he had hidden in his drawers. James and his companions spent a miserable night, waiting for the tide to turn so that they could be taken to Faversham. The seamen lit a fire and smoked all night, ignoring James's complaints. Only a pipemaker was at all civil to James and amused him with a droll explanation of his belief that Catholics went to heaven, but by a very roundabout route.[46]

At noon the next day the seamen and their captives reached Faversham. James was recognized at once, which merely increased his alarm. He entreated all who came near, "begging, praying, tempting, arguing, reproving, etc.", to find him a boat and help him escape. This annoyed the seamen as did the arrival of the Lord Lieutenant and some of the local gentry, who tried to take charge of their prisoners. The sailors were reluctant to let them go: they feared the gentry would let James go or claim from William the glory and rewards for capturing the King. James was moved from an inn to the Mayor's house, but the seamen insisted on guarding him. James was so frightened that he could scarcely write. He reproved the Anglican clergymen who came to see him for their distrustfulness and quoted the Bible at them incessantly (much to their surprise), showing especial fondness for the thoughts of Job on the spiritual benefits of affliction. He wept often. On the 13th he had to listen to some Kentish gentry as they read William's declaration below his window and James came to regard the gentry as a greater threat than the seamen. Sir Basil Dixwell appointed himself James's keeper and complained at James's writing to London for clean clothes without seeking his permission. The lords at the Guildhall were greatly embarrassed by the letter. They did not want to be discourteous to James, but were desperately afraid of offending William. They agreed to send James servants and clothing and (after some hesitation) guards to defend him against the "insolence" of the people. But they rejected Ailesbury's proposal to invite James to return to London and refused to give any indication of what they wished him to do.[47]

Ailesbury set out for Faversham on the night of the 13th. He found James next day with several days' growth of beard, looking like Charles I at his trial. He had the room cleared of the seamen and women who stood around chattering. James was shaved, dressed in a clean shirt and served at dinner with all the formality which the amenities and poor food would allow. Sensing the change in James's condition, the seamen protested their loyalty, saying that their main concern had been to keep James from harm. James left Faversham on the 15th and joined his guards, who escorted him back to London. At first he intended to avoid the City and cross the river at Lambeth, but the large cheering crowds waiting on Blackheath helped to change his mind. He passed through the City and down the Strand with every appearance of triumph. The Tories were especially pleased, as his return revived the possibility of an amicable settlement between James and William. James had at first been irritated by their eagerness to seize power on the 11th—"You were all kings when I left London," he told Ailesbury—but he soon came to accept the loyalists' good intentions. At court that night all seemed much as usual. James dined in public, summoned the council and heard Mass. Many Catholics came out of hiding and appeared at Whitehall. But James was not reassured by the warmth of his reception. He made it clear to Barrillon that he had no intention of coming to terms and that he was still intent on flight.[48]

When William heard that James had been stopped, he was very disturbed and sent to tell him to remain at Rochester. James did not receive the message and his return to London forced William to reconsider his position. Some of his English followers argued that James had forfeited his rights by going away. The loyalists, for their part, soon came to see that the balance of power, military and political, had shifted decisively in William's favour during the six days that James had been away. James no longer had an army while his failure to make any provision for order and government seemed to many criminally irresponsible. Indeed, he had gone out of his way to add to the confusion and to hinder a settlement, throwing away the great seal and destroying two-thirds of the electoral writs. Even so, William was eager to get rid of James without using too much obvious force; it would be best if James appeared to leave the kingdom voluntarily. He therefore decided to order James, for his own safety, to leave London for Ham House. On the night of the 17th a body of Dutch guards arrived at Whitehall to take over from those whom James had posted. There seemed no point in resisting, so James reluctantly acquiesced. Then, at one o'clock in the morning Halifax, Shrewsbury and Delamere arrived with William's orders that James should leave London later that morning.[49]

James was alarmed, but remained outwardly calm. He argued that Ham was too small and poorly furnished and added, "I cannot have any of my people there." Clearly he feared assassination—not unreasonably, since his palace was now surrounded by Dutch soldiers—and gave as one reason for proposing to go to Rochester that some of his foot guards were there. William raised no objection, so on the morning of the 18th a melancholy little convoy of barges set off down river, carrying James, his servants and a guard of a hundred soldiers. James reached Rochester on the 19th and spent the next few days talking, writing and at his devotions, awaiting an opportunity to escape. His loyalist supporters begged him not to go, but his mind was made up. To James's fears for his safety, they replied only with "bare suppositions that they did not believe the Prince of Orange would attempt anything against his majesty's life."[50]

On the night of the 22nd Berwick arrived with some blank passports. That morning a committee of peers and MPs had met to consider the state of the kingdom. James could expect little good from such a meeting and wasted no time in making good his escape. He told the faithful Ailesbury that if he stayed he would be sent to the Tower "and no King ever went out of that place but to his grave." He would return, he added, when his subjects' eyes were opened. They parted with many tears on both sides. Soon after, James slipped out of the back door (which William had deliberately left unguarded), down to where a small boat was waiting. After a wretched crossing he landed at Ambleteuse early on Christmas morning, still talking bitterly of Churchill's ingratitude. Three days later he was reunited with the Queen at St Germain en Laye. Louis greeted the royal refugee with great lavishness and pomp, his earlier niggardliness forgotten. He clearly revelled in the role of a great king, succouring an unfortunate fellow monarch. He placed the palace of St Germain at James's disposal and granted him a pension of fifty thousand francs a month. While James settled down to yet another period of exile, in which to ponder on the infidelity of the English, William advanced steadily towards the crown. By the end of December he controlled the military and civil government. He summoned a Convention or Parliament, which had little real choice but to recognize the accomplished fact that William was exercising the powers of king. It declared that by deserting his people and breaking the laws, James had abdicated the crown, which was thereupon offered jointly to William and Mary on 13th February, 1689.[51]

CHAPTER FOURTEEN

Scotland and Ireland (1685–88)

From James's point of view, England was by far the most important (as well as the richest and most populous) of his three kingdoms. Despite his Scots descent he regarded himself as an Englishman and saw the interests of Scotland and Ireland as subordinate to those of England. Whatever measures he undertook there, he made it clear that they were not to interfere with his plans for England. Nevertheless, he was King of Scotland and Ireland and could not ignore their affairs entirely for three reasons. First, the peers and politicians of the two countries strove constantly to influence James's conduct of their affairs. Secondly, he regarded it as vital to keep the two kingdoms quiet and to keep any dissident elements there in subjection. Thirdly, he felt obliged to do what he could to help the Scots and Irish Catholics. These three concerns were common to Scotland and Ireland, and to some extent to England. There were also important differences between them which ensured that their history in James's reign was very different.

Under James all major decisions on Scots and Irish affairs were made at the English court. Charles, while retaining the final say, had allowed some initiative to the secret committee of the privy council in Edinburgh or the lord lieutenant in Dublin. James did not. As one Scottish commentator noted in 1685:

> "In the last king's time, things were formed here and sent up to court and there passed and remitted down again. But now they come straight down without consulting the secret committee, who are in the head of affairs here and yet are surprised with some orders from his majesty, knowing nothing of them beforehand."

The secret committee occasionally remonstrated that, being on the spot, they were better informed and could give better advice than those in London, but James paid little heed. He concentrated more and more power in the hands of one or two men, notably the Chancellor, the Earl of Perth. Indeed, James's letters to the secret committee were sometimes little more than a list of heads, to which Perth was to add the details.[1] Much the same situation prevailed in Irish affairs. From the time of Ormond's recall, the chief governors lost all influence over military appointments, which were now decided in London. By 1686 Tyrconnell was appointing and dismissing army officers by the dozen without consulting Clarendon, the lord lieutenant, who, indeed, played almost no part in the formulation of policy.

One result of this concentration of Scottish and Irish policy-making in London was that James's policies were based on information that was often inadequate or distorted. Another was that effective power over Scottish and Irish affairs was more or less monopolized by three politicians who had great personal influence with the King. All were Catholics, all were at some time allies of Sunderland and two of them divided their time between London and either Edinburgh or Dublin. First they would procure the King's order for the measures they wanted, then they went to ensure that the governors of Scotland or Ireland obeyed those orders, then they returned to court to plan their next move. In Ireland, Tyrconnell ruled supreme. An old servant of James's and a prodigiously forceful personality, he still needed Sunderland's help, first to secure Clarendon's removal in 1686, then to fend off the attacks of his enemies at court after he had gone to Ireland as lord deputy in 1687. In Scotland the position was more complex. The dominant figures at court were the Drummond brothers, Perth and Melfort, both converts to Catholicism (which naturally endeared them to James). Melfort stayed at court while Perth went periodically to Edinburgh to implement each new set of measures. They too needed Sunderland's help in 1685–86. As Tyrconnell's way was blocked by Clarendon and Sunderland's way was blocked by Rochester, so Perth and Melfort's was blocked by Lord Treasurer Queensberry, Rochester's brother in law. Like Clarendon and Rochester, Queensberry was pushed out of power during 1686. As with Tyrconnell, Sunderland found Perth and Melfort difficult to control once they were firmly esconced in power. Melfort was, in fact, a more dangerous rival than Tyrconnell, as he was always at court: indeed, he contributed substantially to Sunderland's eventual fall.

One prime concern of James's Scottish and Irish policies was the maintenance of order. James was always very sensitive—perhaps over-sensitive—to the dangers of rebellion. The events of 1637–42 had shown clearly the disruptive effects within England of disorders in Scotland and Ireland. James's own experience of the Cameronians confirmed the need for vigilance and repression and he knew that men of similar views could be found across the North Channel among the Ulster Scots. He therefore thought it essential to strengthen the regular army in both kingdoms and to weaken the military potential of the "disaffected". This was seen clearly in his treatment of the militia. The militia was an essentially civilian and amateur body, in which peasants and artisans learned rudimentary drill from gentlemen officers and performed simple, mostly auxiliary, military tasks. James believed that in areas where the bulk of the population was "disaffected", the militia, far from being useful, could be downright dangerous. His belief was strengthened during Argyll and Monmouth's rebellions: in both Scotland and England, part of the militia defected to the rebels. Accordingly, in England James let the militia decay and planned to use the militia rates to help maintain the standing army. In Ireland, Tyrconnell convinced James that Ulster was so disaffected that it was better to have no militia at all, so James ordered the confiscation of the militia's weapons, throughout Ireland. (There are hints of a move to disarm the English militia early in 1688.) For good measure, the arms of "disaffected" private citizens were confiscated as well, which also happened in England, although on a much smaller scale. In Scotland James had made up his mind to abolish the militia even before Argyll's rebellion. He secured an Act of Parliament obliging all men between sixteen and sixty to turn out to serve the King in an emergency, which in effect made the militia redundant, for these general levies and the army could, between them, perform all the tasks which the militia had hitherto performed.[2]

The treatment of the regular armies varied. That of Scotland remained much the same. In 1688 Perth complained that "the hundredth man in it is not a Catholic and we have scarce any officers of that persuasion." It still, however, performed its usual police functions well enough, including suppressing field conventicles. The English army also remained mainly Protestant, presumably because of a shortage of suitable Catholic officers and soldiers. There was no such problem in Ireland. Tyrconnell convinced James (without much difficulty) that most Irish Protestants were inclined to rebellion and republicanism and that only the Catholics were truly loyal. As a result the army was almost wholly Catholic in 1688 and James was so confident of the loyalty of his Irish regiments that he brought some over to reinforce the English army.[3]

As for the promotion of Catholicism, the pattern in Scotland and Ireland was similar to that in England. Again, James's aim was to allow the Catholics freedom of worship and to hold public offices. In Scotland as in England, Parliament proved unco-operative so James resorted to prerogative action. In Ireland there were fewer legal restrictions on Catholicism, so James proceeded by administrative action from the start. In all three kingdoms, he saw it as essential that the religious liberty and civil equality which he had granted should be confirmed and made permanent by a Parliament. In all three, he prepared for this Parliament by sustained interference in the internal affairs of the parliamentary boroughs, backed up (in England and Ireland) by a campaign against the boroughs' charters. In all three, the Revolution came before Parliament could meet and show whether these preparations had been effective.

Despite these similarities, there were crucial differences between the experience of England, Scotland and Ireland in James's reign. First, there were great legal and institutional differences. Parliament was far more powerful and independent in England than in either Scotland or Ireland, while the royal prerogative was far less extensive. On the other hand, England was a more settled and orderly country, untroubled by rapparees, Cameronians or autonomous clan chiefs. Secondly, there were great variations in the balance of religious power in the three kingdoms. In England, the Anglicans were much the largest denomination; the Dissenters were less numerous and the Catholics a tiny minority. In Scotland and Ireland the ruling Episcopalian elite was small. In Scotland most people were Presbyterians of one sort or another, while Catholics were very few. In Ireland, Presbyterians and other Dissenters outnumbered the Episcopalians but the Catholics were much more numerous still. Thus the granting of religious liberty had different effects in the three countries. In England, neither Catholics nor Dissenters made much headway against the Church of England. In Ireland, the main beneficiaries were the Catholics, who already possessed a numerous priesthood and a full ecclesiastical organization. In Scotland, as in England, the work of making converts to Catholicism was impeded both by an acute shortage of priests and by the hostility of all types of Protestants, who agreed in hating the Papists, if in little else. The Catholic mission in Scotland was even less successful than in England. By early 1688 there were only two public Catholic chapels, in Edinburgh and Aberdeen, although there were chapels in many English towns. The main beneficiaries of the religious liberty in Scotland were the Presbyterians. Their numbers swollen by returning exiles, the Presbyterian clergy began to build an ecclesiastical organization and prepared the way for their capture of the Church of Scotland at the Revolution.[4]

* * *

After his return to England in 1682, James still showed considerable interest in Scots affairs, sending a great deal of advice to Queensberry. For this reason, Burnet blamed James for the brutal and often illegal methods used against the radical Dissenters in 1682–84. There is no evidenca that James had anything against such methods, but it seems that the main responsibility for them rested with the men on the spot, above all with Perth. Burnet failed to mention, too, that the indulgence of the more moderate Presbyterians continued.[5]

In the last years of Charles's reign Queensberry and Perth were allies. Together they secured the dismissal of the Lord Chancellor, the Earl of Aberdeen, in the spring of 1684. Perth became chancellor and his brother, Drummond of Lundin, moved into the important post of secretary of state for Scotland. At this stage both were still Protestants: they announced their conversions at the end of 1685. Like Sunderland, they saw that the obvious way to challenge the Rochester–Queensberry interest was with the help of the Catholics, but unlike Sunderland's, their conversions were lasting and, apparently, sincere. When James became king, Lundin (soon created Earl of Melfort) began at once to denigrate Queensberry's handling of affairs, but found it far from easy to undermine James's faith in him. Queensberry served James diligently in the Scottish Parliament in 1685 and had allies among the Scots at court, notably Middleton. Ominously for Queensberry, however, Hamilton joined the Drummonds in pressing for his dismissal. In December James tried to reconcile them all, but their protestations of friendship were insincere. At last, in February 1686, came the Drummonds' chance. Perth had opened a Catholic chapel in Edinburgh. Crowds of youths threw stones—and worse—at his coach and rescued some of their number who had been sentenced to be whipped. To his criticism of Queensberry's finar.cial competence, Perth added allegations that the Treasurer had been behind the riots and tried, unavailingly, to persuade those involved to implicate Queensberry. James's trust in Queensberry was broken. His office was suppressed and a treasury commission set up. Queensberry was a member, but Perth was first commissioner. Queensberry's power was at an end.[6]

When he told Barrillon of these changes, James stressed the need to uphold the royal, Catholic party in Scotland against that of the "zealous Protestants". Clearly Perth and Melfort, like Tyrconnell, were trying to convince James that only the Catholics were truly loyal. Now that Queensberry had gone, Melfort claimed that all would go well. It did not. The Parliament which met in May proved less compliant than expected and refused to allow Catholics to hold offices. Moreover, the Drummonds' control of Scottish affairs was not uncontested. Hamilton had helped them to bring down Queensberry and his influence among the nobility was too great to be ignored. He was a Protestant, but he was also greedy and eager for power. He might dislike the measures which James took to help the Catholics, but he always, eventually, forced his conscience to accept them. His alliance with the Drummonds was bound to be uneasy. Melfort taunted him with claims that no Christian could deny the justice of James's plans for the Catholics. Hamilton's son Arran, who looked after his interests at court, had several furious quarrels with Melfort, but they were always patched up. James still believed he needed Hamilton, and Sunderland supported him as a counterbalance to Melfort. But even if the Drummonds could not break Hamilton's influence, they did far more than he did to shape James's Scottish policy in 1687–88, for their strength (like Sunderland's or Petre's) lay in their zeal for Catholicism and in their telling James what he wished to believe.[7]

Two themes stood out in James's Scottish policy: the strengthening of the state's powers of repression and the promotion of Catholicism. In 1685 Queensberry, helped by the reaction against Argyll's rebellion, pushed through Parliament several measures designed to augment the King's power. The revenue was increased and granted to James for life: financially he was in a stronger position than any of his predecessors. Further measures were taken against radical Dissenters, the Test was extended to all suspected of disaffection (an not just office holders) and Parliament acknowledged the King's "absolute prerogative" more fully and explicitly than ever before. He also tried to procure legislation eroding still further the rights of those accused of treason and reducing the degree of proof required for a conviction, but against the opposition of the lawyers in Parliament he was not entirely successful. Even so, the crown's power was greater than ever before by the end of 1685. Thereafter James's main concern was to be the advancement of Catholicism.[8]

In November 1685 James dispensed from taking the Test twenty-six Catholics named as collectors of the revenue and in December Perth opened his chapel in Edinburgh. In March 1686 James informed the secret committee that he wished Parliament to remove the penal laws, to admit Catholics to office and to replace the Test with a simple oath of allegiance. Perth and Melfort had told him that, with Queensberry's power broken, there should be little difficulty. The secret committee was less sure and said that it wished to consult the bishops. James replied angrily that he could, by his prerogative, employ whomsoever he chose and relieve his subjects from the penalties of unjust laws. He summoned Hamilton and two other members of the committee to

London. They soon raised difficulties about James's proposals, arguing that Parliament would allow Catholics to worship unmolested in their own homes only if the same liberty were allowed to Dissenters. James, who "wanted very much that only the Catholics should be free to practise their religion", was eventually persuaded to agree. As for the Test, they thought Parliament would remove it only if James agreed to cast-iron safeguards for the Protestant religion, which James refused to do. Hamilton and his colleagues then promised to propose its repeal, but held out little hope of success.[9]

Faced with the unexpected stiffness of Hamilton and his colleagues, the court Catholics claimed that they had been tampered with by Rochester and other "zealous Protestants". Such suspicions seemed confirmed when Parliament met. The court had been careful to prepare the way. It dangled the bait of free trade with England before the burghs. Army officers known to oppose the toleration were ordered to their garrisons, other members were advised to stay away and open critics of the measures were dismissed from their offices. But to no avail. A committee was set up, which recommended that Catholics should be allowed to worship freely in private houses but that all the acts against Popery (especially those imposing the oaths and Test on office holders) should be enforced to the full. James hastily sent some proposed modifications, Parliament seemed reluctant to accept them, so James adjourned and then dissolved it.[10]

James blamed the failure of the session on the zealous Protestants and on William's supporters. He remarked that he now knew whom he could trust and that his prerogative gave him ample power to grant liberty to the Catholics. The Act of Supremacy of 1669 gave the King vague and potentially very extensive powers over the Scottish church. Moreover, he possessed a dispensing power, in Scotland as in England, whose limits were uncertain and it was argued that he could suspend laws during his lifetime. (Others claimed that he could dispense only with past, not future, breaches of the law.) In August James wrote to the council, stressing the Catholics' loyalty and declaring that the Test was not intended to debar anyone from voting in Parliament or council. He required the council to support him in allowing the Catholics to practise their religion in private. The council was embarrassed. It saw that it was being asked to endorse James's granting liberty by prerogative. Despite some objections from Hamilton and others, the council offered no serious resistance. The principle had been conceded and James could proceed.[11]

In February 1687 James issued a declaration of indulgence allowing Catholics to worship freely and Presbyterians and Quakers to worship only in private houses. Dissenting clergymen could preach only if they took a special oath. Few Presbyterians would accept toleration under such conditions. In April the oath was waived, but the ban on field conventicles continued and was firmly enforced: James still saw field conventiclers as enemies of both the state and Christianity. As the year went on, the restrictions on Presbyterian worship were relaxed and James tried to win them to the cause of a general liberty of conscience, using such intermediaries as James Stewart. The Presbyterians were willing to embrace the liberty which James offered, but far less prepared to pay the price he demanded—removal of the penal laws and Test Acts. A few warned too loudly against the dangers from Popery and were punished. As in England, there were limits to what James would tolerate.[12]

The eighteen months after the declaration of indulgence saw few new developments. James appointed magistrates in a few large burghs, as if in preparation for a Parliament, but showed no real sign of calling one. He seems now to have been waiting for the indulgence to bear fruit, but few converts appeared. Perth and Melfort, meanwhile, were out to make as much money as they could. As secretary, Melfort received a fee for each official document he issued; he forced people to take out various unnecessary documents in order to collect the fees. Comfortably established in power and growing wealthier by the day, the Drummonds carried on their feuds with Hamilton and Arran, but basically had good reason to be content with things as they were. There was little point in calling Parliament and, until more Catholics appeared, not much could be done. By 1688 James's Scottish policy had run out of impetus, mainly through lack of support.[13]

* * *

Ireland, alone of James's kingdoms, was predominantly Catholic: Petty calculated that there were 100,000 Church of Ireland (Episcopalian) Protestants, 200,000 Dissenters and 800,000 Catholics.[14] The vast majority of these Catholics were of native Irish extraction but there was a small elite of "Old English": heirs of the original conquerors, proud of their English blood and rather contemptuous of the Irish over whom they had ruled for so long. During the seventeenth century, however, a new Protestant elite came to enjoy a monopoly of political power and deprived most of the "Old English" of their estates. For the first time, "Old English" and native Irish Catholics were united by common deprivation and exclusion from power, but they had not given up hope of regaining what they had lost and James's accession seemed to offer them a golden opportunity.

Richard Talbot came of an "Old English" family. Almost thirty years of service had earned him James's trust and respect. He was highly articulate and had the self-confidence to advance specious arguments with an air of utter conviction. He was also prone to ferocious rages before which lesser mortals wilted. Like the Drummonds he used his Catholicism and his influence with James to push his way into a position of great power. Unlike the Drummonds he does not seem to have been motivated by personal ambition or greed*: older than the Drummonds and in poor health, he had no children to inherit his fortune. To Tyrconnell, power was not an end in itself, but a means to a political end: the restoration of the power of the "Old English" Catholics.

In order to achieve this, Tyrconnell had to destroy every aspect of the Protestant ascendancy. He had to disarm the Protestants and restore the arms

---

* A hostile writer accused Tyrconnell and his followers of profiteering in 1689–90; O'Kelly, pp67–70.

confiscated from Catholics. He had to fill the army with Catholic officers and soldiers. He had to give Catholics a monopoly of places in the legal system and administration. He had, above all, to restore the estates confiscated from the "Old English" since 1641. Moreover, he had to do these things quickly. James was already in his fifties. If he died and William and Mary succeeded him, the Catholics' chance would be gone.

In some ways James sympathized with these objectives. He thought it unjust and unnatural that Catholics should be excluded from office on religious grounds and was predisposed to accept Tyrconnell's arguments that the Catholics were the only truly loyal subjects in Ireland. He believed it was vital to have one completely reliable (Catholic) army in his dominions, to repress disorders wherever they arose. He acknowledged, too, that there had been many injustices in the Restoration land settlement. On the other hand, James was an Englishman and put English interests first. He had little but contempt for the native Irish, although he could accept the "Old English" as more or less English. His Irish revenue depended mainly on trade and the business community was mainly Protestant, so that, if the Catholics became too powerful, business confidence would collapse and his revenue would diminish. Finally, any signs of Catholic domination in Ireland would alarm his English subjects and make them reluctant to acquiesce in the granting of greater liberty to the English Catholics.

There were thus cogent objections to James's allowing Tyrconnell to put Ireland into Catholic hands, objections which were stressed repeatedly by James's English advisers, Protestant and Catholic. That Tyrconnell managed despite this to achieve most of his objectives said much for his political skill and determination. Argyll and Monmouth's rising provided a pretext to disarm the militia and other "disaffected" Protestants. Tyrconnell also persuaded James to implement the decision taken at the end of Charles's reign to purge the army of "disaffected" officers and men and put Catholics in their places.

While Tyrconnell was beginning this purge, in the summer of 1685, he heard that James had appointed Clarendon lord lieutenant. The idea had been Sunderland's, an astute counter to Rochester's suggestion that Sunderland himself should be packed off to Dublin. No sooner had Clarendon arrived in Ireland, however, than Tyrconnell came to court to undermine his credit with the King. He joined forces with Sunderland and together they convinced James that the Irish army and administration were riddled with disaffection and that Clarendon and his Protestant colleagues had both concealed this disaffection and exaggerated the difficulty of admitting Catholics to office. James decided that a further purge of the army was needed and that Catholics should be admitted to civilian offices. Clarendon found himself ordered to execute measures which he had not advised and did not like. His remonstrations were ignored, perhaps because Sunderland suppressed his letters but more likely because James did not wish to heed the arguments which they contained.

In the summer of 1686 Tyrconnell returned to Ireland and resumed his purge of the army. He paid little attention and less respect to Clarendon, telling him not to pass on complaints against his conduct "which will anger the King and perplex him". He denounced Protestant officials as "fanatics" or persecutors of Catholics on the flimsiest of evidence: "God damn me, . . . I know nothing of him but what people say and common fame makes him to be a fanatic. . . . I know the King has no ill opinion of him . . . but people tell me things." Clarendon was neither as quick witted nor as tough as Tyrconnell and was quite unable to cope with him. He complained timidly and at length to James, who ignored him. Tyrconnell rampaged on and by October 1686 two-thirds of the soldiers in the Irish army were Catholics.[15]

His task completed, Tyrconnell returned to court, full of complaints against Clarendon: he had refused to admit Catholics to Dublin corporation, he had failed to celebrate James's birthday, and so on. James soon resolved to recall Clarendon, but hesitated to appoint Tyrconnell in his place. The English Catholics disliked him while James feared the effect on English opinion of sending an Irishman to rule Ireland. He may also have feared that Tyrconnell would prove hard to control and might press on too fast. On the other hand, Tyrconnell was utterly loyal and James believed that only a Catholic could be trusted to implement the measures he intended on the Catholics' behalf. Eventually, he compromised. Tyrconnell was to go to Dublin, but with the lesser title of Lord Deputy. Moreover, he appointed two men to watch and report on Tyrconnell's conduct—the new Lord Chancellor, Alexander Fitton, and the Lord Deputy's secretary, Thomas Sheridan.

These constraints proved insufficient to curb Tyrconnell. Fitton was weak and compliant while Tyrconnell rid himself of Sheridan by acccusing him of corruption and suspending him from office.[16] While James protested that he wanted nobody to be dismissed or appointed on religious grounds, more and more Catholics were appointed to civilian and military posts. James reprimanded Tyrconnell for allowing infringement of the navigation acts and complained of other irregularities in his administration. Such complaints were usually far from forceful: James's main concern, it seemed, was to prevent undue "noise". Nevertheless, Tyrconnell's enemies at court were busy, arguing that Tyrconnell's measures would cause a large fall in the Irish revenue. They persuaded James to summon Tyrconnell to Chester in August 1687. James received him coldly but his resolution soon collapsed. He accepted Tyrconnell's claims that the revenue was not falling and that the measures he had taken were in James's best interest. Tyrconnell returned to Ireland more strongly established than ever in James's favour.

He now ruled Ireland virtually unchecked. The only demand which James still resisted was that he should call an Irish Parliament to investigate (in other words, overturn) the Restoration land settlement. Even here, James agreed that Parliament should meet, but insisted that his English Parliament must meet first. Thus by 1688 Tyrconnell had given the Catholics a preponderance of power and was well placed to throw off English rule should James die. In 1687 one of Tyrconnell's associates had sounded Bonrepaus about the chances of French support for such an assertion of independence and had received a favourable response. There is no evidence that Tyrconnell knew of this approach, or that he himself approached the French, but he must have assumed that Louis would be glad to help the Irish against William. James's attitude is hard to fathom. For most of his reign he made it clear that he wished to preserve England's dominance over Ireland. After the meeting at Chester, however, there are hints that he may have changed his mind and that Tyrconnell had persuaded him that it was in the Catholic interest that Ireland should be wholly in Catholic hands and, if need be, separate from England. Such considerations soon became less relevant as the birth of the Prince of Wales reduced the danger of a Protestant succession. Nevertheless, when William invaded England Tyrconnell was in full control of Ireland and seemed quite strong enough to deal with any resistance from the Protestant minority.

CHAPTER FIFTEEN

The Road to the Boyne (1689-90)

As soon as he heard of the collapse of James's regime in England, Tyrconnell began to raise more troops. At the same time, he tried to calm the fears of the Protestants and even entertained some overtures from William. The Protestants were not easily calmed, however; the new levies were unpaid and undisciplined and lived by plunder, while there were many rumours that the Papists planned a general massacre of Protestants. The exodus of Protestants reached panic proportions. The quays at Dublin were jammed with old and young, sick and well, struggling to secure a passage to England. In Ulster, however, the Protestants were strong enough to prepare to defend themselves. On 7th December the citizens of Londonderry closed the gates to keep out a Catholic regiment sent to garrison the town. This news strengthened Tyrconnell's conviction that he could not hold out unaided against the superior might of England and that he needed aid from France. Louis was willing to send arms, but in view of his other commitments he was reluctant to send any men until he knew more of conditions in Ireland. Early in January he sent the Sieur de Pointis to see whether Tyrconnell's army could be made strong enough to resist William. Tyrconnell argued that it could, provided the French sent arms and money. In return, he offered to cede Waterford and Galway to Louis, as cautionary towns. He pressed James to come over in person, asking him "to consider whether you can with honour continue where you are when you may possess a kingdom of your own, plentiful of all things for human life".[1]

James was far from eager to go. The Revolution in England had been a stunning psychological blow. He could explain it, to some extent, in terms of human wickedness. A clique of Williamite conspirators had managed to poison his loyal and well-meaning subjects against him. But how had God allowed this to happen? James's confidence that God approved his actions was shattered and never recovered. The resolution so characteristic of his earlier years never returned. Each new failure merely confirmed his conviction of divine disapproval and increased his fatalism and apathy: indeed there came a point where he almost welcomed failure, since he now believed that God was punishing him for the sins of his youth. He was thus hardly prepared mentally to tear himself away from the peace of St Germain in order to wrestle with the problems of directing a war in Ireland. A contemporary noted that James "is so tranquil and numbed that he would certainly gladly have remained in

France, applying himself only to his exercises of devotion, had it not been for the insistence of the Viceroy of Ireland and of the French."[2]

Louis had decided that James should go to Ireland in the light of Pointis' report, which said that the Irish were very poorly equipped but immensely enthusiastic. Given arms, money and properly trained officers they should be able to defeat the Protestants and carry the war into England. The report convinced Louis that it was worth pouring arms and money into Ireland. He was already at war with the Dutch and it was only a matter of time before William brought England into the war. Louis hoped therefore to divert William's troops and resources from the continent and especially from the Spanish Netherlands which was, for both of them, the focal point of the war. He also expressed a strong desire for James's restoration which was probably sincere. He appointed d'Avaux, just back from the Hague, to act as ambassador to James's court and, in effect, as his first minister. D'Avaux had formed a poor impression of James's capabilities during his years at the Hague and that impression was strengthened by first-hand experience. It should be added, however, that the deficiencies of James's leadership were magnified by the problems which he had to cope with in Ireland. When they landed at Kinsale in March, they found no carts to transport the arms and money, very few horses and very little rope to make into improvised bridles in the absence of proper harness. Nevertheless, the people were friendly and Tyrconnell (now created a duke) was optimistic: if the better units were properly disciplined and the rest were disbanded, he argued, James could have a highly effective army of maybe thirty thousand men. D'Avaux, although worried by the absence of order and method, thought that the soldiers looked well built and eager. As they travelled towards Dublin, old and young turned out to see their king and the country maids danced in his honour. The streets of the capital were strewn with flowers and hung with tapestries. James was gracious and courteous to both Protestants and Catholics and issued a proclamation establishing liberty of conscience, along with another summoning Parliament. Only one piece of news slightly marred the general joy. James heard that the rebels in the north were more numerous than he had thought, so decided to send reinforcements to help to subdue them.[3]

Initially, James had hoped to establish his control over Ireland quickly, and then press on to Scotland or England, but that was impossible while part of Ulster remained outside his control. To subdue Ulster, and especially Derry, would take both skill and time. But skill and experience were sadly lacking in the Irish army. It was not just that it lacked artillery and siege equipment or that its officers had no experience of siege warfare. Since the Restoration the Irish army had been small and dispersed in garrisons and had seen virtually no action, other than the occasional small riot. Since 1685 the army had been altered beyond recognition. Its officer corps had been completely changed: once wholly Protestant it was now wholly Catholic. It had been greatly enlarged in the winter of 1688–89 so that a very high proportion of the regiments were new. (Some of the older regiments had been cut off in England at the Revolution and dispersed.) Moreover, it was now engaged in what was to be a major civil war. Its administration was thus a much larger and more complex business than ever before, but most of the officers responsible for that administration were wholly inexperienced, apart from a few who had seen service abroad. The civilian administration consisted either of inexperienced Catholics or of Protestants whose loyalty was suspect. The revenue administration in particular became notorious for peculation and inaction. For a small bribe officials would allow Protestants to take their goods out of the country or neglect to seize the goods of rebels. Some embezzled the King's stores and requisitioned goods in his name which they sold for their own profit. When not engaged in robbing the King and plundering his subjects, the treasury men devoted their energies to avoiding carrying out his orders, while James lacked either the time or the energy to make them do so. Administratively, the army was a shambles. Officers did not know how to plan a march or how to move arms and provisions from one place to another (assuming that they could find the arms, the provisions and, most difficult of all, the carts and horses with which to transport them). No provision was made for magazines, arsenals or hospitals. Arms rusted at Kinsale and Cork while a regiment at Derry had only seven serviceable muskets. Small wonder that French officers and administrators, trained under the super-efficient Louvois, threw up their hands in horror.*[4]

If James's army was short of skill it was even more short of time. It had been raised in a great hurry; Tyrconnell granted commissions to anyone ready to raise a regiment or company. Nobody knew how many men had been raised: some said a hundred thousand. But Ireland could not afford such a large army. In December 1688 a former revenue commissioner had claimed that half the existing forces could not be maintained by twice the normal revenue. But the revenue was now well below normal. Trade was dead. Protestant merchants had fled to England taking their capital with them. Trade with England had stopped and the English fleet controlled the seas. Agriculture too was disrupted, as the Irish had "turned their ploughshares into swords". So many enlisted as soldiers that large tracts of land remained unsown.[5] By the summer of 1689 estimated expenditure exceeded estimated income by fifty per cent. But the estimate for expenditure made no allowance for waste and speculation while rather over half the estimated income was made up of a Parliamentary grant which was unlikely to produce more than a small fraction of its expected yield. Above all there was a chronic shortage of coin. The Protestants who had fled had taken large quantities with them. The government therefore began, in June 1689, to issue copper money. At first it met a real need for coin, but as more was issued its value fell and the government could not keep up with the demand, even after melting down some brass guns. Attempts to hold down prices proved unavailing. Gold and silver disappeared from circulation and the copper became, in Tyrconnell's words, "our meat, drink and clothes".[6]

---

* James argued, perhaps with reason, that the French were so used to having abundant supplies that they were unable to improvise. TCD, MS E 2. 19, no 4.

There was thus no way out of the basic problem that Ireland now had a much larger army than its economy could support. When Tyrconnell first raised the new forces, he had no money to pay them so left it to the officers to pay the men out of their own pockets. James continued this practice and no serious attempt was made to pay the army until May. Most officers, however, could not or would not pay their men for that length of time. They had expected their commissions to be a source of profit. The soldiers, left to their own devices, lived by theft and pillage, to the detriment of discipline. When James got round to reducing the army to manageable proportions, it proved difficult to cashier officers who had maintained their companies for months at their own expense— or who said that they had done so. So when Tyrconnell organized the scattered companies into regiments he felt obliged to keep on more than he had intended. Regiments which were supposed to have thirteen companies sometimes had over twenty. The first serious attempt to draw up muster rolls was made in May, but in August James still did not know how many men he had in his army. Thus one had the paradox of an army larger than James needed or could afford, but so badly organized and distributed that where he needed large numbers in one place (as at Derry) there were never enough.[7]

The way in which the army had been raised created other problems. The officers usually enrolled their tenants and dependants, but these deserted in droves when ordered away from their own villages. Moreover, the officers' authority over their men was personal rather than military. In order to discipline the soldiers, one had first to discipline the officers, but as the soldiers would obey only their own countrymen James used his more experienced English and Scots officers as subalterns in the hope that they would instruct their superiors. Many officers were idle and self-seeking. Few ensured that their men looked after their muskets, some sold firearms to whoever would buy them.[8] Theft was endemic in the army. Soldiers preyed on the civilian population, as did those on the periphery of the army—disbanded soldiers, the militia and the rapparees (irregular soldiers, something between guerillas and bandits). They also stole from each other (cavalrymen stole one another's horses) and, of course, from the King. The French were soon at their wits' end: "an army of vagabonds and mutineers", they called them, or even "wild bears". An incident which typified the state of the army came when a Captain O'Neill was killed before Derry. Twenty-five of his dragoons laid down their arms, saying they would serve no one else. Rosen, the French commander, had to fire on them to make them stay—but before he could do so he had to borrow the necessary muskets from another regiment.[9]

Thus to pay, deploy, equip, feed and discipline the Irish army raised problems which were well-nigh insoluble. With energetic and determined direction much could still have been done, but James proved incapable of providing such direction. At first he hoped to be out of Ireland and back on the English throne within two or three months. He told d'Avaux "that he had heard nothing from England, but that the greater part of his soldiers had been misled, that the ordinary people loved him and that all his friends would come to him as soon as he landed in England." It was true that both Tories and Whigs soon became disillusioned with William and especially with the taxation which the French wars were to make necessary. The army was mutinous. By March both Danby and Halifax thought that if James would only turn Protestant nothing could prevent his restoration. But if James was to exploit this revulsion of feeling, he needed an army to defeat William's army. Louis was already too fully committed in Germany to spare any troops and anyway the Dutch and English fleets controlled the Channel. The army had to come, therefore, from Ireland or Scotland. Either way the subjugation of Ulster was the first priority and it had to be carried out before William could send an army to relieve the Ulster Protestants. James thus had to turn his thoughts to Derry and to bringing order to the Irish army, but all the time his main objective was to regain the English throne.[10]

James's preoccupation with recovering the English crown shaped the whole of his conduct in Ireland. "His heart is too English for him to agree to anything which could displease the English," grumbled d'Avaux. "He still counts on being re-established soon in the kingdom of England and . . . will do nothing to remove Ireland from its dependence on the English."[11] He delayed as long as he could declaring the English his enemies and struggled hard to prevent the French from taking over England's stranglehold on Irish trade. His opposition was such that Louis at last ordered d'Avaux to press him no further. Where possible he gave commissions to Englishmen in preference to Irishmen and treated the Irish Protestants more mildly than most of his Catholic advisers wished. He was, one complained, "infatuated with this rotten principle, provoke not your Protestant subjects."[12] Even before leaving England, he had ordered Tyrconnell to treat the Protestants with moderation. Once in Ireland, he tried to ensure that Protestants were allowed the liberty of conscience he had granted. He issued an ineffectual proclamation forbidding Catholics to take over Protestant churches. He refused to seize the estate of any "rebel" unless it had been declared forfeit by due process of law or by Act of Parliament—so the Dublin Parliament passed a massive attainder bill branding almost all leading Protestants as rebels. He was reluctant to arrest the leading Protestants of Dublin and other towns as a precautionary measure or to threaten reprisals against them in case of a general Protestant rising. The French and Irish claimed that such mildness never worked and that some rebels taken in arms had James's protections in their pockets. But James insisted that his promises must be honoured.[13]

Besides being unwilling to abandon the English interest, James proved himself incapable of resolute or decisive leadership. "He believes that he does not govern if he does not meddle in everything but he meddles in matters only to spoil them." He agreed with everything d'Avaux said but then did nothing. "He listens to everyone and one has to spend as much time destroying the impressions left on him by bad advice as instilling good advice of one's own." Moreover, both his unwillingness to offend the English and his natural irresolution were intensified by Melfort's influence. Melfort soon became the *bête noire* of both French and Irish. He was a brazen liar, insufferably vain and vindictive, who insisted on handling all business himself while lacking the memory or application to execute it properly. His main objective was to perpetuate his own influence and to this end he flattered and encouraged James's misconceptions and slighted all criticism, however constructive. "He has a blind complaisance for whatever he sees that the King wants," wrote d'Avaux, "What Lord Melfort tells him always seems to him so good and so well considered that he does not consider the representations of others." Melfort played on James's stubbornness and flattered him even when he was wrong. This made James believe "that Lord Melfort is almost the only man who advises him well and loves his interests; and Melfort, to confirm the King in this opinion, makes him distrust everyone else."[14]

In order to maintain his hold over James, Melfort was prepared to use lies and slanders, to sow dissension between d'Avaux and Tyrconnell and to hold up or suppress James's letters. By letters into France, he turned the Queen against d'Avaux (and her letters in turn influenced James). He also tried to mobilize Louis on his behalf. He pandered to James's conviction that his subjects loved him and that he would soon be restored. He encouraged James's distrust of the French and Irish and his suspicion that they put their own interests before his. He led James to believe that Tyrconnell and d'Avaux wanted to manipulate him while only Melfort wanted him to remain a free agent.[15] His advice led James to base his actions on assumptions which were wrong. He led James to believe that the Derry rebels would surrender as soon as they saw him, that the Dutch had no fleet at sea and that William did not have enough troops to invade Ireland that year. He also prepossessed James against criticism of his (Melfort's) conduct of business. Sometimes he ignored such criticism, sometimes he agreed with it and did nothing. When Melfort said that sixty carts which he had promised had "vanished", James remarked blandly, "You see, we are doing everything possible." Later he often became angry at any reflection on Melfort's competence, and took it as a personal insult if he were asked to implement measures which he had agreed weeks before. He was especially sensitive about information sent into France: he did not want the Queen or Louis to know how he was mishandling his affairs.[16]

Yet while he was being misled by Melfort, James seems to have retained some awareness of what was happening. Several times he said that he knew that Melfort's incompetence was harming his affairs, but that he had no one at court who was more able. But even after Melfort was forced to resign in August, James continued to receive his advice and to distrust that of d'Avaux. Not until Louis and the Queen packed Melfort off to Rome (without James's knowledge) did he cease to trouble Irish affairs. James had always been easily led by those who told him what he wished to hear, but his susceptibility seems to have grown with age and he now showed a lack of mental energy which contrasted oddly with his still abundant physical energy. Despite his preoccupation with detail, James showed more glaringly than ever the indecision which had become so marked in the latter part of his reign. Beneath the superficial diligence lay a mental lassitude, born perhaps of fatalism and defeatism. Occasionally he would arouse himself from his lethargy in a sudden burst of naïve optimism or reckless courage, only to sink once more into his torpor. Psychologically, the Revolution had left him a broken man, quite incapable of wrestling with the problems of a disorganized and overburdened Ireland.[17]

Early in April James decided to go to Ulster to encourage his troops. D'Avaux argued that he should stay in Dublin to organize the army and prepare for Parliament, but James was adamant, although he promised to go no further than Armagh. There, on the fringes of Ulster, he saw at first hand the poor state of his forces and the devastation wrought by the war. He saw a regiment armed mostly with pikes and broken muskets. There was no forage or flour and nothing to drink but bad water and worse beer. James, however, was encouraged by Melfort to believe that Derry would surrender at his approach, so forgot his promise and pressed on to Omagh. He found the town in ruins and prepared to withdraw to Dublin. Then on the 17th, he heard that Derry's garrison was ready to discuss terms and that James's presence would persuade them to surrender. When he arrived, he sent a trumpeter to summon the town to capitulate. The townsmen sent word that they would give their answer in an hour and asked that James's forces should advance no further. James never knew whether Rosen heard of this condition. He certainly continued to bring his troops forward and was met with shots from the town. The negotiations were at an end. James stayed in the saddle all day in pouring rain, without food, hoping by his presence to bring his rebellious subjects to their senses. That evening he ordered that the town should be besieged and the next day he decided to return to Dublin.[18]

Whether Derry might have surrendered had James not appeared is a matter for conjecture. Many in the town thought it untenable and had entered into negotiations with James's generals. There is no doubt, however, that the confrontation on 18th April left the inhabitants determined to resist to the last. James's jaunt into Ulster had achieved little but it had shown him that the conquest of Ulster might take all summer and that it was essential to bring more order to his forces. He therefore requested a nucleus of trained French troops. Melfort asked for ten thousand French soldiers and a fleet to transport them so that James could invade England. Louvois treated his request with the contempt it deserved: he believed, indeed, that James should concentrate on holding Ireland and not think of invading England until the following year. Louvois added that Louis was not pleased with what he had heard of James's conduct and that unless James brought some order and discipline to his army, Louis would not feel obliged to go on helping him. As it was, his continental commitments left him unable to spare any troops at all until December.[19]

Meanwhile, on 7th May, James met the Irish Parliament. Its members were almost all Catholics, mostly of Old English extraction. James stressed his attachment to liberty of conscience and promised to assent to bills designed for the good of the nation and the relief of those injured by the Restoration land settlement, "as far forth as may be consistent with reason, justice and the public good of my people." It soon became apparent that the Parliament had little sympathy with James's desire to preserve the English interest. He could do little with the Commons but attended the Lords regularly and was able to use his influence there to block measures which he disliked. In this way he prevented the repeal of Poynings' Law, which laid down that no bill could be put before the Irish Parliament unless it had first been approved by the English privy council. However, he had to assent to a bill stating that the English Parliament could not legislate for Ireland. He thus preserved the crown's control over Irish legislation while allowing the destruction of that of the English Parliament. James also hindered the passage of bills designed to destroy England's control of Ireland's overseas trade. He was forced by circumstances to grant the French some commercial concessions, but these were granted by proclamation and were therefore revocable. The Navigation Acts, which established the Irish economy's "colonial" subjection to that of England, were not repealed, therefore, but merely suspended. As for the land question, Parliament was so vehement and united that James could not stop the repeal of the Acts comprising the Restoration land settlement or the passage of a massive act of attainder, which declared forfeit the property of just about every Protestant of note. Thus the Old English Catholics recovered the lands they had lost in the 1640s and 1650s; but the legislation which established the legal superstructure of the royal supremacy over the Irish church and of England's political and economic dominance over Ireland remained in force, even if its effects were suspended.[20]

While Parliament met, the siege of Derry dragged on. As the besiegers lacked the numbers, artillery and mining skills to take it by force, they had to try to starve it into submission. A boom was stretched across Lough Foyle to prevent relief from the sea. But time was not on the besiegers' side, since sooner or later help was bound to arrive from England. Rosen, the besiegers' commander, became impatient and frustrated. At the end of June he told the inhabitants that if they did not surrender by 1st July he would round up the Protestants of the neighbouring villages, whether or not they had protections from the King, and drive them to the walls. The besieged would then have the choice of watching them starve or letting them in and using up their meagre stock of food more quickly. He accordingly gathered some four thousand people, but the townspeople fired on them and threatened to hang all their prisoners. Rosen abandoned his plan and sent the hostages home. James was furious at what he regarded as this slight on his honour. He persistently ignored Rosen thereafter and asked Louis to recall him. Rosen returned to France, bitter and angry, a few months later.[21]

By July it was common knowledge that William was sending an army to Ireland. D'Avaux urged James to abandon the siege of Derry and to concentrate on preparing to resist the invading army. James and Melfort, however, were reluctant to believe that there would be an invasion and continued to hope that the town would fall. They sent Lord Dover to press Louis once again to send arms, men and money for an invasion of England. On the 22nd James reluctantly agreed to abandon the siege, after all his generals had agreed that the town could not be taken. A week later the blockade was broken and the inhabitants received much needed food. On the 31st James's retreating forces were routed at Newtown Butler.[22]

Thus the Jacobites faced the coming invasion battered and demoralized. For months Tyrconnell and d'Avaux had done all they could to get rid of Melfort, stirring up their friends in Parliament to attack him. James's friends in Scotland wrote that nothing could be done while Melfort remained in charge of Scottish affairs. At St Germain Lauzun and Dover persuaded the Queen to press Melfort to resign. But still he stayed and the Irish began to mutter that they wished James had never come to Ireland. James, meanwhile, seriously considered leaving Ireland, for Melfort had convinced him that without substantial French help all was lost. He was shamed out of this by d'Avaux and Tyrconnell and veered to the opposite extreme, declaring that he would fight at the head of his army.[23]

Then, on 13th August, came news that the veteran general Schomberg had landed in County Down with a large army. James had issued orders to recruit more troops, to raise a Catholic militia and to establish a camp near Dublin, but nothing much had yet been done and the army was in no position to do more than delay Schomberg's progress. The French generals therefore advised James to fall back to the Shannon, with the Gaelic stronghold of Connaught behind them, and wait for help to arrive from France. James and Tyrconnell wanted to advance to Drogheda and challenge the enemy, which d'Avaux thought foolish in the extreme. While these arguments continued and frantic preparations were made to resist the invader, Melfort resigned, claiming that the Irish were plotting to kill him. He set off for France, with a commission from James to inform Louis of the present state of his affairs.[24] Once he had gone, the position began to improve. James was still pessimistic, which was perhaps why he wished to risk all on a battle. He advanced to Drogheda, where his little force was swollen by regiments from all over Ireland, some of them tolerably well armed and disciplined. Schomberg, meanwhile, remained immobile at Dundalk. Gradually the Irish morale improved. On 20th September James took his army within sight of Schomberg's and remained there for three hours, burning the forage. The enemy made no move. Elated, the Irish returned to camp, where they remained another month. For the first time since coming to Ireland, James was enjoying himself. Early in November, he reluctantly dispersed his men into winter quarters leaving Schomberg's at Dundalk to waste away from disease and desertion through a long, wet winter.[25]

By now even d'Avaux shared James's confidence that, given sufficient French help, he could drive Schomberg out of Ireland the following year. But there were ominous signs. Too many of James's soldiers lacked proper clothing, shoes or food. The army still had no magazines of grain and no hospitals, and the economic situation was deteriorating. A summer of disruption and plunder had drastically reduced the amount of food available for winter, while straw and wood were in very short supply. Imported commodities, like wine and salt, were becoming scarce and no new supplies were coming in. Dublin was particularly badly hit, because people from the surrounding countryside would not bring their produce to market for fear that it would be stolen by the soldiers or "requisitioned" by the treasury men. Bakers and other shop-keepers took good care that they profited from the general scarcity. By November the price of grain had trebled and that of coal and wood had quadrupled, and things seem to have got worse in the spring. The copper coin was now depreciating faster than the government could mint it.[26]

A second ominous development was the appointment of the Comte de Lauzun to command the long promised French troops. When James pressed Louis to recall Rosen after the incident at Derry, he had specifically requested that Lauzun should replace him, although he denied this to d'Avaux. Louis agreed, reluctantly. The news was greeted with gloom in Ireland. Lauzun had almost no claim to James's consideration other than his having escorted the Queen to France and his military experience was minimal. For years he had been in disgrace at the French court and Louis still disliked him. Moreover, Louvois hated him and as Louis' leading military adviser Louvois was the last man whom James should have alienated. His insistence on Lauzun's appointment merely convinced Louvois still more that James had no capacity for leadership and that it would be a waste of men and money to prop up the Jacobite cause any further. D'Avaux, too, knew that he could never work with Lauzun and asked permission to return to France, which was granted. James thus lost an able, if nagging adviser, while Tyrconnell was worried by Lauzun's reputation for intrigue. James could hardly have made a worse choice.[27]

James may have asked for Lauzun to command the French force because he was just about the only Frenchman who had any personal obligation to him and who could be expected not to criticize his conduct of affairs. Lauzun's letters certainly praised James for his diligence and industry and formed a sharp contrast to those of d'Avaux. As a general Lauzun proved less bad than many feared. He tried hard to bring order to the army and showed courage in battle. But his reputation for feuds and intrigues was well deserved. Tyrconnell carefully kept on the right side of him, but James's leading English adviser, Lord Dover, had already fallen foul of him at St Germain. Dover was, by his own admission, not much of an administrator: "I have something else to say to you," he wrote to Tyrconnell, "but if my life were at stake I can't think of it; 'tis a great wonder such a head as mine should have thought of so many different things as I have done since my being here." Both Lauzun and Dover tried to get Tyrconnell on their side, which helped to split the council, while Dover tried to extend their quarrel and to exploit the general resentment of the French which grew in Ireland during the first half of 1690.[28]

The elation which had followed the confrontation with Schomberg evaporated with the privations of the winter. Then, in January, William announced that he would come to Ireland in person, with a substantial army. The Jacobites were filled with despondency. Tyrconnell wrote that they would be hard put to resist unless they received much more help from France than had so far been promised. He argued that James's only hope was to invade England before William could invade Ireland, but he suspected that the French wanted

James "to expose himself in this poor country to the last inconveniences and hazards of all kinds to serve them without bettering his own condition". If only the French fleet could sail to the Irish Sea, he wrote later, to stop reinforcements coming from England, James might stand a chance, but he saw little hope for James if William and his army landed, "he having all things in great abundance and fit to attack us and we nothing (almost) to withstand his power." Lauzun, too, wrote that James's only hope lay in a pre-emptive attack on England.[29]

Such appeals fell on deaf ears. Louis had already made it clear that he would send James ships and men for an invasion only when he was assured of a major rising in England in James's favour. He was surprised, wrote Louvois brutally, "that anyone in his right mind could believe, from what we know of the present state of England, that there is the slightest chance that such a design could succeed." When d'Avaux and the French officers returned to court, their information made Louis even less likely to expend men and money in James's cause. Even Lauzun, while he was careful to exonerate James, remarked often how his orders were not carried out: "The King is so used to being robbed and those who serve him are so used to robbing him that it is impossible to bring any remedy." James's friends did what they could to drum up support at Louis' court. Tyrconnell wrote to Barrillon and d'Avaux; the Queen gained the support of Louvois' main rival, Seignelay. But it was Louvois who was most in favour and Louvois who had charge of Louis' military affairs. As Louis' commitments extended during 1690 and as the Dutch and English fleets still controlled the Channel, Louvois argued that it was neither desirable nor possible to send James any more than was required to keep the war going for the coming year.[30]

Such arguments might seem unanswerable at Versailles. At Dublin they seemed wrongheaded and parsimonious, not to say callous. Hostility to the French grew rapidly during the spring. It did not help that the French soldiers were unruly or that the French demanded something in return for their aid. Several thousand Irish soldiers had been sent to France in return for those brought by Lauzun and James and d'Avaux had squabbled about the officers who were to go with them. D'Avaux did not want untrained louts, James did not want his army to lose the few good officers it had. The French also demanded goods in return for their stores and munitions. Ireland had little to offer now except wool, and the French complained that the wool was overvalued and brought to the ports too slowly. Thus Dover found it easy to stir up ill feeling against Lauzun and the French. In April there was a violent row in a council meeting, in which Lauzun boxed the ears of Simon Luttrell, Governor of Dublin. When news came, in June, that William had landed, Dover's resentment spilled over. He claimed that the French aid had been so limited as to be useless and that Louis had betrayed James, whom he advised to make the best terms he could with William. When James refused, Dover retired to Flanders, where he lived out the rest of his days.[31]

William landed near Carrickfergus on 14th June. He brought fifteen thousand men to add to the Protestant forces already there, a train of artillery and two hundred thousand pounds in cash. His aim was to bring an overwhelmingly superior army into the field and to smash James's army in a single campaign. He set out towards Dublin as soon as he could. James, meanwhile, started northwards to meet him, but without much optimism. Lauzun and Tyrconnell both argued that he should avoid a battle unless he saw a real chance of winning, but this Tyrconnell thought most unlikely. William had an army of forty thousand men "provided of all things to subsist . . . they are most of them old disciplined troops; they are paid in gold and silver, in short they want nothing . . . [whereas] we want all things and if we can make in all twenty-five thousand men it will be the most, old and new troopers, well and ill armed and that which is worse we have not above a month's bread to subsist if corn come not out of France." There were thus cogent arguments why James should avoid a battle and try to conserve his army, hoping that the French would beat the Dutch and English at sea and that William's army would waste away as Schomberg's had done. Tyrconnell found such arguments unanswerable on the 24th, but James did not and must have won Tyrconnell over, for two days later he wrote that they should fight rather than let Dublin be taken without a struggle. If they lost Dublin, they would lose all Leinster and Munster and be forced back on to Connaught, the worst corn country in Ireland, where no magazines had been prepared. Besides, the soldiers' morale was now high but would collapse if James abandoned half the country without a fight and the men would desert in droves.[32]

James thus aimed to avoid a battle, but to fight if he had to. Once more he threw himself enthusiastically into the business of command, spending eighteen or twenty hours a day in the saddle. He advanced to Dundalk to eat up the forage, then withdrew, devastating and plundering as he went. On the 29th his army recrossed the River Boyne and encamped on the southern bank, a little to the west of Drogheda. The next day William's army arrived and encamped on the opposite bank. There were some sporadic artillery exchanges, which caused a moment of excitement when a cannon ball grazed William's shoulder and knocked him from his horse. "It's well it came no nearer," he remarked laconically.

The defensive position which James had chosen was far from perfect, but as good as he was likely to find in a country without fortified towns where the rivers were shallow and easily forded. There was certainly nowhere better to the south: "the Boyne is the walls of Dublin." James drew up most of his army on a hillside overlooking Oldbridge, one of several places where the river could be forded at low tide. About four miles upstream from the two armies was another ford at Rosnaree and two miles beyond that, at Slane, there was a bridge. James had had this bridge broken but it clearly worried him, for if William took his army across it he could cut off James's retreat to Dublin. So, on the evening of the 30th, he gave orders to pack up the baggage ready to move next morning and sent Sir Neill O'Neill's dragoons to Slane to hold up the enemy. In the early morning mist next day, James saw part of

William's right wing marching upstream, presumably towards Slane. In fact as the Williamites knew that the bridge was broken they tried to force a crossing at Rosnaree, where O'Neill was waiting for them. His dragoons resisted fiercely, but to no avail. Hearing that his men had a bridgehead on the southern bank, William sent reinforcements which confirmed James's fears that William planned to cut him off. He now committed the whole of his left wing and part of his right to holding the enemy at Rosnaree, "taking it for granted that the main body of the enemy would follow the right wing."[33]

Meanwhile, William, having made his feint at Rosnaree, launched his main assault across the ford at Oldbridge. James had already detached the bulk of his army and had only a few cannon left in his original position, but fording the river in the face of the Jacobite fire was still a fearsome ordeal: "My poor guards, my poor guards," William kept saying. Once his first infantry were across, they were charged repeatedly by Tyrconnell and the Jacobite cavalry, and were in great difficulties until they were relieved by William's cavalry which had forded the river a mile downstream. The Irish infantry broke and fled and the cavalry, despite courageous resistance, were at last beaten back by superior numbers.[34]

Meanwhile, the bulk of James's army was marching parallel with William's right to the south of Rosnaree. James ordered Lauzun to attack, but this proved impossible because of the bogs and ravines between the two forces. Both forces continued to march until an aide arrived with news of William's breakthrough at Oldbridge. James at once turned his forces south-east, towards the village of Duleek and the road to Dublin. As they marched, news of the defeat at Oldbridge became generally known. Then came the first of the fleeing cavalry. James's infantry assumed at once that they were the enemy. (Both sides wore a motley variety of uniforms, the Williamites wearing green sprigs in their hats and the Jacobites white papers.) They broke and fled, "some throwing away their arms, others even their coats and shoes to run the lighter." Fearing William's cavalry was close behind, Lauzun urged James to save himself, take a cavalry escort and head for Dublin. This he did, while Lauzun and Tyrconnell fought a brave and skilful rearguard action, covering the Jacobite retreat.[35]

It was an odd battle, "a skirmish between nine regiments without cannon or entrenchment and an army of thirty-six thousand choice men for the defending and gaining a few passes upon a shallow river." The terrain prevented most of James's army from coming to grips with the enemy. The casualties on both sides were light and the bulk of James's army got away.[36] Yet it was still a major victory, if not an unexpected one. The way to Dublin was open. The morale of the Irish was shattered. To continue the war, they would have to fall back on the bleak and impoverished province of Connaught. The Williamites saw the conquest of the rest of Ireland as a formality and so did James. He reached Dublin at nine that evening. He summoned his privy council, complained that the Irish had "basely" fled the field and concluded that he would never trust the Irish again. "[I] do now resolve to shift for myself and so gentlemen must you." He ordered them to deliver up the city to William and not to harm the Protestants. After some fitful rest, he left the city at four o'clock in the morning. He claimed later that his decision to leave Ireland was carefully considered and that much of his journey to Waterford was a leisurely affair. In fact, he rode as hard as he could go, travelling thirty-six miles by noon and covering the one hundred and twenty miles to Duncannon in only two days. He insisted on going on board ship at once, rather than spend the night ashore. As in 1688, his nerve seems to have cracked and his first thought was self-preservation; he even suffered from nosebleeds again. He sailed from Duncannon on the 3rd, landed at Brest on the 10th and reached St Germain on the 16th.[37]

By that time he had recovered from his panic and put a brave face on his defeat, claiming that he still had twenty thousand men to maintain his cause and talking kindly of the Irish who (he said) were unused to cannon fire. Louis, meanwhile, could afford to be magnanimous. He had just won two great victories which, ironically, would have enabled him to aid the Irish more effectually. The allied armies had been crushed at Fleurus while on 30th June Tourville's victory off Beachy Head had given the French fleet control of the Channel. Louis therefore received James kindly enough, but soon made it clear that he had no intention of letting James use his fleet for an expedition against England or to cut off William's fleet from Ireland. After a while, Louis even feigned illness so as not to offend James by a blunt refusal. As Lady Powis remarked, James "hath quite lost his reputation and I know not what will become of him." It was not just that he had failed: even the most committed Jacobites realized that Ireland's resources were puny compared with England's. It was the manner of his failure—so complete, so ignominious—that made the French unwilling to take him seriously. As James complained plaintively, nobody now believed a word he said. Predictably, he took refuge in his devotions. The Irish débâcle strongly confirmed his belief that God was punishing him for his sins. Soon after his return from Ireland he paid his first visit to the monastery of La Trappe, which was to play such an important part in the remaining years of his life and which was to help him to come to terms with failure.[38]

CHAPTER SIXTEEN

Devotion, Disappointment and Death (1690–1701)

After his return to France, James's devotions came to occupy a still larger place in his life. He heard Mass twice a day and went on retreats to La Trappe or to the English Benedictine house in Paris. He spent much of his time reading devotional works and writing little spiritual meditations. He sought guidance from his spiritual advisers on how to conduct himself on every conceivable occasion. What should he do if he awoke at four in the morning and could not get back to sleep? It hardly seemed fitting to arise and praise God, so what was the most "Christian" way in which he could pass his time? The Church's rituals, with precise instructions on the daily round and the yearly calendar, helped him to organize his time. Now that he had little real work to do and his frail health came to preclude hunting, he took more care than ever to divide his time methodically between devotions, reading and business, "so that he was remarkable for his great exactitude and for his frequently consulting his watch and regulating himself by it, doing everything at its proper time."[1]

His devotions were far more than a way of passing the time. His faith helped him to both explain and atone for his failures in England and Ireland. He explained his failures mainly in terms of God's displeasure. As he could not believe that God could have disapproved of his efforts to help the Catholics, he assumed that God must be angry with him, calling him to account now for the sins of his youth. Although now, as he turned sixty, he was able to bring his own sexuality under control at last, he still had a lifetime's transgressions to atone for, and atonement required suffering. In retrospect, he came to see his expulsion from England as a blessing. Having been deprived of the pomp and power of kingship, he had come to see the emptiness of the things of this world. It was not just that James was trying to reconcile himself psychologically to the loss of something which he could never recover. His belief that God had punished him for his sins and required further expiation became an obsession. He went out of his way to mortify the flesh upon whose weakness he blamed his troubles and imposed suffering on himself in a manner which verged on the masochistic. In his last years he scourged himself and wore around his thighs an iron chain studded with spikes. He would, indeed, have punished his frail body further had not his confessor restrained him. When he made his will, he considered making no provision for prayers and masses to speed his soul through purgatory, arguing that he deserved to suffer to the utmost for his sins.[2]

In James's devotional writings, two themes stand out: a conviction that the things of the world are meaningless and sinful and a longing for death. The puritanism which had long been part of his character now became dominant and stifling. Even innocent pleasures like hunting or tennis were to be enjoyed only in the greatest moderation, while balls, the theatre and light literature were to be avoided if possible. Worldly possessions and acclaim counted for nothing. One should live one's life bearing constantly in mind the need to answer to God for one's sins at any time. Such views—that this imperfect world was a trial to prepare one for the perfect world to come—were common-place in both Catholic and Protestant devotional writings. James, however, went further. While doing nothing to hasten his demise, he made it clear that he wanted to die, to achieve (he hoped) the heavenly crown for which he had lost his earthly crown. "May I always be prepared for death, whenever it pleases You to call me to You," he prayed. "The sooner the better."[3]

Such an attitude led James into fatalism and passivity: he did not really *want* to recover his throne. James denied this: "I am a father and a king and must not abandon the interests of my children and my subjects." Such disclaimers were little more than gestures. More often he expressed passive resignation to God's will: "If Thou will have me obscure and low, Thy blessed will, not mine, be done. Let others be preferred and me neglected; let their affairs succeed and mine miscarry." Such resignation was incompatible with applic-ation and vigorous action. James listened to all the proposals for his restoration and did as his ministers advised him, but his heart was not really in it. As each scheme folded, James remarked "God's will be done" and returned to his devotions with no apparent concern and perhaps even with relief.[4]

* * *

Given James's asceticism and distrust of even innocent enjoyment the court at St Germain was not a jolly place. James insisted that his Catholic servants should perform their devotions regularly while the few Protestants there (although they were allowed to worship in their own way) felt lost and un-comfortable. James handed them little Catholic tracts and told them often that it was impossible to find salvation outside the one true church. Apart from being bigoted, the court was poverty stricken. Louis allowed James fifty thousand *livres* a month (about £45,000 a year) but in 1692 there were over seventy persons lodging in the chateau, plus servants and officers of the guard. In 1697 there were thirty-nine men and women in specific court offices and "a great many chaplains and servants below stairs". As some of James's servants received salaries of up to £450, his revenue did not stretch very far. The English Am-bassador at Paris remarked scathingly in 1698: "King James looks mighty old and worn and stoops in his shoulders; the Queen looks ill and melancholy; their equipage is mighty ragged and their horses are all as lean as Sancho's." Money was desperately short and some of the courtiers went hungry. When James could save a little money, he called favoured servants into his closet and gave them a few coins wrapped in little scraps of paper.[5]

Some of those who had followed James into exile found their loyalty wilting in such an atmosphere. By 1695 it was accepted that anyone who had left St Germain had returned to England. Nobody, remarked Middleton, could reasonably be expected to starve. He, indeed, thought St Germain "next to the Bastille . . . the dreadfullest place in France". But if it was devout and poverty stricken, it was far from peaceful: "Though these people altogether make little more than a private family, they have as much faction and folly amongst them as we can have in England." The habits of intrigue died hard and were intensified by the conspiratorial nature of the court's contacts with England and by the return of Melfort.[6]

There were two main groups among the English Jacobites. The great majority were "Compounders", who were mostly Anglicans, including many clergymen who had refused to swear allegiance to William and Mary. They disliked the new regime for its illegality and for the favour which William showed to Dissenters and Dutchmen. They wished to arrange James's return on the sort of terms the loyalists had proposed at the end of 1688: cast-iron safeguards for the Church and the Ancient Constitution, plus a general pardon and the end of all measures for the advancement of Popery. "He may reign a Catholic in devotion," wrote one, "but he must reign a Protestant in government." The "non-Compounders", however, argued that James should not sacrifice the traditional powers of the monarchy and the interests of the Catholics, nor should he forgive those who had treated him so undutifully, unless they did something positive to atone for their misdeeds. They argued that William's regime was now so unpopular that if James were only patient, the English would throw off the usurper's yoke and restore their rightful king on his own terms.[7]

Neither group's proposals were really very practicable. They exaggerated William's unpopularity and, too often, their heads were "filled with chimeras and noise and nonsense". James could have been restored only by a French army, yet his coming with a French army would have deprived him of the goodwill which William had enjoyed in 1688. Even so, given such deficiencies, the Compounders' arguments were much more realistic than those of their rivals, but the non-Compounders more than held their own in the early 1690s, not because they were numerous in England (which they were not) but because of their power at St Germain. Their strength there owed much to Melfort. When James recalled him from Rome late in 1691 to be his secretary of state, Melfort was determined to monopolize what little power could be exercised in the exiled court. He encouraged his correspondents in England to write only to him, even when Middleton was appointed second secretary in 1693. Hitherto all letters from England had been passed on to Louis' ministers; now Melfort let them have only selected extracts and discouraged the Jacobites from communicating directly with the French court. The French soon became irritated by Melfort's conduct and by his persuading James not to make the concessions which the Compounders demanded. The abbé Renaudot, who translated many letters from England, waged a vigorous and often unscrupulous campaign for Melfort's removal, warmly supported by Middleton. James, however, was very reluctant to dismiss him and accepted his resignation, in May 1694, with regret.[8]

James was reluctant to dismiss Melfort for two reasons. First, he never liked to dismiss a servant whom he liked and trusted. Secondly, James supported whole-heartedly Melfort's opposition to making concessions. He believed that the measures which he had taken had been right in themselves and that it would be morally wrong to renounce them. He believed, too, that he had been expelled because God was angry with him and that he would return if and when God's wrath had been propitiated. That propitiation could come only through personal acts of piety and mortification, not through sacrificing the principles upon which he had acted while king. James was not particularly anxious to recover his throne, certainly not anxious enough to give up all that he had struggled for. To do so would be impious and dishonourable. "The Scots shall not make me, as they would my brother, stand in the stool of repentance," he remarked.[9]

His attitude to concessions can be seen clearly in relation to his declarations of 1692–93. In April 1692 James promulgated a declaration as he prepared to invade England. It was written by Melfort and amended by Herbert (the former Lord Chief Justice). It excepted many from pardon by name and added that others who had not done their duty would be forgiven only if their actions merited it. There were general assurances that James would protect the Church of England and promote liberty of conscience, but no promise to observe the laws or to redress grievances.[10] The French were displeased by the declaration. Louis had long had a low opinion of James's Catholic advisers and in 1689 had advised him to make his peace with the Anglicans. He stressed that James should not lead his subjects to believe that he would rely only on Catholics. Louis' ministers, therefore, joined with the Compounders in pressing James late in 1692 to send a letter into England with more explicit assurances to the Church of England. None was sent. Renaudot blamed Melfort, but Melfort had drawn up a not dissimilar letter, albeit one which ended with threats of what would happen if James's offers were rejected. It seems, then, that it was James himself who was reluctant to give the assurances which were demanded of him.[11]

At last, after months of pressure, James issued a more reassuring declaration in April 1693. It offered a pardon to all who did not oppose his restoration and promised a free Parliament which would redress grievances, provide for regular Parliaments and regulate the dispensing power. It also promised that James would protect and defend the Church of England, including its universities and schools and would respect the Test Acts. The Restoration land settlement in Ireland was to be re-established. It thus offered most of the safeguards which the Tories had wanted in 1688. James, however, was troubled by the explicit assurances to the Church and by the promise not to dispense with the Test. He consulted the great Bossuet and some doctors of the Sorbonne; neither found anything in the declaration against the conscience of a good Catholic. His English priests thought it improperly worded: James should not promise to defend a religion which he thought erroneous, although he could protect those who professed it. The Irish Catholics naturally resented his promise to restore to the Protestants their monopoly of land. Such objections came too late: the declaration was already in print. James apologized to the abbé of La Trappe for some of the expressions it contained, but stressed the good that it would do for the Catholic cause if it helped bring about his restoration. It did not. Despite Middleton's rash claim that James would be restored within six weeks of issuing the declaration, no rising ensued. This can only have strengthened James's conviction of the uselessness and iniquity of such concessions and his determination to make no more.[12]

Such declarations alone could not restore James. He needed Louis' military and naval help on a large scale: the fact that he had come to France ensured that the other Catholic powers would not help him, not even the Papacy, for the Vatican was predominantly anti-French. After the Boyne, however, Louis' advisers were reluctant to waste more arms and money in Ireland. In fact, the Irish army survived the campaign of 1691 and surrendered on terms at Limerick that October. Louis, however, was the more ready to abandon the Irish because the victory at Beachy Head gave him control of the Channel and offered the hope of direct intervention in England. In April 1692 James travelled to Normandy where Louis had assembled a large army, waiting for a fleet to carry him to England. When the fleet arrived, a much superior Anglo-Dutch fleet was waiting. In the battle of La Hogue, the French were decisively beaten and the Allies regained their mastery of the Channel.

James's reaction to this setback was typically fatalistic. "The hand of God appeared very visibly," he wrote, "for without that the design could not have failed, the King having prepared it so well." Louis, meanwhile, had second thoughts about his guest. In 1689 he had seemed a great asset, able to stir up trouble for William in Ireland, Scotland and England. By 1692 Scots and Irish resistance had been broken and the English Jacobites showed no sign of rising. James's own conduct also led Louis to doubt his capacity and determination as a leader. After La Hogue, therefore, Louis thought seriously of abandoning James's cause. At one stage he hoped that William would recognize the Prince of Wales as his heir. James, meanwhile, tried to rally the Pope and the Catholic princes to his cause, but the response was meagre. "Religion is gone and a wicked policy set up in its place," complained Perth, now his Ambassador at Rome.[13]

If the news from Rome was dispiriting, that from England seemed more hopeful. Heartened by Mary's death late in 1694, a group of non-Compounders sent proposals for a rebellion and invasion which sounded promising enough to win Louis' support. By the start of 1696 a second plan had been added to assassinate William. It is uncertain whether James and Louis knew of it—James himself denied that he did—but it is unlikely that they would have disavowed it had it succeeded. In February James prepared yet another declaration, containing fewer guarantees than that of 1693: there was no promise not to dispense with the Test Acts and more were excepted from pardon. Aware of the harm done by his earlier declarations—William's government had published that of 1692, with suitable comments—James decided not to publish this one until he landed. The whole scheme ended in confusion. The Jacobites refused to rise until the French landed, the French refused to sail until they heard that the Jacobites were in arms and, before this misunderstanding could be sorted out, most of the conspirators were arrested in London. James was not unduly perturbed. He had said all along that the design would succeed only if God wished it to do so. Now he remarked placidly that "The good Lord did not wish to restore me" and returned to his devotions. He was coming to accept failure and disappointment as a matter of course.[14]

Further disappointments were to come. In 1697 Louis at last made peace, exhausted by nine years of war. Hitherto he had refused to recognize William as King of Great Britain. Now he agreed, but only after long secret discussions between Bentinck (now Earl of Portland) and Marshal Boufflers. Louis still refused to repudiate James's claims, but agreed not to aid anyone who wished to overthrow William's authority. Other points were left vague. Portland got the impression that James and his family would leave Louis' dominions. He suggested that Mary Beatrice might be paid the £50,000 a year promised as a jointure in her marriage settlement, but implied that this would depend on Louis' giving satisfaction on the other points. These obstacles once removed, peace was signed at Ryswick in September.[15]

James saw the treaty as a betrayal, while Louis felt ashamed at having been driven by his need for peace to compromise his principles. In the next few years, he sought to atone for having sacrificed James's interests. He refused to order James to leave St Germain. William retaliated by refusing to pay Mary Beatrice's jointure, so James remained financially dependent on the French King. James, his wife and their little ragged retinue continued to follow the French court. Louis treated them with elaborate courtesy, but cut their allowance and showed no inclination to seek James's advice. As the chances of James's restoration now seemed virtually nil, more of his followers returned to England. Those who remained became more narrowly devout than ever, with only their faith and their feuds to sustain them.[16]

By now James's health was failing. In March 1701 a stroke partly paralysed his right arm and leg, but he had a strong constitution and within three months he was walking well and beginning to write. In August he had a relapse, complaining of stomach pains and spitting blood, probably a result of two stomach ulcers. On the 22nd he fell ill while hearing Mass. Two days later he suffered a severe internal haemorrhage. He was quickly given extreme unction but his condition then remained stable for a week. For most of the time he was conscious and lucid. He knew he was dying and approached death calmly, without fear, almost with relief. He commanded his son James (now thirteen) and daughter Louisa (aged nine) to remain good Catholics and to remember their obligations to their mother and to Louis. He exhorted his Catholic courtiers to remain firm to the Church and urged the Protestants to seek instruction in the one true faith. (However, in his will he adjured Mary Beatrice to provide for his servants regardless of their religion.) He pardoned William, the Emperor and his other enemies, "having always regarded his enemies as the instruments of divine justice".[17]

On 1st September his condition worsened markedly. He became lethargic and dozed for long periods. His physicians intensified their remedies, inflicting great pain on their patient, which he bore stoically. Next day Louis came and announced that, as Mary Beatrice had requested, he would recognize James's son as James III of England. James tried to embrace Louis, but was too weak. The two parted in floods of tears. By the 4th James was much weaker, with continual shaking and convulsions. On the afternoon of the 5th he died. He had ordered that his body should be buried in the local church with the minimum of pomp, but Louis would not allow this. The corpse was embalmed and cut up. Part of his viscera were buried in the parish church at St Germain, the remainder being sent to the English Jesuit college at St Omers. His brain was interred at the Scots college in Paris where Perth erected "a fair monument" to him. His heart, as he had requested, was deposited at the nunnery of Chaillot where he and his Queen had spent so many edifying hours. The remainder of the corpse was buried in the church of the English Benedictines in Paris. All traces of the body and of the monuments erected to James's memory disappeared in the French Revolution, although there is a later monument in the church at St Germain en Laye.[18]

* * *

To many at Paris and St Germain there was something holy about James's last years and edifying death. The surgeons and bodyguards took away little pieces of his body and clothing to keep as relics, or dipped handkerchiefs in his blood. Many came to the Benedictine church to pray for his soul and miraculous cures were attributed to his intercession. This popular belief in James's sanctity was followed by more official moves to secure his canonization. In 1734 the Archbishop of Paris began to hear the evidence in support of his case, which (like so many schemes associated with James) came to nothing.[19] James's subjects, however, regarded his memory with loathing, and the image of him which has passed into the mainstream of English historical writing is profoundly unfavourable. How can one reconcile these contradictions?

James was not a wicked man. He had high standards of personal honour and integrity, from which he deviated only rarely (as when he lied about his association with Coleman). He was a generous and loyal master and, as Duke of York, showed the same obedience to his brother as he expected others to show to him. He believed that wrongdoers should be punished severely, but was not unusually cruel by the standards of his time and was prepared to forgive many who seemed genuinely to repent of their misdeeds. To his principles of gentlemanly and honourable conduct, he added a stern Christian morality, rejecting the argument that one might use evil means to achieve good ends. He did not set out to undermine the English constitution or to destroy the laws. He believed that the powers which he claimed were his by right and that his interpretation of the law and of his prerogative was the correct one.

If anyone was plotting to subvert the constitution, he thought that it was the republicans who sought to reduce the monarch to a cipher.

If James was not wicked, neither was he idle. He applied himself diligently to the business of government, scrutinizing his accounts and wearing himself out on petty details of military administration in 1688. But application alone was not enough. James lacked the intellect to rise above the minutiae of government, to grasp a problem in its entirety and to formulate informed and coherent policies. Moreover, administrative expertise was only one aspect of the craft of kingship. Other, more political skills were needed and it was here that James was most found wanting. A king needed to be a skilful judge of character and of ministerial talent. Apart from Sunderland and Rochester, whom he inherited from his brother, James placed most trust in men who were at best mediocre and at worst dangerously inept, like Petre and Melfort. Such advisers could do little to rectify the great weakness of James's policies, at home and abroad—his total inability to appreciate the anxieties and principles of others. It might seem to James ridiculous that his subjects should suspect him of wishing to impose Catholicism by force. It might seem wicked that William should suspect him of plotting to alter the succession. It might seem absurd that solid Dutch merchants should fear that James and Louis intended to attack them. But these fears and suspicions existed. They reflected a Protestant view of Catholic behaviour which had grown up over a century and a half and which had been reinforced by Louis' conduct over the past twenty years. Correct or incorrect, rational or irrational, such fears had to be taken into account. James refused to do so.

The story of James's reign, then, is not one of Popish despotism foiled by William's providential intervention but of extreme political incompetence and sheer bad luck. It was bad luck (ironically) that James should have had a son and raised the spectre of a continuing Catholic dynasty. It was bad luck that Louis should have embroiled himself on the Rhine just when James needed his help. Even the wind, in the end, seemed to be on William's side. Yet these pieces of ill fortune would not have mattered had James not already alienated his subjects and convinced the Dutch that he planned to impose Popery at home and to ally with Louis. At the heart of James's failure lay his refusal to take sufficient account of his subjects' aversion to Catholicism. He saw it as the product of self-interest and ignorance. The former, he thought, could be countered by securing the material possessions of the Church of England, the latter by a process of education and propaganda. But anti-Catholicism was too deep rooted to be so easily removed and this James could not, would not understand. His inability to understand was a political failing but it was also a human failing. James was so egocentric, so confident of the rightness of his own views, that he was incapable of understanding the views of others. In a very real sense, he was not interested in other people, except in so far as they served his interests and shared his ideals. This was a particularly serious disability since his ideals (especially on religion) differed so much from those of most of his fellow countrymen. Among his servants and close associates he inspired respect and loyalty rather than love. James II's downfall, therefore, owed much to his inability to cope with the complex demands of kingship and more to his Catholicism. In the last resort, however, it stemmed from a lack of human warmth and, above all, a lack of human understanding.

APPENDIX

Dicconson's *Life of James II*

There has been much dispute among historians about the reliability as historical evidence of the *Life of James II*, edited by JS Clarke. It is generally accepted that the *Life* was written by a Jacobite called Dicconson not long after James's death. It is generally accepted, too, that it was based at least in part on James's "Memoirs". These consisted of memoranda, notes and fragments of narrative, written by James himself and smuggled out of England by Terriesi at the Revolution. They were later deposited in the Scots college in Paris and destroyed in the French Revolution.[1] What is in dispute is the extent to which the *Life* is based on the "Memoirs" and the amount which Dicconson added. There is little dispute about the first section of the *Life*, covering the period up to 1660. A French copy, with some differences of detail, was made under James's supervision in 1696. Moreover, the marginal references to "original memoirs" (parts 1 to 3) in the *Life* show a continuous pagination, which suggests that this section of the "Memoirs" had been written up as a more or less continuous narrative.[2]

For the period after 1660 the question becomes more problematical. Between 1661 and 1677 the *Life* gives no marginal references. From 1678 there are frequent references to "Original Memoirs, tomes 7, 8 and 9", to two large volumes of letters (each 700 to 900 pages), a volume of letters of Charles II, "loose papers" and one or two printed works (Oates's *Narrative*, L'Estrange's *History of the Times*, Baker's *Chronicle*). Such references are common in 1678–85 but become sporadic thereafter. The erratic pagination in the marginal references to these three volumes of "Memoirs" would imply that they consisted of unconnected fragments rather than a coherent narrative. This suggests that Dicconson based at least this part of the *Life* on original sources and quoted from them copiously. The absence of such references for 1661–77 need not mean that the *Life* for that period was not based on documentary evidence: one might, indeed, conjecture that this period was covered by volumes 4 to 6 of the "Memoirs". There is, moreover, evidence that the section on the period "1678 and downwards" was written up separately from the rest.[3] There is also other, more direct evidence.

Several British historians saw the "Memoirs" before they were destroyed. According to Charles James Fox they consisted of four volumes quarto and six volume folio of memoirs and four volumes of letters, which would square quite well with the marginal references in the *Life*.[4] Moreover, Thomas Carte and James Macpherson made notes from the "Memoirs" and letters which Macpherson later edited and published in his *Original Papers*. Now while Carte was an historian of considerable scholarship and integrity, Macpherson is notorious for his "improving" (if not forging) ancient Celtic poems. Moreover, there has been some uncertainty whether the extracts he published were from the *Life* (and therefore of no use in corroborating the material in the *Life*) or from the "Original Memoirs". Sir Winston Churchill was convinced that they had been based on the *Life*. He cited a letter of 1740 which said that the "Memoirs" ended at 1660, ignoring a later passage in the same letter which referred to the *Life* "written by M Dicconson upon his late majesty's Memoirs, letters and papers, both before and since the Restoration." He added the opinions of Fox and of an anonymous writer of 1816 that Macpherson's extracts were based on the *Life*.[5] However, it seems clear that the "Memoirs" described as ending in 1660 were the complete narrative, not the fragments. Moreover, the most superficial correlation of the *Life* and Macpherson's extracts shows such large disparities that it is quite impossible to argue that the latter were based entirely on the former. This led Ranke (whose opinion Churchill casually dismissed) to assert that Macpherson's extracts had been based on James's "Original Memoirs".[6]

That was not entirely correct, however. Carte's notes are preserved in the Bodleian library and are in two parts. The first part (Carte MS 198, ff39–44) is quite clearly based on the *Life* and is, indeed, marked "Life of James II". The second part (Carte MS 198, ff45–54) is chronologically muddled, containing scraps of narrative (sometimes quite lengthy), excerpts from letters and what appear to be extracts from a journal. Thus this set of notes does appear to be based on the "Original Memoirs", an impression confirmed by a single lapse into the first person ("as I remember"). As the passage in question refers to events in the 1640s, it cannot have been written by Dicconson, who was born in 1655.[7] The distinction between Carte's two sets of notes was obscured by Macpherson's mixing them together in roughly chronological order, although he usually (but not invariably) printed notes from the two sources as separate "extracts". He also expanded abbreviations and often added verbs and articles to make the notes more readable. His transcriptions included some errors (not surprisingly, in view of Carte's small and difficult handwriting and use of abbreviations) but on the whole he preserved the sense reasonably well. He also printed some transcripts of his own, which he marked as such in the margin. Macpherson's extracts were apparently taken from both the "Memoirs" and the *Life*. This would support the contention, so much doubted by Fox and Churchill, that the "Memoirs" he had seen were in James's own hand.[8] All in all, the standard of editing and the degree of authenticity of the extracts in Macpherson's *Original Papers* are much higher than his dubious reputation would lead one to expect.

How reliable as historical evidence are the *Life* and the extracts in the *Original Papers*? As far as the *Life* is concerned, I can only repeat the conclusions of

Ranke. The *Life* is most reliable where there are marginal references to some original documentation, whether "Memoirs" or letters. These occur most before 1660 and in 1678–85. Elsewhere it should be regarded as authentic only when corroborated by other evidence.[9] Such evidence can be found in the *Original Papers*, but only in those extracts *not* based on the *Life*.[10] Accordingly, when using the *Life* for the period 1660–78 I have tried where possible to provide corroborating evidence from passages in the *Original Papers* or elsewhere. From 1678 I have normally used only those passages where some documentary citation is given. In using the *Original Papers*, I have cited only those extracts not based on the *Life*.

Abbreviations

AH	*Analecta Hibernica*
AN	Archives Nationales
BL	British Library (Manuscripts Department)
BN, FFr, NA	Bibliothèque Nationale, Fonds Français, Nouvelles Acquisitions
Bodl	Bodleian Library
BT	Baschet transcripts of French ambassadors' dispatches in the PRO (ref PRO 31/3)
Cal Clar SP	*Calendar of Clarendon State Papers* (5 vols, Oxford, 1872–1970)
Carte MSS	Carte papers in the Bodleian Library
CJ	*Commons Journals*
Clar Corr	*Correspondence of Henry Hyde, Earl of Clarendon*, ed SW Singer (2 vols, London, 1828)
Clar MSS	Clarendon papers in the Bodleian Library
Clar SP	*State Papers collected by Edward, Earl of Clarendon* (3 vols, Oxford, 1767–86)
CPA	Archives des Affaires Etrangères, Paris, Correspondance Politique, Angleterre*
CSPD	*Calendar of State Papers, Domestic*
CSPV	*Calendar of State Papers, Venetian*
CSPV (cont)	Typescript continuation of the CSPV for 1676–78, in the PRO (ref E/M/21/58)
CUL	Cambridge University Library
EHR	*English Historical Review*
FO 95/	Foreign Office papers in the PRO (d'Avaux MSS)
HMC	Historical Manuscripts Commission reports
HJ	*Historical Journal*
Life	*Life of James II*, ed JS Clarke (2 vols, London, 1816)
LJ	*Lords Journals*
Morrice	Entering Books of Roger Morrice (MSS 31P and 31Q) in Dr Williams's Library
NS	New Series
PC 2/	Privy Council Registers in the PRO
PRO	Public Record Office

---

* Microfilm copies of CPA, vols 155, 166 and 167 and part of vol 165 (all omitted from BT) can be found in the PRO (ref PRO 28/39–40).

PwA, PwV	Portland papers in Nottingham University Library
Rom Tr	Roman Transcripts in the PRO (ref PRO 31/9)
RPC	*Registers of the Privy Council of Scotland*
SP	State Papers in the PRO
SS Ing	Vatican Archives, Segretaria di Stato, Inghilterra*
TCD	Trinity College, Dublin

---

* A microfilm copy of SS Ing vol 12 (omitted from the Vatican transcripts in the British Library) can be found in the Seeley Historical Library, Cambridge (Microfilm 1499).

Notes

Where full bibliographical details are given in the select bibliography, the notes give only author and (where necessary) a short title.

Unless otherwise stated, all French ambassadors reports were addressed to Louis XIV and all dates are those used by the writer (i.e. new style for foreign ambassadors, old style for Englishmen writing from England).

Chapter One

1. T Birch, *History of the Royal Society* (4 vols, London, 1756–57), IV 539; D McKie, "James, Duke of York, FRS", *Notes and Records of the Royal Society*, XIII. (1958), pp8–15; Campana, II 316; Evelyn, III 306; Pepys, IX 150.
2. *CSPV 1632–36*, p160; *Nicholas Papers*, I 76.
3. *Life*, I 2–5; Clarendon, *History*, II 47–50; Carte MS 180, f33.
4. *Life*, I 27–30; B Whitelocke, *Memorials of the English Affairs* (London, 1732), pp210, 215–17.
5. *CSPV 1643–47*, pp279, 298; *Cal Clar SP*, I 329; *CJ* IV 657, V 27; *Life*, I 30.
6. *CJ* V 198; Clarendon, *History*, IV 236–38, 249–53.
7. *Clar SP*, II Appendix, pp*xliv–xlvi*; *LJ* X 76–77; *CJ* V 470; *Life*, I 32–33; Clar MS 30, f307; *CSPD 1648–49*, p19.
8. Gardiner, *Civil War*, IV 99–101; *Life*, I 33–38; *Clar SP* II Appendix, p*xlvii*.

Chapter Two

1. Clarendon, *History*, V 212, 225n, 329–31, 337–38, 351.
2. *Nicholas Papers*, IV 264; *Cal Clar SP*, III 357; *HMC Bath*, II 144; Geyl, pp131, 159.
3. Thurloe, I 667, II 678, 646; Clarendon, *History*, V 247.
4. Clarendon, *History*, IV 328, 338–39, V 161; *Clar SP*, III Appendix, pp*lxxviii–lxxix*.
5. Clarendon, *History*, IV 336–41, 417; Clar MS 31, f128; *Life*, I 43–44; *Nicholas Papers*, I 97.
6. Gardiner, *Civil War*, IV 210–11; Carte, *Orig Letters*, I 157, 188–89; *Cal Clar SP*, I 445–46; *Clar SP*, II 454; Clarendon, *History*, IV 372–74, 423–24.
7. Geyl, pp66 74; *Cal Clar SP*, I 444–45; Clarendon, *History*, IV 424n; Carte, *Orig Letters*, I 199; *CSPV 1647–52*, p84; *Life*, I 45–46.
8. Thurloe, I 666.
9. BL, Add 15397, f154; *HMC Dartmouth*, I 54; *Life*, I 555, 614; Ranke, VI 80.
10. Burnet, *History*, II 30; Dalrymple, II (a) 218; Prinsterer, V 458.
11. N. Crewe, "Memoirs", p25, in *Camden Miscellany* IX.
12. Clarendon, *History*, V 3, 48, 50, 64–65; *Nicholas Papers*, I 116–17.

13. *Cal Clar SP*, II 50–51; *Nicholas Papers*, I 173–74; Clarendon, *History*, V 107, 162–63.
14. *Nicholas Papers*, I 196–97.
15. *Ibid*, I 195; Clarendon, *History*, V 162–64.
16. Clarendon, *History*, V 164–65; *HMC Bath*, II 97–98; *Nicholas Papers*, I 207–15, 218; *Life*, I 49–50; Geyl, p85; C Wilson, *Profit and Power* (Longman, 1957), p49.
17. *HMC Heathcote*, p5; *Clar SP*, III 29; *Nicholas Papers*, I 247–48.
18. Clarendon, *History*, V 169; *Nicholas Papers*, I 204, 221, 233.
19. *Life*, I 51; Carte, *Orig Letters*, II 40; *HMC Ormond*, NS I 181–82, 208; *Nicholas Papers*, I 265, 274; Clarendon, *History*, V 14, 212, 225n; J Evelyn, *Diary and Correspondence*, ed W Bray (London, 1906), IV 344.
20. *Clar SP*, III 88; Thurloe, II 324.
21. Clarendon, *History*, V 232, 324–28; *Clar SP*, III 52.
22. *Cal Clar SP*, II 128, 132, 153, 195; Clarendon, *History*, V 233–34, 316–18; *Nicholas Papers*, II 7.
23. *Cal Clar SP*, II 136, 169, 281; Gardiner, *Commonwealth*, II 451, 469–73, III 487–88.
24. Carte, *Orig Letters*, I 222; Clarendon, *History*, V 164, 225–27, 247–48; *Clar SP*, III 118, Suppl. p*lxxix*; *Nicholas Papers*, I 281; *Life*, I 273; Sells, p57.
25. *HMC Bath*, II 103.
26. *Nicholas Papers*, II 214–15, 343.
27. *Cal Clar SP*, II 206, 420–35; *Nicholas Papers*, II 118–22, 142, 147.
28. *Cal Clar SP*, II 420, 430, 436; *Nicholas Papers*, II 126–27, III 4.
29. *Cal Clar SP*, II 428–29, 433; *Nicholas Papers*, II 127, 142.
30. *Cal Clar SP*, II 430; *Nicholas Papers*, II 135, 155–56.
31. *Cal Clar SP*, II 409, 415, 430.
32. H Cary, *Memorials of the Great Civil War* (2 vols, London, 1842), II 230–32; Thurloe, I 619; *Cal Clar SP*, II 132; *Nicholas Papers*, I 265; *Clar SP*, III 459 (quoted).
33. *Nicholas Papers*, II 246.
34. *Ibid*, II 185; *HMC Ormond*, I 15; Thurloe, I 685, 687–8; Brown, pp113, 116–17.
35. Gardiner, *Commonwealth*, III 422–24; *Nicholas Papers*, III 125n; Sells, pp217–18; Thurloe, I 666.
36. Gardiner, *Commonwealth*, III 480–81; *Life*, I 265–66; Thurloe, I 667, IV 392, 506; Sells, p219.
37. Carte MS 198, f37; Brown, pp125–26, 129; Sells, pp222–23; Thurloe, V 131, 145 (quoted), 293, 325.
38. Brown, pp108–09; *Life*, I 271–72, 275–80; *Clar SP*, III 322, 350, 370; Thurloe, V 511; *CSPD 1656–57*, p346.
39. *Life*, I 280–84; *Clar SP*, III Suppl. pp*lxxix–lxxx*.
40. *Life*, I 284–89; *Cal Clar SP*, III 223–24; *Clar SP*, III 318.
41. *Life*, I 288–91; *Clar SP*, III 317–18.
42. *Life*, I 291–92; Carte MS 198, f37; *Clar SP*, III 321–24.
43. *Life*, I 292–93; *Clar SP*, III Suppl. p*lxxx*; Thurloe, VI 363.
44. *Clar SP*, III 350; *Cal Clar SP*, III 346–48, 359–60.
45. *CSPD 1657–58*, pp326–28; *Cal Clar SP*, IV 42, 47, 54, 58, 99; Thurloe, VII 420, 428, 453, 503, 508.
46. *Cal Clar SP*, IV 194, 198–99, 250, 521; *Clar SP*, III 475, 607; Carte, *Orig Letters*, II 344; Comminges, 2 April 1663, BT 111.

47. *Cal Clar SP*, IV 54; Thurloe, VIII 420, 503; *Nicholas Papers*, IV 174–75.
48. *Clar SP*, III 347; Sells, pp151–53, 234–37, 241; Pepys, IX 396.
49. Sells, pp252, 266–72; Pepys, V 170; *Nicholas Papers*, IV 56–58; CH Firth, *Last Years of the Protectorate* (2 vols, London, 1909), I 217–19.
50. *Life*, I 381; *CSPV 1659–61*, pp139–40; Clarendon, *History*, VI 141–42.
51. *HMC le Fleming*, pp25–26; *HMC 5*, p167; Clarendon, *History*, VI 234; Evelyn, III 246.

Chapter Three

1. *CSPD 1671*, p563.
2. P Goubert, *The Ancien Regime* (Weidenfeld, 1973), pp46–48, 134 and *passim*; K Wrightson and J Walter, "Dearth and the Social Order in early Modern England", *Past and Present*, no 71 (1976), pp22–42.
3. L Hutchinson, *Memoirs of the Life of Colonel Hutchinson*, ed CH Firth (London, 1906), p7; A Everitt, *The Community of Kent and the Great Rebellion* (Leicester UP, 1973), p36.
4. Cf D Hirst, *The Representative of the People?* (Cambridge, 1975), esp pp7–12, 137–53.
5. Cf JS Morrill, *The Revolt of the Provinces* (Allen and Unwin, 1976); Everitt, *Kent*; and A Fletcher, *A County Community in Peace and War: Sussex 1600–60* (Longman, 1975) (quotation from p113).
6. Everitt, *Kent*, pp323–24.
7. Behrens, pp59–60; JP Kenyon, "The Revolution of 1688: Contract and Resistance", in N McKendrick (ed), *Historical Perspectives: Studies . . . in Honour of JH Plumb* (Europa, 1974), esp p57.
8. Kenyon, *Stuart Constitution*, pp17–18.
9. C Russell, "Introduction", in Russell (ed), *Origins of the English Civil War* (Macmillan, 1973), pp4–6.
10. eg, C Hill, *The Century of Revolution* (Nelson, 1961), pp224–26.
11. Cf Chandaman, esp ch 6.
12. eg, Hill, *Century*, p224; L Stone, *Causes of the English Revolution* (Routledge, 1972), pp146–47.
13. TB Macaulay, *History of England*, ed CH Firth (6 vols, Macmillan, 1913), I 174–75; Hill, *Century*, p228.
14. Newton, *House of Lyme*, pp242–43.
15. C Russell, *The Crisis of Parliaments* (Oxford, 1971), p278.
16. JGA Pocock, *The Ancient Constitution and the Feudal Law* (Cambridge, 1957), ch 8.

Chapter Four

1. Ranke, VI 78; North, *Examen*, p451; Halifax, pp257, 259.
2. Reresby, p182; Halifax, pp256–57; North, *Examen*, p451; Pepys, VII 197, VIII 282.
3. Buckingham, II 59; *CSPV 1661–64*, p84; Pepys, VII 218; Evelyn, IV 410; Ailesbury, I 87.
4. Burnet, *History*, I 170, II 480; Ranke, VI 78; Halifax, pp255–56.
5. L Magalotti, *Travels of Cosimo III, Grand Duke of Tuscany* (London, 1821), pp367–70; D Allen, "The Political Function of Charles II's Chiffinch", *Huntington Library Quarterly* XXXIX (1976), pp277–90.
6. Clarendon, *Life*, II 144, III 61; Colbert to Lionne, 7 Feb 1669, BT 121.

7. *CSPV 1659–61*, p210.

8. Clarendon, *Life*, III 18; Burnet, *History*, I 494, II 1–2; Barrillon, 18 April 1678, BT 139; cf also Ailesbury, I 22.

9. Ailesbury, I 91, 93–94; Burnet, *History*, I 168–69, 501–02, II 22–23; Clarendon, *Life*, II 144–45.

10. Bartet to Mazarin, 7th and 19th Feb 1661, BT 109; Ranke, III 443 and n; Hartmann, p314.

11. Burnet, *Suppl*, p142, *History*, II 481; Pepys, VIII 328–29, 355.

12. Clarendon, *Life*, I 405, II 12–13, III 67–68; *HMC 8/1*, pp279–80.

13. Clar MS 79, ff203, 205, 219, 221; Carte MS 47, f415; Pepys, VIII 286–87.

14. Chandaman, pp117, 120, 132; D Ogg, *England in the Reign of Charles II* (Oxford, 1956), p258; Clar MS 88, ff143–47.

15. *HMC 8/1*, pp278–79; BL Add. 38863, ff1–12; Barrillon to Pomponne, 16th Jan 1678, CPA 133; Campana, I 190–91; Barrillon, 5th Oct 1678, BT 143.

16. *HMC Rye*, pp237, 243; Browning, III 36–38; Reresby, pp40, 62, 118, 131–36, 138–40, 160.

17 *HMC 8/1*, pp278–79; *CSPV 1661–64*, pp18, 185–86; Clarendon, *Life*, III 123–24; Pepys, II 38, V 345.

18. *CSPV 1661–64*, pp28, 87; Pepys, IV 367, V 21, VII 212, 320; Wilson, *Profit and Power*, pp92–93, 112–13, 122–23; Ogg, *Charles II*, pp274–75 and ch. 8.

19. *HMC Heathcote*, pp82, 123; Ogg, *Charles II*, pp676–78; EE Rich, *History of the Hudson's Bay Company* (2 vols, Hudson's Bay Record Soc., 1958–59), I 29–33, 84–85, 144; Clarendon, *Life*, II 231–36; Ruvigny to Lionne, 24 Oct 1667, BT 116; WR Scott, *The Constitution and Finance of English, Scottish and Irish Join Stock Companies to 1720* (3 vols, Cambridge, 1910–12), II 17–21.

20. *Nicholas Papers*, III 4; Sells, p219; *Cal Clar SP* III 45, V 80; Pepys, I 261; Macpherson, I 23; *Life*, I 387.

21. Clarendon, *Life*, I 372–73, 377–84; Pepys, I 260–61; Hamilton, pp163–65; Ruvigny to Mazarin, 17th and 21st Oct 1660, BT 107; Bartet to Mazarin, 10th Feb 1661, BT 109.

22. Clarendon, *Life*, I. 388–89; Ruvigny to Mazarin, 1st Nov 1660, Bartet to Mazarin, 8th, 11th and 16th Nov, Soissons to Mazarin, 15th Nov, Montagu to Mazarin, 15th Nov, all in BT 108; Pepys, I 275.

23. Bartet to Mazarin, 16th, 23rd and 25th Nov, 14th, 16th, 23rd and 30th Dec 1660, 12th Jan 1661, Mazarin to Montagu, 24th Nov 1660, BT 108, 109; Clarendon, *Life*, I 394–97; *HMC 5*, p195.

24. Pepys, II 95, III 75, V 268; Reresby, p55.

25. Hamilton, pp137, 173 and *passim*; Pepys, VII 297, VIII 286, IX 515.

26. Pepys, III 248, VII 8, IX 38, 342; Hamilton, pp273–74; Carte MS 36, f199.

27. Turner, p87; *Life*, I 392–93.

28. Clarendon, *History*, V 326–28; *CSPD 1654*, p408 (quoted); Bordeaux to Mazarin, 14 June 1660, BT 107; *Hatton Corr*, I 34.

29. Clarendon, *Life*, I 321; *Life*, I 393, 435; Macpherson, I 40; Pepys, IX 490; Burnet, *History*, I 286–87; Bristol to Condé, 16 July 1660, Blenheim Palace, MS A1–4, bundle 1; *Rawdon Papers*, p184.

30. Clarendon, *Life*, II 351, III 102–03, 240–45; Pepys, VIII 415, 427; H Roseveare, *The Treasury 1660–1870: The Foundations of Control* (Allen and Unwin, 1973), pp20ff.

31. Clarendon, *Life*, III 64; Buckingham, II 57; Pepys, VI 301–02; Halifax, p256.

32. Clarendon, *Life*, I 507, III 59–66; *CSPV 1661–64*, p206; Carte MS 46, f250; Ranke, VI 82; Pepys, III 238, 290, IV 134, V 21, VII 411.

33. cf GR Abernathy jnr, *The English Presbyterians and the Stuart Restoration* (Transactions of the American Philosophical Society, 1965), chs. 5–7; A Whiteman, "The Restoration of the Church of England", in GF Nuttall and O Chadwick (eds), *From Uniformity to Unity 1662–1962* (SPCK, 1962), pp19–88; Miller, *Popery*, pp94–102; Witcombe, p211.

34. Burnet, *History*, I 325; *LJ* XI 573; Abernathy, pp82–83; *Rawdon Papers*, p143.

35. Vatican Archives, Nunziatura di Fiandra, 45, f283; Abernathy, pp85–89; *HMC* 7, pp167–68; Comminges to Lionne, 8th March 1663, BT 111; Clarendon, *Life*, II 342–50.

36. Burnet, *History*, I 305–06, 333, *Suppl*, p71; *Life*, I 443; Lingard, X 203.

37. Bordeaux to Mazarin, 24th June 1660, BT 107; Ranke, III 390; Clarendon, *Life*, II 236; Comminges, 9th June 1664, BT 113; Pepys, V 239, 264; Verneuil, Comminges and Courtin, 13th Oct 1665, BT 115.

38. Clarendon, *Life*, II 240; Comminges to Lionne, 13th Nov 1664, BT 113; Verneuil et al, 2nd July and 5th Aug 1665, BT 115, CPA 80; Pepys, VIII 379; Macpherson, I 37.

39. *Life*, I 390–91; *CSPV 1661–64*, p91; Pepys, III 15, VI 276–77, 302, VII 55, 395, VIII 332; *Diary of Henry Townshend*, ed JW Willis Bund (2 vols, Worcs. Historical Soc, 1920), I 72; Clarendon, *Life*, III 253–54.

40. Carte MS 35, f478.

41. *Ibid*, ff502, 522; Clarendon, *Life*, III 283–94.

42. Carte MS 217, f405; Pepys, VIII 409; Carte, *Ormond*, V 57; Foxcroft, I 54–55. There was some dispute whether James ever approved the proposal that Clarendon should resign: Pepys, VIII 416, 431, 506, IX 476; Clarendon, *Life*, III 287.

43. Burnet, *Suppl*, p64; Reresby, p66; Hamilton, p142.

44. Pepys, VIII 434, 438, 480; Clarendon, *Life*, III 301–03; Ruvigny, 21st and 28th Oct, 4th and 11th Nov 1667, BT 116, 117; Macpherson, I 39; Carte MS 35, f778.

45. Carte MS 36, f25; Pepys, VIII 518; Clarendon, *Life*, III 332; Carte MS 35, f873; Ruvigny, 28th Nov 1667, BT 117. See also C Roberts, "The Impeachment of the Earl of Clarendon", *Cambridge Hist Jnl*, XIII (1957); Witcombe, pp66–67.

46. Roberts, "Impeachment", pp9–15; Prinsterer, V 482.

Chapter Five

1. Clarendon, *Life*, II 197, 204–11, 313–15; Witcombe, pp78ff and *passim*.

2. BL, Egerton 2539,f170; Pepys, IX 71; Ruvigny, 23rd Feb, 5th and 19th March 1668, BT 118; Witcombe, ch 7.

3. *Life*, I 435; Croissy, 11th and 25th April 1669, BT 121.

4. Pepys, IX 360–61.

5. *Life*, I 437–40; Macpherson, I 44, 47–48, 51; BL, Add 36916, f121; Croissy, 28th March and 13th May 1669, BT 121, 122; Pepys, IX 550–51.

6. Clarendon, *Life*, III 171–79; Burnet, *History*, I 479–82; Croissy to Lionne, 17th March 1670, CPA 97; Macpherson, I 49, 51.

7. Ruvigny to Lionne, 16 April 1668, BT 118; Pepys, IX 417; Croissy, 13th May and 19th Aug 1669, BT 122.

8. Bentinck, p6; *Autobiography of Symon Patrick* (Oxford, 1839), pp112–14; Burnet, *History*, II 25; Mackintosh, p632.

9. Burnet, *History*, II 24, 27.

10. The account of James's conversion is based mainly on Burnet, *History*, I 304–06, II 24–29, *Suppl*, pp51–52; *Life*, I 630–31; Bentinck, pp4–9; Davies, pp23–27.

11. Pepys, IX 397; *Life*, I 440–41, 482–83, 631; Burnet, *History*, I 566–67; Carte MS 180, f34; Treby, I 85–86; Croissy to Lionne, 6th July 1671, CPA 100; Croissy, 21st April 1672, BT 127.

12. *Life*, I 503; Macpherson, I 82; Croissy to Louvois, 2 Nov 1671, CPA 101; Burnet, *History*, II 29, *Suppl*, p52.

13. The main sources for James's conversation with Charles are Carte MS 198, f47 (printed Macpherson, I 48) and *Life* I 441 and for the conference *Life*, I 441–42. Macpherson's version differs from Carte's in substituting "reconciled" for "instructed" and in implying that Charles had already consulted Arundell, Arlington and Clifford, not that he would consult them. The account of the conference in the *Life* is unsubstantiated by Carte's notes. Macpherson's notes appear to be based on the *Life*.

14. Croissy's instructions, 2 Aug 1668, BT 119; Dalrymple, II (a) 9; Croissy, 20th Aug, 17th Sept and 26th Nov 1668, BT 119, 120; Hartmann, pp231–33.

15. Hartmann, p235.

16. Croissy, 5th and 19th Dec 1669, BT 123, 29th Jan, 15th and 30th May 1670, BT 124; Dalrymple, II (a) 59; Hartmann, pp271–74, 312–17.

17. Hartmann, pp250, 265; Croissy, 25th April 1669, BT 121, 29th Jan, 20th March, 11th April, 5th May 1670, BT 124.

18. *Life*, I 444, 448–50; Croissy, 27th May 1670, BT 124; *CSPV 1669–70*, pp197, 202; *HMC Various*, II 145–46, 159.

19. Croissy to Lionne, 19th Jan and 23rd Feb 1671, CPA 100; Croissy, 9th May 1672, BT 127; CH Hartmann, *Clifford of the Cabal* (Heinemann, 1937), pp318–33.

20. Croissy to Lionne, 23rd Feb and 6th July 1671, CPA 100; Croissy, 21st April and 9th May 1672, BT 127.

21. Witcombe, pp115–26; Croissy, 14th July 1671, BT 126 (the passage quoted is printed by Dalrymple, II (a) 80); Croissy, 30th Sept 1672, BT 127.

22. Brown, p66; Hartmann, *Clifford*, pp154–55.

23. Pepys, IV 135; Reresby, pp80–81; Macpherson, I 51; *Lauderdale Papers*, III 87–88.

24. Burnet, *History*, II 26–28, *Suppl*, pp51–52; *Life*, I 656.

25. *CSPD 1671*, p563; *CSPV 1671–72*, pp201, 218, 232–36, 290–91, 295; Croissy, 16th June 1672, BT 127; *Life*, I 478–81.

26. Croissy, 21st April 1672, BT 127; WD Christie, *Life of Shaftesbury* (2 vols, London, 1871), II Appendix, pp*xiv–xv*; *CSPV 1671–72*, p226; Burnet, *History*, I 593; Croissy to Pomponne, 30th June 1672, CPA 103.

27. Croissy, 21st April 1672, BT 127; Croissy to Pomponne, 23rd Jan 1673, CPA 106; *Life*, I 482–83.

Chapter Six

1. Burnet, *History*, II 1; *Williamson Letters*, II 78; above, p35; Marvell, II 301.

2. Burnet, II 1; see also Miller, *Popery*, esp ch 4.

3. See below, ch 9.
4. Temple, *Memoirs 1672–79*, pp153–54.
5. Croissy, 20th Feb 1673, BT 128; Croissy to Pomponne, 27th Feb and 9th March 1673, CPA 106; *CSPV 1673–75*, pp19, 27; Dalrymple, II (a) 93–94; Burnet, *History*, II 9.
6. *CSPV 1673–75*, p29; Croissy to Pomponne, 5th March and 3rd April 1673, CPA 106; Grey, II 25; Newton, *Lyme Letters*, p52; Burnet, *History*, II 7, 11, 103; Croissy, 1st and 3rd April 1673, BT 128.
7. Brown, pp98–105; *CSPV 1673–75*, p13; Croissy, 20th Feb, 6th and 17th April 1673, BT 128; Macpherson, I 68; Carte MS 35, f873.
8. See Haley, *Shaftesbury*, esp pp167, 277–79, 323–26.
9. *CSPV 1673–75*, pp43, 68–69; Croissy, 17th April and 10th July 1673, BT 128; Vatican Archives, Nunziatura di Fiandra 59, ff305–07.
10. *Hatton Corr*, I 111; Croissy, 10th and 24th July 1673, BT 128; *Williamson Letters*, I 58, 116; Macpherson, I 68–69.
11. Croissy, 1st Apr and 10th Aug 1673, BT 128, 129; *CSPV 1673–75*, pp40, 52, 55–56, 73; *Williamson Letters*, I 55, 60.
12. Croissy, 14th Sept and 2nd Oct 1673, BT 129; *Williamson Letters*, I 63, II 27.
13. *HMC 7*, p489; Burnet, *History*, I 566–68; J Evelyn, *Life of Mrs Godolphin*, ed SW Wilberforce (London, 1874), p13.
14. *CSPV 1671–72*, pp38, 114, 132; Croissy, 12th Nov 1671, BT 126; Croissy to Louvois, 2nd Nov 1671, CPA 101; Burnet, *History*, II 16.
15. Croissy, 12th Nov 1671, BT 126, 1st March 1672, BT 127, 17th July 1673, BT 128; *CSPV 1671–72*, pp114, 222; Brown, pp75–104.
16. Croissy, 17th April, 17th and 31st July, 1673, BT 128; R Halstead, *Succinct Genealogies* (London, 1685), pp419–23 (Halstead was Peterborough's pseudonym); Campana, I 3–6.
17. Croissy to Pomponne, 1st Sept 1672, CPA 104; Croissy, 25th Sept 1673, BT 129; *CSPV 1673–75*, p98; Campana, I 18–56.
18. Campana, I 61–89; Halstead, pp428–29; *CSPV 1673–75*, pp 125–26, 130–32.
19. Campana, I 90–91, 150–53; *CSPV 1673–75*, pp129, 142, 144–50, 157, 164, 170–71, 282; Treby, I 85–86, 93–95.
20. CJ IX 281–86; *CSPV 1673–75*, pp161–62; Croissy, 13th Nov 1673, BT 129; *Essex Papers*, I 130.
21. Burnet, *History*, II 37; *Williamson Letters*, II 62; *CSPV 1673–75*, pp174–77, 183, 187; Croissy, 20th Nov and 7th Dec 1673, BT 129; Croissy to Pomponne, 20th and 23rd Nov 1673, CPA 108; *Essex Papers*, I 132, 140, 142; *Lauderdale Papers*, III 6; *Life*, I 487–88.
22. *CSPD 1673–75*, pp40–41; Campana, I 132–33; *CSPV 1673–75*, p197.
23. Halstead, p428; *Essex Papers*, I 145, 159; *The Dispatches of William Perwich*, ed MB Curran (Camden Soc, 1903), pp273–74; *HMC Rutland*, II 34; Burnet, *History*, II 43; All Souls' MS 317, Trumbull's Memoirs, f51.
24. Ruvigny to Pomponne, 1st and 22nd Feb 1674, BT 130; *Williamson Letters*, II 94, 147–48; *CSPV 1673–75*, pp206, 221; Macpherson, I 72; *HMC 9/2*, pp42, 45–46.
25. Evelyn, IV 118; Buckingham, II 63; Browning, II 63–64.
26. Ruvigny, 30th July, 13th Aug and 8th Nov 1674, BT 131; *CSPV 1673–75*, pp206, 298; *Essex Papers*, I 228.
27. Ruvigny, 13th Aug 1674 and 27th Jan 1675, BT 131, 132; Treby, I 1–16, 22–28, 109–10.

28. *CSPD 1673*, pp367–68; *CSPV 1673–75*, pp243, 279, 307–08; for Baber, see Dalrymple, II (a) 256, 282; Burnet, *Letters*, p12; North, *Examen*, pp361–62; Haley, *Shaftesbury*, p385.

29. *CSPV 1673–75*, pp307–50 *passim*; Canaples to Pomponne, 6 Dec, Ruvigny to Pomponne, 20th and 24th Dec 1674, CPA 113; *HMC Portland*, III 348; *Essex Papers*, I 285–88; Ruvigny, 27th Jan 1675, BT 132.

30. *CSPV 1673–75*, pp330, 357–76, 390–91; Ruvigny, 4th Feb and 8th Apr 1675, BT 132; Campana, I 148; Ruvigny to Pomponne, 21st Feb 1675, CPA 115.

31. *CSPV 1673–75*, pp398, 401–02; Burnet, *History*, II 74; *Essex Papers*, II 8; *Morrison Letters: Bulstrode*, I 284; Haley, pp382–84.

32. *CSPV 1673–75*, p407; Haley, p385; Ruvigny, 27th June 1675, BT 132.

33. Ruvigny, 21 Nov 1675, BT 132; *HMC 9/2*, p79; Burnet, *History*, II 93–94.

34. Dalrymple, II (a) 105; Campana, I 176–77; *HMC 7*, p467; Ruvigny to Pomponne, 16th March 1676, CPA 118; *HMC Leeds*, p14; A Browning, *English Historical Documents 1660–1714* (Eyre and Spottiswoode, 1953), pp413–14.

35. Courtin, 8th and 22nd June 1676, BT 132, 12th Oct 1676, BT 134; *Life*, I 502–03 (Macpherson, I 82).

36. Courtin, 28th Sept, 2nd and 30th Nov 1676, BT 133, 134; Courtin to Pomponne, 14th and 28th Dec 1676, CPA 120.

37. Courtin, 10th Dec 1676, BT 134, 3rd Jan 1677, CPA 123A (quoted), 21st Jan, 4th and 11th Feb 1677, BT 135; *CSPD 1676–77*, pp541–42.

38. Courtin, 8th and 18th March 1675, BT 135; Barrillon, 26th Sept 1678, BT 140; *LJ* XIII 75; Sarotti, 5th March 1677, CSPV (cont); *Life*, I 505; Macpherson, I 79–80.

39. Courtin to Pomponne, 22nd and 29th April 1677, CPA 123; Browning, II 70–71; Campana, I 193–95; Courtin, 12th April, 13th May, 3rd and 21st June, 12th July 1677, BT 135, 136; Marvell, II 329.

40. Barrillon, 8th and 11th Nov 1677, BT 137; Temple, *Memoirs, 1672–79*, pp297–98; cf also Geyl; Baxter.

41. Ruvigny, 23rd April, 19th Nov and 20th Dec 1674, BT 131; Temple, *Memoirs, 1672–79*, pp81–84; Macpherson, I 75; Burnet, *History*, II 61n.

42. Temple, *Memoirs, 1672–79*, pp150–55; Courtin, 3rd Sept and 3rd Oct 1676, BT 133, 134.

43. Courtin, 17th June 1677, BT 136; Japikse, II 2, p178; Browning, II 486; Barrillon, 27th and 30th Sept 1677, BT 137; *HMC Ormond*, NS IV 376; Prinsterer, V 348.

44. KHD Haley, "The Anglo-Dutch Rapprochement of 1677", *EHR* LXXIII (1958), pp640–43; Temple, *Memoirs, 1672–79*, pp294–95; *Hatton Corr*, I 51.

45. Barrillon, 1st and 4th Nov 1677, BT 137; Rom Tr 100A, f289; Browning, II 89; cf Burnet, *History*, II 120–23.

46. Barrillon, 30th Sept, 28th and 30th Oct 1677, BT 137.

47. Barrillon, 25th Oct and 15th Nov 1677, BT 137.

48. *Diary of Dr Edward Lake*, ed GP Elliott, p5 in *Camden Miscellany I* (1847); Burnet, *History*, IV 561–62 (quoted); Haley, "Rapprochement", pp647–48; *HMC Athole and Home*, p34.

49. Haley, "Rapprochement", pp643–47.

50. Temple, *Memoirs, 1672–79*, p301; Barrillon, 9th and 13th Dec 1677, 17th Jan 1678, BT 137, 138; Prinsterer, V 359; Sarotti, 7 Jan 1678, CSPV (cont); Campana, I 207–08, 210; *HMC Ormond*, NS IV 395–96.

51. Barrillon, 19 Feb, 9th, 14th and 26th March 1678, BT 138.

52. Dalrymple II (a) 131–32, 142 (quoted); Barrillon, 21st and 26th March, 11th April 1678, BT 138; Sarotti, 8th April 1678, CSPV (cont).
53. Barrillon, 7th Feb 1678, BT 138; Dalrymple, II (a) 146–47, 152, 172–74 (quotation from p174).
54. Barrillon, 21st April 1678, BT 139; Campana, I 213.
55. JP Kenyon, *The Popish Plot* (Heinemann, 1972), pp50–67; *Life*, I 517–18.
56. *HMC Ormond*, NS IV 207; W Cobbett and TB Howell (eds), *State Trials* (33 vols, London, 1809–26), VI 1442, 1457, 1470–71; Kenyon, *Popish Plot*, pp72–73.
57. Treby, I 116.
58. Miller, *Popery*, pp158–59, 171–73; *LJ* XIII 307–09; *CJ* IX 523; Sarotti, 11 Nov 1678, CSPV (cont). I hope soon to publish an article on Coleman and his letters.
59. Barrillon, 27th Oct, 3rd and 14th Nov 1678, BT 141; Barrillon to Pomponne, 24th Nov 1678, CPA 131; *HMC Ormond*, NS IV 484; *CSPD 1678*, p 550; *HMC Fitzherbert*, pp137, 145–46.
60. Barrillon, 10th, 13th and 27th Oct, 3rd and 7th Nov, 22nd Dec 1678, BT 141; Kenyon, *Popish Plot*, p150; *HMC Savile Foljambe*, p123; Sarotti, 23rd Dec 1678, CSPV (cont); *HMC Ormond*, NS IV 465–66; Carte MS 38, f678.
61. *Life*, I 530; Carte MS 39, f1; *HMC Ormond*, NS IV 496; Burnet, *History*, II 173; Barrillon, 12th Dec 1678, 5th and 9th Jan 1679, BT 141, 142.
62. *HMC Ormond*, NS IV 340; *Clar Corr*, II 466–71; *Life*, I 537–41; Dalrymple, II (a) 213–14; *HMC Ormond*, I 27; *HMC 14/9*, p401; Carte, *Ormond*, V 142; Barrillon, 13th March 1679, BT 142.

Chapter Seven

1. C Blount (?), "An Appeal from the Country to the City", in *State Tracts* (2 vols, London, 1689–92), I 401–02.
2. Campana, I 362 (Barrillon, 28th July 1681).
3. Reresby, pp205, 209.
4. Browning, II 379–80; see also Miller, *Popery*, pp182–88; for the Whigs' constitutional views see Behrens, esp p50.
5. eg, Temple, *Memoirs, Part III*, pp 48–49.
6. See Kenyon, *Sunderland*, esp ch 10.
7. Temple, *Memoirs, Part III*, pp38–41; *Life*, I. 556; Burnet, *History*, II 239.
8. *HMC Ormond*, NS IV 512–15; Barrillon, 8th May 1679, BT 142; North, *Examen*, pp77–78; Dalrymple, II (a) 217–20.
9. *HMC Dartmouth*, I 34.
10. Sidney, I 129–30, II 78–79, 120; Prinsterer, V 422–24, 493–94; *Life*, I 691.
11. Dalrymple II (a) 218, 221, 224, 265; *HMC Dartmouth*, I 34.
12. *HMC Ormond*, I 28; Sidney, I 16n; Dalrymple, II (a) 226; *HMC Dartmouth*, I 36; *Clar Corr*, I 45.
13. *Life*, I 562–67; Campana, I 295–96; Reresby, p187.
14. Temple, *Memoirs, Part III*, pp74–75, 79–80; Sidney, I 176; *Life*, I 564–68; Campana, I 295–96; Rom Tr 100A, ff197–99; Dalrymple, II (a) 247; *Hatton Corr*, I 195; *CSPD 1679–80*, pp243–44; Kenyon, *Sunderland*, p31n.
15. Temple, *Memoirs, Part III*, pp74–75, 85–86; Kenyon, *Sunderland*, pp32–33; Rom Tr 100A, ff199–200.
16. Blathwayt to Southwell, 9th Sept 1679, PwV 51; *Life*, I 567–69; *Hatton Corr*, I 203–06; Barrillon, 11th Dec 1679, 6th and 13th June 1680, BT 143, 145.

17. *HMC Ormond*, NS IV 537, 542, 545–46; E Newdigate—Newdegate, *Cavalier and Puritan in the Days of the Stuarts* (London, 1901), pp67–68; Wood, II 466–67; *Hatton Corr*, I 198.

18. *Life*, I 573–75; *HMC Ormond*, NS V 234–35; *Morrison Letters*, 1st Series, III 171–72; Reresby, pp190–91.

19. *Lauderdale Papers*, III 181–86; BL Add 23245, ff35, 51; *Clar Corr*, I 81–82; *HMC Dartmouth*, I 41–42; *Life*, I 586.

20. *Life*, I 583–84; *HMC Ormond*, NS V 269–70, 276; Prinsterer, V 393, 399; *Letters of Algernon Sidney to Henry Savile* (London, 1742), pp151–52; Barrillon, 21st Sept 1679, BT 143, 7th March 1680, BT 144, 29th April, 13th and 24th June 1680, BT 145, 22nd July 1680, BT 146.

21. Barrillon, 22nd April and 13th June 1680, BT 145; Prinsterer, V 415, 417, 422.

22. *Life*, I 591–92; Barrillon, 3rd Aug, 12th, 16th and 19th Sept (quoted) 1680, BT 146; Sidney, II 107; Prinsterer, V 422–24; Temple, *Memoirs, Part III*, 113–16.

23. Barrillon, 12th and 19th Sept, 24th and 28th Oct 1680, BT 146; Prinsterer, V 426; Dalrymple, II (a) 269–72; *HMC Ormond*, NS V 454; *Life*, I 598–99.

24. Barrillon, 22nd, 25th and 28th Nov 1680, BT 147; *HMC Ormond*, NS V 486–87, 490.

25. Barrillon, 5th, 9th and 16th Dec 1680, 9th, 13th and 20th Jan 1681, BT 147, 148; Burnet, *History*, II 259; Grey, VII 406; *HMC Finch*, II 98–99; BL, Add 18730, f80.

26. Clar MS 87, ff331, 334; *HMC Ormond*, I 30–31; *HMC Dartmouth*, I 40, 46–47 (both misdated), 53–55; *Clar. Corr*, I 47–51.

27. Barrillon, 8th Jan, 15th April and 16th Dec 1680, BT 144, 145, 147; Dalrymple, II (a) 301–02; *His Majesty's Declaration to all his Loving Subjects* (1681); *CSPD 1680–81*, pp175, 182, etc; *HMC 7*, p533; Reresby, p202; North, *Lives*, I 239.

28. Wolf, pp497–501.

29. Sidney, II 120; Dalrymple, II (a) 305–06; Prinsterer, V 452–53, 481–82, 493–94, 512–13; *Clar Corr*, I 56, 58; *Life*, I 691–92; Macpherson, I 125; Barrillon, 7th, 11th and 25th Aug 1681, BT 149.

30. This and the previous paragraph are based mainly on JM Buckroyd, "The Duke of Lauderdale and the Evolution of Scottish Ecclesiastical Policy, 1660–81" (unpublished PhD thesis, Cambridge, 1976).

31. *HMC Hamilton (Suppl)* pp89, 91; Burnet, *History*, II 54, 140; *Lauderdale Papers*, III 160.

32. Burnet, *History*, II 229, 236–37, 300; *HMC Dartmouth*, I 41.

33. *HMC Dartmouth*, I 41; Burnet, *History*, II 300–03, 326–31; *Lauderdale Papers*, III 188; Donaldson, pp371–73; *CSPD 1680–81*, p526; Buckroyd, pp312–13.

34. Buckroyd, pp287–90; *Life*, I 694–95, 704–05; *CSPD 1680–81*, p343; Burnet, *History*, II 304–06, 309.

35. *HMC Dartmouth*, I 66, 70–71; Prinsterer, V 514, 533; *HMC Hamilton*, p197; Donaldson, pp379–80; *Lauderdale Papers*, III 225; Morrice P, p315; Burnet, *History*, II 317–18.

36. Burnet, *History*, II 318–21; *Life*, I 706–13; Prinsterer, V 538; Barrillon, 5th Jan and 5th Feb 1682, BT 151; Morrice P, pp324–25; *HMC Dartmouth*, I 43; *Lauderdale Papers*, III 225.

37. Barrillon, 25th Aug 1681, 4th May 1682, BT 149, 152; Macpherson, I 129; *Life*, I 724–29; Luttrell, I 179–80.

38. Wolf, pp508–09; *Clar Corr*, I 69–73; Dalrymple, II (a) 68–72.

Chapter Eight

1. R Beddard, "The Commission for Ecclesiastical Promotions, 1681–4: an instrument of Tory Reaction", *HJ* X (1967), pp11–40, esp pp25–30; Burnet, *History*, II 304–05; Miller, *Popery*, pp189–94.
2. AF Havighurst, "The Judiciary and Politics in the Reign of Charles II", *Law Quarterly Rev*, LXVI (1950), pp250–52; Luttrell, I 199.
3. *CSPD 1676–77*, p232; Jones, pp43–50.
4. *CSPD 1682*, pp238–40, 274–75, 472, *Jan–June 1683*, pp95–96, *July–Sept 1683*, pp104, 150; North, *Examen*, pp625–26; *HMC House of Lords 1689–90*, pp298–99.
5. Reresby, pp194, 259.
6. Burnet, *History*, II 444; *Life*, I 665–66, 722–25, 729–30; Barrillon, 29th June and 27th July 1682, BT 152.
7. Reresby, p210; Barrillon, 27th July 1682 and 31st July 1684, BT 152, 158.
8. Barrillon, 5th Nov 1682, CPA 148; Carte MS 70, ff558–60; Reresby, pp288–90; *HMC Ormond*, NS VI 542; Chandaman, pp72–75, 102–09.
9. Barrillon, 5th, 12th, 15th and 22nd July 1683, BT 155; Burnet, *History*, II 359–60, 380 and n, 382, 418; Evelyn, IV 329–31; Ailesbury, I 77; Havighurst, *Law Quart Rev* (1950), pp245–46, 251.
10. Barrillon, 5th, 8th, 15th and 19th July 1683, BT 155; Prinsterer, V 578.
11. *HMC 7*, pp368, 375; Barrillon, 5th, 6th, 9th, 13th, 16th, 20th and 23rd Dec 1683, BT 156; Carte MSS 70, ff570–71, 118, ff210–11; Reresby, pp320–24; *CSPD 1683–84*, pp153–54; Dalrymple, II (b) 54–55.
12. Burnet, *History*, II 416; Dalrymple, II (b) 56–57, 62–63, 65; d'Avaux, 11 Jan, 1st Feb and 1st March 1685, FO 95/571; Barrillon, 25th Dec 1684, 1st, 15th and 18th Jan 1685, BT 159, 160.
13. Miller, *Popery*, pp194–95; Carte MS 217, f51; Barrillon, 13th Nov 1684, BT 159.
14. Barrillon, 24th, 27th and 31st July, 28th and 31st Aug, 4th and 17th Sept 1684, BT 158, 159; *Clar Corr*, I 93–96.
15. Barrillon, 19th March 1684, BT 157; All Souls' MS 317, Trumbull's Memoirs, f15; Burnet, *History*, II 460; Fox, Appendix, p*xvii*; Barrillon, 28 Dec 1684, 8(?) Jan 1685, BT 159, 160; Kenyon, *Sunderland*, pp107–09.
16. Fox, Appendix, pp*xii–xv*; *HMC Stuart*, I 3–4; *HMC Egmont*, I 145–47; Evelyn, IV 408–09; Madan, I 258–59; Ellis, *Orig Letters*, III 335–37; *CSPD 1685*, no 2143.

Chapter Nine

1. BL Add 41805, ff148, 152, 154; E Calamy, *An Historical Account of My Own Life*, ed JT Rutt (2 vols, London, 1829), I 116–17; Wood, III 129–30. But see also BL, Add 29561, f55.
2. PC 2/71, p1; Fox, Appendix, p*xvi*; Ellis, *Orig Letters*, III 339; see also *HMC Buccleuch*, I 215.
3. Burnet, *Suppl*, pp144–45; Fox, Appendix, pp*xxxix, lxvi–lxvii*; CUL, Add MS 4836, f27; *HMC Ormond*, NS VII 327; *HMC Buccleuch*, II 219.
4. eg, Pepys, IX 317; S Pepys, *Letters and the Second Diary*, ed RG Howarth (London, 1932), pp83, 113.
5. CUL, Add MS 4880, f187; Campana, II 25; Chandaman, pp260–61.
6. CUL, Add MS 4880, ff186–87; Campana, II 25; BL, Add 41823, f14; *Hatton Corr*, II 53; Barrillon, 5th April 1685, BT 161; *HMC Frankland–*

Russell–Astley, p60; PC 2/71, p208; Sunderland to Skelton, 28th Feb 1687, SP 104/19.

7. Pepys, IX 5–6, 443; Ailesbury, I 105; Newton, *House of Lyme*, p326.
8. Clarendon, *Life*, III 64; Burnet, *History*, I 304; All Souls' MS 317, Trumbull's Memoirs, f52; see also North, *Lives*, I 358.
9. cf Kenyon, *Sunderland*.
10. Kenyon, *Stuart Constitution*, pp12–14; RM Hatton, *Europe in the Age of Louis XIV* (Thames and Hudson, 1969), p79; see below, p176.
11. Kenyon, *Stuart Constitution*, p14; Dalrymple, II (a) 224; *Life*, II 620–21.
12. *HMC Dartmouth*, I 36; for James's views on Providence, see *Life*, I 5–6, 546, 690.
13. *HMC Stuart*, I 63; Barrillon, 28th June 1688, CPA 165; Burnet, *History*, II 27–28, *Suppl*, p52; *Life*, I 656; Ellis, *Orig Letters*, III 339.
14. A Whiteman, "The Census that Never Was", in A Whiteman, JS Bromley and PGM Dickson (eds), *Statesmen, Scholars and Merchants: Essays in Honour of Lucy S Sutherland* (Oxford, 1973), pp1–17; Miller, *Popery*, pp9–12; Miller, "Officers", pp46–49.
15. James to Albeville, c 29th March 1687, CPA 164, f28 (this is a retranslation of a French translation).
16. *HMC Dartmouth*, I 36; Lingard, X 203; see also *Life*, II 621–22.
17. Fox, Appendix, p*cvi*. See also BL, Add 15396, f156, Add 15397, ff14–5; Mackintosh, p653; Barrillon, 4th Feb 1686, Bonrepaus to Seignelay, 21st July 1687, BT 164, 171.
18. Barrillon, 9th Oct 1687, BT 174; BL, Add 15395, f493.
19. Wood, III 239.
20. WB Gardner, "The Later Years of Lauderdale", *Journal of Modern History* XX (1948), p122.
21. The foregoing account of Louis' foreign policy is based primarily on Hatton, esp pp. 30–34; Symcox, pp180–88; Wolf, *passim*.
22. For the Dutch republic in the later seventeenth century, see KHD Haley, *The Dutch in the Seventeenth Century* (Thames and Hudson, 1972); P Geyl, *The Netherlands in the Seventeenth Century, II 1648–1715* (Benn, 1964); JL Price, *Culture and Society in the Dutch Republic in the Seventeenth Century* (Batsford, 1975); Baxter.
23. See Barrillon, 24th May and 20th Dec 1683, 25th May 1684, BT 155, 156, 158.
24. Japikse, I 1, pp33–34; Burnet, *History*, III 134, 173.

Chapter Ten

1. PC 2/71, pp8, 12–13; Bramston, pp200–01; *HMC Ormond* NS VII 322; CUL Add MS 4880, f175.
2. Barrillon, 19th April 1685, BT 161.
3. See Barrillon's dispatches, *passim* and Fox, Appendix, pp*lxiii–lxiv*.
4. Burnet, *History*, III 17 and n, 94–95; Ailesbury, I 98; Fox Appendix, pp*xxxii–xxxiii, lxvi;* CUL Add MS 4880, f176; Evelyn, IV 479.
5. Lingard, X 203 (Barrillon's dispatch of 12th March 1685 is not in BT and has been torn out of CPA 154); Ranke, IV 228–29; BL, Add 25369, ff278, 285–86; Campana, II 25; CUL, Add MS 4880, ff183–85; Reresby, pp363–64.
6. *CJ* IX 714; Evelyn, IV 442–43; Ailesbury, I 100–01.

7. Chandaman, pp256–59. See the same author's "The Financial Settlement in the Parliament of 1685", in H Hearder and HR Loyn (eds), *British Government and Administration: Studies Presented to SB Chrimes* (University of Wales Press, 1974), pp144–54.

8. Reresby, pp 368–69; Fox, Appendix, pp*xcv–xcvi, clii–clvi*; Barrillon, 12th July, CPA 155.

9. D'Avaux, 1st March, FO 95/571; Fox, Appendix, p*xliii;* Barrillon, 19th and 29th March, BT 160; BL, Add 41823, f5; Dalrymple, II (b) 116–17.

10. Sidney, II 249–50; d'Avaux, 10th and 19th April, FO 95/571; *Clar Corr*, I 119–25; BL, Add 41812, ff1–2, 15.

11. *HMC* 7, pp325–26.

12. *CSPD 1685*, no 358; Barrillon, 23rd April, BT 161; BL, Add 34508, ff10–11, 14; d'Avaux, 3rd May, FO 95/571.

13. BL, Add 41812, ff38, 53–57, 104, Add 41817, ff67–68, 109, Add 41822, ff244, 251, 262–64, Add 34512, ff18–21.

14. BL, Add 41812, ff47, 74, 104; d'Avaux, 28th June, FO 95/571; *Clar Corr*, I 128; Dalrymple, II (b) 129–30; Barrillon, 31st May, CPA 155; SP 84/220, ff5–6; Japikse, I 1, pp20–21.

15. Japikse, I 1, pp21–22, 24–25, 28.

16. BL, Add 41812, ff121–23; GH Rose (ed), *Papers of the Earls of Marchmont* (3 vols, London, 1831), III 35–37.

17. Dalrymple, II (b) 124–25; BL, Add 34508, ff15–16, 53, Add 34512, ff21–22; Barrillon, 21st June, CPA 155.

18. Fox, Appendix, pp*xcix–cxi*.

19. Japikse, I 1, pp28–29; *Clar Corr*, I 153; *CSPD* 1685, nos 1462, 1503; BL, Add 34508, ff66–67, Add 41823, f27.

20. *CSPD 1685*, nos 864, 981; Dalrymple, II (b) 129–31; *HMC Stopford Sackville*, pp5, 9; Newton, *House of Lyme*, p336.

21. G Duckett (ed), "Original Letters of the Duke of Monmouth", pp4–6, in *Camden Miscellany; VIII* Barrillon, 26th July, CPA 155; Dalrymple, II (b) 134.

22. *CSPD 1685*, nos 1102, 1575, 1629, 1644; Kenyon, *Constitution*, p422.

23. A Fletcher, *Tudor Rebellions* (Longman, 1968), pp100–01; L Stone, *Crisis of the Aristocracy* (Oxford, 1965), pp413–14; Gardiner, *Commonwealth*, I 328, 465–66, III 194–96; G Davies, *Essays on the Later Stuarts* (Huntington Library Publications, 1958), pp49–50; *HMC Ormond*, NS VII 405.

24. CUL, Add MS 4836, ff11, 23; *CSPD 1685*, nos 1629, 1663; Dalrymple, II (b) 166.

25. Dalrymple, II (b) 137, 165, 169–70; Barrillon, 19th and 30th July, 9th Aug, CPA 155; Miller, "Officers", pp42–46; Miller, "Militia", pp661–62.

26. *Royal Tracts*, pp71–72. The authenticity of this passage is not certain, but some of the other pieces in the collection are genuine and this one has much in common with an earlier one (Davies, *Papers*, pp107–09).

27. Barrillon, 2 Aug, CPA 155.

28. Louis to d'Avaux, 25th Oct (quoted) and 6th Dec, d'Avaux, 29th Nov and 20th Dec, FO 95/571.

29. D'Avaux, 29th Nov, FO 95/571.

30. Evelyn, IV 484–87; Barrillon, 1st and 22nd Oct, 8th Nov, BT 161, 162; Bodl, Ballard MS 12, f15; Newton, *Lyme Letters*, pp137–38; *HMC Egmont*, II 164; Morrice P, p491.

31. BL, Add 34502, ff61, 77, Add 34512, ff35, 48; Burnet, *History*, III 87, 176; Dalrymple, II (b) 176–77.
32. BL, Add 34508, f88, Add 34512, f35; *HMC Downshire*, I 130; *CSPD 1686–87*, nos 611, 630; Bodl, Tanner MS 31, f279; Barrillon, 13th and 16th May 1686, BT 166.
33. Sunderland's correspondence with Trumbull is in SP 78/150 and SP 104/19 (partly printed in *HMC Downshire*, I). For the above incident, see SP 78/150, ff99–101, 105–08; *HMC Downshire*, I 192, 197–98; Louis to Barrillon, 9th Aug 1686, CPA 159.
34. Barrillon, 6th and 16th Aug 1685, CPA 155, 10th Sept and 1st Oct 1685, BT 161; Bonrepaus to Seignelay, 3rd Jan 1686, BT 163. My ideas on this point owe much to a seminar paper given by Rowland Gwynn at the Institute of Historical Research early in 1976.
35. Fox, Appendix, p*lxxvii*; Barrillon, 22th Oct, 1st and 5th Nov 1685, BT 161, 162; Foxcroft, I 454–6.
36. Barrillon, 22 Nov, BT 162; *CJ*, IX 756.
37. Bramston, pp210–12; Barrillon, 19th Nov, BT 162; Morrice P, pp493–95; Grey, VIII 355–60; Reresby, pp394–95; Fox, Appendix, pp*cxxxix–cxl*.
38. *CJ*, IX 757–58; Grey, VIII 369; Reresby, p397; Fox, Appendix, pp*cxl–cxli*; Ailesbury, I 126–27.
39 Reresby, pp397–98; Barrillon, 29th and 30th Nov, 3rd Dec, BT 162; BL, Add 25371, ff140, 148; Ranke, IV 277–79; Bramston, pp216–17.

Chapter Eleven

1. *HMC Egmont*, II 167–68; *HMC Ormond*, NS VII 405.
2. Fox, Appendix, p*xlviii*; *HMC Stuart*, VI 3; *Life*, II 74, 99–100; Barrillon, 22nd Feb 1685, 25th March 1686, BT 160, 165.
3. See below, ch 14.
4. *Letters of Algernon Sidney to Henry Savile*, pp130–31; Barrillon, 17th June 1686 and 10th March 1687, BT 166, 168.
5. Barrillon, 22nd Nov, 3rd, 6th and 13th Dec 1685, BT 162; Fox, Appendix, pp*cxliii–cxlv*; BL, Add 15395, ff284–85, 298–99, 315–17.
6. Fox, Appendix, p*cxliii*; Barrillon, 28th March 1686, BT 165; Bonrepaus to Seignelay, 31st Jan, 4th and 11th Feb 1686, BT 163, 164; *HMC Rutland*, II 102–03.
7. Barrillon, 11th March, 18th July 1686, BT 165, 166; BL, Add 15395, f441; North, *Lives*, II 192–93; *Ellis Corr*, I 133–34, 138; Kenyon, *Sunderland*.
8. Barrillon, 4th Oct 1685, BT 161; Fox, Appendix, p*cxxix*.
9. Bodl, Rawl MS A257, ff243–44.
10. Bodl, MS Arch FC6, ff38, 103; *CSPD 1687–89*, no 486; TCD, MS 1184, no 21; Carte MS 181, ff158–59; Carte MS 209, ff15, 64, 66–67 (quoted), 345.
11. See above, p73–74; also Miller, *Popery*, ch 12. The Pope denied that Howard had opposed Petre's candidature: CUL, Add MS 4881, f583.
12. See above, p136; Bodl, Tanner MS 31, ff123, 156, 198–99; Morrice P, pp492, 520; Wood, III 141; *Ellis Corr*, I 3–5
13. Ranke, IV 293–94; *Clar Corr*, I 258; Bodl, Tanner MS 31, ff268, 270; *CSPD 1686–87*, nos 227–28.
14. Bodl, Tanner MS 31, f250; BL, Add 34508, f133; *Ellis Corr*, I 4; T Sharp, *Life of Archbishop John Sharp* (2 vols, London, 1825), I 69–74).

15. D Ogg, *England in the Reigns of James II and William III* (Oxford, 1955) pp175–78.

16. Buranelli, pp69, 99 (this work is far from reliable on James, but its account of Penn's motives carries conviction); *HMC Buccleuch*, I 215; Miller, *Popery*, pp210–12; Morrice P, p594.

17. *CSPD 1685*, nos 1936, 1959; Barrillon, 3rd Dec 1685, BT 162; Bramston, p222; BL, Add 34508, ff97, 102, Add 15395, ff322, 328–29, 335–36.

18. Barrillon, 10th Dec 1685, 10th Jan 1686, BT 162, 163; BL, Add 15395, ff337–38, 468–69, Add 34508, ff105, 107; Kenyon, *Constitution*, pp422–23, 438–39.

19. Holdsworth, VI 217–21, 223–25; GR Elton, *The Tudor Constitution* (Cambridge, 1960), p19.

20. Gutch, I 436; *Clar Corr*, II 160–62; BL, Add 15395, f492; Buranelli, pp104–07.

21. Dalrymple, II (b) 166–67. See also BL, Add 34508, f117.

22. BL, Add 41812, f70, Add 41813, ff86, 204, Add 41819, f245.

23. For Peyton, see BL, Add 34508, f52, Add 41814, f139, Add 41820, ff175–76; Sunderland to Skelton, 10th Jan 1687, SP 104/19; d'Avaux, 25th Oct 1686, FO 95/572; *CSPD 1686–87*, nos 1582, 1680; Barrillon, 21st April 1687, BT 168.

24. D'Avaux, 17th Oct and 12th Nov 1686, FO 95/572; Barrillon, 28th Oct, BT 167.

25. BL, Add 41813, f141, Add 41814, ff135, 176, 41823, f40; Japikse, II 2, pp731–32, 736; Dalrymple, II (b) 138–40; BL, Add 15396, f105; Barrillon, 23rd Sept 1686, 9th Feb 1688, BT 167, 175; Campana, II 131.

26. Sunderland to Trumbull, 19th Oct, 19th Nov and 7th Dec 1685, SP 104/19; *HMC Downshire*, I 106, 116; SP 78/148, ff136, 157; Louis to Barrillon, 14th Dec 1685, CPA 156, ff294–95.

27. *CSPD 1685*, nos 1775, 1915; Japikse, II 2, pp725–26; BL, Add 41813, f59; d'Avaux, 17th Jan 1686, FO 95/572.

28. Burnet, *History*, III 86; Bonrepaus to Seignelay, 11th Feb 1686, BT 164; d'Avaux, 4th April 1686, 5th Aug 1688, FO 95/572, 574; Dalrymple, II (b) 158–60; *Clar Corr*, I 168–69.

29. BL, Add 41814, f85, Add 41818, ff244, 250; d'Avaux, 21st and 28th Feb 1686, FO 95/572; Barrillon, 7th and 18th March 1686, BT 165.

30. Citters, 28th May 1686, FO 95/553; BL, Add 15396, ff186–87, 214; Bonrepaus to Seignelay, 17th Jan 1686, BT 163; Seignelay to Bonrepaus, 9th Feb 1686, CPA 160; Symcox, p184.

31. Louis to Barrillon, 28th Feb 1686, CPA 158; Bonrepaus to Seignelay, 11th and 25th Feb 1686, BT 164.

32. Symcox, p186; Louis to Barrillon, 26th Dec 1686, CPA 159; Barrillon, 25th Oct 1685, 17th and 21st April 1687, BT 161, 168; Bonrepaus to Seignelay, 14th March 1686, BT 165.

33. Burnet, *History*, III 176; BL, Add 15397, ff240–41; see also BL, Add 15396, ff355, 400–03, 424–25; SS Ing 12, f250.

34. BL, Add 34512, ff38–39, Add 34893, ff10–11.

35. BL, Add 34512, ff39–48, Add 15396, ff243–48.

36. Barrillon, 22nd and 29th Aug, 5th, 12th and 16th Sept, 7th Oct and 12th Dec 1686, BT 166, 167; BL, Add 41819, ff254–56; Citters, 15th Oct 1686, FO 95/553 (back of volume); Burnet, *Suppl*, p221; Japikse, I 2, p8; BL, Add 34508, ff133–34.

37. BL, Add 41814, ff40–41.

38. *CSPD 1686–87*, no 619; Japikse, I 2, p8; d'Avaux, 21st Jan 1687, FO 95/573; *Papers of the Earls of Marchmont*, III 71–72; BL, Add 41814, f194.

39. Barrillon, 23rd Sept and 26th Dec 1686, BT 167; CUL, Add MS 4836, ff182, 184; BL, Add 15396, ff189–90; *Ellis Corr*, I 206–07; Kenyon, *Sunderland*, pp141–44.

40. Barrillon, 23rd Sept, 4th, 18th and 21st Nov, 12th, 16th and 23rd Dec 1686, 6th and 9th Jan 1687, BT 167, 168; *Clar Corr*, II 62–64, 90–91, 116–18 (quoted); SS Ing 12, ff2–6.

41. BL, Add 15396, ff139–40, 230–31; Miller, *Popery*, p272; Mackintosh, p636; BL, Add 25373, f87; SS Ing 12, f11; Barrillon, 20th Jan 1687, BT 168; *HMC Beaufort*, pp89–90.

42. SS Ing 12, ff21, 30; BL, Add 34512, ff57–58; Reresby, pp448–49; Bramston, pp267–69; Barrillon, 17th March 1687, BT 168.

43. *Ellis Corr*, I 256; Ranke, IV 310n; Barrillon, 10th, 20th and 24th March 1687, BT 168; Burnet, *Suppl*, p281; Mackintosh, p641.

44. Kenyon, *Constitution*, pp410–13, 442–45; Gutch, I 352.

45. Kenyon, *Constitution*, pp402–03; Holdsworth, VI 221–23; Ailesbury, I 151; Barrillon, 21st June 1688, CPA 165.

46. PC 2/71, p413; *HMC Portland*, III 398; Kenyon, *Constitution*, pp410–13; *Ellis Corr*, I 269; Povey to Southwell, 5th April 1687, PwV 61; Barrillon, 31st March, 3rd and 21st April 1687, BT 168; SS Ing. 12, ff81–82, 87–88.

Chapter Twelve

1. Ailesbury, I 105–06; BL, Add 34510, ff52–53, 113, Add 25374, ff326–27; Luttrell, I 416–17; North, *Lives*, III 186–87; PC 2/72, pp473–74, 648–49, 659–60, 664, 725–27.

2. *CSPV 1673–75*, pp310–11; J Miller, "Thomas Sheridan and his Narrative", to be published in *Irish Hist Studies* during 1977.

3. *Petty–Southwell Correspondence*, ed marquis of Lansdowne (London, 1928), pp231ff (quotation from p240); *The Petty Papers*, ed Lansdowne (2 vols, London, 1927), I 259–60; for Penn, see Buranelli, esp pp128–35.

4. Scott, *English, Scottish and Irish Joint Stock Companies*, II 148–49; *Petty–Southwell Corr*, p234; Ellis, I 307–08; *CSPD 1686–87*, no 1805, *1687–89*, nos 28, 43, 104.

5. See especially Bonrepaus to Seignelay, 4th March 1686, 12th June, 28th July and 14th Sept 1687, BT 165, 170, 171, 172; Instructions to Bonrepaus and Barrillon, 5th May 1687, BT 169.

6. Barrillon, 28th June 1688, CPA 165; Bodl, Ballard MS 12, f25 (quoted); Foxcroft, I 480n; Evelyn, IV 555ff.

7. *CSPD 1686–87*, no 1712; Cartwright, pp47–51; BL, Add 34487, f5; Bodl, Ballard MS 12, f27; "Trelawney Papers", pp18–20, *Camden Miscellany II*; Wood, III 220; *A Copy of An Address to the King by the Bishop of Oxon* (1687); Morrice Q, pp107, 137.

8. Barrillon, 19th May 1687, BT 169; BL, Add 32095, ff243–46; *HMC Leybourne Popham*, p265.

9. *CSPD 1686–87*, nos 342, 1062, 1340; BL, Add 15396, ff41–42.

10. JR Bloxam (ed), *Magdalen College and James II* (Oxford Historical Soc, 1886), pp29–30, 51–52.

11. Bloxam, pp85, 91 and *passim*; Wood, III 238; Bonrepaus to Seignelay,

14th Sept 1687, BT 172; *Hatton Corr*, II 71–72; *HMC Leybourne Popham*, p265.

12. Bloxam, pp24, 89, 269–70; BL, Add 15397, f284 (misdated 1688).

13. Bloxam, pp219, 221–23, 230, 235; SS Ing 12, ff280–83.

14. Bloxam, pp88, 93, 105–06; Morrice Q, p168; Barrillon, 1st Dec 1687, BT 174.

15. CG Bolam, J Goring, HL Short and R Thomas, *The English Presbyterians* (Allen and Unwin, 1968), pp94–101; R Beddard, "Vincent Alsop and the Emancipation of Restoration Dissent", *Journal of Ecclesiastical History* XXIV (1973), pp175ff; Morrice Q, pp84–85, 89–90, 181.

16. Morrice Q, pp102, 88–89; Dalrymple, II (b) 182.

17. BL, Add 28876, f23; *HMC 7*, p504; Bodl, Tanner MS 29, f75; Campana, 199–200; PwA 2162; Reresby, p495.

18. BL, Add 29562, f148; Bodl, Ballard MS 12, f21, Tanner MS 29, ff8–10, 59; Evelyn, IV 546; Beddard, "Vincent Alsop", pp178, 182–83.

19. SS Ing 12, ff214, 216; Barrillon, 20th and 29th Sept (quoted) 1687, BT 172; Cartwright, pp74–75; *CSPD 1687–89*, no 255; *HMC Portland*, III 404; *HMC Kenyon*, p212; *HMC 10/4*, p376.

20. Mackintosh, pp643–45.

21. All Souls' MS 317, Trumbull's Memoirs, f48; *HMC Ormond*, NS VII 483; *Ellis Corr*, I 305; BL, Add 25373, f180; attendance at council meetings was recorded in PC 2/71–72.

22. AN, K 1351, no 4, f58. For the political role of the court, see A Hassell Smith, *County and Court: Government and Politics in Norfolk 1558–1603* (Oxford, 1974).

23. *CSPD 1687–89*, no 1472; Mackintosh, pp643–45; Bonrepaus to Seignelay, 22nd Sept and 9th Oct 1687, BT 172, 173; Kenyon, *Sunderland*, ch 6.

24. Burnet, *History*, III 140–41, 175–77; Dalrymple, II (b) 184, 188; BL, Add 34510, ff5–7; Barrillon, 12th June 1687, BT 170; Albeville to d'Avaux, c 17th May 1687, FO 95/573.

25. Burnet, *History*, III 173, 175; CPA 164, f28 (quoted above, p126); Barrillon, 30th Jan, 12th June 1687, BT 168, 170.

26. Albeville to d'Avaux, c 17th May 1687, FO 95/573.

27. Burnet, *History*, III 175, 178; CPA 164, ff28–29 (quoted) ; SS Ing 12, f100; Barrillon, 22nd May, 2nd, 9th and 12th June 1687, Bonrepaus to Seignelay, 4th June, all BT 170; Dalrymple, II (b) 183–85 (quoted).

28. Burnet, *History*, III 173–74; d'Avaux, 10th and 23rd Jan 1687, FO 95/573; Morrice Q, p42; Barrillon, 17th March, 3rd and 7th April, BT 168; Bonrepaus to Seignelay, 22nd Sept, BT 172.

29. Morrice P, p628, Q, pp124–25; Dalrymple, II (b) 192–95, 202–07; Halifax, pp335–37; Jones, pp221–22, 225–26; d'Avaux, 18th Sept and 30th Oct, FO 95/573.

30. Bonrepaus to Seignelay, 21st June 1687, BT 170; d'Avaux, 6th July 1687, 15th Jan and 25th March 1688, FO 95/573, 574; Japikse, I 1, pp33–34; Burnet, *History*, III 213–17; *State Tracts*, II (1692), pp334–37.

31. *HMC le Fleming*, pp205–07; *CSPD 1687–89*, no 523.

32. Burnet, *History*, III 193n; *HMC Lindsey (Suppl)*, pp271–72; figures based on information in Duckett.

33. J Carswell, *The Descent on England* (Cresset, 1969), pp238–43; Jones, pp166–68.

34. Bodl, Tanner MS 259, f55.

35. *HMC House of Lords, 1689–90*, pp294, 300; *HMC Rutland*, II 118; North, *Lives*, II 221–22; BL, Add 34510, ff81–82, Add 34512, ff77–78, 84; Carte MS 130, f23.

36. Jones, pp43–45 and ch 6; JR Jones, "James II's Whig Collaborators", *HJ* III (1960), pp65–73; Vellacott, pp51–54.

37. PC 2/72, p534 onwards; Luttrell, I 420–21; *HMC Laing*, I 458; North, *Lives*, II 221; Ailesbury, I 174–75; Morrice Q, pp238–39 (3), 243–45. For Brent, see Jones, p145; *HMC Ormond*, NS V 32; All Souls' MS 317, Trumbull's memoirs, f50; Campana, II 366; BL, Add 41813, f171.

38. Barrillon, 15th and 22nd Dec 1687, BT 174; Morrice Q, p181; BL, Add 34512, f66, Add 15396, f405; SS Ing 12, f279.

39. BL, Add 34512, ff65–66, 15396, ff364–65; Bonrepaus to Seignelay, 24th Nov 1687, BT 173; PwA 2112, 2149, 2159, 2169; Kenyon, *Sunderland*, ch 6.

40. Buranelli, pp91–92; PwA 2126–27, 2129, 2135, 2141; Barrillon, 16th Oct 1687, BT 173.

41. BL, Add 34512, f76, Add 34509, ff151–54; *HMC le Fleming*, p210; see also Halifax, pp121–43 ("The Anatomy of an Equivalent"), which appeared early in Sept 1688: *Ellis Corr*, II 172.

42. PwA 2126, 2141; Barrillon, 16th Feb and 18th March 1688, BT 175, 176; Mackintosh, pp649–50.

43. Morrice Q, p170; BL, Add 34510, f68, Add 15397, ff45–46; *CSPD 1687–89*, no 2126; Mackintosh, pp651–52; PC 2/72, pp 655–58.

44. BL, Add 34512, f77, Add 29563, f130 (quoted); PC 2/72, p661.

45. BL, Add 38493, f136; d'Avaux, 21st Aug 1687, FO 95/573.

46. BL, Add 34508, f128; Barrillon, 2nd and 23rd Sept 1686, BT 167; d'Avaux, 13th Sept and 10th Oct 1686, 20th Feb 1687, FO 95/572, 573.

47. D'Avaux, 8th May, 6th July and 14th Aug, Louis to d'Avaux, 17th July 1687, FO 95/573; Bonrepaus to Seignelay, 21st Aug, BT 172; Mackintosh, p646; BL, Add 41814, f259, Add 41815, ff3–4, 13–14.

48. BL, Add 41814, f206; Barrillon, 23rd Sept, 10th, 13th and 17th Nov, 8th Dec 1687, 26th Jan and 2nd Feb 1688, BT 173, 174, 175; Louis to Barrillon, 24th Oct 1687, CPA 162; Albeville's memorial, 25th Dec 1687, BT 174; Dalrymple, II (b) 257–59, 268–72; BL, Add 41823, ff58–59.

49. BL, Add 34512, ff68–70, Add 34510, ff83–84; Barrillon, 9th Feb 1688, BT 175; Mackintosh, p648.

50. BL, Add 41823, f61, Add 41822, ff209–12 (quoted), 223–27; Barrillon, 22nd March and 15th April 1688, BT 176.

51. Dalrymple, II (b) 217–18; Barrillon, 8th and 11th March, BT 176; BL, Add 32095, f256 (quoted), Add 41815, ff178, 189, Add 38493, ff48–49, 53; CUL, Add 4817, pp22–23; AN, K 1351, no 6; Mackintosh, p650.

52. Burnet, *Suppl*, pp261–65, 277–78; BL, Add 41821, f81, Add 32095, ff261–62; d'Avaux, 29th April, 13th and 20th May, FO 95/574; Baxter, pp224–25.

53. *Clar Corr*, II 171; Gutch, I 329, 336–40; see also R Thomas, "The Seven Bishops and their Petition", *Journal of Ecclesiastical History*, XII (1961), pp56–70.

54. *Life*, II 210–11; BL, Add 38175, f132; Thomas, "Seven Bishops", pp61–62; Campana, II 206; Mackintosh, pp660–61.

55. *Clar Corr*, II 177; BL, Add 34510, ff121, 123; Mackintosh, pp656–57; PwA 2161.

56. PwA 2167, 2171, 2177; Campana, II 221–22, 249–50; Louis to Barrillon,

30th June, CPA 165; CUL, Add MS 4881, f467; BL, Add 15397, ff203–07.

57. PwA 2167; Barrillon, 28th June and 1st July, CPA 165, 166; Thomas, "Seven Bishops", pp68–69; *Ellis Corr*, II 3; Mackintosh, pp660–61.

58. AF Havighurst, "James II and the Twelve Men in Scarlet", *Law Quarterly Review*, LXIX (1953), pp534–39; Kenyon, *Constitution*, pp442–47.

59. *HMC 6*, p473; Campana, II 235–36; BL, Add 25376, f209; EN Williams, *The Eighteenth Century Constitution* (Cambridge, 1960), pp8–10.)

Chapter Thirteen

1. Barrillon, 12th, 16th and 19th July, CPA 166; Mackintosh, pp662–64.

2. Reresby, p507; Gutch, I 393–97; BL, Add 36707, f38, Add 25376, ff188–89, 235–36; *Ellis Corr*, II 100–02, 108–09; *HMC Portland*, III 415.

3. Symcox, pp187–90.

4. Louis to Barrillon, 13th Feb and 15th April, CPA 165; Barrillon, 22nd and 29th March, 12th, 15th and 26th April, BT 165; Louis to d'Avaux, 22nd April, FO 95/574.

5. Louis to Barrillon, 4th May, CPA 165; BL, Add 34510, ff114, 117; Luttrell, I 437–38; Campana, II 190; Barrillon, 10th and 24th May, BT 177.

6. Louis to Barrillon, 2nd and 7th June, CPA 165.

7. Louis to Barrillon, 7th June, CPA 165; Louis to d'Avaux, 6th June, d'Avaux, 10 June, FO 95/574; Japikse, I 1, p41; Symcox, pp193–95.

8. BL, Add 15397, ff120, 159; Barrillon, 14th, 17th and 24th June, CPA 165; CUL, Add MS 4817, pp150–51; SP 78/151, f193; Campana, II 237–39.

9. D'Avaux, 10th June and 21st Aug, Louis to d'Avaux, 26th Aug and 2nd Sept, FO 95/574; Louis to Barrillon, 17th June and 5th Aug, CPA 165, 166; Japikse, I 1, pp48–49; PwA 2173.

10. Louis to d'Avaux, 16th Sept, d'Avaux 7th and 9th Sept, FO 95/574; BL, Add 41816, ff175, 213–15, Add 34512, ff4–6.

11. BL, Add 34512, ff6, 12–15; Dalrymple, II (b) 254–55; BL, Add 41821, ff271–72; *Lexington Papers*, ed HM Sutton (London, 1851), pp327ff and 354–55; Symcox, pp197–202; Louis to d'Avaux, 14th Oct, FO 95/574.

12. Bentinck, pp73–75; BL, Add 41816, f152.

13. Louis to Barrillon, 5th Aug (relevant passage crossed out in draft) and 3rd Sept, Barrillon, 26th Aug, CPA 166; AN, K 1351, no 4, ff1–4, 14–18, 24–25, 32; Campana, II 255–56.

14. Barrillon, 9th, 18th and 27th Sept, CPA 166; Sunderland to Skelton, 30th Aug, SP 104/19; BL, Add 15397, ff244–47; Dalrymple, II (b) 295.

15. AN, K 1351, no 4, f21; d'Avaux, 18th Sept, Louis to d'Avaux, 14th Oct, FO 95/574; Barrillon, 30th Aug, 7th (quoted), 11th and 25th Oct, Louis to Barrillon, 17th Oct and 1st Nov, CPA 166; Barrillon, 11th and 25th Nov, CPA 167.

16. D'Avaux, 21st Aug, FO 95/574; BL, Add 34487, f23, Add 38495, f31; EB Powley, *The English Navy in the Revolution of 1688* (Cambridge, 1928), p19; AN, K 1351, no 4, f 10; Barrillon, 13th and 27th Sept, CPA 166.

17. Powley, pp29, 35–36, 47; Miller, "Militia", p672n; Miller, "Officers", p46; BL, Add 34510, f160, Add 34517, ff68–69; *HMC Hastings*, II 188.

18. Reresby, p503; Miller, "Officers", pp47–49; *Ellis Corr*, II 184–85; Barrillon, 18th Sept, CPA 166; Burnet, *Suppl*, p282.

19. Jones, pp133, 150; Barrillon, 2nd Sept, CPA 166.

20. Jones, p150n; *Ellis Corr*, II 19–20; *CSPD 1687–89*, nos 1498–99, 1504–09; Reresby, pp506–08; Duckett, I 102–03, II 225ff and *passim*.

21. Duckett, I 102; BL, Add 15397, ff214–15; AN, K 1351, no 4, ff21, 36, 54.

22. AN, K 1351, no 4, ff55–56; PC 2/72, p736; Gutch, I 409; *Clar Corr*, II 188–90.

23. *Clar Corr*, II 191–93; Gutch, I 410–13, 420; Barrillon, 14th Oct, CPA 166; PC 2/72, pp749–51.

24. Barrillon, 18th and 25th Oct, CPA 166; Campana, II 290; Mackintosh, pp675–76.

25. BL, Add 15397, ff371–73; Barrillon, 8th and 11th Nov, CPA 167; Campana, II 312.

26. Evelyn, IV 600; PC 2/72, pp757–82; Louis to Barrillon, 10th Nov, CPA 167.

27. Williams, *Eighteenth Century Constitution*, pp10–18; Japikse, I 1, pp49–50; CUL, Add MS 4817, pp104–05.

28. AN, K 1351, no 4, f4; Campana, II 291; *HMC Dartmouth*, I 220; Barrillon, 15th Nov, CPA 167.

29. Japikse, I 2, pp612–13; Campana, II 318–19; Miller, "Militia", pp673–74.

30. Barrillon, 25th Nov, CPA 167; Burnet, *History*, III 331n.

31. CUL, Add MS 4817, pp79–81; Campana, II 337; Ailesbury, I 190; Burnet, *History*, III 333; *CSPD 1687–89*, nos 1978, 1983; Barrillon, 1st and 9th Dec, CPA 167.

32. Barrillon, 22–27 Nov, CPA 167; BL, Add 34510, ff175–76, Add 15397, ff421–22, 431–32; *Clar Corr*, II 205; Morrice Q, p320.

33. *Life*, II 222, 645–67; Macpherson, I 281–84; CUL, Add MS 4817, p98; Barrillon, 1st and 3rd Dec, CPA 167; *CSPD 1687–89*, no 1983; *HMC 7*, p416; Dalrymple, II (b) 335.

34. *Life*, II 223–26; Barrillon, 3–5th Dec, CPA 167; *HMC Leybourne Popham*, p267.

35. BC Brown (ed), *Letters of Queen Anne* (Cassell, 1968), esp pp33–34, 43; *Clar Corr*, II 191, 194, 216.

36. Miller, "Militia", pp667–76; Bramston, p338 (quoted); BL Add 34510, ff180, 183.

37. BL, Add 36707, f50; *Royal Tracts*, pp74–79.

38. GH Jones, *Charles Middleton* (Chicago UP, 1967), p227; Barrillon, 13th Dec, CPA 167.

39. Japikse, II 3, pp77, 80–81; *Clar Corr*, II 214–23; Burnet, *History*, III 341, *Suppl*, p532.

40. Barrillon, 11–18th Dec, CPA 167; BL, Add 15397, ff475–78, 485–89; Campana, II 355–56, 370–02; *Life*, II 249.

41. *Clar Corr*, II 208–11, 219–23; BL, Add 34510, ff191, 193; *Life*, II 239; CUL, Add MS 4817, pp109–10; Foxcroft, II 23–30; All Souls' MS 273, back of vol, nos 1, 3.

42. Foxcroft, II 24–26; BL, Add 15397, f500; Barrillon, 20th Dec, CPA 167; *HMC 7*, p351; *HMC 8/1*, p555; Campana, II 377–78; All Souls' MS 273, back of vol, nos. 21–22; Ailesbury, I 174–77.

43. *HMC Dartmouth*, I 230–33; Miller, "Militia", pp676–77; BL, Add 32095, f297; *HMC 8/1*, p556; Barrillon, 22nd Dec, CPA 167.

44. Newton, *House of Lyme*, p354; *Clar Corr*, II 224–25; *Hatton Corr*, II 127; Japikse, I 2, pp632–33; Carte MS 40, f502.

45. R Beddard, "The Guildhall Declaration and the Counter Revolution of the

Loyalists", *HJ* XI (1968), pp403–20; cf Beddard, "A Letter of Dr Francis Turner on the Revolution of 1688", *Bulletin of the Institute of Historical Research*, XL (1967), p106.

46. Vellacott, p58; *Life*, II 252–54; BL, Add 5842, p241, Add 32095, ff303–05, 308–09, Harl 6852, f402.

47. Vellacott, pp59–61; *Life*, II 254–56; BL, Add 32095, ff304–11, Add 5842, pp241–42, Harl 6852, ff402–03; Burnet, *History*, III 346n; Foxcroft, II 58; Barrillon, 23rd and 24th Dec, CPA 167; Ailesbury, I 201–02.

48. Vellacott, pp61–62; Ailesbury, I 209–15; *Life*, II 261; *Universal Intelligence*, no 3 (15–18 Dec); Beddard, "Letter of Francis Turner", p107; Barrillon, 27th Dec, CPA 167.

49. *Clar Corr*, II 226–30; Burnet, *History*, III 354–57; *Life*, II 264–66.

50. *Life*, II 266–67, 270–72; S Pepys, *Private Corr and Miscellaneous Papers*, ed JR Tanner (2 vols, London, 1926), I 25–26; *Clar Corr*, II 232–34.

51. Ailesbury, I 222–25; *Life*, II 275–77; *AH*, XXI 60–61; CUL, Add MS 4817, pp273–76.

Chapter Fourteen

1. Fountainhall, pp624 (quoted), 866–67; *HMC Buccleuch*, I 132; *RPC 1686*, pp434–35.

2. Miller, "Militia", pp661–62; *CSPD 1687–89*, no 727; Reresby, p440; *Clar Corr*, I 148; *HMC Buccleuch*, I 92, 133.

3. *HMC Stuart*, I 31.

4. Miller, *Popery*, ch 13; *HMC Stuart*, I 30–1; Donaldson, pp381–83.

5. *HMC Buccleuch*, I 168–215, II 162; Burnet, *History*, II 425–35; Ailesbury, I. 18.

6. *HMC Buccleuch*, II 52ff; *HMC Hamilton*, pp169–72; Fountainhall, pp708–11; Barrillon, 18th Feb 1686, BT 164; BL, Add 15395, ff377–78, 385.

7. Barrillon, 11th March 1686, 18th Dec 1687, BT 165, 174; SS Ing 12, ff266–67; *HMC Hamilton*, p173; *HMC Hamilton (Suppl.)*, pp105–08; PwA 2143, 2161, 2175.

8. *HMC Buccleuch*, I 91–93, 136–43; Burnet, *History*, III 34–37.

9. Fountainhall, pp676–77, 694; *HMC Laing*, I 443–44; BL, Add 15395, ff385, 440–43; *HMC 9/2*, p251; Barrillon, 29th April 1686, BT 165 (quoted).

10. Fountainhall, pp717, 734–36; BL, Add 15395, ff495–98, 513–14; *HMC Laing*, I 446–47.

11. Barrillon, 27th May, 1st and 22nd July 1686, BT 166; Burnet, *History*, I 520–22; Fountainhall, pp676, 750–51, 796; *Cal Clar SP*, V 666 (endorsed, incorrectly, as being addressed to the Scottish Parliament).

12. *Life*, II 108; Fountainhall, pp792, 806, 818–22, 839; Burnet, *History*, III 183; C Lindsay, Earl of Balcarres, *Memoirs touching the Revolution in Scotland, 1688–90*, ed AWC Lindsay (Bannatyne Club, 1841), p5.

13. *RPC 1686*, pp511–15, 540; Barrillon, 29th April 1686, BT 165; *HMC Stuart*, I 31; Fountainhall, pp755, 775, 816, 839, 875; Balcarres, *Memoirs*, p4.

14. Simms, p8; much of the material which follows appears, in a different and much more extended form, in my article, "The Earl of Tyrconnell and James II's Irish Policy, 1685–8", to be published by the *HJ* in 1977.

15. *Clar Corr*, I 432, 458.

16. For Sheridan, see my article in *Irish Hist Studies*, 1977.

Chapter Fifteen

1. Campana, II 529–34; d'Avaux, p62; *Life*, II 319–20.
2. Campana, II 528; also *ibid* 551–52.
3. *Ibid*, 537–39, 578–79; d'Avaux, pp 23–30, 37, 48, 241, 490; Steele, II, no 1029; Carte MS 181, f76a.
4. D'Avaux, pp140, 217–18, 263; BN, FFr, NA 9392, ff45–49; Ranke, VI 108.
5. Macpherson, I 175; Ranke, VI 131; Carte MS 217, f310; *HMC House of Lords, 1689–90*, p182; BL, Add 28876, f182.
6. D'Avaux, pp 128–29, 642–43; *HMC Ormond*, NS VIII 372, 377–85; *AH* IV 103, 107–10; Carte MS 181, f254.
7. D'Avaux, pp26–29, 92, 119, 139, 182–84; Macpherson, I 175, 181, 194–95; Carte MS 181, f86 (Macpherson, I 191 gives 30 instead of 13); *AH*, XXI 201.
8. Ranke, VI 132, 134–35; *AH*, XXI 137; d'Avaux, pp357, 459; d'Avaux, *Supplement*, p37.
9. *AH*, XXI 149, 167; *HMC Ormond*, NS VIII 378; Macpherson, I 211n.
10. D'Avaux, pp39, 90, 112 (quoted), 147; Reresby, pp564–65.
11. D'Avaux, pp255, 105; cf also O'Kelly, pp30–31.
12. D'Avaux, pp51, 55–56, 80, 223–24, 340–42, 390, 490; Gilbert, p63.
13. Campana, II 413; W King, *The State of the Protestants of Ireland under the late King James's Government* (London, 1691), pp210–15; *HMC Ormond*, NS VIII 373–75; d'Avaux, pp137–38, 268, 378–79, 446, 550–51; Macpherson, I 203–4n, 210n.
14. D'Avaux, pp23, 36, 247, 344, 498.
15. *Ibid*, pp104–05, 250–52, 317–18, 506–12, etc; *AH*, IV 100.
16. D'Avaux, pp247, 250–53, 261, 288–90, 353–54 (quoted), 431, 521; *AH*, XXI 202.
17. D'Avaux, pp218, 343, 498, 548–49; Macpherson, I 319–33, 337–41. James had no part in sending Melfort to Rome, d'Avaux, pp611–12, 615.
18. D'Avaux, pp59, 86–87, 96–98, 101–05; Macpherson, I 180–87; *AH*, XXI 93; *Life*, II 332–35.
19. Simms, pp98–100; *AH*, XXI 36, 103–05, 131–33; d'Avaux, pp110–12, 159, 271–86.
20. *Life*, II 355–56; King, *State of the Protestants*, p151; d'Avaux, pp 226, 340–42; Steele, II, no 1044; Carte MS 181, f250.
21. Carte MS 181, f229; Macpherson, I 203–14n, 311–12; Gilbert, pp79–80; *AH*, XXI 193–94; d'Avaux, p356.
22. D'Avaux, pp301–02, 310, 323, 352; *HMC 8/1*, pp495–96; Macpherson, I 217–18n, 220, 309–11.
23. D'Avaux, pp149, 225–26, 248, 278, 344, 379–80, 544–45.
24. *Ibid*, pp345–46, 377, 426, 433, 442–44, 509; Macpherson, I 221; *AH*, IV 100; *Life*, II 373, 376–78; *HMC Stuart*, I 46.
25. D'Avaux, pp458–65, 475–80, 563–64.
26. Macpherson, I 314–15; d'Avaux, pp493, 546–47, 551.
27. Macpherson, I 311–12; d'Avaux, pp317–18, 515, 521, 609–11; *AH*, IV 101.
28. BN, FFr, NA 9392, ff26–27, 50; Ranke, VI 102; *AH*, IV 117, 127–28, 130; National Library of Ireland, MS 37, Dover to Tyrconnell, 23rd March 1689 (1690).
29. D'Avaux, p630; *AH*, IV 108, 111–14, 119 (quoted), 121–22, 126–27; BN, FFr, NA 9392, ff41–43, 46, 59.

30. D'Avaux, pp649–50, 655–56; BN, FFr, NA 9392, ff22, 46, 49; *AH*, IV 113, 123–25; Ranke, VI 103, 108; *Life*, II 405.

31. *HMC Ormond*, NS VIII 380, 384; d'Avaux, pp517–20, 668, 678; *AH*, IV 112–16, 121; BN, FFr, NA 9392, ff38, 56–57; Ranke, VI 111.

32. Simms, pp141–43; BN, FFr, NA 9392, f52; Ranke, VI 114–15; *Life*, II 393–94; *AH*, IV 132–33, 129–30 (the second of these letters is misplaced: the date must be 26th June Old Style, not New Style, as the army was at the camp at Ardee from 24th to 28th June).

33. Ranke, VI 113–14, 140–41; Baxter, p265; Simms, pp 146–48; *HMC Finch*, II 327; *Life*, II 395–96.

34. *Life*, II 394–400; Ranke, VI 118–19; *HMC Finch*, II 329; Simms, pp149–50.

35. *Life*, II 396–401; Ranke, VI 119–20, 141–43; *HMC Finch*, II 328.

36. Gilbert, p102; *HMC Finch*, II 329; Simms, p151.

37. *HMC Ormond*, NS VIII 387, 401–02; *Royal Tracts*, pp31–32; *Life*, II 401–04; *HMC Finch*, II 344–45, 352, 362, 371–72.

38. *HMC Finch*, II 362, 369; *Morrison Letters*, 1st Series, IV between 332 and 333; *Life*, II 411–13; Macpherson, I 230–31n; Gilbert, p37.

Chapter Sixteen

1. Davies, pp71–75, 79–80; Acton, p19; Carte MS 208, f368.

2. Madan, II 272–73, 328, 331; Davies, pp162–63; *Life*, II 585–86.

3. Davies, pp50, 72–73, 98–100 and *passim*; Carte MS 208, f328 (quoted).

4. Madan, II 326; *Royal Tracts*, pp89–90; cf also Davies, p92.

5. GH Jones, *The Mainstream of Jacobitism* (Harvard UP, 1954), pp35–36; Carte MS 208, ff287–88, 369; PwA 1032, 2725; *HMC Bath*, III 257 (quoted).

6. *HMC Stuart*, VI 72; Carte MS 208, ff121, 267; *HMC Bath*, III 208.

7. *HMC Dartmouth*, I 254; Macpherson, I 409–10; BN, FFr, NA 7487, f126. See also Jones, *Jacobitism*, chs 1–2.

8. Ailesbury, I 352; BN, FFr, NA 7487, ff21–22, 60, 260–61 and *passim*, 7492, ff10–11, 355–57; *HMC Bath*, I 319; CUL, Add MS 4880, f844.

9. *HMC Stuart*, VI 66.

10. BN, FFr, NA 7487, ff77, 167; *Life*, II 479–88.

11. Louis to Barrillon, 21st Oct 1688, CPA 166; d'Avaux, pp420–21; CPA 172, ff197–99; BN, FFr, NA 7487, ff58, 100–01; Macpherson, I 426–31.

12. *Life*, II 501–12; Royal Archives, Stuart MS M7, pp97–101, 104 (microfilm copy in University of London Library, microfilm no 150/550); CPA 172, ff286–90; Acton, pp21–23.

13. Acton, p15; C Nordmann, "Louis XIV and the Jacobites", in RM Hatton (ed), *Louis XIV and Europe* (Macmillan, 1976), pp86–88.

14. Jones, *Jacobitism*, pp46–47; *Life*, II 530–46; Acton, pp46–47.

15. MA Thomson, "William III and Louis XIV, 1689–97", in R Hatton and JS Bromley (eds), *William III and Louis XIV: Essays by and for Mark A Thomson* (Liverpool UP, 1968), pp40–46.

16. *Ibid*, p47; *HMC Bath*, III 276–77, 285, 290–91, 297, 305, 311.

17. Madan, I 49–52, II 273–74, 338–39, 343–44, 349–50; *Life*, II 592–96; Carte MS 181, f701.

18. Madan, II 270–71; *Life*, II 595–604; Hatton, p23.

19. Carte MS 180, ff4–31, Carte MS 208, ff370–71; *HMC 10/5*, pp188–89.

Appendix

1. Simms, pp281–84; WS Churchill, *Marlborough, his Life and Times* (4 vols, Sphere, 1967), I 302–03, 306; *Life*, I *xvii–xviii*; MV Hay, *Blairs Papers* (Sands, 1929), p9.

2. Sells, pp25–31; Ranke, VI 31–32.

3. Ranke, VI 32–45; *HMC Stuart*, I 209.

4. Fox, Introduction, p*xxv* (footnote). The four volumes quarto probably made up a copy of the complete *Life*, of which there were two (*Life*, I *xv*). One is now in the Stuart papers in Windsor, the other is in the Blairs College papers in Edinburgh. The section of the "Memoirs" which formed the basis of the first part of the *Life* (up to 1660) consisted of three quarto volumes, which were already in poor condition in 1740 (Churchill, I 308). What Fox saw half a century later was probably a complete copy of the *Life*, plus volumes 4 to 9 of the "Memoirs".

5. Churchill, I 305n, 306–09.

6. Ranke, VI 36, 45; Churchill, I 305n.

7. Macpherson, I 46; Sells, p28. For James's keeping a journal, see Burnet, *History*, II 28.

8. Macpherson, I 6, 14 (but Macpherson, I 50–51 follows the *Life* closely); Clarke, I *xv;* Churchill, I 306–07.

9. Ranke, VI 29–45.

10. The sections of Macpherson's *Original Papers* based on the *Life* are as follows: 1660–68, Extract I for each year; 1669, Extract II; 1670, Extracts I, VI and IX; 1671, Extract II; 1672, Extracts II and IV; 1673, Extracts II and IV; 1674, Extract II; 1675, Extract I; 1676, Extract II; 1677, Extract II; 1678, Extract II; 1679, Extracts I, V, VIII, X, XIII, XV and the first parts of XI and XII; 1680, Extracts I, IV, VIII, X; 1681, Extracts I, IV, VII; 1682, Extract V; 1683, Extract I; 1685, Extracts II, IV (i) (which also includes some Macpherson extracts), V; 1686, Extracts I, III; 1687, Extracts I, II; 1688, Extracts I and III.

Select Bibliography

Acton, Lord (ed), *Letters of James II to the Abbot of La Trappe* (Philobiblon Soc Miscellanies, XIV, 1872–76)

Ailesbury, T Bruce, Earl of, *Memoirs*, ed WE Buckley (2 vols, Roxburgh Club, 1890)

D'Avaux, Comte, *Négociations en Irlande 1689–90* (Irish Manuscripts Commission, 1934) (Supplement, 1958)

Baxter, SB, *William III* (Longman, 1966)

Behrens, B, "The Whig Theory of the Constitution in the Reign of Charles II," *Cambridge Historical Journal*, VII (1941)

Bentinck, M (ed), *Lettres et Mémoires de Marie, Reine d'Angleterre* (The Hague, 1880)

Bramston, Sir J, *Autobiography*, ed Lord Braybrooke (Camden Soc, 1845)

Brown, T, *Miscellanea Aulica* (London, 1702)

Browning, A, *Thomas Earl of Danby* (3 vols, Jackson, 1951)

Buckingham, J Sheffield, Duke of, *Works* (2 vols, London, 1753)

Buranelli, V, *The King and the Quaker* (Pennsylvania UP, 1962)

Burnet, G, *History of My Own Time* (6 vols, Oxford, 1833)
    "Some Unpublished Letters," ed HC Foxcroft (*Camden Miscellany* XI)
    Supplement to the History of My Own Time, ed HC Foxcroft (Oxford, 1902)

Campana di Cavelli, E, *Les Derniers Stuarts à St Germain en Laye* (2 vols, London, 1871)

Carte, T(ed), *Original Letters, 1641–60* (2 vols, London, 1739)
    Life of James, Duke of Ormond (6 vols, Oxford, 1851)

Cartwright, T, *Diary*, ed J Hunter (Camden Soc 1843)

Chandaman, CD, *The English Public Revenue 1660–88* (Oxford, 1975)

Clarendon, E Hyde, Earl of, *History of the Rebellion*, ed WD Macray (6 vols, Oxford, 1888)
    The Life of (3 vols, Oxford, 1827)

Dalrymple, Sir J, *Memoirs of Great Britain and Ireland* (2 vols, London, 1771–73) (Volume II is divided into three parts, with separate pagination, designated "Appendix", "Appendix Part I" and "Appendix Part II". For brevity's sake I have referred to these as (a), (b) and (c))

Davies, G(ed), *Papers of Devotion of James II* (Roxburgh Club, 1925)

Donaldson, G, *Scotland: James V to James VII* (Oliver and Boyd, 1965)

Duckett, Sir G (ed), *Penal Laws and Test Acts, 1687–88* (2 vols, London, 1882–83)

Ellis Correspondence, ed GJW Agar Ellis (2 vols, London, 1829)

Ellis, Sir H(ed), *Original Letters Illustrative of English History* (2nd edn, 3 vols, London, 1825)

Essex Papers: vol I ed O Airy, vol II ed CE Pike, (Camden Soc, 1890, 1913)

Evelyn, J, *Diary*, ed ES de Beer (6 vols, Oxford, 1955)

Fountainhall, Sir J Lauder of, *Historical Notices* (2 vols, but with continuous pagination, Bannatyne Club, 1848)

Fox, CJ, *A History of the Early Part of the Reign of James II* (London, 1808)

Foxcroft, HC, *Life and Letters of Halifax* (2 vols, London, 1898)

Gardiner, SR, *History of the Commonwealth and Protectorate* (3 vols, London, 1894–1901)

    History of the Great Civil War (4 vols, London, 1893)

Geyl, P, *Orange and Stuart, 1641–72* (Weidenfeld, 1969)

Gilbert, JT(ed), *A Jacobite Narrative of the Wars in Ireland* (Irish UP, 1971)

Grey, A, *Debates in the House of Commons, 1667–94* (10 vols, London, 1763)

Gutch, J(ed), *Collectanea Curiosa* (2 vols, London, 1781)

Haley, KHD, *The First Earl of Shaftesbury* (Oxford, 1968)

Halifax, G Savile, Marquis of, *Complete Works*, ed JP Kenyon, (Penguin, 1969)

(Hamilton, A), *Memoirs of Count Grammont*, ed Sir W Scott (Bohn, 1846)

Hartmann, CH, *The King my Brother* (Heinemann, 1954)

Hatton, RM, "Louis XIV and his Fellow Monarchs", in Hatton, (ed), *Louis XIV and Europe* (Macmillan, 1976)

Hatton Correspondence, ed EM Thompson (2 vols, Camden Soc, 1878)

Holdsworth, WS, *History of English Law* (14 vols, Methuen, 1922–64)

Hulton, R, *Charles II, King of England, Scotland and Ireland* (Oxford, 1989)

Japikse, N(ed), *Correspondentie van Willem III en van Hans Willem Bentinck* (vol I in two parts, vol II in three parts, The Hague, 1927–37)

Jones, JR, *The Revolution of 1688 in England* (Weidenfeld, 1972)

Kenyon, JP, *Robert Spencer, Earl of Sunderland* (Longman, 1958)

    The Stuart Constitution (Cambridge, 1966)

Lauderdale Papers, ed O Airy (3 vols, Camden Soc, 1884–85)

Lingard, J, *History of England* (6th edn, 10 vols, London, 1855)

Luttrell, N, *A Brief Historical Relation of State Affairs, 1678–1714* (6 vols, Oxford, 1857)

Mackintosh, Sir J, *History of the Revolution of 1688* (London, 1834)

Macpherson, J, *Original Papers containing the Secret History of Great Britain* (2 vols, London, 1775)

Madan, F(ed), *Stuart Papers* (2 vols, Roxburgh Club, 1889)

Marvell, A, *Poems and Letters*, ed H Margoliouth (3rd edn, 2 vols, Oxford, 1971)

Miller, J, "Catholic Officers in the Later Stuart Army", *EHR* LXXXVIII (1973)

    "The Militia and the Army in the Reign of James II", *HJ* XVI (1973)

    Popery and Politics in England, 1660–88 (Cambridge, 1973)

Morrison Letters: Autograph Letters in the Collection of Alfred Morrison, ed EW Thibaudeau (1st Series, 6 vols, London, 1883–92; 2nd Series, 3 vols, 1893–96; *Bulstrode Papers*, 1 vol only, 1897)

Newton, Lady, *The House of Lyme* (Heinemann, 1917)

    Lyme Letters, 1660–1760 (Heinemann, 1925)

Nicholas Papers, ed GF Warner (4 vols, Camden Soc, 1886–1920)

North, R, *Examen* (London, 1740)

    Lives of the Norths, ed A Jessopp (3 vols, London, 1890)

O'Kelly, C, "Macariae Excidium or the Destruction of Cyprus", in TC Croker (ed), *Narratives Illustrative of the Contests in Ireland in 1641 and 1690* (Camden Soc, 1841)

Pepys, S, *Diary*, ed RC Latham and W Matthews (11 vols, Bell 1970–——) (Vols 1–9 have appeared at the time of writing.)

Prinsterer, G Groen van, *Archives de la Maison Orange Nassau* (2nd series, 5 vols, The Hague, 1858–61)

Ranke, L von, *A History of England, Principally in the Seventeenth Century* (6 vols, Oxford, 1875)

Rawdon Papers, ed E Berwick (London, 1819)

Reresby, Sir J, *Memoirs*, ed A Browning (Jackson, 1936)

Royal Tracts. In Two Parts (Paris, 1692)

Seaward, P, *The Cavalier Parliament and the Reconstruction of the old Regime 1661–7* (Cambridge, 1989)

Sells, AL(ed), *Memoirs of James II: His Campaigns while Duke of York, 1652–60* (Chatto and Windus, 1962)

Sidney, H, *Diary of the Times of Charles II*, ed RW Blencowe (2 vols, London, 1843)

Simms, JG, *Jacobite Ireland, 1685–91* (Routledge, 1969)

Steele, R (ed), *Tudor and Stuart Proclamations* (2 vols, Bibliotheca Lindesiana, Oxford, 1910)

Symcox, G, "The Origins of the Nine Years' Wars", in RM Hatton (ed), *Louis XIV and Europe* (Macmillan, 1976)

Temple, Sir W, *Memoirs, 1672–9* (London, 1692)

Memoirs, Part III (London, 1709)

Thurloe, J, *State Papers of John Thurloe*, ed T Birch (7 vols London, 1742)

Treby, G(ed), *A Collection of Letters and Other Writings* and *The Second Part of the Collection* (2 vols, London, 1681)

Turner, FC, *James II* (Eyre and Spottiswoode, 1948)

Vellacott, PC, "The Diary of a Country Gentleman in 1688", *Cambridge Historical Journal*, II (1926)

Williamson Letters: Letters addressed from London to Sir Joseph Williamson 1673–74, ed WD Christie (2 vols, Camden Soc, 1874)

Witcombe, DT, *Charles II and the Cavalier House of Commons, 1663–74* (Manchester UP, 1966)

Wolf, JB, *Louis XIV* (Panther, 1970)

Wood, A à, *Life and Times*, ed A Clark (5 vols, Oxford Historical Soc, 1891–1900)

The following books and articles appeared after the writing of the first edition

Bennett, G.V., "The Seven Bishops: A Reconsideration" in D. Baker (ed), *Religious Motivation: Biographical and Sociological Problems for the Church Historian*, (Studies in Church History, XV, Blackwell, 1978)

Childs, J., *The Army, James II and the Glorious Revolution*, (Manchester UP, 1980)

Clifton, R., *The Last Popular Rebellion: The Western Rising of 1685*, (Temple Smith, 1984)

Coleby, A.M., *Central Government and the Localities: Hampshire 1649–89*, (Cambridge UP, 1987)

Glassey, L.K.J., *Politics and the Appointment of Justices of the Peace, 1675–1725*, (Oxford UP, 1979)

Gwynn, R.D., "James II in the Light of his Treatment of Huguenot Refugees in England, 1685–6", *EHR* XCII (1977)

Jones, C. (ed), *Britain in the First Age of Party, 1680–1750* (Hambledon Press, 1987)

Jones, J.R. (ed), *The Restored Monarchy 1660–88*, (Macmillan, 1979)

Miller, J., "The Initial Impact of the Revocation in England" in C.E.J. Caldicott, H. Gough and J-P. Pittion (eds), *The Huguenots and Ireland: Anatomy of an Emigration* (Glendale Press, Dublin, 1987)

Miller, J., "James II and Toleration" in E. Cruickshanks (ed), *By Force or by Default? The Revolution of 1688* (John Donald, 1989)

Miller, J., "The Potential for 'Absolutism' in Later Stuart England", *History* LXIX (1984)

Miller, J., "Proto-Jacobitism? The Tories in the Revolution of 1688–9" in E. Cruickshanks and J. Black (eds), *The Jacobite Challenge* (John Donald, 1988)

Murrell, P.E., "Bury St Edmunds and the Campaign to Pack Parliament, 1687–8", *Bulletin of the Institute of Historical Research*, LIV (1981)

Speck, W.A., *Reluctant Revolutionaries: Englishmen and the Revolution of 1688* (Oxford UP, 1988)

Index